Native American Ways
Four Paths to Enlightenment

Native American Ways

Four Paths to Enlightenment

The Sacred Formulas of the Cherokees
Blackfoot Lodge Tales
Truth of a Hopi
Navaho Myths, Prayers, and Songs

©2007 A & D Publishing

A & D Publishing
PO Box 3005
Radford VA 24143-3005
www.wilderpublications.com

ISBN 10: 1-934451-94-0
ISBN 13: 978-1-934451-94-6

First Edition

The Sacred Formulas of the Cherokees.
By James Mooney

This is an ethnographic description of Cherokee shamanistic practice. Based on several manuscripts written by Cherokee shamans of the 19th Century, this includes the actual text of the rituals to treat various diseases, information on herbs used, love spells, hunting rituals, weather spells, as well as a spell for victory in the ball game.

Table of Contents

though the prophets of the old religion still have much
ence with the people, they are daily losing ground and will
be without honor in their own country.

uch an exposition of the aboriginal religion could be obtained
no other tribe in North America, for the simple reason that
ther tribe has an alphabet of its own in which to record its
ed lore. It is true that the Crees and Micmacs of Canada and
Tukuth of Alaska have so-called alphabets or ideographic
ems invented for their use by the missionaries, while, before
Spanish conquest, the Mayas of Central America were
stomed to note down their hero legends and priestly
monials in hieroglyphs graven upon the walls of their temples
ainted upon tablets made of the leaves of the maguey. But it
ns never to have occurred to the northern tribes that an
abet coming from a missionary source could be used for any
r purpose than the transcription of bibles and catechisms,
le the sacred books of the Mayas, with a few exceptions, have
since met destruction at the hands of fanaticism, and the
ern copies which have come down to the present day are
tten out from imperfect memory by Indians who had been
cated under Spanish influences in the language, alphabet and
as of the conquerors, and who, as is proved by an examination
he contents of the books themselves, drew from European
rces a great part of their material. Moreover, the Maya tablets
re so far hieratic as to be understood, only by the priests and
se who had received a special training in this direction, and
y seem therefore to have been entirely unintelligible to the
mmon people.

The Cherokee alphabet, on the contrary, is the invention or
aptation of one of the tribe, who, although he borrowed most of
e Roman letters, in addition to the forty or more characters of
s own devising, knew nothing of their proper use or value, but
versed them or altered their forms to suit his purpose, and gave
em a name and value determined by himself. This alphabet was
once adopted by the tribe for all purposes for which writing can
used, including the recording of their shamanistic prayers and
tualistic ceremonies. The formulas here given, as well as those of
e entire collection, were written out by the shamans
emselves—men who adhere to the ancient religion and speak
ly their native language in order that their sacred knowledge
ight be preserved in a systematic manner for their mutual

The sacred formulas here given are select
about six hundred, obtained on the Cherokee
Carolina in 1887 and 1888, and covering eve
to the daily life and thought of the Indian,
love, hunting, fishing, war, self-protection, de
witchcraft, the crops, the council, the ball pl
embodying almost the whole of the anci
Cherokees. The original manuscripts, now in t
Bureau of Ethnology, were written by the shar
their own use, in the Cherokee characters in
(Sequoyah) in 1821, and were obtained, witl
either from the writers themselves or fro
relatives.

Some of these manuscripts are known to be ε
old, and many are probably older. The medic
kinds constitute perhaps one-half of the whole
love charms come next in number, closely foll
and prayers used in hunting and fishing. The gr
charms will doubtless be a surprise to thos
educated in the old theory that, the Indian is
attractions of woman. The comparatively sma
formulas is explained by the fact that the last
Cherokees, as a tribe, were engaged on their ow
with the Revolutionary period, so that these thin
forgotten before the invention of the alphabet, a
The Cherokees who engaged in the Creek w
American civil war fought in the interests of the
leaders were subordinated to white officers, hen
the same opportunity for the exercise of shama
there would have been had Indians alone been
prayers for hunting, fishing, and the ball play
constant demand, have been better preserved,

These, formulas had been handed down orall
antiquity until the early part of the present cen
invention of the Cherokee syllabary enabled the pri
to put them into writing. The same invention mad
their rivals, the missionaries, to give to the India
their own language, so that the opposing forces of C
shamanism alike profited by the genius of Sikwâya
of the new civilization was too strong to be withst

and
influ
soon
S
from
no o
sacr
the
syst
the
accu
cere
or p
seer
alph
othe
whi
long
mo
wri
edu
ide
of
sou
we
the
the
co

ad
th
hi
re
th
at
be
ri
th
th
o
m

benefit. The language, the conception, and the execution are all genuinely Indian, and hardly a dozen lines of the hundreds of formulas show a trace of the influence of the white man or his religion. The formulas contained in these manuscripts are not disjointed fragments of a system long since extinct, but are the revelation of a living faith which still has its priests and devoted adherents, and it is only necessary to witness a ceremonial ball play, with its fasting, its going to water, and its mystic bead manipulation, to understand how strong is the hold which the old faith yet has upon the minds even of the younger generation. The numerous archaic and figurative expressions used require the interpretation of the priests, but, as before stated, the alphabet in which they are written is that in daily use among the common people.

In all tribes that still retain something of their ancient organization we find this sacred knowledge committed to the keeping of various secret societies, each of which has its peculiar ritual with regular initiation and degrees of advancement. From this analogy we may reasonably conclude that such was formerly the case with the Cherokees also, but by the breaking down of old customs consequent upon their long contact with the whites and the voluntary adoption of a civilized form of government in 1827, all traces of such society organization have long since disappeared, and at present each priest or shaman is isolated and independent, sometimes confining himself to a particular specialty, such as love or medicine, or even the treatment of two or three diseases, in other cases broadening his field of operations to include the whole range of mystic knowledge.

It frequently happens, however, that priests form personal friendships and thus are led to divulge their secrets to each other for their mutual advantage. Thus when one shaman meets another who he thinks can probably give him some valuable information, he says to him, "Let us sit down together." This is understood by the other to mean, "Let us tell each other our secrets." Should it seem probable that the seeker after knowledge can give as much as he receives, an agreement is generally arrived at, the two retire to some convenient spot secure from observation, and the first party begins by reciting one of his formulas with the explanations. The other then reciprocates with one of his own, unless it appears that the bargain is apt to prove a losing one, in which case the conference comes to an abrupt ending.

It is sometimes possible to obtain a formula by the payment of a coat, a quantity of cloth, or a sum of money. Like the Celtic Druids of old, the candidate for the priesthood in former times found it necessary to cultivate a long memory, as no formula was repeated more than once for his benefit. It was considered that one who failed to remember after the first hearing was not worthy to be accounted a shaman. This task, however, was not so difficult as might appear on first thought, when once the learner understood the theory involved, as the formulas are all constructed on regular principles, with constant repetition of the same set of words. The obvious effect of such a regulation was to increase the respect in which this sacred knowledge was held by restricting it to the possession of a chosen few.

Although the written formulas can be read without difficulty by any Cherokee educated in his own language, the shamans take good care that their sacred writings shall not fall into the hands of the laity or of their rivals in occult practices, and in performing the ceremonies the words used are uttered in such a low tone of voice as to be unintelligible even to the one for whose benefit the formula is repeated. Such being the case, it is in order to explain how the formulas collected were obtained.

HOW THE FORMULAS WERE OBTAINED.

On first visiting the reservation in the summer of 1887, I devoted considerable time to collecting plants used by the Cherokees for food or medicinal purposes, learning at the same time their Indian names and the particular uses to which each was applied and the mode of preparation. It soon became evident that the application of the medicine was not the whole, and in fact was rather the subordinate, part of the treatment, which was always accompanied by certain ceremonies and "words." From the workers employed at the time no definite idea could be obtained as to the character of these words. One young woman, indeed, who had some knowledge of the subject, volunteered to write the words which she used in her prescriptions, but failed to do so, owing chiefly to the opposition of the half-breed shamans, from whom she had obtained her information.

THE SWIMMER MANUSCRIPT.

Some time afterward an acquaintance was formed with a man named A`yûn'inï or "Swimmer," who proved to be so intelligent that I spent several days with him, procuring information in regard to myths and old customs. He told a number of stories in very good style, and finally related the Origin of the Bear. The bears were formerly a part of the Cherokee tribe who decided to leave their kindred and go into the forest. Their friends followed them and endeavored to induce them to return, but the Ani-Tsâ'kahï, as they were called, were determined to go. Just before parting from their relatives at the edge of the forest, they turned to them and said, "It is better for you that we should go; but we will teach you songs, and some day when you are in want of food come out to the woods and sing these songs and we shall appear and give you meat." Their friends, after warning several songs from them, started back to their homes, and after proceeding a short distance, turned around to take one last look, but saw only a number of bears disappearing in the depths of the forest. The songs which they learned are still sung by the hunter to attract the bears.

When Swimmer had finished the story he was asked if he knew these songs. He replied that he did, but on being requested to sing one he made some excuse and was silent. After some further efforts the interpreter said it would be useless to press the matter then as there were several other Indians present, but that to-morrow we should have him alone with us and could then make another attempt.

The next day Swimmer was told that if he persisted in his refusal it would be necessary to employ some one else, as it was unfair in him to furnish incomplete information when he was paid to tell all he knew. He replied that he was willing to tell anything in regard to stories and customs, but that these songs were a part of his secret knowledge and commanded a high price from the hunters, who sometimes paid as much as $5 for a single song, "because you can't kill any bears or deer unless you sing them."

He was told that the only object in asking about the songs was to put them on record and preserve them, so that when he and the half dozen old men of the tribe were dead the world might be aware how much the Cherokees had known. This appeal to his professional pride proved effectual, and when he was told that a great many similar songs had been sent to Washington by medicine men of other tribes, he promptly declared that he knew as much as any of them, and that he would give all the information in his possession, so that others might be able to judge for themselves who knew most. The only conditions he made were that these secret matters should be heard by no one else but the interpreter, and should not be discussed when other Indians were present.

As soon as the other shamans learned what was going on they endeavored by various means to persuade him to stop talking, or failing in this, to damage his reputation by throwing out hints as to his honesty or accuracy of statement. Among other objections which they advanced was one which, however incomprehensible to a white man, was perfectly intelligible to an Indian, viz.: That when he had told everything this information would be taken to Washington and locked up there, and thus they would be deprived of the knowledge. This objection was one of the most difficult to overcome, as there was no line of argument with which to oppose it.

These reports worried Swimmer, who was extremely, sensitive in regard to his reputation, and he became restive under the insinuations of his rivals. Finally on coming to work one day he produced a book from under his ragged coat as he entered the house, and said proudly: "Look at that and now see if I don't know something." It was a small day-book of about 240 pages, procured originally from a white man, and was about half filled with writing in the Cherokee characters. A brief examination disclosed the fact that it contained just those matters that had proved so difficult to procure. Here were prayers, songs, and prescriptions for the cure of all kinds of diseases—for chills, rheumatism, frostbites, wounds, bad dreams, and witchery; love charms, to gain the affections of a woman or to cause her to hate a detested rival; fishing charms, hunting charms—including the songs without which none could ever hope to kill, any game; prayers to make the corn grow, to frighten away storms, and to drive off witches; prayers for long life, for safety among strangers, for acquiring influence in council and success in the ball play. There were prayers to the Long Man, the Ancient White, the Great Whirlwind, the Yellow Rattlesnake, and to a hundred other gods of the Cherokee pantheon. It was in fact an Indian ritual and pharmacopoeia.

After recovering in a measure from the astonishment produced by this discovery I inquired whether other shamans had such books. "Yes," said Swimmer, "we all have them." Here then was a clew to follow up. A bargain was made by which be was to have another blank book into which to copy the formulas, after which the original was bought. It is now deposited in the library of the Bureau of Ethnology. The remainder of the time until the return was occupied in getting an understanding of the contents of the book.

THE GATIGWANASTI
MANUSCRIPT.

Further inquiry elicited the names of several others who might be supposed to have such papers. Before leaving a visit was paid to one of these, a young man named Wilnoti, whose father, Gatigwanasti, had been during his lifetime a prominent shaman, regarded as a man of superior intelligence. Wilnoti, who is a professing Christian, said that his father had had such papers, and after some explanation from the chief he consented to show them. He produced a box containing a lot of miscellaneous papers, testaments, and hymn-books, all in the Cherokee alphabet. Among them was his father's chief treasure, a manuscript book containing 122 pages of foolscap size, completely filled with formulas of the same kind as those contained in Swimmer's book. There were also a large number of loose sheets, making in all nearly 200 foolscap pages of sacred formulas.

On offering to buy the papers, he replied that he wanted to keep them in order to learn and practice these things himself—thus showing how thin was the veneer of Christianity, in his case at least. On representing to him that in a few years the new conditions would render such knowledge valueless with the younger generation, and that even if he retained the papers he would need some one else to explain them to him, he again refused, saying that they might fall into the hands of Swimmer, who, he was determined, should never see his father's papers. Thus the negotiations came to an end for the time.

On returning to the reservation in July, 1888, another effort was made to get possession of the Gatigwanasti manuscripts and any others of the same kind which could be procured. By this time the Indians had had several months to talk over the matter, and the idea had gradually dawned upon them that instead of taking their knowledge away from them and looking it up in a box, the intention was to preserve it to the world and pay them for it at the same time. In addition the writer took every opportunity to impress upon them the fact that he was acquainted with the secret knowledge of other tribes and perhaps could give them as much as they gave. It was now much easier to approach them, and on again visiting Wilnoti, in company with the interpreter, who explained the matter fully to him, he finally consented to lend the papers for a time, with the same condition that neither Swimmer nor anyone else but the chief and interpreter should see them, but he still refused to sell them. However, this allowed the use of the papers, and after repeated efforts during a period of several weeks, the matter ended in the purchase of the papers outright, with unreserved permission to show them for copying or explanation to anybody who might be selected. Wilnoti was not of a mercenary disposition, and after the first negotiations the chief difficulty was to overcome his objection to parting with his father's handwriting, but it was an essential point to get the originals, and he was allowed to copy some of the more important formulas, as he found it utterly out of the question to copy the whole.

These papers of Gatigwanasti are the most valuable of the whole, and amount to fully one-half the entire collection, about fifty pages consisting of love charms. The formulas are beautifully written in bold Cherokee characters, and the directions and headings are generally explicit, bearing out the universal testimony that he was a man of unusual intelligence and ability, characteristics inherited by his son, who, although a young man and speaking no English, is one of the most progressive and thoroughly reliable men of the band.

THE GAHUNI MANUSCRIPT.

The next book procured was obtained from a woman named Ayâsta, "The Spoiler," and had been written by her husband, Gahuni, who died about 30 years ago. The matter was not difficult to arrange, as she had already been employed on several occasions, so that she understood the purpose of the work, besides which her son had been regularly engaged to copy and classify the manuscripts already procured. The book was claimed as common property by Ayâsta and her three sons, and negotiations had to be carried on with each one, although in this instance the cash amount involved was only half a dollar, in addition to another book into which to copy some family records and personal memoranda. The book contains only eight formulas, but these are of a character altogether unique, the directions especially throwing a curious light on Indian beliefs. There had been several other formulas of the class called Y'û'nnwëhï, to cause hatred between man and wife, but these had been torn out and destroyed by Ayâsta on the advice of an old shaman, in order that her sons might never learn them. In referring to the matter she spoke in a whisper, and it was evident enough that she had full faith in the deadly power of these spells.

In addition to the formulas the book contains about twenty pages of Scripture extracts in the same handwriting, for Gahuni, like several others of their shamans, combined the professions of Indian conjurer and Methodist preacher. After his death the book fell into the hands of the younger members of the family, who filled it with miscellaneous writings and scribblings. Among other things there are about seventy pages of what was intended to be a Cherokee-English pronouncing dictionary, probably written by the youngest son, already mentioned, who has attended school, and who served for some time as copyist on the formulas. This curious Indian production, of which only a few columns are filled out, consists of a list of simple English words and phrases, written in ordinary English script, followed by Cherokee characters intended to give the approximate pronunciation, together with the corresponding word in the Cherokee language and characters. As the language lacks a number of sounds which are of frequent occurrence in English, the attempts to indicate the pronunciation sometimes give amusing results. Thus we find: Fox (English script); *kwâgisï'* (Cherokee characters); *tsú`lû'* (Cherokee characters). As the Cherokee language lacks the labial *f* and has no compound sound equivalent to our *x*, *kwâgisï"* is as near as the Cherokee speaker can come to pronouncing our word fox. In the same way "bet" becomes *wëtï*, and "sheep" is *síkwï*, while "if he has no dog" appears in the disguise of *ikwï hâsï nâ dâ'ga*.

THE INÂLI MANUSCRIPT.

In the course of further inquiries in regard to the whereabouts of other manuscripts of this kind we heard a great deal about Inâ'lï, or "Black Fox," who had died a few years before at an advanced age, and who was universally admitted to have been one of their most able men and the most prominent literary character among them, for from what has been said it must be sufficiently evident that the Cherokees have their native literature and literary men. Like those already mentioned, he was a full-blood Cherokee, speaking no English, and in the course of a long lifetime he had filled almost every position of honor among his people, including those of councilor, keeper of the townhouse records, Sunday-school leader, conjurer, officer in the Confederate service, and Methodist preacher, at last dying, as he was born, in the ancient faith of his forefathers.

On inquiring of his daughter she stated that her father had left a great many papers, most of which were still in her possession, and on receiving from the interpreter an explanation of our purpose she readily gave permission to examine and make selections from them on condition that the matter should be kept secret from outsiders. A day was appointed for visiting her, and on arriving we found her living in a comfortable log house, built by Inâ'lï himself, with her children and an ancient female relative, a decrepit old woman, with snow-white hair and vacant countenance. This was the oldest woman of the tribe, and though now so feeble and childish, she had been a veritable savage in her young days, having carried a scalp in the scalp dance in the Creek war 75 years before.

Having placed chairs for us in the shade Inâ'lï's daughter brought out a small box filled with papers of various kinds, both Cherokee and English. The work of examining these was a tedious business, as each paper had to be opened out and enough of it read to get the general drift of the contents, after which the several classes were arranged in separate piles. While in the midst of this work she brought out another box nearly as large as a small trunk, and on setting it down there was revealed to the astonished gaze such a mass of material as it had not seemed possible could exist in the entire tribe.

In addition to papers of the sort already mentioned there were a number of letters in English from various officials and religious organizations, and addressed to "Enola," to "Rev. Black Fox," and to "Black Fox, Esq," with a large number of war letters written to him by Cherokees who had enlisted in the Confederate service. These latter are all written in the Cherokee characters, in the usual gossipy style common among friends, and several of them contain important historic material in regard to the movements of the two armies in East Tennessee. Among other things was found his certificate as a Methodist preacher, dated in 1848. "Know all men by these presents that Black Fox (Cherokee) is hereby authorized to exercise his Gifts and Graces as a local preacher in M. E. Church South. "

There was found a manuscript book in Inâ'lï's handwriting containing the records of the old council of Wolftown, of which he had been secretary for several years down to the beginning of the war. This also contains some valuable materials.

There were also a number of miscellaneous books, papers, and pictures, together with various trinkets and a number of conjuring stones.

In fact the box was a regular curiosity shop, and it was with a feeling akin to despair that we viewed the piles of manuscript which had to be waded through and classified. There was a day's hard work ahead, and it was already past noon; but the woman was not done yet, and after rummaging about inside the house for a while longer she appeared with another armful of papers, which she emptied on top of the others. This was the last straw; and finding it impossible to examine in detail such a mass of material we contented ourselves with picking out the sacred formulas and the two manuscript books containing the town-house records and scriptural quotations and departed.

The daughter of Black Fox agreed to fetch down the other papers in a few days for further examination at our leisure; and she kept her promise, bringing with her at the same time a number of additional formulas which she had not been able to obtain before. A large number of letters and other papers were selected from the miscellaneous lot, and these, with the others obtained from her, are now deposited also with the Bureau of Ethnology. Among other things found at this house were several beads of the old shell wampum, of whose use the Cherokees have now lost even the recollection. She knew only that they were very old and different from the common beads, but she prized them as talismans, and firmly refused to part with them.

OTHER MANUSCRIPTS.

Subsequently a few formulas were obtained from an old shaman named Tsiskwa or "Bird," but they were so carelessly written as to be almost worthless, and the old mail who wrote them, being then on his dying bed, was unable to give much help in the matter. However, as he was anxious to tell what he knew all attempt was made to take down some formulas from his dictation. A few more were obtained in this way but the results were not satisfactory and the experiment was abandoned. About the same time A`wani'ta or "Young Deer," one of their best herb doctors, was engaged to collect the various plants used in medicine and describe their uses. While thus employed he wrote in a book furnished him for the purpose a number of formulas used by him in his practice, giving at the same time a verbal explanation of the theory and ceremonies. Among these was one for protection in battle, which had been used by himself and a number of other Cherokees in the late war. Another doctor named Takwati'hï or "Catawba Killer," was afterward employed on the same work and furnished some additional formulas which he had had his son write down from his dictation, he himself being unable to write. His knowledge was limited to the practice of a few specialties, but in regard to these his information was detailed and accurate. There was one for bleeding with the cupping horn. All these formulas obtained from Tsiskwa, A`wanita, and Takwtihi are now in possession of the Bureau.

THE KANÂHETA ANI-TSALAGI ETI.

Among the papers thus obtained was a large number which for various reasons it was found difficult to handle or file for preservation. Many of them had been written so long ago that the ink had almost faded from the paper; others were written with lead pencil, so that in handling them the characters soon became blurred and almost illegible; a great many were written on scraps of paper of all shapes and sizes; and others again were full of omissions and doublets, due to the carelessness of the writer, while many consisted simply of the prayer, with nothing in the nature of a heading or prescription to show its purpose.

Under the circumstances it was deemed expedient to have a number of these formulas copied in more enduring form. For this purpose it was decided to engage the services of Ayâsta's youngest son, an intelligent young man about nineteen years of age, who had attended school long enough to obtain a fair acquaintance with English in addition to his intimate knowledge of Cherokee. He was also gifted with a ready comprehension, and from his mother and uncle Tsiskwa had acquired some familiarity with many of the archaic expressions used in the sacred formulas. He was commonly known as "Will West," but signed himself W. W. Long, Long being the translation of his father's name, Gûnahi'ta. After being instructed as to how the work should be done with reference to paragraphing, heading, etc., he was furnished a blank book of two hundred pages into which to copy such formulas as it seemed desirable to duplicate. He readily grasped the idea and in the course of about a month, working always under the writer's personal supervision, succeeded in completely filling the book according to the plan outlined. In addition to the duplicate formulas he wrote down a number of dance and drinking songs, obtained originally from A`yûn'inï, with about thirty miscellaneous formulas obtained from various sources. The book thus prepared is modeled on the plan of an ordinary book, with headings, table of contents, and even with an illuminated title page devised by the aid of the interpreter according to the regular Cherokee idiomatic form, and is altogether a unique specimen of Indian literary art. It contains in all two hundred and fifty-eight formulas and songs, which of course are native aboriginal productions, although the mechanical arrangement was performed under the direction of a white man. This book also, under its Cherokee title, *Kanâhe'ta Ani-Tsa'lagï E'tï* or "Ancient Cherokee Formulas," is now in the library of the Bureau.

There is still a considerable quantity of such manuscript in the hands of one or two shamans with whom there was no chance for negotiating, but an effort will be made to obtain possession of these on some future visit, should opportunity present. Those now in the Bureau library comprised by far the greater portion of the whole quantity held by the Indians, and as only a small portion of this was copied by the owners it can not be duplicated by any future collector.

CHARACTER OF THE FORMULAS
THE CHEROKEE RELIGION.

It is impossible to overestimate the ethnologic importance of the materials thus obtained. They are invaluable as the genuine production of the Indian mind, setting forth in the clearest light the state of the aboriginal religion before its contamination by contact with the whites. To the psychologist and the student of myths they are equally precious. In regard to their linguistic value we may quote the language of Brinton, speaking of the sacred books of the Mayas, already referred to:

Another value they have, and it is one which will be properly appreciated by any student of languages. They are, by common consent of all competent authorities, the genuine productions of native minds, cast in the idiomatic forms of the native tongue by those born to its use. No matter how fluent a foreigner becomes in a language not his own, he can never use it as does one who has been familiar with it from childhood. This general maxim is tenfold true when we apply it to a European learning an American language. The flow of thought, as exhibited in these two linguistic families, is in such different directions that no amount of practice can render one equally accurate in both. Hence the importance of studying a tongue as it is employed by natives; and hence the very high estimate I place on these "Books of Chilan Balam" as linguistic material—an estimate much increased by the great rarity of independent compositions in their own tongues by members of the native races of this continent.

The same author, in speaking of the internal evidences of authenticity contained in the Popol Vuh, the sacred book of the Kichés, uses the following words, which apply equally well to these Cherokee formulas:

To one familiar with native American myths, this one bears undeniable marks of its aboriginal origin. Its frequent puerilities and inanities, its generally low and coarse range of thought and expression, its occasional loftiness of both, its strange metaphors and the prominence of strictly heathen names and potencies, bring it into unmistakable relationship to the true native myth.

These formulas furnish a complete refutation of the assertion so frequently made by ignorant and prejudiced writers that the Indian had no religion excepting what they are pleased to call the meaning less mummeries of the medicine man. This is the very reverse of the truth. The Indian is essentially religious and contemplative, and it might almost be said that every act of his life is regulated and determined by his religious belief. It matters not that some may call this superstition. The difference is only relative. The religion of to-day has developed from the cruder superstitions of yesterday, and Christianity itself is but an outgrowth and enlargement of the beliefs and ceremonies which have been preserved by the Indian in their more ancient form. When we are willing to admit that the Indian has a religion which he holds sacred, even though it be different from our own, we can then admire the consistency of the theory, the particularity of the ceremonial and the beauty of the expression. So far from being a jumble of crudities, there is a wonderful completeness about the whole system which is not surpassed even by the ceremonial religions of the East. It is evident from a study of these formulas that the Cherokee Indian was a polytheist and that the spirit world was to him only a shadowy counterpart of this. All his prayers were for temporal and tangible blessings—for health, for long life, for success in the chase, in fishing, in war and in love, for good crops, for protection and for revenge. He had no Great Spirit, no happy hunting ground, no heaven, no hell, and consequently death had for him no terrors and he awaited the inevitable end with no anxiety as to the future. He was careful not to violate the rights of his tribesman or to do injury to his feelings, but there is nothing to show that he had any idea whatever of what is called morality in the abstract.

THE ORIGIN OF DISEASE AND MEDICINE.

In the old days quadrupeds, birds, fishes, and insects could all talk, and they and the human race lived together in peace and friendship. But as time went on the people increased so rapidly that their settlements spread over the whole earth and the poor animals found themselves beginning to be cramped for room. This was bad enough, but to add to their misfortunes man invented bows, knives, blowguns, spears, and hooks, and began to slaughter the larger animals, birds and fishes for the sake of their flesh or their skins, while the smaller creatures, such as the frogs and worms, were crushed and trodden upon without mercy, out of pure carelessness or contempt. In. this state of affairs the animals resolved to consult upon measures for their common safety.

The bears were the first to meet in council in their townhouse in Kuwa'hï, the "Mulberry Place," and the old White Bear chief presided.

After each in turn had made complaint against the way in which man killed their friends, devoured their flesh and used their skins for his own adornment, it was unanimously decided to begin war at once against the human race. Some one asked what weapons man used to accomplish their destruction. "Bows and arrows, of course," cried all the bears in chorus. "And what are they made of?" was the next question. "The bow of wood and the string of our own entrails," replied one of the bears. It was then proposed that they make a bow and some arrows and see if they could not turn man's weapons against himself. So one bear got a nice piece of locust wood and another sacrificed himself for the good of the rest in order to furnish a piece of his entrails for the string. But when everything was ready and the first bear stepped up to make the trial it was found that in letting the arrow fly after drawing back the bow, his long claws caught the string and spoiled the shot. This was annoying, but another suggested that he could overcome the difficulty by cutting his claws, which was accordingly done, and on a second trial it was found that the arrow went straight to the mark. But here the chief, the old White Bear, interposed and said that it was necessary that they should have long claws in order to be able to climb trees. "One of us has already died to furnish the bowstring, and if we now cut off our claws we shall all have to starve together. It is better to trust to the teeth and claws which nature has given us, for it is evident that man's weapons were not intended for us."

No one could suggest any better plan, so the old chief dismissed the council and the bears dispersed to their forest haunts without having concerted any means for preventing the increase of the human race. Had the result of the council been otherwise, we should now be at war with the bears, but as it is the hunter does not even ask the bear's pardon when he kills one.

The deer next held a council under their chief, the Little Deer, and after some deliberation resolved to inflict rheumatism upon every hunter who should kill one of their number, unless he took care to ask their pardon for the offense. They sent notice of their decision to the nearest settlement of Indians and told them at the same time how to make propitiation when necessity forced them to kill one of the deer tribe. Now, whenever the hunter brings down a deer, the Little Deer, who is swift as the wind and can not be wounded, runs quickly up to the spot and bending over the blood stains asks the spirit of the deer if it has heard the prayer of the hunter for pardon. If the reply be "Yes" all is well and the Little Deer goes on his way, but if the reply be in the negative he follows on the trail of the hunter, guided by the drops of blood on the ground, until he arrives at the cabin in the settlement, when the Little Deer enters invisibly and strikes the neglectful hunter with rheumatism, so that he, is rendered on the instant a helpless cripple. No hunter who has regard for his health ever fails to ask pardon of the deer for killing it, although some who have not learned the proper formula may attempt to turn aside the Little Deer from his pursuit by building a fire behind them in the trail.

Next came the fishes and reptiles, who had their own grievances against humanity. They held a joint council and determined to make their victims dream of snakes twining about them in slimy folds and blowing their fetid breath in their faces, or to make them dream of eating raw or decaying fish, so that they would lose appetite, sicken, and die. Thus it is that snake and fish dreams are accounted for.

Finally the birds, insects, and smaller animals came together for a like purpose, and the Grubworm presided over the deliberations. It was decided that each in turn should express an opinion and then vote on the question as to whether or not man should be deemed guilty. Seven votes were to be sufficient to condemn him. One after another denounced man's cruelty and injustice toward the other animals and voted in favor of his death. The Frog (walâ'sï) spoke first and said: "We must do something to check the increase of the race or people will become so numerous that we shall be crowded from off the earth. See how man has kicked me about because I'm ugly, as he says, until my back is covered with sores;" and here he showed the spots on his skin. Next came the Bird (tsi'skwa; no particular species is indicated), who condemned man because "he burns my feet off," alluding to the way in which the hunter barbecues birds by impaling them on a stick set over the fire, so that their feathers and tender feet are singed and burned. Others followed in the same strain. The Ground Squirrel alone ventured to say a word in behalf of man, who seldom hurt him because he was so small; but this so enraged the others that they fell upon the Ground Squirrel and tore him with their teeth and claws, and the stripes remain on his back to this day.

The assembly then began to devise and name various diseases, one after another, and had not their invention finally failed them not one of the human race would have been able to survive. The Grubworm in his place of honor hailed each new malady with delight, until at last they had reached the end of the list, when some one suggested that it be arranged so that menstruation should sometimes prove fatal to woman. On this he rose up in his place and cried: "Wata'n! Thanks! I'm glad some of them will die, for they are getting so thick that they tread on me." He fairly shook with joy at the thought, so that he fell over backward and could not get on his feet again, but had to wriggle off on his back, as the Grubworm has done ever since.

When the plants, who were friendly to man, heard what had been done by the animals, they determined to defeat their evil designs. Each tree, shrub, and herb, down even to the grasses and mosses, agreed to furnish a remedy for some one of the diseases named, and each said: "I shall appear to help man when he calls upon me in his need." Thus did medicine originate, and the plants, every one of which has its use if we only knew it, furnish the antidote to counteract the evil wrought by the revengeful animals. When the doctor is in doubt what treatment to apply for the relief of a patient, the spirit of the plant suggests to him the proper remedy.

THEORY OF DISEASE—ANIMALS, GHOSTS, WITCHES.

Such is the belief upon which their medical practice is based, and whatever we may think of the theory it must be admitted that the practice is consistent in all its details with the views set forth in the myth. Like most primitive people the Cherokees believe that disease and death are not natural, but are due to the evil influence of animal spirits, ghosts, or witches. Haywood, writing in 1823, states on the authority of two intelligent residents of the Cherokee nation:

In ancient times the Cherokees had no conception of anyone dying a natural death. They universally ascribed the death of those who perished by disease to the intervention or agency of evil spirits and witches and conjurers who had connection with the Shina (Anisgi'na) or evil spirits. A person dying by disease and charging his death to have been procured by means of witchcraft or spirits, by any other person, consigns that person to inevitable death. They profess to believe that their conjurations have no effect upon white men.

On the authority of one of the same informants, he also mentions the veneration which "their physicians have for the numbers four and seven, who say that after man was placed upon the earth four and seven nights were instituted for the cure of diseases in the human body and the seventh night as the limit for female impurity."

Viewed from a scientific standpoint, their theory and diagnosis are entirely wrong, and consequently we can hardly expect their therapeutic system to be correct. As the learned Doctor Berendt states, after an exhaustive study of the medical books of the Mayas, the scientific value of their remedies is "next to nothing." It must be admitted that many of the plants used in their medical practice possess real curative properties, but it is equally true that many others held in as high estimation are inert. It seems probable that in the beginning the various herbs and other plants were regarded as so many fetiches and were selected from some fancied connection with the disease animal, according to the idea known to modern folklorists as the doctrine of signatures. Thus at the present day the doctor puts into the decoction intended as a vermifuge some of the red fleshy stalks of the common purslane or chickweed (Portulaca oleracea), because these stalks somewhat resemble worms and consequently must have some occult influence over worms. Here the chickweed is a fetich precisely as is the flint arrow bead which is put into the same decoction, in order that in the same mysterious manner its sharp cutting qualities may be communicated to the liquid and enable it to cut the worms into pieces. In like manner, biliousness is called by the Cherokees dalâ'nï or "yellow," because the most apparent symptom of the disease is the vomiting by the patient of the yellow bile, and hence the doctor selects for the decoction four different herbs, each of which is also called dalânï, because of the color of the root, stalk, or flower. The same idea is carried out in the tabu which generally accompanies the treatment. Thus a scrofulous patient must abstain from eating the meat of a turkey, because the fleshy dewlap which depends from its throat somewhat resembles an inflamed scrofulous eruption. On killing a deer the hunter always makes an incision in the hind quarter and removes the hamstring, because this tendon, when severed, draws up into the flesh; ergo, any one who should unfortunately partake of the hamstring would find his limbs draw up in the same manner.

There can be no doubt that in course of time a haphazard use of plants would naturally lead to the discovery that certain herbs are efficacious in certain combinations of symptoms. These plants would thus come into more frequent use and finally would obtain general recognition in the Indian materia medica. By such a process of evolution an empiric system of medicine has grown up among the Cherokees, by which they are able to, treat some classes of ailments with some degree of success, although without any intelligent idea of the process involved. It must be remembered that our own medical system has its remote origin in the same mythic conception of disease, and that within two hundred years judicial courts have condemned women to be burned to death for producing sickness by spells and incantations, while even at the present day our faith-cure professors reap their richest harvest among people commonly supposed to belong to the intelligent classes. In the treatment of wounds the Cherokee doctors exhibit a considerable degree of skill, but as far as any internal ailment is concerned the average farmer's wife is worth all the doctors in the whole tribe.

The faith of the patient has much to do with his recovery, for the Indian has the same implicit confidence in the shaman that a child has in a more intelligent physician. The ceremonies and prayers are well calculated to inspire this feeling, and the effect thus produced upon the mind of the sick man undoubtedly reacts favorably upon his physical organization.

The following list of twenty plants used in Cherokee practice will give a better idea of the extent of their medical knowledge than could be conveyed by a lengthy dissertation. The names are given in the order in which they occur in the botanic notebook filled on the reservation, excluding names of food plants and species not identified, so that no attempt has been made to select in accordance with a preconceived theory. Following the name of each plant are given its uses as described by the Indian doctors, together with its properties as set forth in the United States Dispensatory, one of the leading pharmacopœias in use in this country. For the benefit of those not versed in medical phraseology it may be stated that aperient, cathartic, and deobstruent are terms applied to medicines intended to open or purge the bowels, a diuretic has the property of exciting the flow of urine, a diaphoretic excites perspiration, and a demulcent protects or soothes irritated tissues, while hæmoptysis denotes a peculiar variety of blood-splitting and aphthous is an adjective applied to ulcerations in the mouth.

SELECTED LIST OF PLANTS USED.

1. UNASTE'TSTYÛ = "very small root "—Aristolochia serpentaria—Virginia or black snakeroot: Decoction of root blown upon patient for fever and feverish head ache, and drunk for coughs; root chewed and spit upon wound to cure snake bites; bruised root placed in hollow tooth for toothache, and held against nose made sore by constant blowing in colds. Dispensatory: "A stimulant tonic, acting also as a diaphoretic or diuretic, according to the mode of its application; also been highly recommended in intermittent fevers, and though itself generally inadequate to the cure often proves serviceable as an adjunct to Peruvian bark or sulphate of quinia." Also used for typhous diseases, in dyspepsia, as a gargle for sore throat, as a mild stimulant in typhoid fevers, and to promote eruptions. The genus derives its scientific name from its supposed efficacy in promoting menstrual discharge, and some species have acquired the "reputation of antidotes for the bites of serpents."

2. UNISTIL'ÛnISTÎ = "they stick on"—Cynoglossum Morrisoni—Beggar lice: Decoction of root or top drunk for kidney troubles; bruised root used with bear oil as an ointment for cancer; forgetful persons drink a decoction of this plant, and probably also of other similar bur plants, from an idea that the sticking qualities of the burs will thus be imparted to the memory. From a similar connection of ideas the root is also used in the preparation of love charms. Dispensatory: Not named. C. officinale "has been used as a demulcent and sedative in coughs, catarrh, spitting of blood, dysentery, and diarrhea, and has been also applied externally in bums, ulcers, scrofulous tumors and goiter."

2. The Cherokee plant names here given are generic names, which are the names commonly used. In many cases the same name is applied to several species and it is only when it is necessary to distinguish between them that the Indians use what might be called specific names. Even then the descriptive term used serves to distinguish only the particular plants under discussion and the introduction of another variety bearing the same generic name would necessitate a new classification of species on a different basis, while hardly any two individuals would classify the species by the same characteristics.]

3. ÛnNAGÉI = "olack"—Cassia Marilandica—Wild senna: Root bruised and moistened with water for poulticing sores; decoction drunk for fever and for a disease also called ûnnage'i, or "black" (same name as plant), in which the hands and eye sockets are said

to turn black; also for a disease described as similar to ûnnage'i, but more dangerous, in which the eye sockets become black, while black spots appear on the arms, legs, and over the ribs on one side of the body, accompanied by partial paralysis, and resulting in death should the black spots appear also on the other side. Dispensatory: Described as "an efficient and safe cathartic, most conveniently given in the form of infusion."

4. KÂSD'ÚTA = "simulating ashes," so called on account of the appearance of the leaves—Gnaphalium decurrens—Life everlasting: Decoction drunk for colds; also used in the sweat bath for various diseases and considered one of their most valuable medical plants. Dispensatory: Not named. Decoctions of two other species of this genus are mentioned as used by country people for chest and bowel diseases, and for hemorrhages, bruises, ulcers, etc., although "probably possessing little medicinal virtue."

5. ALTSA'STI = "a wreath for the head"—Vicia Caroliniana—Vetch: Decoction drunk for dyspepsia and pains in the back, and rubbed on stomach for cramp; also rubbed on ball-players after scratching, to render their muscles tough, and used in the same way after scratching in the disease referred to under ûnnage'i, in which one side becomes black in spots, with partial paralysis; also used in same manner in decoction with Kâsduta for rheumatism; considered one of their most valuable medicinal herbs. Dispensatory: Not named.

6. DISTAI'YÏ = "they (the roots) are tough"—Tephrosia Virginiana—Catgut, Turkey Pea, Goat's Rue, or Devil's Shoestrings: Decoction drunk for lassitude. Women wash their hair in decoction of its roots to prevent its breaking or falling out, because these roots are very tough and hard to break; from the same idea ball-players rub the decoction on their limbs after scratching, to toughen them. Dispensatory: Described as a cathartic with roots tonic and aperient.

7. U'GA-ATASGI'SKÏ = "the pus oozes out"—Euphorbia hypericifolia—Milkweed: Juice rubbed on for skin eruptions, especially on children's heads; also used as a purgative; decoction drunk for gonorrhœa and similar diseases in both sexes, and held in high estimation for this purpose; juice used as an ointment for sores and for sore nipples, and in connection with other herbs for cancer. Dispensatory: The juice of all of the genus has the property of "powerfully irritating the skin when applied to it," while nearly all are powerful emetics, and cathartics. This species "has been

highly commended as a remedy in dysentery after due depletion, diarrhea, menorrhagia, and leucorrhea."

8. GÛ'NÏGWALÏ'SKÏ = "It becomes discolored when bruised"—Scutellaria lateriflora—Skullcap. "The name refers to the red juice which comes out of the stalk when bruised or chewed. A decoction of the four varieties of Gûnigwalï'skï—lateriflora, S. pilosa, Hypericum corymbosum, and Stylosanthes elatior—is drunk to promote menstruation, and the same decoction is also drunk and used as a wash to counteract the ill effects of eating food prepared by a woman in the menstrual condition, or when such a woman by chance comes into a sick room or a house under the tabu; also drunk for diarrhea and used with other herbs in decoction for breast pains. Dispensatory: This plant "produces no very obvious effects," but some doctors regard it as possessed of nervine, antispasmodic and tonic properties. None of the other three species are named.

9. KÂ'GA SKÛ'nTAGÏ = "crow shin"—Adiantum pedatum—Maidenhair Fern: Used either in decoction or poultice for rheumatism and chills, generally in connection with some other fern. The doctors explain that the fronds of the different varieties of fern are curled up in the young plant, but unroll and straighten out as it grows, and consequently a decoction of ferns causes the contracted muscles of the rheumatic patient to unbend and straighten out in like manner. It is also used in decoction for fever. Dispensatory: The leaves "have been supposed to be useful in chronic catarrh and other pectoral affections."

10. ANDA'NKALAGI'SKI = "it removes things from the gums"—Geranium maculatum—Wild Alum, Cranesbill: Used in decoction with Yânû Unihye stï (Vitis cordifolia) to wash the mouths of children in thrush; also used alone for the same purpose by blowing the chewed fiber into the mouth. Dispensatory: "One of our best indigenous astringents diarrhea, chronic dysentery, cholora infantum in the latter stages, and the various hemorrhages are the forms of disease in which it is most commonly used." Also valuable as "an application to indolent ulcers, an injection in gleet and leucorrhea, a gargle in relaxation of the uvula and aphthous ulcerations of the throat." The other plant sometimes used with it is not mentioned.

11. Û'nLË, UKÏ'LTÏ = "the locust frequents it"—Gillenia trifoliata—Indian Physic. Two doctors state that it is good as a tea for bowel complaints, with fever and yellow vomit; but another

says that it is poisonous and that no decoction is ever drunk, but that the beaten root is a good poultice for swellings. Dispensatory: "Gillenia is a mild and efficient emetic, and like most substances belonging to the same class occasionally acts upon the bowels. In very small doses it has been thought to be tonic."

12. SKWA'LÏ = Hepatica acutiloba—Liverwort, Heartleaf: Used for coughs either in tea or by chewing root. Those who dream of snakes drink a decoction of this herb and I'natû Ga'n`ka = "snake tongue"—(Camptosorus rhizophyllus or Walking Fern) to produce vomiting, after which the dreams do not return. The traders buy large quantities of liverwort from the Cherokees, who may thus have learned to esteem it more highly than they otherwise would. The appearance of the other plant, Camptosorus rhizophyllus, has evidently determined its Cherokee name and the use to which it is applied. Dispensatory: "Liverwort is a very mild demulcent tonic and astringent, supposed by some to possess diuretic and deobstruent virtues. It was formerly used in Europe in various complaints, especially chronic hepatic affections, but has fallen into entire neglect. In this country, some years since, it acquired considerable reputation, which, however, it has not maintained as a remedy in hæmoptysis and chronic coughs." The other plant is not named.

13. DA'YEWÛ = "it sews itself up," because the leaves are said to grow together again when torn—Cacalia atriplicifolia—Tassel Flower: Held in great repute as a poultice for cuts, bruises, and cancer, to draw out the blood or poisonous matter. The bruised leaf is bound over the spot and frequently removed. The dry powdered leaf was formerly used to sprinkle over food like salt. Dispensatory—Not named.

14. Â'TALÏ KÛLÏ' = "it climbs the mountain."—Aralia quinquefolia—Ginseng or "Sang:" Decoction of root drunk for headache, cramps, etc., and for female troubles; chewed root blown on spot for pains in the side. The Cherokees sell large quantities of sang to the traders for 50 cents per pound, nearly equivalent there to two days' wages, a fact which has doubtless increased their idea of its importance. Dispensatory: "The extraordinary medical virtues formerly ascribed to ginseng had no other existence than in the imagination of the Chinese. It is little more than a demulcent, and in this country is not employed as a medicine." The Chinese name, ginseng, is said to refer to the fancied resemblance of the root to a human figure, while in the

Cherokee formulas it is addressed as the "great man" or "little man," and this resemblance no doubt has much to do with the estimation in which it is held by both peoples.

15. Û'TSATÏ UWADSÏSKA = "fish scales," from shape of leaves—Thalictrum anemonoides—Meadow Rue: Decoction of root drunk for diarrhea with vomiting. Dispensatory: Not named.

16. K'KWË ULASU'LA = "partridge moccasin"—Cypripedium parviflorum—Ladyslipper: Decoction of root used for worms in children. In the liquid are placed some stalks of the common chickweed or purslane (Cerastium vulgatum) which, from the appearance of its red fleshy stalks, is supposed to have some connection with worms. Dispensatory: Described as "a gentle nervous stimulant" useful in diseases in which the nerves are especially affected. The other herb is not named.

17. A'HAWÏ' AKÄ'TÄ'—"deer eye," from the appearance of the flower-Rudbeckia fulgida—Cone Flower: Decoction of root drunk for flux and for some private diseases; also used as a wash for snakebites and swellings caused by (mythic) tsgâya or worms; also dropped into weak or inflamed eyes. This last is probably from the supposed connection between the eye and the flower resembling the eye. Dispensatory: Not named.

18. UTÏSTUGÏ'—Polygonatum multiflorum latifolium—Solomon's Seal: Root heated and bruised and applied as a poultice to remove an ulcerating swelling called tu'stï', resembling a boil or carbuncle. Dispensatory: This species acts like P. uniflorum, which is said to be emetic, In former times it was used externally in bruises, especially those about the eyes, in tumors, wounds, and cutaneous eruptions and was highly esteemed as a cosmetic. At present it is not employed, though recommended by Hermann as a good remedy in gout and rheumatism." This species in decoction has been found to produce nausea, a cathartic effect and either diaphoresis or diuresis, "and is useful as an internal remedy in piles, and externally in the form of decoction, in the affection of the skin resulting from the poisonous exhalations of certain plants."

19. ÄMÄDITA`TÏ—"water dipper," because water can be sucked up through its hollow stalk—Eupatorium purpureum—Queen of the Meadow, Gravel Root: Root used in decoction with a somewhat similar plant called Ämäditá`tï ü'tanu, or "large water dipper" (not identified) for difficult urination. Dispensatory: "Said to operate as a diuretic. Its vulgar name of gravel root indicates the popular

estimation of its virtues." The genus is described as tonic, diaphoretic, and in large doses emetic and aperient.

20. YÂNA UTSËSTA = "the bear lies on it"—Aspidium acrostichoides—Shield Fern: Root decoction drunk to produce vomiting, and also used to rub on the skin, after scratching, for rheumatism—in both cases some other plant is added to the decoction; the warm decoction is also held in the mouth to relieve toothache. Dispensatory: Not named.

The results obtained from a careful study of this list maybe summarized as follows: Of the twenty plants described as used by the Cherokees, seven (Nos. 2, 4, 5, 13, 15, 17, and 20) are not noticed in the Dispensatory even in the list of plants sometimes used although regarded as not officinal. It is possible that one or two of these seven plants have medical properties, but this can hardly be true of a larger number unless we are disposed to believe that the Indians are better informed in this regard than the best educated white physicians in the country. Two of these seven plants, however (Nos. 2 and 4), belong to genera which seem to have some of the properties ascribed by the Indians to the species. Five others of the list (Nos. 8, 9, 11, 14, and 16) are used for entirely wrong purposes, taking the Dispensatory as authority, and three of these are evidently used on account of some fancied connection between the plant and the disease, according to the doctrine of signatures. Three of the remainder (Nos. 1, 3, and 6) may be classed as uncertain in their properties, that is, while the plants themselves seem to possess some medical value, the Indian mode of application is so far at variance with recognized methods, or their own statements are so vague and conflicting, that it is doubtful whether any good can result from the use of the herbs. Thus the Unaste'tstiyû, or Virginia Snakeroot, is stated by the Dispensatory to have several uses, and among other things is said to have been highly recommended in intermittent fevers, although alone it is "generally inadequate to the cure." Though not expressly stated, the natural inference is that it must be applied internally, but the Cherokee doctor, while he also uses it for fever, takes the decoction in his mouth and blows it over the head and shoulders of the patient. Another of these, the Distai'yï, or Turkey Pea, is described in the Dispensatory as having roots tonic and aperient. The Cherokees drink a decoction of the roots for a feeling of weakness and languor, from which it might be supposed that they understood the tonic properties of the plant had not the same decoction been used by the women as a hair wash, and by the ball players to bathe their limbs, under the impression that the toughness of the roots would thus be communicated to the hair or muscles. From this fact and from the name of the plant, which means at once hard, tough, or strong, it is quite probable that its roots are believed to give strength to the patient solely because they themselves are so strong and not because they have been proved to be really efficacious. The remaining five plants have generally pronounced medicinal qualities, and are used by the Cherokees for the very purposes for which, according to the Dispensatory, they are best adapted; so that we must admit that so much of their practice is correct, however false the reasoning by which they have arrived at this result.

MEDICAL PRACTICE.

Taking the Dispensatory as the standard, and assuming that this list is a fair epitome of what the Cherokees know concerning the medical properties of plants, we find that five plants, or 25 per cent of the whole number, are correctly used; twelve, or 60 per cent, are presumably either worthless or incorrectly used, and three plants, or 15 per cent, are so used that it is difficult to say whether they are of any benefit or not. Granting that two of these three produce good results as used by the Indians, we should have 35 per cent, or about one-third of the whole, as the proportion actually possessing medical virtues, while the remaining two-thirds are inert, if not positively injurious. It is not probable that a larger number of examples would change the proportion to any appreciable extent. A number of herbs used in connection with these principal plants may probably be set down as worthless, inasmuch as they are not named in the Dispensatory.

The results here arrived at will doubtless be a surprise to those persons who hold that an Indian must necessarily be a good doctor, and that the medicine man or conjurer, with his theories of ghosts, witches, and revengeful animals, knows more about the properties of plants and the cure of disease than does the trained botanist or physician who has devoted a lifetime of study to the patient investigation of his specialty, with all the accumulated information contained in the works of his predecessors to build upon, and with all the light thrown upon his pathway by the discoveries of modern science. It is absurd to suppose that the savage, a child in intellect, has reached a higher development in any branch of science than has been attained by the civilized man, the product of long ages of intellectual growth. It would be as unreasonable to suppose that the Indian could be entirely ignorant of the medicinal properties of plants, living as he did in the open air in close communion with nature; but neither in accuracy nor extent can his knowledge be compared for a moment with that of the trained student working upon scientific principles.

Cherokee medicine is an empiric development of the fetich idea. For a disease caused by the rabbit the antidote must be a plant called "rabbit's food," "rabbit's ear," or "rabbit's tail;" for snake dreams the plant used is "snake's tooth;" for worms a plant resembling a worm in appearance, and for inflamed eyes a flower having the appearance and name of "deer's eye." A yellow root must be good when the patient vomits yellow bile, and a black one when dark circles come about his eyes, and in each case the disease and the plant alike are named from the color. A decoction of burs must be a cure for forgetfulness, for there is nothing else that will stick like a bur; and a decoction of the wiry roots of the "devil's shoestrings" must be an efficacious wash to toughen the ballplayer's muscles, for they are almost strong enough to stop the plowshare in the furrow. It must be evident that under such a system the failures must far outnumber the cures, yet it is not so long since half our own medical practice was based upon the same idea of correspondences, for the mediaeval physicians taught that similia similibus curantur, and have we not all heard that "the hair of the dog will cure the bite?"

Their ignorance of the true medical principles involved is shown by the regulations prescribed for the patient. With the exception of the fasting, no sanitary precautions are taken to aid in the recovery of the sick man or to contribute to his comfort. Even the fasting is as much religious as sanative, for in most cases where it is prescribed the doctor also must abstain from food until sunset, just as in the Catholic church both priest and communicants remain fasting from midnight until after the celebration of the divine mysteries. As the Indian cuisine is extremely limited, no delicate or appetizing dishes are prepared for the patient, who partakes of the same heavy, sodden cornmeal dumplings and bean bread which form his principal food in health. In most cases certain kinds of food are prohibited, such as squirrel meat, fish, turkey, etc.; but the reason is not that such food is considered deleterious to health, as we understand it, but because of some fanciful connection with the disease spirit. Thus if squirrels have caused the illness the patient must not eat squirrel meat. If the disease be rheumatism, he must not eat the leg of any animal, because the limbs are generally the seat of this malady. Lye, salt, and hot food are always forbidden when there is any prohibition at all; but here again, in nine cases out of ten, the regulation, instead of being beneficial, serves only to add to his discomfort. Lye enters into almost all the food preparations of the Cherokees, the alkaline potash taking the place of salt, which is seldom used among them, having been introduced by the whites. Their bean and chestnut bread, cornmeal dumplings' hominy, and gruel are all boiled in a pot, all contain lye, and are all, excepting the last, served up hot from the fire. When cold their bread is about as hard and tasteless as a lump of yesterday's dough, and to condemn a sick man to a diet of such dyspeptic food, eaten cold without even a pinch of salt to give it a relish, would seem to be sufficient to kill him with, out any further aid from the doctor. The salt or lye so strictly prohibited is really a tonic and appetizer, and in many diseases acts with curative effect. So much for the health regimen.

In serious cases the patient is secluded and no strangers are allowed to enter the house. On first thought this would appear to be a genuine sanitary precaution for the purpose of securing rest and quiet to the sick man. Such, however, is not the case. The necessity for quiet has probably never occurred to the Cherokee doctor, and this regulation is intended simply to prevent any direct or indirect contact with a woman in a pregnant or menstrual condition. Among all primitive nations, including the ancient Hebrews, we find an elaborate code of rules in regard to the conduct and treatment of women on arriving at the age of puberty, during pregnancy and the menstrual periods, and at childbirth. Among the Cherokees the presence of a woman under any of these conditions, or even the presence of any one who has come from a house where such a woman resides, is considered to neutralize all the effects of the doctor's treatment. For this reason all women, excepting those of the household, are excluded. A man is forbidden to enter, because he may have had intercourse with a tabued woman, or may have come in contact with her in some other way; and children also are shut out, because they may have come from a cabin where dwells a woman subject to exclusion. What is supposed to be the effect of the presence of a menstrual woman in the family of the patient is not clear; but judging from analogous customs in other tribes and from rules still enforced among the Cherokees, notwithstanding their long contact with the whites, it seems probable that in former times the patient was removed to a smaller house or temporary bark lodge built for his accommodation whenever the tabu as to women was prescribed by the doctor. Some of the old men assert that in former times sick persons were removed to the public townhouse, where they remained under the care of the doctors until they either recovered or died. A curious instance of this prohibition is given in the second Didûnlë'skï (rheumatism) formula from the Gahuni manuscript (see page 350), where the patient is required to abstain from touching a squirrel, a dog, a cat, a mountain trout, or a woman, and must also have a chair appropriated to his use alone during the four days that he is under treatment.

In cases of the children's disease known as Gûnwani'gista'ï (see formulas) it is forbidden to carry the child outdoors, but this is not to procure rest for the little one, or to guard against exposure to cold air, but because the birds send this disease, and should a bird chance to be flying by overhead at the moment the flapping of its wings would fan the disease back into the body of the patient.

ILLUSTRATION OF THE TABU.

On a second visit to the reservation the writer once had a practical illustration of the gaktû'nata or tabu, which may be of interest as showing how little sanitary ideas have to do with these precautions. Having received several urgent invitations from Tsiskwa (Bird), an old shaman of considerable repute, who was anxious to talk, but confined to his bed by sickness, it was determined to visit him at his house, several miles distant. On arriving we found another doctor named Sû'nkï (The Mink) in charge of the patient and were told that he had just that morning begun a four days' gaktûnta, which, among other provisions, excluded all visitors. It was of no use to argue that we had come by the express request of Tsiskwa. The laws of the gaktûnta were as immutable as those of the Medes and Persians, and neither doctor nor patient could hope for favorable results from the treatment unless the regulations were enforced to the letter. But although we might not enter the house; there was no reason why we should not talk to the old man, so seats were placed for us outside the door, while Tsiskwa lay stretched out on the bed just inside and The Mink perched himself on the fence a few yards distant to keep an eye on the proceedings. As there was a possibility that a white man might unconsciously affect the operation of the Indian medicine, the writer deemed it advisable to keep out of sight altogether, and accordingly took up a position just around the corner of the house, but within easy hearing distance, while the interpreter sat facing the doorway within a few feet of the sick man inside. Then began an animated conversation, Tsiskwa inquiring, through the interpreter, as to the purpose of the Government in gathering such information, wanting to know how we had succeeded with other shamans and asking various questions in regard to other tribes and their customs. The replies were given in the same manner, an attempt being also made to draw him out as to the extent of his own knowledge. Thus we talked until the old man grew weary, but throughout the whole of this singular interview neither party saw the other, nor was the gaktûnta violated by entering the house. From this example it must be sufficiently evident that the tabu as to visitors is not a hygienic precaution for securing greater quiet to the patient, or to prevent the spread of contagion, but that it is simply a religious observance of the tribe, exactly parallel to many of the regulations among the ancient Jews, as laid down in the book of Leviticus.

NEGLECT OF SANITARY REGULATIONS.

No rules are ever formulated as to fresh air or exercise, for the sufficient reason that the door of the Cherokee log cabin is always open, excepting at night and on the coldest days in winter, while the Indian is seldom in the house during his waking hours unless when necessity compels him. As most of their cabins are still built in the old Indian style, without windows, the open door furnishes the only means by which light is admitted to the interior, although when closed the fire on the hearth helps to make amends for the deficiency. On the other hand, no precautions are taken to guard against cold, dampness, or sudden drafts. During the greater part of the year whole families sleep outside upon the ground, rolled up in an old blanket. The Cherokee is careless of exposure and utterly indifferent to the simplest rules of hygiene. He will walk all day in a pouring rain clad only in a thin shirt and a pair of pants. He goes barefoot and frequently bareheaded nearly the entire year, and even on a frosty morning in late November, when the streams are of almost icy coldness, men and women will deliberately ford the river where the water is waist deep in preference to going a few hundred yards to a foot-log. At their dances in the open air men, women, and children, with bare feet and thinly clad, dance upon the damp ground from darkness until daylight, sometimes enveloped in a thick mountain fog which makes even the neighboring treetops invisible, while the mothers have their infants laid away under the bushes with only a shawl between them and the cold ground. In their ball plays also each young man, before going into the game, is subjected to an ordeal of dancing, bleeding, and cold plunge baths, without food or sleep, which must unquestionably waste his physical energy.

In the old days when the Cherokee was the lord of the whole country from the Savannah to the Ohio, well fed and warmly clad and leading an active life in the open air, he was able to maintain a condition of robust health notwithstanding the incorrectness of his medical ideas and his general disregard of sanitary regulations. But with the advent of the white man and the destruction of the game all this was changed. The East Cherokee of to-day is a dejected being; poorly fed, and worse clothed, rarely tasting meat, cut off from the old free life, and with no incentive to a better, and constantly bowed down by a sense of helpless degradation in the presence of his conqueror. Considering all the circumstances, it may seem a matter of surprise that any of them are still in existence. As a matter of fact, the best information that could be obtained in the absence of any official statistics indicated a slow but steady decrease during the last five years. Only the constitutional vigor, inherited from their warrior ancestors, has enabled them to sustain the shock of the changed conditions of the last half century. The uniform good health of the children in the training school shows that the case is not hopeless, however, and that under favorable conditions, with a proper food supply and a regular mode of living, the Cherokee can hold his own with the white man.

THE SWEAT BATH-BLEEDING—
RUBBING— BATHING.

In addition to their herb treatment the Cherokees frequently resort to sweat baths, bleeding, rubbing, and cold baths in the running stream, to say nothing of the beads and other conjuring paraphernalia generally used in connection with the ceremony. The sweat bath was in common use among almost all the tribes north of Mexico excepting the central and eastern Eskimo, and was considered the great cure-all in sickness and invigorant in health. Among many tribes it appears to have been regarded as a ceremonial observance, but the Cherokees seem to have looked upon it simply as a medical application, while the ceremonial part was confined to the use of the plunge bath. The person wishing to make trial of the virtues of the sweat bath entered the â'sï, a small earth-covered log house only high enough to allow of sitting down. After divesting himself of his clothing, some large bowlders, previously heated in a fire, were placed near him, and over them was poured a decoction of the beaten roots of the wild parsnip. The door was closed so that no air could enter from the outside, and the patient sat in the sweltering steam until he was in a profuse perspiration and nearly choked by the pungent fumes of the decoction. In accordance with general Indian practice it may be that he plunged into the river before resuming his clothing; but in modern times this part of the operation is omitted and the patient is drenched with cold water instead. Since the âsï has gone out of general use the sweating takes place in the ordinary dwelling, the steam being confined under a blanket wrapped around the patient. During the prevalence of the smallpox epidemic among the Cherokees at the close of the late war the sweat bath was universally called into requisition to stay the progress of the disease, and as the result about three hundred of the band died, while many of the survivors will carry the marks of the visitation to the grave. The sweat bath, with the accompanying cold water application, being regarded as the great panacea, seems to have been resorted to by the Indians in all parts of the country whenever visited by smallpox—originally introduced by the whites—and in consequence of this mistaken treatment they have died, in the language of an old writer, "like rotten sheep" and at times whole tribes have been almost swept away. Many of the Cherokees tried to ward off the disease by eating the flesh of the buzzard, which they believe to enjoy entire immunity from sickness, owing to its foul smell, which keeps the disease spirits at a distance.

Bleeding is resorted to in a number of cases, especially in rheumatism and in preparing for the ball play. There are two methods of performing the operation, bleeding proper and scratching, the latter being preparatory to rubbing on the medicine, which is thus brought into more direct contact with the blood. The bleeding is performed with a small cupping horn, to which suction is applied in the ordinary manner, after scarification with a flint or piece of broken glass. In the blood thus drawn out the shaman claims sometimes to find a minute pebble, a sharpened stick or something of the kind, which he asserts to be the cause of the trouble and to have been conveyed into the body of the patient through the evil spells of an enemy. He frequently pretends to suck out such an object by the application of the lips alone, without any scarification whatever. Scratching is a painful process and is performed with a brier, a flint arrowhead, a rattlesnake's tooth, or even with a piece of glass, according to the nature of the ailment, while in preparing the young men for the ball play the shaman uses an instrument somewhat resembling a comb, having seven teeth made from the sharpened splinters of the leg bone of a turkey. The scratching is usually done according to a particular pattern, the regular method for the ball play being to draw the scratcher four times down the upper part of each arm, thus making twenty-eight scratches each about 6 inches in length, repeating the operation on each arm below the elbow and on each leg above and below the knee. Finally, the instrument is drawn across the breast from the two shoulders so as to form a cross; another curving stroke is made to connect the two upper ends of the cross, and the same pattern is repeated on the back, so that the body is thus gashed in nearly three hundred places. Although very painful for a while, as may well be supposed, the scratches do not penetrate deep enough to result seriously, excepting in some cases where erysipelas sets in. While the blood is still flowing freely the medicine, which in this case is intended to toughen the muscles of the player, is rubbed into the wounds after which the sufferer plunges into the stream and washes off the blood. In order that the blood may flow the longer without clotting it is frequently scraped off with a small switch as it flows. In rheumatism and other local diseases the scratching is confined to the part affected. The instrument used is selected in accordance with the mythologic theory, excepting in the case of the piece of glass, which is merely a modern makeshift for the flint arrowhead.

Rubbing, used commonly for pains and swellings of the abdomen, is a very simple operation performed with the tip of the finger or the palm of the hand, and can not be dignified with the name of massage. In one of the Gahuni formulas for treating snake bites (page 351) the operator is told to rub in a direction contrary to that in which the snake coils itself, because "this is just the same as uncoiling it." Blowing upon the part affected, as well as upon the head, hands, and other parts of the body, is also an important feature of the ceremonial performance. In one of the formulas it is specified that the doctor must blow first upon the right hand of the patient, then upon the left foot, then upon the left hand, and finally upon the right foot, thus making an imaginary cross.

Bathing in the running stream, or "going to water," as it is called, is one of their most frequent medico-religious ceremonies, and is performed on a great variety of occasions, such as at each new moon, before eating the new food at the green corn dance, before the medicine dance and other ceremonial dances before and after the ball play, in connection with the prayers for long life, to counteract the effects of bad dreams or the evil spells of an enemy, and as a part of the regular treatment in various diseases. The details of the ceremony are very elaborate and vary according to the purpose for which it is performed, but in all cases both shaman and client are fasting from the previous evening, the ceremony being generally performed just at daybreak. The bather usually dips completely under the water four or seven times, but in some cases it is sufficient to pour the water from the hand upon the head and breast. In the ball play the ball sticks are dipped into the water at the same time. While the bather is in the water the shaman is going through with his part of the performance on the bank and draws omens from the motion of the beads between his thumb and finger, or of the fishes in the water. Although the old customs are fast dying out this ceremony is never neglected at the ball play, and is also strictly observed by many families on occasion of eating the new corn, at each new moon, and on other special occasions, even when it is necessary to break the ice in the stream for the purpose, and to the neglect of this rite the older people attribute many of the evils which have come upon the tribe in later days. The latter part of autumn is deemed the most suitable season of the year for this ceremony, as the leaves which then cover the surface of the stream are supposed to impart their medicinal virtues to the water.

SHAMANS AND WHITE PHYSICIANS.

Of late years, especially since the establishment of schools among them, the Cherokees are gradually beginning to lose confidence in the abilities of their own doctors and are becoming more disposed to accept treatment from white physicians. The shamans are naturally jealous of this infringement upon their authority and endeavor to prevent the spread of the heresy by asserting the convenient doctrine that the white man's medicine is inevitably fatal to an Indian unless eradicated from the system by a continuous course of treatment for four years under the hands of a skillful shaman. The officers of the training school established by the Government a few years ago met with considerable difficulty on this account for some time, as the parents insisted on removing the children at the first appearance of illness in order that they might be treated by the shamans, until convinced by experience that the children received better attention at the school than could possibly be had in their own homes. In one instance, where a woman was attacked by a pulmonary complaint akin to consumption, her husband, a man of rather more than the usual amount of intelligence, was persuaded to call in the services of a competent white physician, who diagnosed the case and left a prescription. On a second visit, a few days later, he found that the family, dreading the consequences of this departure from old customs, had employed a shaman, who asserted that the trouble was caused by a sharpened stick which some enemy bad caused to be imbedded in the woman's side. He accordingly began a series of conjurations for the removal of the stick, while the white physician and his medicine were disregarded, and in due time the woman died. Two children soon followed her to the grave, from the contagion or the inherited seeds of the same disease, but here also the sharpened sticks were held responsible, and, notwithstanding the three deaths under such treatment, the husband and father, who was at one time a preacher still has faith in the assertions of the shaman. The appointment of a competent physician to look after the health of the Indians would go far to eradicate these false ideas and prevent much sickness and suffering; but, as the Government has made no such provision, the Indians, both on and off the reservation, excepting the children in the home school, are entirely without medical care.

MEDICINE DANCES.

The Cherokees have a dance known as the Medicine Dance, which is generally performed in connection with other dances when a number of people assemble for a night of enjoyment. It possesses no features of special interest and differs in no essential respect from a dozen other of the lesser dances. Besides this, however, there was another, known as the Medicine Boiling Dance, which, for importance and solemn ceremonial, was second only to the great Green Corn Dance. It has now been discontinued on the reservation for about twenty years. It took place in the fall, probably preceding the Green Corn Dance, and continued four days. The principal ceremony in connection with it was the drinking of a strong decoction of various herbs, which acted as a violent emetic and purgative. The usual fasting and going to water accompanied the dancing and medicine-drinking.

DESCRIPTION OF SYMPTOMS.

It is exceedingly difficult to obtain from the doctors any accurate statement of the nature of a malady, owing to the fact that their description of the symptoms is always of the vaguest character, while in general the name given to the disease by the shaman expresses only his opinion as to the occult cause of the trouble. Thus they have definite names for rheumatism, toothache, boils, and a few other ailments of like positive character, but beyond this their description of symptoms generally resolves itself into a statement that the patient has bad dreams, looks black around the eyes, or feels tired, while the disease is. assigned such names as "when they dream of snakes," "when they dream of fish," "when ghosts trouble them," "when something is making something else eat them," or "when the food is changed," i.e., when a witch causes it to sprout and grow in the body of the patient or transforms it into a lizard, frog, or sharpened stick.

THE PAY OF THE SHAMAN.

The consideration which the doctor receives for his services is called ugista"tï, a word of doubtful etymology, but probably derived from the verb tsï'giû, "I take" or "I eat." In former times this was generally a deer-skin or a pair of moccasins, but is now a certain quantity of cloth, a garment, or a handkerchief. The shamans disclaim the idea that the ugista"tï is pay, in our sense of the word, but assert that it is one of the agencies in the removal and banishment of the disease spirit. Their explanation is somewhat obscure, but the cloth seems to be intended either as an offering to the disease spirit, as a ransom to procure the release of his intended victim, or as a covering to protect the hand of a shaman while engaged in pulling the disease from the body of the patient. The first theory, which includes also the idea of vicarious atonement, is common to many primitive peoples. Whichever maybe the true explanation, the evil influence of the disease is believed to enter into the cloth, which must therefore be sold or given away by the doctor, as otherwise it will cause his death when the pile thus accumulating reaches the height of his head. No evil results seem to follow its transfer from the shaman to a third party. The doctor can not bestow anything thus received upon a member of his own family unless that individual gives him something in return. If the consideration thus received, however, be anything eatable, the doctor may partake along with the rest of the family. As a general rule the doctor makes no charge for his services, and the consideration is regarded as a free-will offering. This remark applies only to the medical practice, as the shaman always demands and receives a fixed remuneration for performing love charms, hunting ceremonials, and other conjurations of a miscellaneous character. Moreover, whenever the beads are used the patient must furnish a certain quantity of new cloth upon which to place them, and at the close of the ceremony the doctor rolls up the cloth, beads and all, and takes them away with him. The cloth thus received by the doctor for working with the beads must not be used by him, but must be sold. In one instance a doctor kept a handkerchief which he received for his services, but instead sold a better one of his own. Additional cloth is thus given each time the ceremony is repeated, each time a second four days' course of treatment is begun, and as often as the doctor sees fit to change his method of procedure. Thus, when he begins to treat a sick man for a disease caused by rabbits, he expects to receive a certain ugista"tï; but, should he decide after a time that the terrapin or the red bird is responsible for the, trouble, he adopts a different course of treatment, for which another ugista"tï is necessary. Should the sickness not yield readily to his efforts, it is because the disease animal requires a greater ugista"tï, and the quantity of cloth must be doubled, so that on the whole the doctrine is a very convenient one for the shaman. In many of the formulas explicit directions are given as to the pay which the shaman is to receive for performing the ceremony. In one of the Gatigwanasti formulas, after specifying the amount of cloth to be paid, the writer of it makes the additional proviso that it must be "pretty good cloth, too," asserting as a clincher that "this is what the old folks said a long time ago."

The ugista"tï can not be paid by either one of a married couple to the other, and, as it is considered a necessary accompaniment of the application, it follows that a shaman can not treat his own wife in sickness, and vice versa. Neither can the husband or wife of the sick person send for the doctor, but the call must come from some one of the blood relatives of the patient. In one instance within the writer's knowledge a woman complained that her husband was very sick and needed a doctor's attention, but his relatives were taking no steps in the matter and it was not permissible for her to do so.

CEREMONIES FOR GATHERING PLANTS AND PREPARING MEDICINE.

There are a number of ceremonies and regulations observed in connection with the gathering of the herbs, roots, and barks, which can not be given in detail within the limits of this paper. In searching for his medicinal plants the shaman goes provided with a number of white and red beads, and approaches the plant from a certain direction, going round it from right to left one or four times, reciting certain prayers the while. He then pulls up the plant by the roots and drops one of the beads into the hole and covers it up with the loose earth. In one of the formulas for hunting ginseng the hunter addresses the mountain as the "Great Man" and assures it that he comes only to take a small piece of flesh (the ginseng) from its side, so that it seems probable that the bead is intended as a compensation to the earth for the plant thus torn from her bosom. In some cases the doctor must pass by the first three plants met until he comes to the fourth, which he takes and may then return for the others. The bark is always taken from the east side of the tree, and when the root or branch is used it must also be one which runs out toward the east, the reason given being that these have imbibed more medical potency from the rays of the sun.

When the roots, herbs, and barks which enter into the prescription have been thus gathered the doctor ties them up into a convenient package, which he takes to a running stream and casts into the water with appropriate prayers. Should the package float, as it generally does, he accepts the fact as an omen that his treatment will be successful. On the other band, should it sink, he concludes that some part of the preceding ceremony has been improperly carried out and at once sets about procuring a new package, going over the whole performance from the beginning. Herb-gathering by moonlight, so important a feature in European folk medicine, seems to be no part of Cherokee ceremonial. There are fixed regulations in regard to the preparing of the decoction, the care of the medicine during the continuance of the treatment, and the disposal of what remains after the treatment is at an end. In the arrangement of details the shaman frequently employs the services of a lay assistant. Id these degenerate days a number of upstart pretenders to the healing art have arisen in the tribe and endeavor to impose upon the ignorance of their fellows by posing as doctors, although knowing next to nothing of the prayers and ceremonies, without which there can be no virtue in the application. These impostors are sternly frowned down and regarded with the utmost contempt by the real professors, both men and women, who have been initiated into the sacred mysteries and proudly look upon themselves as conservators of the ancient ritual of the past.

THE CHEROKEE GODS AND THEIR ABIDING PLACES.

After what has been said in elucidation of the theories involved in the medical formulas, the most important and numerous of the series, but little remains to be added in regard to the others, beyond what is contained in the explanation accompanying each one. A few points, however, may be briefly noted.

The religion of the Cherokees, like that of most of our North American tribes, is zootheism or animal worship, with the survival of that earlier stage designated by Powell as hecastotheism, or the worship of all things tangible, and the beginnings of a higher system in which the elements and the great powers of nature are deified. Their pantheon includes gods in the heaven above, on the earth beneath, and in the waters under the earth, but of these the animal gods constitute by far the most numerous class, although the elemental gods are more important. Among the animal gods insects and fishes occupy a subordinate place, while quadrupeds, birds, and reptiles are invoked almost constantly. The uktena (a mythic great horned serpent), the rattlesnake, and the terrapin, the various species of hawk, and the rabbit, the squirrel, and the dog are the principal animal gods. The importance of the god bears no relation to the size of the animal, and in fact the larger animals are but seldom invoked. The spider also occupies a prominent place in the love and life-destroying formulas, his duty being to entangle the soul of his victim in the meshes of his web or to pluck it from the body of the doomed man and drag it way to the black coffin in the Darkening Land.

Among what may be classed as elemental gods the principal are fire, water, and the sun, all of which are addressed under figurative names. The sun is called Une`lanû'hï, "the apportioner," just as our word moon means originally "the measurer." Indians and Aryans alike, having noticed how these great luminaries divide and measure day and night, summer and winter, with never varying regularity, have given to each a name which should indicate these characteristics, thus showing how the human mind constantly moves on along the same channels. Missionaries have naturally, but incorrectly, assumed this apportioner of all things to be the suppositional "Great Spirit" of the Cherokees and hence the word is used in the Bible translation as synonymous with God. In ordinary conversation and in the lesser myths the sun is called Nû'ntâ. The sun is invoked chiefly by the ball-player, while the hunter prays to the fire; but every important ceremony—whether connected with medicine, love, hunting, or the ball play—contains a prayer to the "Long Person," the formulistic name for water, or, more strictly speaking, for the river. The wind, the storm, the cloud, and the frost are also invoked in different formulas.

But few inanimate gods are included in the category, the principal being the Stone, to which the shaman prays while endeavoring to find a lost article by means of a swinging pebble suspended by a string; the Flint, invoked when the shaman is about to scarify the patient with a flint arrow-head before rubbing on the medicine; and the Mountain, which is addressed in one or two of the formulas thus far translated. Plant gods do not appear prominently, the chief one seeming to be the ginseng, addressed in the formulas as the "Great Man" or "Little Man," although its proper Cherokee name signifies the "Mountain Climber."

A number of personal deities are also invoked, the principal being the Red Man. He is one of the greatest of the gods, being repeatedly called upon in formulas of all kinds, and is hardly subordinate to the Fire, the Water, or the Sun. His identity is as yet uncertain, but he seems to be intimately connected with the Thunder family. In a curious marginal note in one of the Gahuni formulas , it is stated that when the patient is a woman the doctor must pray to the Red Man, but when treating a man he must pray to the Red Woman, so that this personage seems to have dual sex characteristics. Another god invoked in the hunting songs is Tsu'l`kalû', or "Slanting Eyes" (see Cherokee Myths), a giant hunter who lives in one of the great mountains of the Blue Ridge and owns all the game. Others are the Little Men, probably the two Thunder boys; the Little People, the fairies who live in the rock cliffs; and even the De'tsata, a diminutive sprite who holds the place of our Puck. One unwritten formula, which could not be obtained correctly by dictation, was addressed to the "Red-Headed Woman, whose hair hangs down to the ground."

The personage invoked is always selected in accordance with the theory of the formula and the duty to be performed. Thus, when a sickness is caused by a fish, the Fish-hawk, the Heron, or some other fish-eating bird is implored to come and seize the intruder and destroy it, so that the patient may find relief. When the trouble is caused by a worm or an insect, some insectivorous bird is called in for the same purpose. When a flock of redbirds is pecking at the vitals of the sick man the Sparrow-hawk is brought down to scatter them, and when the rabbit, the great mischief-maker, is the evil genius, he is driven out by the Rabbit-hawk. Sometimes after the intruder has been thus expelled "a small portion still remains," in the words of the formula, and accordingly the Whirlwind is called down from the treetops to carry the remnant to the uplands and there scatter it so that it shall never reappear. The hunter prays to the fire, from which he draws his omens; to the reed, from which he makes his arrows; to Tsu'l`kalû, the great lord of the game, and finally addresses in songs the very animals which he intends to kill. The lover prays to the Spider to hold fast the affections of his beloved one in the meshes of his web, or to the Moon, which looks down upon him in the dance. The warrior prays to the Red War-club, and the man about to set out on a dangerous expedition prays to the Cloud to envelop him and conceal him from his enemies.

Each spirit of good or evil has its distinct and appropriate place of residence. The Rabbit is declared to live in the broomsage on the hillside, the Fish dwells in a bend of the river under the pendant hemlock branches, the Terrapin lives in the great pond in the West, and the Whirlwind abides in the leafy treetops. Each disease animal, when driven away from his prey by some more powerful animal, endeavors to find shelter in his accustomed haunt. It must be stated here that the animals of the formulas are not the ordinary, everyday animals, but their great progenitors, who live in the upper world (galû'nlati) above the arch of the firmament.

COLOR SYMBOLISM.

Color symbolism plays an important part in the shamanistic system of the Cherokees, no less than in that of other tribes. Each one of the cardinal points has its corresponding color and each color its symbolic meaning, so that each spirit invoked corresponds in color and local habitation with the characteristics imputed to him, and is connected with other spirits of the same name, but of other colors, living in other parts of the upper world and differing widely in their characteristics. Thus the Red Man, living in the east, is the spirit of power, triumph, and success, but the Black Man, in the West, is the spirit of death. The shaman therefore invokes the Red Man to the assistance of his client and consigns his enemy to the fatal influences of the Black Man.

The symbolic color system of the Cherokees, which will be explained more fully in connection with the formulas, is as follows:

East	red	success; triumph.
North	blue	defeat; trouble.
West	black	death.
South	white	peace; happiness.
Above?	brown	unascertained, but propitious.
yellow	about the same as blue.	

There is a great diversity in the color systems of the various tribes, both as to the location and significance of the colors, but for obvious reasons black was generally taken as the symbol of death, while white and red signified, respectively, peace and war. It is somewhat remarkable that red was the emblem of power and triumph among the ancient Oriental nations no less than among the modern Cherokees.

IMPORTANCE ATTACHED TO NAMES.

In many of the formulas, especially those relating to love and to life-destroying, the shaman mentions the name and clan of his client, of the intended victim, or of the girl whose affections it is desired to win. The Indian regards his name, not as a mere label, but as a distinct part of his personality, just as much as are his eyes or his teeth, and believes that injury will result as surely from the malicious handling of his name as from a wound inflicted on any part of his physical organism. This belief was found among the various tribes from the Atlantic to the Pacific, and has occasioned a number of curious regulations in regard to the concealment and change of names. It may be on this account that both Powhatan and Pocahontas are known in history under assumed appellations, their true names having been concealed from the whites until the pseudonyms were too firmly established to be supplanted. Should his prayers have no apparent effect when treating a patient for some serious illness, the shaman sometimes concludes that the name is affected, and accordingly goes to water, with appropriate ceremonies, and christens the patient with a new name, by which he is henceforth to be known. He then begins afresh, repeating the formulas with the new name selected for the patient, in the confident hope that his efforts will be crowned with success.

LANGUAGE OF THE FORMULAS.

A few words remain to be said in regard to the language of the formulas. They are full of archaic and figurative expressions, many of which are unintelligible to the common people, and some of which even the shamans themselves are now unable to. explain. These archaic forms, like the old words used by our poets, lend a peculiar beauty which can hardly be rendered in a translation. They frequently throw light on the dialectic evolution of the language, as many words found now only in the nearly extinct Lower Cherokee dialect occur in formulas which in other respects are written in the Middle or Upper dialect. The R sound, the chief distinguishing characteristic of the old Lower dialect, of course does not occur, as there are no means of indicating it in the Cherokee syllabary. Those who are accustomed to look to the Bible for all beauty in sacred expression will be surprised to find that these formulas abound in the loftiest flights of poetic imagery. This is especially true of the prayers used to win the love of a woman or to destroy the life of an enemy, in which we find such expressions as—"Now your soul fades away—your spirit shall grow less and dwindle away, never to reappear;" "Let her be completely veiled in loneliness—O Black Spider, may you hold her soul in your web, so that it may never get through the meshes;" and the final declaration of the lover, "Your soul has come into the very center of my soul, never to turn away."

In the translation it has been found advisable to retain as technical terms a few words which could not well be rendered literally, such as ada'wëhï and ugistâ`tï. These words will be found explained in the proper place. Transliterations of the Cherokee text of the formulas are given, but it must be distinctly understood that the translations are intended only as free renderings of the spirit of the originals, exact translations with grammatic and glossarial notes being deferred until a more extended study of the language has been made, when it is hoped to present with more exactness of detail the whole body of the formulas, of which the specimens here given are but a small portion.

The facsimile formulas are copies from the manuscripts now in possession of the Bureau of Ethnology, and the portraits are from photographs taken by the author in the field.

SPECIMEN FORMULAS.
NOTE ON THE ORTHOGRAPHY AND TRANSLATION.

In the Cherokee text both d and g have a medial sound, approximating the sounds of t and k respectively. The other letters are pronounced in regular accordance with the alphabet of the Bureau of Ethnology. The language abounds in nasal and aspirate sounds, the most difficult of the latter being the aspirate `l, which to one familiar only with English sounds like tl.

A few words whose meaning could not be satisfactorily ascertained have been distinctively indicated in the Cherokee text by means of italics. In the translation the corresponding expression has been queried, or the space left entirely blank. On examining the text the student can not fail to be struck by the great number of verbs ending in iga. This is a peculiar form hardly ever used excepting in these formulas, where almost every paragraph contains one or more such verbs. It implies that the subject has just come and is now performing the action, and that he came for that purpose. In addition to this, many of these verbs may be either assertive or imperative (expressing entreaty), according to the accent. Thus hatû'n-gani'ga means "you have just come and are listening and it is for that purpose you came." By slightly accenting the final syllable it becomes "come at once to listen." It will thus be seen that the great majority of the formulas are declarative rather than petitional in form-laudatory rhapsodies instead of prayers, in the ordinary sense of the word.

FORMULA FOR TREATING THE CRIPPLER (RHEUMATISM).

Listen! Ha! In the Sun Land you repose, O Red Dog, O now you have swiftly drawn near to hearken. O great ada'wëhï, you never fail in anything. O, appear and draw near running, for your prey never escapes. You are now come to remove the intruder. Ha! You have settled a very small part of it far off there at the end of the earth.

Listen! Ha! In the Frigid Land you repose, O Blue Dog. O now you have swiftly drawn near to hearken. O great ad'âw hï, you never fail in anything. O, appear and draw near running, for your prey never escapes. You are now come to remove the intruder. Ha! You have settled a very small part of it far off there at the end of the earth.

Listen! Ha! In the darkening land you repose, O Black Dog. O, now you have swiftly drawn near to hearken. O great ada'wëhi, you never fail in anything. O, appear and draw near running, for your prey never escapes. You are now come to remove the intruder. Ha! You have settled a very small part of it far off there at the end of the earth.

Listen! On Wa'halä you repose, O White Dog. Oh, now you have swiftly drawn near to hearken. O great ada'wëhï, you never fail in anything. Oh, appear and draw near running, for your prey never escapes. You are now come to remove the intruder. Ha! You have settled a very small part of it far off there at the end of the earth.

Listen! On Wa'halä, you repose, O White Terrapin. O, now you have swiftly drawn near to hearken. O great ada'wëhï, you never fail in anything. Ha! It is for you to loosen its hold on the bone. Relief is accomplished.

(Prescription.)—Lay a terrapin shell upon (the spot) and keep it there while the five kinds (of spirits) listen. On finishing, then blow once. Repeat four times, beginning each time from the start. On finishing the fourth time, then blow four times. Have two white beads lying in the shell, together with a little of the medicine. Don't interfere with it, but have a good deal boiling in another vessel—a bowl will do very well—and rub it on warm while treating by applying the hands. And this is the medicine: What is called Yâ'na-Utsë'sta ("bear's bed," the Aspidium acrostichoides or Christmas fern); and the other is called Kâ'ga-Asgû'ntagï ("crow's shin," the Adianthum pedatum or Maidenhair fern); and the other is the common Egû'nlï (another fern); and the other is the Little Soft (-leaved) Egû'nlï (Osmunda Cinnamonea or cinnamon fern), which grows in the rocks and resembles Yâna-Utsë'sta and is a small and soft (-leaved) Egû'nlï. Another has brown roots and another has black roots. The roots of all should be (used).

Begin doctoring early in the morning; let the second (application) be while the sun is still near the horizon; the third when it has risen to a considerable height (10 a. m.); the fourth when it is above at noon. This is sufficient. (The doctor) must not eat, and the patient also must be fasting.

Ada'wëhï is a word used to designate one supposed to have supernatural powers, and is applied alike to human beings and to the spirits invoked in the formulas. Some of the mythic heroes famous for their magic deeds are spoken of as ada'wëhï (plural anida'wëhï or anida'we), but in its application to mortals the term is used only of the very greatest shamans. None of those now belonging to the band are considered worthy of being thus called, although the term was sometimes applied to one, Usawï, who died some years ago. In speaking of himself as an ada'wëhï, as occurs in some of the formulas, the shaman arrogates to himself the same powers that belong to the gods. Our nearest equivalent is the word magician, but this falls far short of the idea conveyed by the Cherokee word. In the bible translation the word is used as the equivalent of angel or spirit.

EXPLANATION. As this formula is taken from the manuscript of Gahuni, who died nearly thirty years ago, no definite statement of the theory of the disease, or its treatment, can be given, beyond what is contained in the formula itself, which, fortunately, is particularly explicit; most doctors contenting themselves with giving only the words of the prayer, without noting the ceremonies or even the medicine used. There are various theories as to the cause of each disease, the most common idea in regard to rheumatism being that it is caused by the spirits of. the slain animals, generally the deer, thirsting for vengeance on the hunter, as has been already explained in the myth of the origin of disease and medicine.

The measuring-worm (Catharis) is also held to cause rheumatism, from the resemblance of its motions to those of a rheumatic patient, and the name of the worm wahïlï' is frequently applied also to the disease.

There are formulas to propitiate the slain animals, but these are a part of the hunting code and can only be noticed here, although it may be mentioned in passing that the hunter, when about to return to the settlement, builds a fire in the path behind him, in order that the deer chief may not be able to follow him to his home. The disease, figuratively called the intruder (ulsgéta), is regarded as a living being, and the verbs used in speaking of it show that it is considered to be long, like a snake or fish. It is brought by the deer chief and put into the body, generally the limbs, of the hunter, who at once begins to suffer intense pain. It can be driven out only by some more powerful animal spirit which is the natural enemy of the deer, usually the dog or the wolf. These animal gods live up above beyond the seventh heaven and are the great prototypes of which the earthly animals are only diminutive copies. They are commonly located at the four cardinal points, each of which has a peculiar formulistic name and a special color which applies to everything in the same connection. Thus the east, north, west, and south are respectively the Sun Land, the Frigid Land, the Darkening Land, and Wä'halä', while their respective mythologic colors are Red, Blue, Black, and White. Wä'halä' is said to be a mountain far to the south. The white or red spirits are generally invoked for peace, health, and other blessings, the red alone for the success of an under taking, the blue spirits to defeat the schemes of an enemy or bring down troubles upon him, and the black to compass his death. The white and red spirits are regarded as the most powerful, and one of these two is generally called upon to accomplish the final result.

In this case the doctor first invokes the Red Dog in the Sun Land, calling him a great adáwehi, to whom nothing is impossible and who never fails to accomplish his purpose. He is addressed as if out of sight in the distance and is implored to appear running swiftly to the help of the sick man. Then the supplication changes to an assertion and the doctor declares that the Red Dog has already arrived to take the disease and has borne away a small portion of it to the uttermost ends of the earth. In the second, third, and fourth paragraphs the Blue Dog of the Frigid Land, the Black Dog of the Darkening Land, and the White Dog of Wä'halä' are successively invoked in the same terms and each bears away a portion of the disease and disposes of it in the same way. Finally, in the fifth paragraph, the White Terrapin of Wä'halä' is invoked. He bears off the remainder of the disease and the doctor declares that relief is accomplished. The connection of the terrapin in this formula is not evident, beyond the fact that he is regarded as having great influence in disease, and in this case the beads and a portion of the medicine are kept in a terrapin shell placed upon the diseased part while the prayer is being recited.

The formulas generally consist of four paragraphs, corresponding to four steps in the medical ceremony. In this case there are five, the last being addressed to the terrapin instead of to a dog. The prayers are recited in an undertone hardly audible at the distance of a few feet, with the exception of the frequent ha, which seems to be used as an interjection to attract attention and is always uttered in a louder tone. The beads—which are here white, symbolic of relief—are of common use in connection with these formulas, and are held between the thumb and finger, placed upon a cloth on the ground, or, as in this case, put into a terrapin shell along with a small portion of the medicine. According to directions, the shell has no other part in the ceremony.

The blowing is also a regular part of the treatment, the doctor either holding the medicine in his mouth and blowing it upon the patient, or, as it seems to be the case here, applying the medicine by rubbing, and blowing his breath upon the spot afterwards. In some formulas the simple blowing of the breath constitutes the whole application. In this instance the doctor probably rubs the medicine upon the affected part while reciting the first paragraph in a whisper, after which he blows once upon the spot. The other paragraphs are recited in the same manner, blowing once after each. In this way the whole formula is repeated four times, with four blows at the end of the final repetition. The directions imply that the doctor blows only at the end of the whole formula, but this is not in accord with the regular mode of procedure and seems to be a mistake.

The medicine consists of a warm decoction of the roots of four varieties of fern, rubbed on with the hand. The awkward description of the species shows how limited is the Indian's power of botanic classification. The application is repeated four times during the same morning, beginning just at daybreak and ending at noon. Four is the sacred number running through every detail of these formulas, there being commonly four spirits invoked in four paragraphs, four blowings with four final blows, four herbs in the decoction, four applications, and frequently four days' gaktun'ta or tabu. In this case no tabu is specified beyond the fact that both doctor and patient must be fasting. The tabu generally extends to salt or lye, hot food and women, while in rheumatism some doctors forbid the patient to eat the foot or leg of any animal, the reason given being that the limbs are generally the seat of the disease. For a similar reason the patient is also forbidden to eat or even to touch a squirrel, a buffalo, a eat, or any animal which "humps" itself. In the same way a scrofulous patient must not eat turkey, as that bird seems to have a scrofulous eruption on its head, while ball players must abstain from eating frogs, because the bones of that animal are brittle and easily broken.

AND THIS ALSO IS FOR TREATING
THE CRIPPLER.

Yû! O Red Woman, you have caused it. You have put the intruder under him. Ha! now you have come from the Sun Land. You have brought the small red seats, with your feet resting upon them. Ha! now they have swiftly moved away from you. Relief is accomplished. Let it not be for one night alone. Let the relief come at once.

(Prescription)—(corner note at top.) If treating a man one must say Red Woman, and if treating a woman one must say Red Man.

This is just all of the prayer. Repeat it four times while laying on the hands. After saying it over once, with the hands on (the body of the patient), take off the hands and blow once, and at the fourth repetition blow four times. And this is the medicine. Egû'nlï (a species of fern). Yâ'-na-Utsë'sta ("bear's bed," the Aspidium acrostichoides or Christmas fern), two varieties of the soft-(leaved) Egû'nlï (one, the small variety, is the Cinnamon fern, Osmunda cinnamonea), and what is called Kâ'ga Asgû'ntagë ("crow's shin," the Adiantum pedatum or Maidenhair fern) and what is called Da'yï-Uwâ'yï ("beaver's paw"—not identified). Boil the roots of the six varieties together and apply the hands warm with the medicine upon them. Doctor in the evening. Doctor four consecutive nights. (The pay) is cloth and moccasins; or, if one does not have them, just a little dressed deerskin and some cloth.

And this is the tabu for seven nights. One must not touch a squirrel, a dog, a cat, the mountain trout, or women. If one is treating a married man they (sic) must not touch his wife for four nights. And he must sit on a seat by himself for four nights, and must not sit on the other seats for four nights.

EXPLANATION. The treatment and medicine in this formula are nearly the same as in that just given, which is also for rheumatism, both being written by Gahuni. The prayer differs in several respects from any other obtained, but as the doctor has been dead for years it is impossible to give a full explanation of all the points. This is probably the only formula in the collection in which the spirit invoked is the "Red Woman," but, as explained in the corner note at the top, this is only the form used instead of "Red Man," when the patient is a man. The Red Man, who is considered perhaps the most powerful god in the Cherokee pantheon, is in some way connected with the thunder, and is invoked in a large number of formulas. The change in the formula, according to the sex of the patient, brings to mind a belief in Irish folk medicine, that in applying certain remedies the doctor and patient must be of opposite sexes. The Red Man lives in the east, in accordance with the regular mythologic color theory, as already explained. The seats also are red, and the form of the verb indicates that the Red Woman is either standing upon them (plural) or sitting with her feet resting upon the rounds. These seats or chairs are frequently mentioned in the formulas, and always correspond in color with the spirit invoked. It is not clear why the Red Woman is held responsible for the disease, which is generally attributed to the revengeful efforts of the game, as already explained. In agreement with the regular form, the disease is said to be put under (not into) the patient. The assertion that the chairs "have swiftly moved away" would seem from analogy to mean that the disease has been placed upon the seats and thus borne away. The verb implies that the seats move by their own volition. Immediately afterward it is declared that relief is accomplished. The expression "usû'hita nutanû'na" occurs frequently in these formulas, and may mean either "let it not be for one night alone," or "let it not stay a single night," according to the context.

The directions specify not only the medicine and the treatment, but also the doctor's fee. From the form of the verb the tabu, except as regards the seat to be used by the sick person, seems to apply to both doctor and patient. It is not evident why the mountain trout is prohibited, but the dog, squirrel, and cat are tabued, as already explained, from the fact that these animals frequently assume positions resembling the cramped attitude common to persons afflicted by rheumatism. The cat is considered especially uncanny, as coming from the whites. Seven, as well as four, is a sacred number with the tribe, being also the number of their gentes. It will be noted that time is counted by nights instead of by days.

THIS IS TO TREAT THEM IF THEY ARE BITTEN BY A SNAKE.

1. Dûnu'wa, dûnu'wa, dûnu'wa, dûnu'wa, dûnu'wa, dûnu'wa. Listen! Ha! It is only a common frog which has passed by and put it (the intruder) into you. Dayuha', dayuha, dayuha, dayuha, dayuha. Listen! Ha! It is only an Us`gï which has passed by and put it into you.

(Prescription.)—Now this at the beginning is a song. One should say it twice and also say the second line twice. Rub tobacco (juice) on the bite for some time, or if there be no tobacco just rub on saliva once. In rubbing it on, one must go around four times. Go around toward the left and blow four times in a circle. This is because in lying down the snake always coils to the right and this is just the same (lit. "means like") as uncoiling it.

EXPLANATION. This is also from the manuscript book of Gahuni, deceased, so that no explanation could be obtained from the writer. The formula consists of a song of two verses, each followed by a short recitation.

The whole is repeated, according to the directions, so as to make four verses or songs; four, as already stated, being the sacred number running through most of these formulas. Four blowings and four circuits in the rubbing are also specified. The words used in the songs are sometimes composed of unmeaning syllables, but in this case dûnuwa and dayuha seem to have a meaning, although neither the interpreter nor the shaman consulted could explain them, which may be because the words have become altered in the song, as frequently happens. Dûnu'wa appears to be an old verb, meaning "it has penetrated," probably referring to the tooth of the reptile. These medicine songs are always sung in a low plaintive tone, somewhat resembling a lullaby. Usu`gï also is without explanation, but is probably the name of some small reptile or batrachian.

As in this case the cause of the trouble is evident, the Indians have no theory to account for it. It may be remarked, however, that when one dreams of being bitten, the same treatment and ceremonies must be used as for the actual bite; otherwise, although perhaps years afterward, a similar inflammation will appear on the spot indicated in the dream, and will be followed by the same fatal consequences, The rattlesnake is regarded as a supernatural being or ada'wehi, whose favor must be propitiated, and great pains are taken not to offend him. In consonance with this idea it is never said among the people that a person has been bitten by a snake, but that he has been "scratched by a brier." In the same way, when an eagle has been shot for a ceremonial dance, it is announced that "a snowbird has been killed," the purpose being to deceive the rattlesnake or eagle spirits which might be listening.

The assertion that it is "only a common frog" or" only an Usu'?gï brings out another characteristic idea of these formulas. Whenever the ailment is of a serious character, or, according to the Indian theory, whenever it is due to the influence of some powerful disease spirit the doctor always endeavors to throw contempt upon the intruder, and convince it of his own superior power by asserting the sickness to be the work of some inferior being, just as a white physician might encourage a patient far gone with consumption by telling him that the, illness was only a slight cold. Sometimes there is a regular scale of depreciation, the doctor first ascribing the disease to a rabbit or groundhog or some other weak animal, then in succeeding paragraphs mentioning other still less important animals and finally declaring it to be the work of a mouse, a small fish, or some other insignificant creature. In this instance an ailment caused by the rattlesnake, the most dreaded of the animal spirits, is ascribed to a frog, one of the least importance.

In applying the remedy the song is probably sung while rubbing the tobacco juice around the wound. Then the short recitation is repeated and the doctor blows four times in a circle about the spot.

The whole ceremony is repeated four times. The curious directions for uncoiling the snake have parallels in European folk medicine.

TO TREAT THEM WHEN SOMETHING IS CAUSING SOMETHING TO EAT THEM.

Listen! Ha! I am a great ada'wehi, I never fail in anything. I surpass all others-I am a great ada'wehi. Ha! It is a mere screech owl that has frightened him. Ha! now I have put it away in the laurel thickets. There I compel it to remain,

Listen! Ha! I am a great ada'wehi, I never fail in anything. I surpass all others—I am a great ada'wehi. Ha! It is a mere hooting owl that has frightened him. Undoubtedly that has frightened him. Ha! At once I have put it away in the spruce thickets. Ha! There I compel it to remain.

Listen! Ha! I am a great ada'wehi, I never fail in anything. I surpass all others—I am a great ada'wehi. Ha! It is only a rabbit that has frightened him. Undoubtedly that has frightened him. Ha! Instantly I have put it away on the mountain ridge. Ha! There in the broom sage I compel it to remain.

Listen! Ha! I am a great ada'wehi, I never fail in anything. I surpass all others—I am a great ada'wehi. Ha! It is only a mountain sprite that has frightened him. Undoubtedly that has frightened him. Ha! Instantly I have put it away on the bluff. Ha! There I compel it to remain.

(Prescription)—Now this is to treat infants if they are affected by crying and nervous fright. (Then) it is said that something is causing something to eat them. To treat them one may blow water on them for four nights. Doctor them just before dark. Be sure not to carry them about outside the house.

EXPLANATION. The Cherokee name for this disease is Gunwani'gistâï', which signifies that "something is causing something to eat," or gnaw the vitals of the patient. The disease attacks only infants of tender age and the symptoms are nervousness and troubled sleep, from which the child wakes suddenly crying as if frightened. The civilized doctor would regard these as symptoms of the presence of worms, but although the Cherokee name might seem to indicate the same belief, the real theory is very different.

Cherokee mothers sometimes hush crying children by telling them that the screech owl is listening out in the woods or that the De'tsata—a malicious little dwarf who lives in caves in the river bluffs—will come and get them. This quiets the child for the time and is so far successful, but the animals, or the De'tsata, take offense at being spoken of in this way, and visit their displeasure upon the children born to the mother afterward. This they do by sending an animal into the body of the child to gnaw its vitals. The disease is very common and there are several specialists who devote their attention to it, using various formulas and prescriptions. It is also called ätawi'nëhï, signifying that it is caused by the "dwellers in the forest," i. e., the wild game and birds, and some doctors declare that it is caused by the revengeful comrades of the animals, especially birds, killed by the father of the child, the animals tracking the slayer to his home by the blood drops on the leaves. The next formula will throw more light upon this theory.

In this formula the doctor, who is certainly not overburdened with modesty, starts out by asserting that he is a great ada'wehi, who never fails and who surpasses all others. He then declares that, the disease is caused by a more screech owl, which he at once banishes to the laurel thicket. In the succeeding paragraphs he reiterates his former boasting, but asserts in turn that the trouble is caused by a mere hooting owl, a rabbit, or even by the De'tsata, whose greatest exploit is hiding the arrows of the boys, for which the youthful hunters do not hesitate to rate him soundly. These various mischief-makers the doctor banishes to their proper haunts, the hooting owl to the spruce thicket, the rabbit to the broom sage. on the mountain side, and the, De'tsata to the bluffs along the river bank.

Some doctors use herb decoctions, which are blown upon the body of the child, but in this formula the only remedy prescribed is water, which must be blown upon the body of the little sufferer just before dark for four nights. The regular method is to blow once each at the end of the first, second, and third paragraphs and four times at the end of the fourth or last. In diseases of this kind, which are not supposed to be of a local character, the doctor blows first upon the back of the head, then upon the left shoulder, next upon the right shoulder, and finally upon the breast, the patient being generally sitting, or propped up in bed, facing the east. The child must not be taken out of doors during the four days, because should a bird chance to fly overhead so that its shadow would fall upon the infant, it would fan the disease back into the body of the little one.

TO TREAT GûnWANI'GISTÛ'nÏ (SECOND).

Yû! Listen! Quickly you have drawn near to hearken, O Blue Sparrow-Hawk; in the spreading tree tops you are at rest. Quickly you have come down. The intruder is only a bird which has, overshadowed him. Swiftly you have swooped down upon it. Relief is accomplished. Yû!

Yû! Listen! Quickly you have drawn near to hearken, O Brown Rabbit-Hawk; you are at rest there above. Ha! Swiftly now you have come down. It is only the birds which have come together for a council. Quickly you have come and scattered them. Relief is accomplished. Yû!

EXPLANATION. This formula, also for Gûnwani'gistû'nï or Atawinë'hï, was obtained from A`wan'ita (Young Deer), who wrote down only the prayer and explained the treatment orally. He coincides in the opinion that this disease in children is caused by the birds, but says that it originates from the shadow of a bird. flying overhead having fallen upon the pregnant mother. He says further that the disease is easily recognized in children, but that it sometimes does not develop until the child has attained maturity, when it is more difficult to discern the cause of the trouble, although in the latter case dark circles around the eyes are unfailing symptoms.

The prayer—like several others from the same source—seems incomplete, and judging from analogy is evidently incorrect in some respects, but yet exemplifies the disease theory in a striking manner. The disease is declared to have been caused by the birds, it being asserted in the first paragraph that a bird has cast its shadow upon the sufferer, while in the second it is declared that they have gathered in council (in his body). This latter is a favorite expression in these formulas to indicate the great number of the disease animals.

Another expression of frequent occurrence is to the effect that the disease animals have formed a settlement or established a townhouse in the patient's body. The disease animal, being a bird or birds, must be dislodged by something which preys upon birds, and accordingly the Blue Sparrow-Hawk from the tree tops and the Brown Rabbit-Hawk (Diga'tiskï—"One who snatches up"), from above are invoked to drive out the intruders. The former is then said to have swooped down upon them as a hawk darts upon its prey, while the latter is declared to have scattered the birds which were holding a council. This being done, relief is accomplished. Yû! is a meaningless interjection frequently used to introduce or close paragraphs or songs.

The medicine used is a warm decoction of the bark of Kûnstû'tsï (Sassafras—Sassafras officinale), Kanûnsi'ta (Flowering Dogwood—Cornus florida), Udâ'lana (Service tree—Amelanchier Canadensis), and Uni'kwa (Black Gum—Nyssa multiflora), with the roots of two species (large and small) of Da'yakalï'skï (Wild Rose—Rosa lucida). The bark in every case is taken from the east side of the tree, and the roots selected are also generally, if not always, those growing toward the east. In this case the roots and barks are not bruised, but are simply steeped in warm water for four days. The child is then stripped and bathed all over with the decoction morning and night for four days, no formula being used during the bathing. It is then made to hold up its hands in front of its face with the palms turned out toward the doctor, who takes some of the medicine in his mouth and repeats the prayer mentally, blowing the medicine upon the head and hands of the patient at the, final Yû! of each paragraph. It is probable that the prayer originally consisted of four paragraphs, or else that these two paragraphs were repeated. The child drinks a little of the medicine at the end of each treatment.

The use of salt is prohibited during the four days of the treatment, the word (amä') being understood to include lye, which enters largely into Cherokee food preparations. No chicken or other feathered animal is allowed to enter the house during the same period, for obvious reasons, and strangers are excluded for reasons already explained.

THIS TELLS ABOUT MOVING PAINS IN THE TEETH (NEURALGIA?).

Listen! In the Sunland you repose, O Red Spider. Quickly you have brought and laid down the red path. O great ada'wehi, quickly you have brought down the red threads from above. The intruder in the tooth has spoken and it is only a worm. The tormentor has wrapped itself around the root of the tooth. Quickly you have dropped down the red threads, for it is just what you eat. Now it is for you to pick it up. The relief has been caused to come. Yû!

O Ancient White, you have drawn near to hearken, for you have said, "When I shall hear my grandchildren, I shall hold up their heads." Because you have said it, now therefore you have drawn near to listen. The relief has been caused to come. Yû!

Listen! In the Frigid Land you repose, O Blue Spider. Quickly you have brought and laid down the blue path. O great ada'wehi, quickly you have brought down the blue threads from above. The intruder in the tooth has spoken and it is only a worm. The tormentor has wrapped itself around the root of the tooth. Quickly you have dropped down the blue threads, for it is just what you eat. Now it is for you to pick it up. The relief has been caused to come. Yû!

O Ancient White, you have drawn near to hearken, for you have said, "When I shall hear my grandchildren, I shall hold up their heads." Because you have said it, now therefore you have drawn near to listen. The relief has been caused to come. Yû!

Listen! In the Darkening Land you repose, O Black Spider. Quickly you have brought and laid down the black path. O great ada'wehi, quickly you have brought down the black threads from above. The intruder in the tooth has spoken and it is only a worm. The tormentor has wrapped itself around the root of the tooth. Quickly you have dropped down the black threads, for it is just what you eat. Now it is for you to pick it up. The relief has been caused to come. Yû!

O Ancient White, you have drawn near to hearken, for you have said, "When I shall hear my grandchildren, I shall hold up their heads." Because you have said it, now therefore you have drawn near to listen. The relief has been caused to come. Yû!

Listen! You repose on high, O White Spider. Quickly you have brought and laid down the white path. O great ada'wehi, quickly you have brought down the white threads from above. The intruder in the tooth has spoken and it is only a worm. The tormentor has wrapped itself around the root of the tooth. Quickly you have dropped down the white threads, for it is just what you eat. Now it is for you to pick it up. The relief has been caused to come. Yû!

O Ancient White, you have drawn near to hearken, for you have said, "When I shall hear my grandchildren, I shall hold up their heads." Because you have said it, now therefore you have drawn near to listen. The relief has been caused to come. Yû!

(Prescription)—This is to treat them if there are pains moving about in the teeth. It is only (necessary) to lay on the hands, or to blow, if one should prefer. One may use any kind of a tube, but usually they have the medicine in the mouth. It is the Yellow-rooted Grass (kane'ska dalâ'nige unaste'tla; not identified.) One must abstain four nights from cooked corn (hominy), and kanâhe'na (fermented corn gruel) is especially forbidden during the same period.

EXPLANATION. This formula is taken from the manuscript book of Gatigwanasti, now dead, and must therefore be explained from general analogy. The ailment is described as "pains moving about in the teeth"—that is, affecting several teeth simultaneously—and appears to be neuralgia. The disease spirit is called "the intruder" and "the tormentor" and is declared to be a mere worm (tsgâ'ya), which has wrapped itself around the base of the tooth. This is the regular toothache theory. The doctor then calls upon the Red Spider of the Sunland to let down the red threads from above, along the red path, and to take up the intruder, which is just what the spider eats. The same prayer is addressed in turn to the Blue Spider in the north, the Black Spider in the west and the White Spider above (galûn'lati). It may be stated here that all these spirits are supposed to dwell above, but when no point of the compass is assigned, galûn'lati is understood to mean directly overhead, but far above everything of earth. The dweller in this overhead galûn'lati may be red, white, or brown in color. In this formula it is white, the ordinary color assigned spirits dwelling in the south. In another toothache formula the Squirrel is implored to take the worm and put it between the forking limbs of a tree on the north side of the mountain.

Following each supplication to the spider is another addressed to the Ancient White, the formulistic name for fire. The name refers to its antiquity and light-giving properties and perhaps also to the fact that when dead it is covered with a coat of white ashes. In those formulas in which the hunter draws omens from the live coals it is frequently addressed as the Ancient Red.

The directions are not explicit and must be interpreted from analogy. "Laying on the hands" refers to pressing the thumb against the jaw over the aching tooth, the hand having been previously warmed over the fire, this being a common method of treating toothache. The other method suggested is to blow upon the spot (tooth or outside of jaw?) a decoction of an herb described rather vaguely as "yellow-rooted grass" either through a tube or from the mouth of the operator. Igawï', a toothache specialist, treats this ailment either by pressure with the warm thumb, or by blowing tobacco smoke from a pipe placed directly against the tooth. Hominy and fermented corn gruel (kanâhe'na) are prohibited for the regular term of four nights, or, as we are accustomed to say, four days, and special emphasis is laid upon the gruel tabu.

The prayer to the Spider is probably repeated while the doctor is warming his hands over the fire, and the following paragraph to the Ancient White (the Fire) while holding the warm thumb upon the aching spot. This reverses the usual order, which is to address the fire while warming the hands. In this connection it must be noted that the fire used by the doctor is never the ordinary fire on the hearth, but comes from four burning chips taken from the hearth fire and generally placed in an earthen vessel by the side of the patient. In some cases the decoction is heated by putting into it seven live coals taken from the fire on the hearth.

TO TREAT THE GREAT CHILL.

Listen! On high you dwell, On high you dwell—you dwell, you dwell. Forever you dwell, you anida'we, forever you dwell, forever you dwell. Relief has come—has come. Hayï!

Listen! On Ûnwadâ'hï you dwell, On Ûnwadâ'hï you dwell—you dwell, you dwell. Forever you dwell, you anida'we, forever you dwell, forever you dwell. Relief has come—has come. Hayï!

Listen! In the pines you dwell, In the pines you dwell—you dwell, you dwell. Forever you dwell, you anida'we, forever you dwell, forever you dwell. Relief has come—has come. Hayï!

Listen! In the water you dwell, In the water you dwell, you dwell, you dwell. Forever you dwell, you anida'we, forever you dwell, forever you dwell. Relief has come—has come. Hayï!

Listen! O now you have drawn near to hearken, O Little Whirlwind, O ada'wehi, in the leafy shelter of the lower mountain, there you repose. O ada'wehi, you can never fail in anything. Ha!

Now rise up. A very small portion [of the disease] remains. You have come to sweep it away into the small swamp on the upland. You have laid down your paths near the swamp. It is ordained that you shall scatter it as in play, so that it shall utterly disappear. By you it must be scattered. So shall there be relief.

Listen! O now again you have drawn near to hearken, O Whirlwind, surpassingly great. In the leafy shelter of the great mountain there you repose. O Great Whirlwind, arise quickly. A very small part [of the disease] remains. You have come to sweep the intruder into the great swamp on the upland. You have laid down your paths toward the great swamp. You shall scatter it as in play so that it shall utterly disappear. And now relief has come. All is done. Yû!

(Prescription.)—(This is to use) when they are sick with the great chill. Take a decoction of wild cherry to blow upon them. If you have Tsâ'l-agayû'nlï ("old tobacco"—Nicotiana rustica) it also is very effective.

EXPLANATION. Unawa'stï, "that which chills one," is a generic name for intermittent fever, otherwise known as fever and ague. It is much dreaded by the Indian doctors, who recognize several varieties of the disease, and have various theories to account for them. The above formula was obtained from A`yûnni (Swimmer), who described the symptoms of this variety, the "Great Chill," as blackness in the face, with alternate high fever and shaking chills. The disease generally appeared in spring or summer, and might return year after year. In the first stages the chill usually came on early in the morning, but came on later in the day as the disease progressed. There might be more than one chill during the day. There was no rule as to appetite, but the fever always produced an excessive thirst. In one instance the patient fainted from the heat and would even lie down in a stream to cool himself. The doctor believed the disease was caused by malicious tsgâ'ya, a general name for all small insects and worms, excepting intestinal worms. These tsgâ'ya—that is, the disease tsgâ'ya, not the real insects and worms—are held responsible for a large number of diseases, and in fact the tsgâ'ya doctrine is to the Cherokee practitioner what the microbe theory is to some modern scientists. The tsgâ'ya live in the earth, in the water, in the air, in the foliage of trees, in decaying wood, or wherever else insects lodge, and as they are constantly being crushed, burned or otherwise destroyed through the unthinking carelessness of the human race, they are continually actuated by a spirit of revenge. To accomplish their vengeance, according to the doctors, they "establish towns" under the skin of their victims, thus producing an irritation which results in fevers, boils, scrofula and other diseases.

The formula begins with a song of four verses, in which the doctor invokes in succession the spirits of the air, of the mountain, of the forest, and of the water. Galûnlatï, the word used in the first verse, signifies, as has been already explained, "on high" or "above everything," and has been used by translators to mean heaven. Ûnwadâ'hï in the second verse is the name of a bald mountain east of Webster, North Carolina, and is used figuratively to denote any mountains of bold outline. The Cherokees have a tradition to account for the name, which is derived from Ûnwadâ'lï, "provision house." Nâ'tsihï' in the third verse signifies "pinery," from nâ`tsï, "pine," but is figuratively used to denote a forest of any kind.

In the recitation which follows the song, but is used only in serious cases, the doctor prays to the whirlwind, which is considered to dwell, among the trees on the mountain side, where the trembling of the leaves always gives the first intimation of its presence. He declares that a small portion of the disease still remains, the spirits invoked in the song having already taken the rest, and calls upon the whirlwind to lay down a path for it and sweep it away into the swamp on the upland, referring to grassy marshes common in the small coves of the higher mountains, which, being remote from the settlements, are convenient places to which to banish the disease. Not satisfied with this he goes on to direct the whirlwind to scatter the disease as it scatters the leaves of the forest, so that it shall utterly disappear. In the Cherokee formula the verb a`ne'tsâge'ta, means literally "to play," and is generally understood to refer to the ball play, a`ne'tsâ, so that to a Cherokee the expression conveys the idea of catching up the disease and driving it onward as a player seizes the ball and sends it spinning through the air from between his ball sticks. Niga'gï is a solemn expression about equivalent to the Latin *consummatum est*.

The doctor beats up some bark from the trunk of the wild cherry and puts it into water together with seven coals of fire, the latter being intended to warm the decoction The leaves of Tsâl-agayû'nli (Indian tobacco—Nicotiana rustica) are sometimes used in place of the wild cherry bark. The patient is placed facing the sunrise, and the doctor, taking the medicine in his mouth, blows it over the body of the sick man. First, standing between the patient and the sunrise and holding the medicine cup in his hand, he sings the first verse in a low tone. Then, taking some of the liquid in his mouth, he advances and blows it successively upon the top of the head, the right shoulder, left shoulder, and breast or back of the patient, making four blowings in all. He repeats the same ceremony with the second, third, and fourth verse, returning each time to his original position. The ceremony takes place in the morning, and if necessary is repeated in the evening. It is sometimes necessary also to repeat the treatment for several—generally four—consecutive days.

The recitation is not used excepting in the most serious cases, when, according to the formula, "a very small portion" of the disease still lingers. It is accompanied by blowing of the breath alone, without medicine, probably in this case typical of the action of the whirlwind. After repeating the whole ceremony accompanying the song, as above described, the doctor returns to his position in front of the patient and recites in a whisper the first paragraph to the Little Whirlwind, after which he advances and blows his breath upon the patient four times as he has already blown the medicine upon him. Then going around to the north he recites the second paragraph to the Great Whirlwind, and at its conclusion blows in the same manner. Then moving around to the west—behind the patient—he again prays to the Little Whirlwind with the same ceremonies, and finally moving around to the south side he closes with the prayer to the Great Whirlwind, blowing four times at its conclusion. The medicine must be prepared anew by the doctor at the house of the patient at each application morning or evening. Only as much as will be needed is made at a time, and the patient always drinks what remains after the blowing. Connected with the preparation and care of the medicine are a number of ceremonies which need not be detailed here. The wild cherry bark must always be procured fresh; but the Tsâl-agayû'nlï ("Old Tobacco") leaves may be dry. When the latter plant is used four leaves are taken and steeped in warm water with the fire coals, as above described.

THIS IS TO MAKE CHILDREN JUMP DOWN.

Listen! You little man, get up now at once. There comes an old woman. The horrible [old thing] is coming, only a little way off. Listen! Quick! Get your bed and let us run away. Yû!

Listen! You little woman, get up now at once. There comes your grandfather. The horrible old fellow is coming only a little way off. Listen! Quick! Get your bed and let us run away. Yû!

EXPLANATION. In this formula for childbirth the idea is to frighten the child and coax it to come, by telling it, if a boy, that an ugly old woman is coming, or if a girl, that her grandfather is coming only a short distance away. The reason of this lies in the fact that an old woman is the terror of all the little boys of the neighborhood, constantly teasing and frightening them by declaring that she means to live until they grow up and then compel one of them to marry her, old and shriveled as she is. For the same reason the maternal grandfather, who is always a privileged character in the family, is especially dreaded by the little girls, and nothing will send a group of children running into the house more quickly than the announcement that an old "granny," of either sex is in sight.

As the sex is an uncertain quantity, the possible boy is always first addressed in the formulas, and if no result seems to follow, the doctor then concludes that the child is a girl and addresses her in similar tones. In some cases an additional formula with the beads is used to determine whether the child will be born alive or dead. In most instances the formulas were formerly repeated with the appropriate ceremonies by some old female relative of the mother, but they are now the property of the ordinary doctors, men as well as women.

This formula was obtained from the manuscript book of A`yû'ninï, who stated that the medicine used was a warm decoction of a plant called Dalâ'nige Unaste'tsï ("yellow root"—not identified), which was blown successively upon the top of the mother's head, upon the breast, and upon the palm of each hand. The doctor stands beside the woman, who is propped up in a sitting position, while repeating the first paragraph and then blows. If this produces no result he then recites the paragraph addressed to the girl and again blows. A part of the liquid is also given to the woman to drink. A`yû'ninï claimed this was always effectual.

THIS IS TO MAKE CHILDREN JUMP DOWN.

Little boy, little boy, hurry, hurry, come out, come out!
Little boy, hurry; a bow, a bow; let's see who'll get it, let's see who'll get it!
Little girl, little girl, hurry, hurry, come out, come out, Little girl, hurry; a sifter, a sifter; let's see who'll get it, let's see who'll get it!

EXPLANATION. This formula was obtained from Takwati'hï, as given to him by a specialist in this line. Takwatihi himself knew nothing of the treatment involved, but a decoction is probably blown upon the patient as described in the preceding formula. In many cases the medicine used is simply cold water, the idea being to cause a sudden muscular action by the chilling contact. In this formula the possible boy or girl is coaxed out by the promise of a bow or a meal-sifter to the one who can get it first. Among the Cherokees it is common, in asking about the sex of a new arrival, to inquire, "Is it a bow or a sifter?" or "Is it ball sticks or bread?"

TO TREAT THE BLACK YELLOWNESS.
Yuha'ahi', yuha'ahi', yuha'ahi', yuha'ahi',
Yuha'ahi', yuha'ahi', yuha'ahi' Yû!

Listen! In the great lake the intruder reposes. Quickly he has risen up there. Swiftly he has come and stealthily put himself (under the sick man).

Listen! Ha! Now you two have drawn near to hearken, there in the Sun Land you repose, O Little Men, O great anida'wehi! The intruder has risen up there in the great lake. Quickly you two have lifted up the intruder. His paths have laid themselves down toward the direction whence he came. Let him never look back (toward us). When he stops to rest at the four gaps you will drive him roughly along. Now he has plunged into the great lake from which he came. There he is compelled to remain, never to look back. Ha! there let him rest. (Yû!)

(Directions.)—This is to treat them when their breast swells. Fire (coals) is not put down.

EXPLANATION. This formula, from A`yûninï's manuscript, is used in treating a disease known as Dalâni, literally, "yellow." From the vague description of symptoms given by the doctors, it appears to be an aggravated form of biliousness, probably induced by late suppers and bad food. According to the Indian theory it is caused by revengeful animals, especially by the terrapin and its cousin, the turtle.

The doctors recognize several forms of the disease, this variety being distinguished as the "black dalâni (Dalâni Ûnnage'ï) and considered the most dangerous. In this form of dalânï, according to their account, the navel and abdomen of the patient swell, the ends of his fingers become black, dark circles appear about his eyes, and the throat contracts spasmodically and causes him to fall down suddenly insensible. A`yûninï's method of treatment is to rub the breast and abdomen of the patient with the hands, which have been previously rubbed together in the warm infusion of wild cherry (ta'ya) bark. The song is sung while rubbing the hands together in the liquid, and the prayer is repeated while rubbing the swollen abdomen of the patient. The operation may be repeated several times on successive days.

The song at the beginning has no meaning and is sung in a low plaintive lullaby tone, ending with a sharp Yu! The prayer possesses a special interest, as it brings out several new points in the Cherokee mythologic theory of medicine. The "intruder," which is held to be some amphibious animal—as a terrapin, turtle, or snake—is declared to have risen up from his dwelling place in the great lake, situated toward the sunset, and to have come by stealth under the sick man. The verb implies that the disease spirit creeps under as a snake might crawl under the coverlet of a bed.

The two Little Men in the Sun Land are now invoked to drive out the disease. Who these Little Men are is not clear, although they are regarded as most powerful spirits and are frequently invoked in the formulas. They are probably the two Thunder Boys, sons of Kanati.

The Little Men come instantly when summoned by the shaman, pull out the intruder from the body of the patient, turn his face toward the sunset, and begin to drive him on by threats and blows (expressed in the word gû'ntsatatagi'yû) to the great lake from which he came. On the road there are four gaps in the mountains, at each of which the disease spirit halts to rest, but is continually forced onward by his two pursuers, who finally drive him into the lake, where he is compelled to remain, without being permitted even to look back again. The four gaps are mentioned also in other formulas for medicine and the ball play and sometimes correspond with the four stages of the treatment. The direction "No fire (coals) is put down" indicates that no live coals are put into the decoction, the doctor probably using water warmed in the ordinary manner.

Takwati'hï uses for this disease a decoction of four herbs applied in the same manner. He agrees with A`yû'ninï in regard to the general theory and says also that the disease may be contracted by neglecting to wash the hands after handling terrapin shells, as, for instance, the shell rattles used by women in the dance. The turtle or water tortoise (seligu'gï) is considered as an inferior being, with but little capacity for mischief, and is feared chiefly on account of its relationship to the dreaded terrapin or land tortoise (tûksï'). In Takwatihï's formula he prays to the Ancient White (the fire), of which these cold-blooded animals are supposed to be afraid, to put the fish into the water, the turtle into the mud, and to send the terrapin and snake to the hillside.

TO TREAT FOR ORDEAL DISEASES.

Listen! Ha! Now you have drawn near to hearken and are resting directly overhead. O Black Raven, you never fail in anything. Ha! Now you are brought down. Ha! There shall be left no more than a trace upon the ground where you have been. It is an evolute ghost. You have now put it into a crevice in Sanigalagi, that it may never find the way back. You have put it to rest in the Darkening Land, so that it may never return. Let relief come.

Listen! Ha! Now you have drawn near to hearken, O Red Raven, most powerful ada'wehi. Ha! You never fail in anything, for so it was ordained of you. Ha! You are resting directly overhead. Ha! Now you are brought down. There shall remain but a trace upon the ground where you have been. It is an evolute ghost. Ha! You have put the Intruder into a crevice of Sanigalagi and now the relief shall come. It (the Intruder) is sent to the Darkening Land. You have put it to rest in the Darkening Land. Let the relief come.

Listen! Ha! Now you have drawn near to hearken, O Blue Raven; you are resting directly overhead, ada'wehi. You never fail in anything, for so it was ordained of you. Ha! Now you are brought down. There shall be left but a trace upon the ground where you have been. You have put the Intruder into a crevice in Sanigalagi, that it may never find the way back. You have put it to rest in the Darkening Land, so that it may never return. Let the relief come.

Listen! Ha! Now you have drawn near to hearken; you repose on high on Wa'hïlï, O White Raven, ada'wehi. You never fail in anything. Ha! Now you are brought down. There shall be left but a trace upon the ground where you have been. Ha! Now you have taken it up. You have put the Intruder into a crevice in Sanigalagi, that it may never find the way back. You have put it to rest in the Darkening Land, never to return. Let the relief come.

(Directions)—This is to treat them for a painful sickness. One must suck. Use Tsâ'lagayûn'-li ("Old Tobacco"—Nicotiana rustica), blossoms, and just have them in the mouth, and Kanasâ'la (Wild Parsnip), goes with it, and four red beads also must lie there, and Tsâliyu'sti Usdi'ga ("Little (plant) Like Tobacco"—Indian Tobacco—Lobelia inflata.) And if there should be anything mixed with it (i. e., after sucking the place), just put it about a hand's-length into the mud.

EXPLANATION. The Cherokee name for this disease gives no idea whatever of its serious nature. The technical term, Tsundaye'liga'ktanû'hï, really refers to the enthusiastic outburst of sociability that ensues when two old friends meet. In this instance it might be rendered "an ordeal." The application of such a name to what is considered a serious illness is in accordance with the regular formulistic practice of making light of a dangerous malady in order to convey to the disease spirit the impression that the shaman is not afraid of him. A`yûninï, from whom the formula was obtained, states also that the disease is sometimes sent to a man by a friend or even by his parents, in order to test his endurance and knowledge of counter spells.

As with most diseases, the name simply indicates the shaman's theory of the occult cause of the trouble, and is no clue to the symptoms, which may be those usually attendant upon fevers, indigestion, or almost any other ailment.

In some cases the disease is caused by the conjurations of an enemy, through which the patient becomes subject to an inordinate appetite, causing him to eat until his abdomen is unnaturally distended. By the same magic spells tobacco may be conveyed into the man's body, causing him to be affected by faintness and languor. The enemy, if bitterly revengeful, may even put into the body of his victim a worm or insect (tsgâya), or a sharpened stick of black locust or "fat" pine, which will result in death if not removed by a good doctor. Sometimes a weed stalk is in some occult manner conveyed into the patient's stomach, where it is transformed into a worm. As this disease is very common, owing to constant quarrels and rival jealousies, there are a number of specialists who devote their attention to it.

The prayer is addressed to the Black, Red, Blue, and White Ravens, their location at the four cardinal points not being specified, excepting in the case of the white raven of Wa'hilï, which, as already stated, is said to be a mountain in the south, and hence is used figuratively to mean the south. The ravens are each in turn declared to have put the disease into a crevice in Sanigala'gi—the Cherokee name of Whiteside Mountain, at the head of Tuckasegee River, in North Carolina, and used figuratively for. any high precipitous mountain—and to have left no more than a trace upon the ground where it has been. The adjective translated "evolute" (udanûhï) is of frequent occurrence in the formulas. but has no exact equivalent in English. It signifies springing into being or life from an embryonic condition. In this instance it would imply that whatever object the enemy has put into the body of the sick man has there developed into a ghost to trouble him.

The directions are expressed in a rather vague manner, as is the case with most of A`yûnini's attempts at original composition. The disease is here called by another name, agi`li'ya unitlûngû'nï, signifying "when they are painfully sick." The treatment consists in sucking the part most affected, the doctor having in his mouth during the operation the blossoms of Tsâ'l-agayû'nlï (Nicotiana rustica), Kanasâ'la (wild parsnip,) and Tsâliyusti Usdiga (Lobelia inflata.) The first and last of these names signify "tobacco" and "tobacco-like," while the other seems to contain the same word, tsâ'la, and the original idea may have been to counteract the witchcraft by the use of the various species of "tobacco," the herb commonly used to drive away a witch or wizard. During the sticking process four red beads lie near upon a piece of (white) cloth, which afterward becomes the perquisite of the doctor. Though not explicitly stated, it is probable that the doctor holds in his mouth a decoction of the blossoms named, rather than the blossoms themselves. On withdrawing his mouth from the spot and ejecting the liquid into a bowl, it is expected that there will be found "mixed" with it a small stick, a pebble, an insect, or something of the kind, and this the shaman then holds up to view as the cause of the disease. It is afterward buried a "hand's length" (awâ'hilû) deep in the mud. No directions were given as to diet or tabu.

CONCERNING HUNTING.

Give me the wind. Give me the breeze. Yû! O Great Terrestrial Hunter, I come to the edge of your spittle where you repose. Let your stomach cover itself; let it be covered with leaves. Let it cover itself at a single bend, and may you never be satisfied.

And you, O Ancient Red, may you hover above my breast while I sleep. Now let good (dreams?) develop; let my experiences be propitious. Ha! Now let my little trails be directed, as they lie down in various directions(?). Let the leaves be covered with the clotted blood, and may it never cease to be so. You two (the Water and the Fire) shall bury it in your stomachs. Yû!

EXPLANATION. This is a hunting formula, addressed to the two great gods of the hunter, Fire and Water. The evening before starting the hunter "goes to water," as already explained, and recites the appropriate formula. In the morning he sets out, while still fasting, and travels without eating or drinking until nightfall. At sunset he again goes to water, reciting this formula during the ceremony, after which he builds his camp fire, eats his supper and lies down for the night, first rubbing his breast with ashes from the fire. In the morning he starts out to look for game.

"Give me the wind," is a prayer that the wind may be in his favor, so that the game may not scent him. The word rendered here "Great Terrestrial Hunter," is in the original "Ela-Kana'tï." In this e'la is the earth and kana'tï is a term applied to a successful hunter. The great Kanatï, who, according to the myth, formerly kept all the game shut up in his underground caverns, now dwells above the sky, and is frequently invoked by hunters. The raven also is often addressed as Kanatï in these hunting formulas. Ela-Kana'tï, the Great Terrestrial Hunter—as distinguished from the other two—signifies the river, the name referring to the way in which the tiny streams and rivulets search out and bring down to the great river the leaves and débris of the mountain forests. In formulas for medicine, love, the ball play, etc., the river is always addressed as the Long Person (Yû'nwï Gûnahi'ta). The "spittle" referred to is the foam at the edge of the water. "Let your stomach be covered with leaves" means, let the blood-stained leaves where the stricken game shall fall be so numerous as to cover the surface of the water. The hunter prays also that sufficient game may be found in a single bend of the river to accomplish this result without the necessity of searching through the whole forest, and to that end he further prays that the river may never be satisfied, but continually longing for more. The same idea is repeated in the second paragraph, The hunter is supposed to feed the river with blood washed from the game. In like manner he feeds the fire, addressed in the second paragraph as the "Ancient Red," with a piece of meat cut from the tongue of the deer. The prayer that the fire may hover above his breast while he sleeps and brings him favorable dreams, refers to his rubbing his breast with ashes from his camp fire before lying down to sleep, in order that the fire may bring him dream omens of success for the morrow. The Fire is addressed either as the Ancient White or the Ancient Red, the allusion in the first case being to the light or the ashes of the fire; in the other case, to the color of the burning coals. "You two shall bury it in your stomachs" refers to the bloodstained leaves and the piece of meat which are cast respectively into the river and the fire. The formula was obtained from A`yûninï, who explained it in detail.

THIS IS FOR HUNTING BIRDS.

Listen! O Ancient White, where you dwell in peace I have come to rest. Now let your spirit arise. Let it (the game brought down) be buried in your stomach, and may your appetite never be satisfied. The red hickories have tied themselves together. The clotted blood is your recompense.

O Ancient White, Accept the clotted blood (?).

O Ancient White. put me in the successful hunting trail. Hang the mangled things upon me. Let me come along the successful trail with them doubled up (under my belt). It (the road) is clothed with the mangled things.

O Ancient White, O Kanati, support me continually, that I may never become blue. Listen!

EXPLANATION. This formula, from A`yûninï's manuscript, is recited by the bird-hunter in the morning while standing over the fire at his hunting camp before starting out for the day's hunt. A`yû'nini stated that seven blowgun arrows are first prepared, including a small one only a "hand-length" (awâ'hilû) long. On rising in the morning the hunter, standing over the fire, addresses it as the "Ancient White," rubbing his hands together while repeating the prayer. He then sets out for the hunting ground, where he expects to spend the day, and on reaching it he shoots away the short arrow at random, without attempting to trace its flight. There is of course some significance attached to this action and perhaps an accompanying prayer, but no further information upon this point was obtainable. Having shot away the magic arrow, the hunter utters a peculiar hissing sound, intended to call up the birds, and then goes to work with his remaining arrows. On all hunting expeditions it is the regular practice, religiously enforced, to abstain from food until sunset.

A favorite method with the bird-hunter during the summer season is to climb a gum tree, which is much frequented by the smaller birds on account of its berries, where, taking up a convenient position amid the branches with his noiseless blowgun and arrows, he deliberately shoots down one bird after another until his shafts are exhausted, when he climbs down, draws out the arrows from the bodies of the birds killed, and climbs up again to repeat the operation. As the light darts used make no sound, the birds seldom take the alarm, and are too busily engaged with the berries to notice their comrades dropping to the ground from time to time, and pay but slight attention even to the movements of the hunter.

The prayer is addressed to the Ancient White (the Fire), the spirit most frequently invoked by the hunter, who, as before stated, rubs his hands together over the fire while repeating the words. The expressions used are obscure when taken alone, but are full of meaning when explained in the light of the hunting customs. The "clotted blood" refers to the bloodstained leaves upon which the fallen game has lain. The expression occurs constantly in the hunting formulas. The hunter gathers up these bloody leaves and casts them upon the fire, in order to draw omens for the morrow from the manner in which they burn. A part of the tongue, or some other portion of the animal, is usually cast upon the coals also for the same purpose. This subject will be treated at length in a future account of the hunting ceremonies.

"Let it be buried in your stomach" refers also to the offering made the fire. By the red hickories are meant the strings of hickory bark which the bird hunter twists about his waist for a belt. The dead birds are carried by inserting their heads under this belt. Red is, of course, symbolic of his success. "The mangled things" (unigwalû'ngï) are the wounded birds. Kana'tï is here used to designate the fire, on account of its connection with the hunting ceremonies.

TO SHOOT DWELLERS IN THE WILDERNESS.

Instantly the Red Selagwû'tsï strike you in the very center of your soul—instantly. Yû!

EXPLANATION. This short formula, obtained from A`wani'ta, is recited by the hunter while taking aim. The bowstring is let go—or, rather, the trigger is pulled—at the final Yû! He was unable to explain the meaning of the word selagwû'tsï further than that it referred to the bullet. Later investigation, however, revealed the fact that this is the Cherokee name of a reed of the genus Erianthus, and the inference follows that the stalk of the plant was formerly used for arrow shafts. Red implies that the arrow is always successful in reaching the mark aimed at, and in this instance may refer also to its being bloody when withdrawn from the body of the animal. Inagë'hï, "dwellers in the wilderness," is the generic term for game, including birds, but A`wani'ta has another formula intended especially for deer.

BEAR SONG.

He! Hayuya'haniwä', hayuya'haniwä', hayuya'haniwä', hayuya'haniwä'.

In Rabbit Place you were conceived (repeat)—Yoho' +! He! Hayuya'haniwä', hayuya'haniwä', hayuya'haniwä', hayuya'haniwä'.

In Mulberry Place you were conceived (repeat)—Yoho' +! He! Hayuya'haniwä', hayuya'haniwä', hayuya'haniwä', hayuya'haniwä'.

In Uyâ''yë you were conceived (repeat)—Yoho' +! He! Hayuya'haniwä', hayuya'haniwä', hayuya'haniwä', hayuya'haniwä'.

In the Great Swamp (?) you were conceived (repeat)—Yoho' +! And now surely we and the good black things, the best of all, shall see each other.

EXPLANATION. This song, obtained from A`yû'ninï in connection with the story of the Origin of the Bear, as already mentioned, is sung by the bear hunter, in order to attract the bears, while on his way from the camp to the place where he expects to hunt during the day. It is one of those taught the Cherokees by the Ani-Tsâ'kahï before they lost their human shape and were transformed into bears. The melody is simple and plaintive.

The song consists of four verses followed by a short recitation. Each verse begins with a loud prolonged He! and ends with Yoho'! uttered in the same manner. Hayuya'haniwä' has no meaning. Tsistu'yï, Kuwâ'hï, Uyâ''yë, and Gâte'kwâhï are four mountains, in each of which the bears have a townhouse and hold a dance before going into their dens for the winter. The first three named are high peaks in the Smoky Mountains, on the Tennessee line, in the neighborhood of Clingman's Dome and Mount Guyot. The fourth is southeast of Franklin, North Carolina, toward the South Carolina line, and may be identical with Fodderstack Mountain. In Kuwahi dwells the great bear chief and doctor, in whose magic bath the wounded bears are restored to health. They are said to originate or be conceived in the mountains named, because these are their headquarters. The "good black things" referred to in the recitation are the bears.

THIS IS FOR CATCHING LARGE FISH.

Listen! Now you settlements have drawn near to hearken. Where you have gathered in the foam you are moving about as one. You Blue Cat and the others, I have come to offer you freely the white food. Let the paths from every direction recognize each other. Our spittle shall be in agreement. Let them (your and my spittle) be together as we go about. They (the fish) have become a prey and there shall be no loneliness. Your spittle has become agreeable. I am called Swimmer. Yû!

EXPLANATION. This formula, from A`yûnini's' book, is for the purpose of catching large fish. According to his instructions, the fisherman must first chew a small piece of Yugwilû' (Venus' Flytrap—Dionæa muscipula) and spit it upon the bait and also upon the hook. Then, standing facing the stream, he recites the formula and puts the bait upon the hook. He will be able to pull out a fish at once, or if the fish are not about at the moment they will come in a very short time.

The Yugwilû' is put upon the bait from the idea that it will enable the hook to attract and hold the fish as the plant itself seizes and holds insects in its cup. The root is much prized by the Cherokees for this purpose, and those in the West, where the plant is not found, frequently send requests for it to their friends in Carolina.

The prayer is addressed directly to the fish, who are represented as living in settlements. The same expression as has already been mentioned is sometimes used by the doctors in speaking of the tsgâ'ya or worms which are supposed to cause sickness by getting under the skin of the patient. The Blue Cat (Amiurus, genus) is addressed as the principal fish and the bait is spoken of as the "white food," an expression used also of the viands prepared at the feast of the green corn dance, to indicate their wholesome character. "Let the paths from every direction recognize each other," means let the fishes, which are supposed to have regular trails through the water, assemble together at the place where the speaker takes his station, as friends recognizing each other at a distance approach to greet each other, uWâhisâ'nahï tigiwatsi'la, rendered "our spittle shall be in agreement," is a peculiar archaic expression that can not be literally translated. It implies that there shall be such close sympathy between the fisher and the fish that their spittle shall be as the spittle of one individual. As before stated, the spittle is believed to exert an

important influence upon the whole physical and mental being.
The expression "your spittle has become agreeable" is explained by
A`yûninï as an assertion or wish that the fish may prove palatable,
while the words rendered "there shall be no loneliness" imply that
there shall be an abundant catch.

CONCERNING LIVING HUMANITY (LOVE).

Kû! Listen! In Alahi'yï you repose, O Terrible Woman, O you have drawn near to hearken. There in Elahiyï you are at rest, O White Woman. No one is ever lonely when with you. You are most beautiful. Instantly and at once you have rendered me a white man. No one is ever lonely when with me. Now you have made the path white for me. It shall never be dreary. Now you have put me into it. It shall never become blue. You have brought down to me from above the white road. There in mid-earth (mid-surface) you have placed me. I shall stand erect upon the earth. No one is ever lonely when with me. I am very handsome. You have put me into the white house. I shall be in it as it moves about and no one with me shall ever be lonely. Verily, I shall never become blue. Instantly you have caused it to be so with me.

And now there in Elahiyï you have rendered the woman blue. Now you have made the path blue for her. Let her be completely veiled in loneliness. Put her into the blue road. And now bring her down. Place her standing upon the earth. Where her feet are now and wherever she may go, let loneliness leave its mark upon her. Let her be marked out for loneliness where she stands.

Ha! I belong to the Wolf clan, that one alone which was allotted into for you. No one is ever lonely with me. I am handsome. Let her put her soul the very center of my soul, never to turn away. Grant that in the midst of men she shall never think of them. I belong to the one clan alone which was allotted for you when the seven clans were established.

Where (other) men live it is lonely. They are very loathsome. The common polecat has made them so like himself that they are fit only for his company. They have became mere refuse. They are very loathsome. The common opossum has made them so like himself that they are fit only to be with him. They are very loathsome. Even the crow has made them so like himself that they are fit only for his company. They are very loathsome. The miserable rain-crow has made them so like himself that they are fit only to be with him.

The seven clans all alike make one feel very lonely in their company. They are not even good looking. They go about clothed with mere refuse. They even go about covered with dung. But I—I was ordained to be a white man. I stand with my face toward the Sun Land. No one is ever lonely with me. I am very handsome. I shall certainly never become blue. I am covered by the everlasting white house wherever I go. No one is ever lonely with me. Your soul has come into the very center of my soul, never to turn away. I—(Gatigwanasti,) (O O)—I take your soul. Sgë!

EXPLANATION. This unique formula is from one of the loose manuscript sheets of Gatigwanasti, now dead, and belongs to the class known as Yûnwë'hï or love charms (literally, concerning "living humanity") including all those referring in any way to the marital or sexual relation. No explanation accompanies the formula, which must therefore be interpreted from analogy. It appears to be recited by the lover himself—not by a hired shaman—perhaps while painting and adorning himself for the dance. (See next two formulas.)

The formula contains several obscure expressions which require further investigation. Elahiyï or Alahiyï, for it is written both ways in the manuscript, does not occur in any other formula met with thus far, and could not be explained by any of the shamans to whom it was submitted. The nominative form may be Elahï, perhaps from ela, "the earth," and it may be connected with Wa'hïlï, the formulistic name for the south. The spirit invoked is the White Woman, white being the color denoting the south.

Uhisa''tï, rendered here "lonely," is a very expressive word to a Cherokee and is of constant recurrence in the love formulas. It refers to that intangible something characteristic of certain persons which inevitably chills and depresses the spirits of all who may be so unfortunate as to come within its influence. Agisa''tï nige'sûnna, "I never render any one lonely," is an intensified equivalent for, "I am the best company in the world," and to tell a girl that a rival lover is uhisa''tï is to hold out to her the sum of all dreary prospects should she cast in her lot with him.

The speaker, who evidently has an exalted opinion of himself, invokes the aid of the White Woman, who is most beautiful and is never uhisa''tï. She at once responds by making him a white—that is, a happy—man, and placing him in the white road of happiness, which shall never become blue with grief or despondency. She then places him standing in the middle of the earth, that he may be seen and admired by the whole world, especially by the female portion. She finally puts him into the white house, where happiness abides forever. The verb implies that the house shelters him like a cloak and goes about with him wherever he may go

There is something comical in the extreme self-complacency with which he asserts that he is very handsome and will never become blue and no one with him is ever lonely. As before stated, white signifies peace and happiness, while blue is the emblem of sorrow and disappointment.

Having thus rendered himself attractive to womankind, he turns his attention to the girl whom he particularly desires to win. He begins by filling her soul with a sense of desolation and loneliness. In the beautiful language of the formula, her path becomes blue and she is veiled in loneliness. He then asserts, and reiterates, that he is of the one only clan which was allotted for her when the seven clans were established.

He next pays his respects to his rivals and advances some very forcible arguments to show that she could never be happy with any of them. He says that they are all "lonesome" and utterly loathsome—the word implies that they are mutually loathsome—and that they are the veriest trash and refuse. He compares them to so many polecats, oppossums, and crows, and finally likens them to the raincrow (cuckoo; Coccygus), which is regarded with disfavor on account of its disagreeable note. He grows more bitter in his denunciations as he proceeds and finally disposes of the matter by saying that all the seven clans alike are uhisa`tï and are covered with filth. Then follows another glowing panegyric of himself, closing with the beautiful expression, "your soul has come into the very center of mine, never to turn away," which reminds one forcibly of the sentiment in the German love song, "Du liegst mir im Herzen." The final expression, "I take your soul," implies that the formula has now accomplished its purpose in fixing her thoughts upon himself.

When successful, a ceremony of this kind has the effect of rendering the victim so "blue" or lovesick that her life is in danger until another formula is repeated to make, her soul "white" or happy again. Where the name of the individual or clan is mentioned in these formulas the blank is indicated in the manuscript by crosses + + or ciphers O O or by the word iyu'stï, "like."

THIS TELLS ABOUT GOING INTO THE WATER.

Listen! O, now instantly, you have drawn near to hearken, O Agë``yagu'ga. You have come to put your red spittle upon my body. My name is (Gatigwanasti.) The blue had affected me. You have come and clothed me with a red dress. She is of the (Deer) clan. She has become blue. You have directed her paths straight to where I have my feet, and I shall feel exultant. Listen!

EXPLANATION. This formula, from Gatigwanasti's book, is also of the Yûnwë'hï class, and is repeated by the lover when about to bathe in the stream preparatory to painting himself for the dance. The services of a shaman are not required, neither is any special ceremony observed. The technical word used in the heading, ä'tawasti'yï, signifies plunging or going entirely into a liquid. The expression used for the ordinary "going to water," where the water is simply dipped up with the hand, is ämâ'yï dita`ti'yï, "taking them to water."

The prayer is addressed to Agë``yaguga, a formulistic name for the moon, which is supposed to exert a great influence in love affairs, because the dances, which give such opportunities for love making, always take place at night. The shamans can not explain the meaning of the term, which plainly contains the word agë``ya, "woman," and may refer to the moon's supposed influence over women. In Cherokee mythology the moon is a man. The ordinary name is nû'ndâ, or more fully, nû'ndâ sûnnâyë'hï, "the sun living in the night," while the sun itself is designated as nû'nndâ igë'hï, "the sun living in the day."

By the red spittle of Agë``yagu'ga and the red dress with which the lover is clothed are meant the red paint which he puts upon himself. This in former days was procured from a deep red clay known as ela-wâ'tï, or "reddish brown clay." The word red as used in the formula is emblematic of success in attaining his object, besides being the actual color of the paint. Red, in connection with dress or ornamentation, has always been a favorite color with Indians throughout America, and there is some evidence that among the Cherokees it was regarded also as having a mysterious protective power. In all these formulas the lover renders the woman blue or disconsolate and uneasy in mind as a preliminary to fixing her thoughts upon himself. (See next formula.)

SONG FOR PAINTING.

Yû'nwëhï, yû'nwëhï, yû'nwëhï, yû'nwëhï.
I am come from above—
Yû'nwëhï, yû'nwëhï, yû'nwëhï, yû'nwëhï.
I am come down from the Sun Land—yû'nwëhï.
O Red Agë`yagu'ga. you have come and put your red spittle
upon my body—Yû'nwëhï, yû'nwëhï, yû'nwëhï!.

And this above is to recite while one is painting himself.

EXPLANATION. This formula, from Gatigwanasti, immediately follows the one last given, in the manuscript book, and evidently comes immediately after it also in practical use. The expressions used have been already explained. The one using the formula first bathes in the running stream, reciting at the same time the previous formula "Amâ'yï Ä'tawasti'yï." He then repairs to some convenient spot with his paint, beads, and other paraphernalia and proceeds to adorn himself for the dance, which usually begins about an hour after dark, but is not fairly under way until nearly midnight. The refrain, yû'nwëhï, is probably sung while mixing the paint, and the other portion is recited while applying the pigment, or vice versa. Although these formula are still in use, the painting is now obsolete, beyond an occasional daubing of the face, without any plan or pattern, on the occasion of a dance or ball play.

TO ATTRACT AND FIX THE AFFECTIONS.

Listen! O, now you have drawn near to hearken—
—Your spittle, I take it, I eat it.
—Your body, I take it, I eat it.
—Your flesh, I take it, I eat it
—Your heart, I take it, I eat it
Each sung four times.

Listen! O, now you have drawn near to hearken, O, Ancient One. This man's (woman's) soul has come to rest at the edge of your body. You are never to let go your hold upon it. It is ordained that you shall do just as you are requested to do. Let her never think upon any other place. Her soul has faded within her. She is bound by the black threads.

EXPLANATION. This formula is said by the young husband, who has just married an especially engaging wife, who is liable to be attracted by other men. The same formula may also be used by the woman to fix her husband's affections. On the first night that they are together the husband watches until his wife is asleep, when, sitting up by her side, he recites the first words: Sgë! Ha-nâ'gwa hatû'ngani'ga nihï', and then sings the next four words: Tsawatsi'lû tsïkï' tsïkû' ayû', "Your spittle, I take it, I eat it," repeating the words four times. While singing he moistens his fingers with spittle, which he rubs upon the breast of the woman. The next night he repeats the operation, this time singing the words, "I take your body." The third night, in the same way, he sings, "I take your flesh," and the fourth and last night, he sings "I take your heart," after which he repeats the prayer addressed to the Ancient One, by which is probably meant the Fire (the Ancient White). A`yûninï states that the final sentences should be masculine, i. e., His soul has faded, etc., and refer to any would-be seducer. There is no gender distinction in the third person in Cherokee. He claimed that this ceremony was so effective that no husband need have any fears for his wife after performing it.

FOR SEPARATION (OF LOVERS).

Yû! On high you repose, O Blue Hawk, there at the far distant lake. The blue tobacco has come to be your recompense. Now you have arisen at once and come down. You have alighted midway between them where they two are standing. You have spoiled their souls immediately. They have at once become separated.

I am a white man; I stand at the sunrise. The good sperm shall never allow any feeling of loneliness. This white woman is of the Paint (iyustï) clan; she is called (iyustï) Wâyï'. We shall instantly turn her soul over. We shall turn it over as we go toward the Sun Land. I am a white man. Here where I stand it (her soul) has attached itself to (literally, "come against") mine. Let her eyes in their sockets be forever watching (for me). There is no loneliness where my body is.

EXPLANATION. This formula, from A`yûninï's book, is used to separate two lovers or even a husband and wife, if the jealous rival so desires. In the latter case the preceding formula, from the same source, would be used to forestall this spell. No explanation of the ceremony is given, but the reference to tobacco may indicate that tobacco is smoked or thrown into the fire during the recitation. The particular hawk invoked (giya'giya') is a large species found in the coast region but seldom met with in the mountains. Blue indicates that it brings trouble with it, while white in the second paragraph indicates that the man is happy and attractive in manner.

In the first part of the formula the speaker calls upon the Blue Hawk to separate the lovers and spoil their souls, i. e., change their feeling toward each other. In the second paragraph he endeavors to attract the attention of the woman by eulogizing himself. The expression, "we shall turn her soul over," seems here to refer to turning her affections, but as generally used, to turn one's soul is equivalent to killing him.

TO FIX THE AFFECTIONS.

Yû! Ha! Now the souls have come together. You are of the Deer (x x) clan. Your name is (x x) Ayâsta, I am of the Wolf (o-o) clan. Your body, I take it, I eat it. Yû! Ha! Now the souls have come together. You are of the Deer clan. Your name is Ayâsta. I am of the Wolf clan. Your flesh I take, I eat. Yû!

Yû! Ha! Now the souls have come together. You are of the Deer clan. Your name is Ayâsta. I am of the Wolf clan. Your spittle I take, I eat. I! Yû!

Yû! Ha! Now the souls have come together. You are of the Deer clan. Your name is Ayâsta. I am of the Wolf clan. Your heart I take, I eat. Yû!

Listen! "Ha! Now the souls have met, never to part," you have said, O Ancient One above. O Black Spider, you have been brought down from on high. You have let down your web. She is of the Deer clan; her name is Ayâsta. Her soul you, have wrapped up in (your) web. There where the people of the seven clans are continually coming in sight and again disappearing (i. e. moving about, coming; and going), there was never any feeling of loneliness.

Listen! Ha! But now you have covered her over with loneliness. Her eyes have faded. Her eyes have come to fasten themselves on one alone. Whither can her soul escape? Let her be sorrowing as she goes along, and not for one night alone. Let her become an aimless wanderer, whose trail may never be followed. O Black Spider, may you hold her soul in your web so that it shall never get through the meshes. What is the name of the soul? They two have come together. It is mine!

Listen! Ha! And now you have hearkened, O Ancient Red. Your grandchildren have come to the edge of your body. You hold them yet more firmly in your grasp, never to let go your hold. O Ancient One, we have become as one. The woman has put her (x x x) soul into our hands. We shall never let it go! Yû!

(Directions.)—And this also is for just the same purpose (the preceding formula in the manuscript book is also a love charm). It must be done by stealth at night when they are asleep. One must put the hand on the middle of the breast and rub on spittle with the hand, they say. The other formula is equally good.

EXPLANATION. This formula to fix the affections of a young wife is taken from the manuscript sheets of the late Gatigwanasti. It very much resembles the other formula for the same purpose, obtained from A`yû'ninï, and the brief directions show that the ceremony is alike in both. The first four paragraphs are probably sung, as in the other formula, on four successive nights, and, as explained in the directions and as stated verbally by A`yû'ninï, this must be done. stealthily at night while the woman is asleep, the husband rubbing his spittle on her breast with his hand while chanting the song in a low tone, hardly above a whisper. The prayer to the Ancient One, or Ancient Red (Fire), in both formulas, and the expression, "I come to the edge of your body," indicate that the hands are first warmed over the fire, in accordance with the general practice when laying on the hands. The prayer to the Black Spider is a beautiful specimen of poetic imagery, and hardly requires an explanation. The final paragraph indicates the successful accomplishment of his purpose. "Your grandchildren" (tsetsûli'sï) is an expression frequently used in addressing the more important deities.

TO SHORTEN A NIGHT-GOER ON THIS SIDE.

Listen! In the Frigid Land above you repose, O Red Man, quickly we two have prepared your arrows for the soul of the Imprecator. He has them lying along the path. Quickly we two will take his soul as we go along.

Listen! In the Frigid Land above you repose, O Purple Man, Ha! Quickly now we two have prepared your arrows for the soul of the Imprecator. He has them lying along the path. Quickly we two will cut his soul in two.

EXPLANATION. This formula, from A`yû'ninïs' book, is for the purpose of driving away a witch from the house of a sick person, and opens up a most interesting chapter of Cherokee beliefs. The witch is supposed to go about chiefly under cover of darkness, and hence is called sûnnâ'yï edâ'hï, "the night goer." This is the term in common use; but there are a number of formulistic expressions to designate a witch, one of which, u'ya igawa'stï, occurs in the body of the formula and may be rendered "the imprecator," i. e., the sayer of evil things or curses. As the counteracting of a deadly spell always results in the death of its author, the formula is stated to be not merely to drive away the wizard, but to kill him, or, according to the formulistic expression, "to shorten him (his life) on this side."

When it becomes known that a man is dangerously sick the witches front far and near gather invisibly about his house after nightfall to worry him and even force their way in to his bedside unless prevented by the presence of a more powerful shaman within the house. They annoy the sick man and thus hasten his death by stamping upon the roof and beating upon the sides of the house; and if they can manage to get inside they raise up the dying sufferer from the bed and let him fall again or even drag him out upon the floor. The object of the witch in doing this is to prolong his term of years by adding to his own life as much as he can take from that of the sick man. Thus it is that a witch who is successful in these practices lives to be very old. Without going into extended details, it may be sufficient to state that the one most dreaded, alike by the friends of the sick man and by the lesser witches, is the Kâ'lana-ayeli'skï or Raven Mocker, so called because he flies through the air at night in a shape of fire, uttering sounds like the harsh croak of a raven.

The formula here given is short and simple as compared with some others. There is evidently a mistake in regard to the Red Man, who is here placed in the north, instead of in the east, as it should be. The reference to the arrows will be explained further on. Purple, mentioned in the second paragraph, has nearly the same symbolic meaning as blue, viz: Trouble, vexation and defeat; hence the Purple Man is called upon to frustrate the designs of the witch.

To drive away the witch the shaman first prepares four sharpened sticks, which he drives down into the ground outside the house at each of the four corners, leaving the pointed ends projecting upward and outward. Then, about noontime he gets ready the Tsâl-agayû'nlï or "Old Tobacco" (Nicotiana rustica), with which he fills his pipe, repeating this formula during the operation, after which he wraps the pipe thus filled in a black cloth. This sacred tobacco is smoked only for this purpose. He then goes out into the forest, and returns just before dark, about which time the witch may be expected to put in an appearance. Lighting his pipe, he goes slowly around the house, puffing the smoke in the direction of every trail by which the witch might be. able to approach, and probably repeating the same or another formula the while. He then goes into the house and awaits results. When the witch approaches under cover of the darkness, whether in his own proper shape or in the form of some animal, the sharpened stick on that side of the house shoots up into the air and comes down like an arrow upon his head, inflicting such a wound as proves fatal within seven days. This explains the words of the formula, "We have prepared your arrows for the soul of the Imprecator. He has them lying along the path". A`yû'ninï said nothing about the use of the sharpened sticks in this connection, mentioning only the tobacco, but the ceremony, as here described, is the one ordinarily used. When wounded the witch utters a groan which is heard by those listening inside the house, even at the distance of half a mile. No one knows certainly who the witch is until a day or two afterward, when some old man or woman, perhaps in a remote settlement, is suddenly seized with a mysterious illness and before seven clays elapse is dead.

I HAVE LOST SOMETHING.

Listen! Ha! Now you have drawn near to hearken, O Brown Rock; you never lie about anything. Ha! Now I am about to seek for it. I have lost a hog and now tell me about where I shall find it. For is it not mine? My name is_____.

EXPLANATION. This formula, for finding anything lost, is so simple as to need but little explanation. Brown in this instance has probably no mythologic significance, but refers to the color of the stone used in the ceremony. This is a small rounded water-worn pebble, in substance resembling quartz and of a reddish-brown color. It is suspended by a string held between the thumb and finger of the shaman, who is guided in his search by the swinging of the pebble, which, according to their theory, will swing farther in the direction of the lost article than in the contrary direction! The shaman, who is always fasting, repeats the formula, while closely watching the motions of the swinging pebble. He usually begins early in the morning, making the first trial at the house of the owner of the lost article. After noting the general direction toward which it seems to lean he goes a considerable distance in that direction, perhaps half a mile or more, and makes a second trial. This time the pebble may swing off at an angle in another direction. He follows up in the direction indicated for perhaps another half mile, when on a third trial the stone may veer around toward the starting point, and a fourth attempt may complete the circuit. Having thus arrived at the conclusion that the missing article is somewhere within a certain circumscribed area, he advances to the center of this space and marks out upon the ground a small circle inclosing a cross with arms pointing toward the four cardinal points. Holding the stone over the center of the cross he again repeats the formula and notes the direction in which the pebble swings. This is the final trial and he fiow goes slowly and carefully over the whole surface in that direction, between the center of the circle and the limit of the circumscribed area until in theory, at least, the article is found. Should he fail, he is never at a loss for excuses, but the specialists in this line are generally very shrewd guessers well versed in the doctrine of probabilities.

There are many formulas for this purpose, some of them being long and elaborate. When there is reason to believe that the missing article has been stolen, the specialist first determines the clan or settlement to which the thief belongs and afterward the name of the individual. Straws, bread balls, and stones of various kinds are used in the different formulas, the ceremony differing according to .the medium employed. The stones are generally pointed crystals or antique arrowheads, and are suspended as already described, the point being supposed to turn finally in the direction of the missing object. Several of these stones have been obtained on the reservation and are now deposited in the National Museum. It need excite no surprise to find the hog mentioned in the formula, as this animal has been domesticated among the Cherokees for more than a century, although most of them are strongly prejudiced against it.

THIS IS TO FRIGHTEN A STORM.

Yuhahi', yuhahi', yuhahi', yuhahi', yuhahi',
Yuhahi', yuhahi', yuhahi', yuhahi', yuhahi'—Yû!

Listen! O now you are coming in rut. Ha! I am exceedingly afraid of you. But yet you are only tracking your wife. Her footprints can be seen there directed upward toward the heavens. I have pointed them out for you. Let your paths stretch out along the tree tops (?) on the lofty mountains (and) you shall have them (the paths) lying down without being disturbed, Let (your path) as you go along be where the waving branches meet. Listen!

EXPLANATION. This formula, from A`yû'ninï's book, is for driving away, or "frightening" a storm, which threatens to injure the growing corn. The first part is a meaningless song, which is sting in a low tone in the peculiar style of most of the sacred songs. The storm, which is not directly named, is then addressed and declared to be coming on in a fearful manner on the track of his wife, like an animal in the rutting season. The shaman points out her tracks directed toward the upper regions and begs the storm spirit to follow her along the waving tree tops of the lofty mountains, where he shall be undisturbed.

The shaman stands facing the approaching storm with one hand stretched out toward it. After repeating the song and prayer he gently blows in the direction toward which he wishes it to go, waving his hand in the same direction as though pushing away the storm. A part of the storm is usually sent into the upper regions of the atmosphere. If standing at the edge of the field, he holds a blade of corn in one hand while repeating the ceremony.

WHAT THOSE WHO HAVE BEEN TO WAR DID TO HELP THEMSELVES.

Hayï'! Yû! Listen! Now instantly we have lifted up the red war club. Quickly his soul shall be without motion. There under the earth, where the black war clubs shall be moving about like ball sticks in the game, there his soul shall be, never to reappear. We cause it to be so. He shall never go and lift up the war club. We cause it to be so. There under the earth the black war club (and) the black fog have come together as one for their covering. It shall never move about (i. e., the black fog shall never be lifted from them). We cause it to be so.

Instantly shall their souls be moving about there in the seventh heaven. Their souls shall never break in two. So shall it be. Quickly we have moved them (their souls) on high for them, where they shall be going about in peace. You have shielded yourselves with the red war club. Their souls shall never be knocked about. Cause it to be so. There on high their souls shall be going about. Let them shield themselves with the white war whoop. Instantly (grant that) they shall never become blue. Yû!

EXPLANATION. This formula, obtained from A`wani'ta, may be repeated by the doctor for as many as eight men at once when about to go to war. It is recited for four consecutive nights, immediately before setting out. There is no tabu enjoined and no beads are used, but the warriors "go to water" in the regular way, that is, they stand at the edge of the stream, facing the east and looking down upon the water, while the shaman, standing behind them, repeats the formula. On the fourth night the shaman gives to each man a small charmed root which has the power to confer invulnerability. On the eve of battle the warrior after bathing in the running stream chews a portion of this and spits the juice upon his body in order that the bullets of the enemy may pass him by or slide off from his skin like drops of water. Almost every man of the three hundred East Cherokees who served in the rebellion had this or a similar ceremony performed before setting out—many of them also consulting the oracular ulû'nsû'tï stone at the same time—and it is but fair to state that not more than two or three of the entire number were wounded in actual battle.

In the formula the shaman identifies himself with the warriors, asserting that "we" have lifted up the red war club, red being the color symbolic of success and having no reference to blood, as might be supposed from the connection. In the first paragraph he invokes curses upon the enemy, the future tense verb It shall be, etc., having throughout the force of let it be. He puts the souls of the doomed enemy in the lower regions, where the black war clubs are constantly waving about, and envelops them in a black fog, which shall never be lifted and out of which they shall never reappear. From the expression in the second paragraph, "their souls shall never be knocked about," the reference to the black war clubs moving about like ball sticks in the game would seem to imply that they are continually buffeting the doomed souls under the earth. The spirit land of the Cherokees is in the west, but in these formulas of malediction or blessing the soul of the doomed man is generally consigned to the underground region, while that of the victor is raised by antithesis to the seventh heaven.

Having disposed of the enemy, the shaman in the second paragraph turns his attention to his friends and at once raises their souls to the seventh heaven, where they shall go about in peace, shielded by (literally, "covered with") the red war club of success, and never to be knocked about by the blows of the enemy. "Breaking the soul in two" is equivalent to snapping the thread of life, the soul being regarded as an intangible something having length, like a rod or a string. This formula, like others written down by the same shaman, contains several evident inconsistencies both as to grammar and mythology, due to the fact that A`wanita is extremely careless with regard to details and that this particular formula has probably not been used for the last quarter of a century. The warriors are also made to shield themselves with the white war whoop, which should undoubtedly be the red war whoop, consistent with the red war club, white being the color emblematic of peace, which is evidently an incongruity. The war whoop is believed to have a positive magic power for the protection of the warrior, as well as for terrifying the foe.

The mythologic significance of the different colors is well shown in this formula. Red, symbolic of success, is the color of the war club with which the warrior is to strike the enemy and also of the other one with which he is to shield or "cover" himself. There is no doubt that the war whoop also should be represented as red. In conjuring with the beads for long life, for recovery from sickness, or for success in love, the ball play, or any other undertaking, the red beads represent the party for whose benefit the magic spell is wrought, and he is figuratively clothed in red and made to stand upon a red cloth or placed upon a red seat. The red spirits invoked always live in the east and everything pertaining to them is of the same color.

Black is always typical of death, and in this formula the soul of the enemy is continually beaten about by black war clubs and enveloped in a black fog. In conjuring to destroy an enemy the shaman uses black beads and invokes the black spirits—which always live in the west—bidding them tear out the man's soul, carry it to the west, and put it into the black coffin deep in the black mud, with a black serpent coiled above it.

Blue is emblematic of failure, disappointment, or unsatisfied desire. "They shall never become blue" means that they shall never fail in anything they undertake. In love charms the lover figuratively covers himself with red and prays that his rival shall become entirely blue and walk in a blue path. The formulistic expression, "He is entirely blue," closely approximates in meaning the common English phrase, "He feels blue." The blue spirits live in the north.

White—which occurs in this formula only by an evident error—denotes peace and happiness. In ceremonial addresses, as at the green corn dance and ball play, the people figuratively partake of white food and after the dance or the game return along the white trail to their white houses. In love charms the man, in order to induce the woman to cast her lot with his, boasts "I am a white man," implying that all is happiness where he is. White beads have the same meaning in the bead conjuring and white was the color of the stone pipe anciently used in ratifying peace treaties. The white spirits live in the south (Wa'halä).

Two other colors, brown and yellow, are also mentioned in the formulas. Wâtige'ï, "brown," is the term used to include brown, bay, dun, and similar colors, especially as applied to animals. It seldom occurs in the formulas and its mythologic significance is as yet undetermined. Yellow is of more frequent occurrence and is typical of trouble and all manner of vexation, the yellow spirits being generally invoked when the shaman wishes to bring down calamities upon the head of his victim, without actually destroying him. So far as present knowledge goes, neither brown nor yellow can be assigned to any particular point of the compass.

Usïnuli'yu, rendered "instantly," is the intensive form of usïnu'lï "quickly," both of which words recur constantly in the formulas, in some entering into almost every sentence. This frequently gives the translation an awkward appearance. Thus the final sentence above, which means literally "they shall never become blue instantly," signifies "Grant that they shall never become blue, i. e., shall never fail in their purpose, and grant our petition instantly."

TO DESTROY LIFE.

Listen! Now I have come to step over your soul. You are of the (wolf) clan. Your name is (A`yû'ninï). Your spittle I have put at rest under the earth. Your soul I have put at rest under the earth. I have come to cover you over with the black rock. I have come to cover you over, with the black cloth. I have come to cover you with the black slabs, never to reappear. Toward the black coffin of the upland in the Darkening Land your paths shall stretch out. So shall it be for you. The clay of the upland has come (to cover you). Instantly the black clay has lodged there where it is at rest at the black houses in the Darkening Land. With the black coffin and with the black slabs I have come to cover you. Now your soul has faded away. It has become blue. When darkness comes your spirit shall grow less and dwindle away, never to reappear. Listen!

EXPLANATION. This formula is from the manuscript book of A`yû'ninï, who explained the whole ceremony. The language needs but little explanation. A blank is left for the name and clan of the victim, and is filled in by the shaman. As the purpose of the ceremony is to bring about the death of the victim, everything spoken of is symbolically colored black, according to the significance of the colors as alreadyexplained. The declaration near the end, "It has become blue," indicates that the victim now begins to feel in himself the effects of the incantation, and that as darkness comes on his spirit will shrink and gradually become less until it dwindles away to nothingness.

When the shaman wishes to destroy the life of another, either for his own purposes or for hire, he conceals himself near the trail along which the victim is likely to pass. When the doomed man appears the shaman waits until he has gone by and then follows him secretly until he chances to spit upon the ground. On coming up to the spot the shaman collects upon the end of a stick a little of the dust thus moistened with the victim's spittle. The possession of the man's spittle gives him power over the life of the man himself. Many ailments are said by the doctors to be due to the fact that some enemy has by this means "changed the spittle" of the patient and caused it to breed animals or sprout corn in the sick man's body. In the love charms also the lover always figuratively "takes the spittle" of the girl in order to fix her affections upon himself. The same idea in regard to spittle is found in European folk medicine.

The shaman then puts the clay thus moistened into a tube consisting of a joint of the Kanesâ'la or wild parsnip, a poisonous plant of considerable importance in life-conjuring ceremonies. He also puts into the tube seven earthworms beaten into a paste, and several splinters from a tree which has been struck by lightning. The idea in regard to the worms is not quite clear, but it may be that they are expected to devour the soul of the victim as earthworms are supposed to feed upon dead bodies, or perhaps it is thought that from their burrowing habits they may serve to hollow out a grave for the soul under the earth, the quarter to which the shaman consigns it. In other similar ceremonies the dirt-dauber wasp or the stinging ant is buried in the same manner in order that it may kill the soul, as these are said to kill other more powerful insects by their poisonous sting or bite. The wood of a tree struck by lightning is also a potent spell for both good and evil and is used in many formulas of various kinds.

Having prepared the tube, the shaman goes into the forest to a tree which has been struck by lightning. At its base he digs a hole, in the bottom of which he puts a large yellow stone slab. He then puts in the tube, together with seven yellow pebbles, fills in the earth and finally builds a fire over the spot to destroy all traces of his work. The yellow stones are probably chosen as the next best substitute for black stones, which are not always easy to find. The formula mentions "black rock," black being the emblem of death, while yellow typifies trouble. The shaman and his employer fast until after the ceremony.

If the ceremony has been properly carried out, the victim becomes blue, that is, he feels the effects in himself at once, and, unless he employs the countercharms of some more powerful shaman, his soul begins to shrivel up and dwindle, and within seven days he is dead. When it is found that the spell has no effect upon the intended victim it is believed that he has discovered the plot and has taken measures for his own protection, or that, having suspected a design against him—as, for instance, after having won a girl's affections from a rival or overcoming him in the ball play—he has already secured himself from all attempts by counterspells. It then becomes a serious matter, as, should he succeed in turning the curse aside from himself, it will return upon the heads of his enemies.

The shaman and his employer then retire to a lonely spot in the mountains, in the vicinity of a small stream, and begin a new series of conjurations with the beads. After constructing a temporary shelter of bark laid over poles, the two go down to the water, the shaman taking with him two pieces of cloth, a yard or two yards in length, one white, the other black, together with seven red and seven black beads. The cloth is the shaman's pay for his services, and is furnished by his employer, who sometimes also supplies the beads. There are many formulas for conjuring with the beads, which are used on almost all important occasions, and differences also in the details of the ceremony, but the general practice is the same in all cases. The shaman selects a bend in the river where his client can look toward the east while facing up stream. The man then takes up his position on the bank or wades into the stream a short distance, where—in the ceremonial language—the water is a "hand length" (awâ'hilû) in depth and stands silently with his eyes fixed upon the water and his back to the shaman on the bank. The shaman then lays upon the ground the two pieces of cloth, folded into convenient size, and places the red beads—typical of success and his client—upon the white cloth, while the black beads—emblematic of death and the intended victim—are laid upon the black cloth. It is probable that the first cloth should properly be red instead of white, but as it is difficult to get red cloth, except in the shape of handkerchiefs, a substitution has been made, the two colors having a close mythologic relation. In former days a piece of buckskin and the small glossy seeds of the Viper's Bugloss (Echium vulgare) were used instead of the cloth and beads. The formulistic name for the bead is sû'nïkta, which the priests are unable to analyze, the ordinary word for beads or coin being adélâ.

The shaman now takes a red bead, representing his client, between the thumb and index finger of his right hand, and a black bead, representing the victim, in like manner, in his left hand. Standing a few feet behind his client he turns toward the east, fixes his eyes upon the bead between the thumb and finger of his right hand, and addresses it as the Sû'nïkta Gigäge'ï, the Red Bead, invoking blessings upon his client and clothing him with the red garments of success. The formula is repeated in a low chant or intonation, the voice rising at intervals, after the manner of a revival speaker. Then turning to the black bead in his left hand he addresses it in similar manner, calling down the most withering curses upon the head of the victim. Finally looking up he addresses the stream, under the name of Yû'nwï Gûnahi'ta, the "Long

Person," imploring it to protect his client and raise him to the seventh heaven, where he will be secure from all his enemies. The other, then stooping down, dips up water in his hand seven times and pours it upon his head, rubbing it upon his shoulders and breast at the same time. In some cases he dips completely under seven times, being stripped, of course, even when the water is of almost icy coldness. The shaman, then stooping down, makes a small hole in the ground with his finger, drops into it the fatal black bead, and buries it out of sight with a stamp of his foot. This ends the ceremony, which is called "taking to water."

While addressing the beads the shaman attentively observes them as they are held between the thumb and finger of his outstretched hands. In a short time they begin to move, slowly and but a short distance at first, then faster and farther, often coming down as far as the first joint of the finger or even below, with an irregular serpentine motion from side to side, returning in the same manner. Should the red bead be more lively in its movements and come down lower on the finger than the black bead, he confidently predicts for the client the speedy accomplishment of his desire. On the other hand, should the black bead surpass the red in activity, the spells of the shaman employed by the intended victim are too strong, and the whole ceremony must be gone over again with an additional and larger quantity of cloth. This must be kept up until the movements of the red beads give token of success or until they show by their sluggish motions or their failure to move down along the finger that the opposing shaman can not be overcome. In the latter case the discouraged plotter gives up all hope, considering himself as cursed by every imprecation which he has unsuccessfully invoked upon his enemy, goes home and—theoretically—lies down and dies. As a matter of fact, however, the shaman is always ready with other formulas by means of which he can ward off such fatal results, in consideration of a sufficient quantity of cloth.

Should the first trial, which takes place at daybreak, prove unsuccessful, the shaman and his client fast until just before sunset. They then eat and remain awake until midnight, when the ceremony is repeated, and if still unsuccessful it may be repeated four times before daybreak (or the following noon?), both men remaining awake and fasting throughout the night. If still unsuccessful, they continue to fast all day until just before sundown. Then they eat again and again remain awake until midnight, when the previous night's

programme is repeated. It has now become a trial of endurance between the revengeful client and his shaman on the one side and the intended victim and his shaman on the other, the latter being supposed to be industriously working countercharms all the while, as each party must subsist upon one meal per day and abstain entirely from sleep until the result has been decided one way or the other. Failure to endure this severe strain, even so much as closing the eyes in sleep for a few moments or partaking of the least nourishment excepting just before sunset, neutralizes all the previous work and places the unfortunate offender at the mercy of his more watchful enemy. If the shaman be still unsuccessful on the fourth day, he acknowledges himself defeated and gives up the contest. Should his spells prove the stronger, his victim will die within seven days, or, as the Cherokees say, seven nights. These "seven nights," however, are frequently interpreted, figuratively, to mean seven years, a rendering which often serves to relieve the shaman from a very embarrassing position.

With regard to the oracle of the whole proceeding, the beads do move; but the explanation is simple, although the Indians account for it by saying that the beads become alive by the recitation of the sacred formula. The shaman is laboring under strong, though suppressed, emotion. He stands with his hands stretched out in a constrained position, every muscle tense, his breast heaving and voice trembling from the effort, and the natural result is that before he is done praying his fingers begin to twitch involuntarily and thus cause the beads to move. As before stated, their motion is irregular; but the peculiar delicacy of touch acquired by long practice probably imparts more directness to their movements than would at first seem possible.

THIS CONCERNS THE BALL PLAY TO TAKE THEM TO WATER WITH IT.

Listen! Ha! Now where the white thread has been let down, quickly we are about to examine into (the fate of) the admirers of the ball play. They are of—such a (iyu'stï) descent. They are called—so and so (iyu'stï). They are shaking the road which shall never be joyful. The miserable Terrapin has come and fastened himself upon them as they go about. They have lost all strength. They have become entirely blue.

But now my admirers of the ball play have their roads lying along in this direction. The Red Bat has come and made himself one of them. There in the first heaven are the pleasing stakes. Therein the second heaven are the pleasing stakes. The Pewee has come and joined them. The immortal ball stick shall place itself upon the whoop, never to be defeated.

As for the lovers of the ball play on the other side, the common Turtle has come and fastened himself upon them as they go about. Under the earth they have lost all strength.

The pleasing stakes are in the third heaven. The Red Tläniwä has come and made himself one of them, that they may never be defeated. The pleasing stakes are in the fourth heaven. The Blue Fly-catcher has made himself one of them, that they may never be defeated. The pleasing stakes are in the fifth heaven. The Blue Martin has made himself one of them, that they may never be defeated. The other lovers of the ball play, the Blue Mole has come and fastened upon them, that they may never be joyous. They have lost all strength.The pleasing stakes are there in the sixth heaven. The Chimney Swift has made himself one of them, that they may never be defeated. The pleasing stakes are in the seventh heaven. The Blue Dragon-fly has made himself one of them, that they may never be defeated.As for the other admirers of the ball play, the Bear has just come and fastened him upon them, that they may never be happy. They have lost all strength. He has let the stakes slip from his grasp and there shall be nothing left for their share.The examination is ended.

Listen! Now let me know that the twelve are mine, O White Dragon-fly. Tell me that the share is to be mine—that the stakes are mine. As for the player there on the other side, he has been forced to let go his hold upon the stakes.Now they are become exultant and happy. Yû!

EXPLANATION. This formula, from the A`yûninï manuscript is one of those used by the shaman in taking the ball players to water before the game. The ceremony is performed in connection with red and black beads, as described in the formula just given for destroying life. The formulistic name given to the ball players signifies literally, "admirers of the ball play." The Tlä'niwä (sä'niwä, in the Middle dialect) is the mythic great hawk, as large and powerful as the roc of Arabian tales. The shaman begins by declaring that it is his purpose to examine or inquire into the fate of the ball players, and then gives his attention by turns to his friends and their opponents, fixing his eyes upon the red bead while praying for his clients, and upon the black bead while speaking of their rivals. His friends he raises gradually to the seventh or highest *galû'nlati*. This word literally signifies height, and is the name given to the abode of the gods dwelling above the earth, and is also used to mean heaven in the Cherokee bible translation. The opposing players, on the other hand, are put down under the earth, and are made to resemble animals slow and clumsy of movement, while on behalf of his friends the shaman invokes the aid of swift-flying birds, which, according to the Indian belief, never by any chance fail to secure their prey. The birds invoked are the He'nilû or wood pewee (*Contopus virens*), the Tläniwä or mythic hawk, the Gulï'sgulï' or great crested flycatcher (*Myiarchus crinitus*), the Tsûtsû or martin (*Progne subis*), and the A'nigâsta'ya or chimney swift (*Chœtura pelasgia*). In the idiom of the formulas it is said that these "have just come and are sticking to them" (the players), the same word (*danûtsgû'lani?ga*) being used to express the devoted attention of a lover to his mistress. The Watatuga, a small species of dragon-fly, is also invoked, together with the bat, which, according to a Cherokee myth, once took sides with the birds in a great ball contest with the four-footed animals, and won the victory for the birds by reason of his superior skill in dodging. This myth explains also why birds, and no quadrupeds, are invoked by the shaman to the aid of his friends. In accordance with the regular color symbolism the flycatcher, martin, and dragonfly, like the bat and the tlä'niwä, should be red, the color of success, instead of blue, evidently so written by mistake. The white thread is frequently mentioned in the formulas, but in this instance the reference is not clear. The twelve refers to the number of runs made in the game.

Blackfoot Lodge Tales

by George Bird Grinnell

Table of Contents

Note

We were sitting about the fire in the lodge on Two Medicine. Double Runner, Small Leggings, Mad Wolf, and the Little Blackfoot were smoking and talking, and I was writing in my note-book. As I put aside the book, and reached out my hand for the pipe, Double Runner bent over and picked up a scrap of printed paper, which had fallen to the ground. He looked at it for a moment without speaking, and then, holding it up and calling me by name, said:—

"*Pi-nut-ú-ye is-tsím-okan,* this is education. Here is the difference between you and me, between the Indians and the white people. You know what this means. I do not. If I did know, I should be as smart as you. If all my people knew, the white people would not always get the best of us."

"*Nísah* (elder brother), your words are true. Therefore you ought to see that your children go to school, so that they may get the white man's knowledge. When they are men, they will have to trade with the white people; and if they know nothing, they can never get rich. The times have changed. It will never again be as it was when you and I were young."

"You say well, *Pi-nut-ú-ye is-tsím-okan,* I have seen the days; and I know it is so. The old things are passing away, and the children of my children will be like white people. None of them will know how it used to be in their father's days unless they read the things which we have told you, and which you are all the time writing down in your books."

"They are all written down, *Nísah,* the story of the three tribes, Sík-si-kau, Kaínah, and Pikŭ′ni."

INDIANS AND THEIR STORIES

The most shameful chapter of American history is that in which is recorded the account of our dealings with the Indians. The story of our government's intercourse with this race is an unbroken narrative of injustice, fraud, and robbery. Our people have disregarded honesty and truth whenever they have come in contact with the Indian, and he has had no rights because he has never had the power to enforce any.

Protests against governmental swindling of these savages have been made again and again, but such remonstrances attract no general attention. Almost every one is ready to acknowledge that in the past the Indians have been shamefully robbed, but it appears to be believed that this no longer takes place. This is a great mistake. We treat them now much as we have always treated them. Within two years, I have been present on a reservation where government commissioners, by means of threats, by bribes given to chiefs, and by casting fraudulently the votes of absentees, succeeded after months of effort in securing votes enough to warrant them in asserting that a tribe of Indians, entirely wild and totally ignorant of farming, had consented to sell their lands, and to settle down each upon 160 acres of the most utterly arid and barren land to be found on the North American continent. The fraud perpetrated on this tribe was as gross as could be practised by one set of men upon another. In a similar way the Southern Utes were recently induced to consent to give up their reservation for another.

Americans are a conscientious people, yet they take no interest in these frauds. They have the Anglo-Saxon spirit of fair play, which sympathizes with weakness, yet no protest is made against the oppression which the Indian suffers. They are generous; a famine in Ireland, Japan, or Russia arouses the sympathy and calls forth the bounty of the nation, yet they give no heed to the distress of the Indians, who are in the very midst of them. They do not realize that Indians are human beings like themselves.

For this state of things there must be a reason, and this reason is to be found, I believe, in the fact that practically no one has any personal knowledge of the Indian race. The few who are acquainted with them are neither writers nor public speakers, and for the most part would find it easier to break a horse than to write a letter. If the general public knows little of this race, those who legislate about them are equally ignorant. From the congressional page who distributes the copies of a pending bill, up through the representatives and senators who vote for it, to the president whose signature makes the measure a law, all are entirely unacquainted with this people or their needs.

Many stories about Indians have been written, some of which are interesting and some, perhaps, true. All, however, have been written by civilized people, and have thus of necessity been misleading. The reason for this is plain. The white person who gives his idea of a story of Indian life inevitably looks at things from the civilized point of view, and assigns to the Indian such motives and feelings as govern the civilized man. But often the feelings which lead an Indian to perform a particular action are not those which would induce a white man to do the same thing, or if they are, the train of reasoning which led up to the Indian's motive is not the reasoning of the white man.

In a volume about the Pawnees, I endeavored to show how Indians think and feel by letting some of them tell their own stories in their own fashion, and thus explain in their own way how they look at the every-day occurrences of their life, what motives govern them, and how they reason.

In the present volume, I treat of another race of Indians in precisely the same way. I give the Blackfoot stories as they have been told to me by the Indians themselves, not elaborating nor adding to them. In all cases except one they were written down as they fell from the lips of the storyteller. Sometimes I have transposed a sentence or two, or have added a few words of explanation; but the stories as here given are told in the words of the original narrators as nearly as it is possible to render those words into the simplest every-day English. These are Indians' stories, pictures of Indian life drawn by Indian artists, and showing this life from the Indian's point of view. Those who read these stories will have the narratives just as they came to me from the lips of the Indians themselves; and from the tales they can get a true notion of the real man who is speaking. He is not the Indian of the newspapers, nor of the novel, nor of the Eastern sentimentalist, nor of the Western boomer, but the real Indian as he is in his daily life among his own people, his friends, where he is not embarrassed by the presence of strangers, nor trying to produce effects, but is himself—the true, natural man.

And when you are talking with your Indian friend, as you sit beside him and smoke with him on the bare prairie during a halt in the day's march, or at night lie at length about your lonely camp fire in the mountains, or form one of a circle of feasters in his home lodge, you get very near to nature. Some of the sentiments which he expresses may horrify your civilized mind, but they are not unlike those which your own small boy might utter. The Indian talks of blood and wounds and death in a commonplace, matter-of-fact way that may startle you. But these things used to be a part of his daily life; and even to-day you may sometimes hear a dried-up, palsied survivor of the ancient wars cackle out his shrill laugh when he tells as a merry jest, a bloodcurdling story of the torture he inflicted on some enemy in the long ago.

I have elsewhere expressed my views on Indian character, the conclusions founded on an acquaintance with this race extending over more than twenty years, during which time I have met many tribes, with some of whom I have lived on terms of the closest intimacy.

The Indian is a man, not very different from his white brother, except that he is undeveloped. In his natural state he is kind and affectionate in his family, is hospitable, honest and straightforward with his fellows,—a true friend. If you are his guest, the best he has is at your disposal; if the camp is starving, you will still have set before you your share of what food there may be in the lodge. For his friend he will die, if need be. He is glad to perform acts of kindness for those he likes. While travelling in the heats of summer over long, waterless stretches of prairie, I have had an Indian, who saw me suffering from thirst, leave me, without mentioning his errand, and ride thirty miles to fetch me a canteen of cool water.

The Indian is intensely religious. No people pray more earnestly nor more frequently. This is especially true of all Indians of the Plains.

The Indian has the mind and feelings of a child with the stature of a man; and if this is clearly understood and considered, it will readily account for much of the bad that we hear about him, and for many of the evil traits which are commonly attributed to him. Civilized and educated, the Indian of the better class is not less intelligent than the average white man, and he has every capacity for becoming a good citizen.

This is the view held not only by myself, but by all of the many old frontiersmen that I have known, who have had occasion to live much among Indians, and by most experienced army officers. It was the view held by my friend and schoolmate, the lamented

Lieutenant Casey, whose good work in transforming the fierce Northern Cheyennes into United States soldiers is well known among all officers of the army, and whose sad death by an Indian bullet has not yet, I believe, been forgotten by the public.

It is proper that something should be said as to how this book came to be written.

About ten years ago, Mr. J.W. Schultz of Montana, who was then living in the Blackfoot camp, contributed to the columns of the *Forest and Stream*, under the title "Life among the Blackfeet," a series of sketches of that people. These papers seemed to me of unusual interest, and worthy a record in a form more permanent than the columns of a newspaper; but no opportunity was then presented for filling in the outlines given in them.

Shortly after this, I visited the Pi-kŭn-i tribe of the Black-feet, and I have spent more or less time in their camps every year since. I have learned to know well all their principal men, besides many of the Bloods and the Blackfeet, and have devoted much time and effort to the work of accumulating from their old men and best warriors the facts bearing on the history, customs, and oral literature of the tribe, which are presented in this volume.

In 1889 my book on the Pawnees was published, and seemed to arouse so much interest in Indian life, from the Indian's standpoint, that I wrote to Mr. Schultz, urging him, as I had often done before, to put his observations in shape for publication, and offered to edit his work, and to see it through the press. Mr. Schultz was unwilling to undertake this task, and begged me to use all the material which I had gathered, and whatever he could supply, in the preparation of a book about the Blackfeet.

A portion of the material contained in these pages was originally made public by Mr. Schultz, and he was thus the discoverer of the literature of the Blackfeet. My own investigations have made me familiar with all the stories here recorded, from original sources, but some of them he first published in the columns of the *Forest and Stream*. For this work he is entitled to great credit, for it is most unusual to find any one living the rough life beyond the frontier, and mingling in daily intercourse with Indians, who has the intelligence to study their traditions, history, and customs, and the industry to reduce his observations to writing.

Besides the invaluable assistance given me by Mr. Schultz, I acknowledge with gratitude the kindly aid of Miss Cora M. Ross, one of the school teachers at the Blackfoot agency, who has furnished me with a version of the story of the origin of the Medicine Lodge; and of Mrs. Thomas Dawson, who gave me help on the story of the Lost Children. William Jackson, an educated half-breed, who did good service from 1874 to 1879, scouting under Generals Custer and Miles, and William Russell, half-breed, at one time government interpreter at the agency, have both given me valuable assistance. The latter has always placed himself at my service, when I needed an interpreter, while Mr. Jackson has been at great pains to assist me in securing several tales which I might not otherwise have obtained, and has helped me in many ways. The veteran prairie man, Mr. Hugh Monroe, and his son, John Monroe, have also given me much information. Most of the stories I owe to Blackfeet, Bloods, and Piegans of pure race. Some of these men have died within the past few years, among them the kindly and venerable Red Eagle; Almost-a-Dog, a noble old man who was regarded with respect and affection by Indians and whites; and that matchless orator, Four Bears. Others, still living, to whom I owe thanks, are Wolf Calf, Big Nose, Heavy Runner, Young Bear Chief, Wolf Tail, Rabid Wolf, Running Rabbit, White Calf, All-are-his-Children, Double Runner, Lone Medicine Person, and many others.

The stories here given cover a wide range of subjects, but are fair examples of the oral literature of the Blackfeet. They deal with religion, the origin of things, the performances of medicine men, the bravery and single-heartedness of warriors.

It will be observed that in more than one case two stories begin in the same way, and for a few paragraphs are told in language which is almost identical. In like manner it is often to be noted that in different stories the same incidents occur. This is all natural enough, when it is remembered that the range of the Indians' experiences is very narrow. The incidents of camp life, of hunting and war excursions, do not offer a very wide variety of conditions; and of course the stories of the people deal chiefly with matters with which they are familiar. They are based on the every-day life of the narrators.

The reader of these Blackfoot stories will not fail to notice many curious resemblances to tales told among other distant and different peoples. Their similarity to those current among the Ojibwas, and other Eastern Algonquin tribes, is sufficiently obvious and altogether to be expected, nor is it at all remarkable that we should find, among the Blackfeet, tales identical with those told by tribes of different stock far to the south; but it is a little startling to see in the story of the Worm Pipe a close parallel to the classical myth of Orpheus and Eurydice. In another of the stories is an incident which might have been taken bodily from the Odyssey.

Well-equipped students of general folk-lore will find in these tales much to interest them, and to such may be left the task of commenting on this collection.

STORIES OF ADVENTURE

THE PEACE WITH THE SNAKES

I

In those days there was a Piegan chief named Owl Bear. He was a great chief, very brave and generous. One night he had a dream: he saw many dead bodies of the enemy lying about, scalped, and he knew that he must go to war. So he called out for a feast, and after the people had eaten, he said:—

"I had a strong dream last night. I went to war against the Snakes, and killed many of their warriors. So the signs are good, and I feel that I must go. Let us have a big party now, and I will be the leader. We will start to-morrow night."

Then he told two old men to go out in the camp and shout the news, so that all might know. A big party was made up. Two hundred men, they say, went with this chief to war. The first night they travelled only a little way, for they were not used to walking, and soon got tired.

In the morning the chief got up early and went and made a sacrifice, and when he came back to the others, some said, "Come now, tell us your dream of this night."

"I dreamed good," said Owl Bear. "I had a good dream. We will have good luck."

But many others said they had bad dreams. They saw blood running from their bodies.

Night came, and the party started on, travelling south, and keeping near the foot-hills; and when daylight came, they stopped in thick pine woods and built war lodges. They put up poles as for a lodge, and covered them very thick with pine boughs, so they could build fires and cook, and no one would see the light and smoke; and they all ate some of the food they carried, and then went to sleep.

Again the chief had a good dream, but the others all had bad dreams, and some talked about turning back; but Owl Bear laughed at them, and when night came, all started on. So they travelled for some nights, and all kept dreaming bad except the chief. He always had good dreams. One day after a sleep, a person again asked Owl Bear if he dreamed good. "Yes," he replied. "I have again dreamed of good luck."

"We still dream bad," the person said, "and now some of us are going to turn back. We will go no further, for bad luck is surely ahead." "Go back! go back!" said Owl Bear. "I think you are cowards; I want no cowards with me." They did not speak again. Many of them turned around, and started north, toward home.

Two more days' travel. Owl Bear and his warriors went on, and then another party turned back, for they still had bad dreams. All the men now left with him were his relations. All the others had turned back.

They travelled on, and travelled on, always having bad dreams, until they came close to the Elk River. Then the oldest relation said, "Come, my chief, let us all turn back. We still have bad dreams. We cannot have good luck."

"No," replied Owl Bear, "I will not turn back."

Then they were going to seize him and tie his hands, for they had talked of this before. They thought to tie him and make him go back with them. Then the chief got very angry. He put an arrow on his bow, and said: "Do not touch me. You are my relations; but if any of you try to tie me, I will kill you. Now I am ashamed. My relations are cowards and will turn back. I have told you I have always dreamed good, and that we would have good luck. Now I don't care; I am covered with shame. I am going now to the Snake camp and will give them my body. I am ashamed. Go! go! and when you get home put on women's dresses. You are no longer men."

They said no more. They turned back homeward, and the chief was all alone. His heart was very sad as he travelled on, and he was much ashamed, for his relations had left him.

II

Night was coming on. The sun had set and rain was beginning to fall. Owl Bear looked around for some place where he could sleep dry. Close by he saw a hole in the rocks. He got down on his hands and knees and crept in. Here it was very dark. He could see nothing, so he crept very slowly, feeling as he went. All at once his hand touched something strange. He felt of it. It was a person's foot, and there was a moccasin on it. He stopped, and sat still. Then he felt a little further. Yes, it was a person's leg. He could feel the cowskin legging. Now he did not know what to do. He thought perhaps it was a dead person; and again, he thought it might be one of his relations, who had become ashamed and turned back after him.

Pretty soon he put his hand on the leg again and felt along up. He touched the person's belly. It was warm. He felt of the breast, and could feel it rise and fall as the breath came and went; and the heart was beating fast. Still the person did not move. Maybe he was afraid. Perhaps he thought that was a ghost feeling of him.

Owl Bear now knew this person was not dead. He thought he would try if he could learn who the man was, for he was not afraid. His heart was sad. His people and his relations had left him, and he had made up his mind to give his body to the Snakes. So he began and felt all over the man,—of his face, hair, robe, leggings, belt, weapons; and by and by he stopped feeling of him. He could not tell whether it was one of his people or not.

Pretty soon the strange person sat up and felt all over Owl Bear; and when he had finished, he took the Piegan's hand and opened it and held it up, waving it from side to side, saying by signs, "Who are you?"

Owl Bear put his closed hand against the person's cheek and rubbed it; he said in signs, "Piegan!" and then he asked the person who he was. A finger was placed against his breast and moved across it *zigzag*. It was the sign for "Snake."

"*Hai yah!*" thought Owl Bear, "a Snake, my enemy." For a long time he sat still, thinking. By and by he drew his knife from his belt and placed it in the Snake's hand, and signed, "Kill me!" He waited. He thought soon his heart would be cut. He wanted to die. Why live? His people had left him.

Then the Snake took Owl Bear's hand and put a knife in it and motioned that Owl Bear should cut his heart, but the Piegan would not do it. He lay down, and the Snake lay down beside him. Maybe they slept. Likely not.

So the night went and morning came. It was light, and they crawled out of the cave, and talked a long time together by signs. Owl Bear told the Snake where he had come from, how his party had dreamed bad and left him, and that he was going alone to give his body to the Snakes.

Then the Snake said: "*I* was going to war, too. I was going against the Piegans. Now I am done. Are you a chief?"

"I am the head chief," replied Owl Bear. "I lead. All the others follow."

"I am the same as you," said the Snake. "I am the chief. I like you. You are brave. You gave me your knife to kill you with. How is your heart? Shall the Snakes and the Piegans make peace?"

"Your words are good," replied Owl Bear. "I am glad."

"How many nights will it take you to go home and come back here with your people?" asked the Snake.

Owl Bear thought and counted. "In twenty-five nights," he replied, "the Piegans will camp down by that creek."

"My trail," said the Snake, "goes across the mountains. I will try to be here in twenty-five nights, but I will camp with my people just behind that first mountain. When you get here with the Piegans, come with one of your wives and stay all night with me. In the morning the Snakes will move and put up their lodges beside the Piegans."

"As you say," replied the chief, "so it shall be done." Then they built a fire and cooked some meat and ate together.

"I am ashamed to go home," said Owl Bear. "I have taken no horses, no scalps. Let me cut off your side locks?"

"Take them," said the Snake.

Owl Bear cut off the chiefs braids close to his head, and then the Snake cut off the Piegan's braids. Then they exchanged clothes and weapons and started out, the Piegan north, the Snake south.

III

"Owl Bear has come! Owl Bear has come!" the people were shouting.

The warriors rushed to his lodge. *Whish*! how quickly it was filled! Hundreds stood outside, waiting to hear the news.

For a long time the chief did not speak. He was still angry with his people. An old man was talking, telling the news of the camp. Owl Bear did not look at him. He ate some food and rested. Many were in the lodge who had started to war with him. They were now ashamed. They did not speak, either, but kept looking at the fire. After a long time the chief said: "I travelled on alone. I met a Snake. I took his scalp and clothes, and his weapons. See, here is his scalp!" And he held up the two braids of hair.

No one spoke, but the chief saw them nudge each other and smile a little; and soon they went out and said to one another:

"What a lie! That is not an enemy's scalp; there is no flesh on it He has robbed some dead person."

Some one told the chief what they said, but he only laughed and replied:—

"*I* do not care. They were too much afraid even to go on and rob a dead person. They should wear women's dresses."

Near sunset, Owl Bear called for a horse, and rode all through camp so every one could hear, shouting out: "Listen! listen! To-morrow we move camp. We travel south. The Piegans and Snakes are going to make peace. If any one refuses to go, I will kill him. All must go."

Then an old medicine man came up to him and said: "*Kyi*, Owl Bear! listen to me. Why talk like this? You know we are not afraid of the Snakes. Have we not fought them and driven them out of this country? Do you think we are afraid to go and meet them? No. We will go and make peace with them as you say, and if they want to fight, we will fight. Now you are angry with those who started to war with you. Don't be angry. Dreams belong to the Sun. He gave them to us, so that we can see ahead and know what will happen. The Piegans are not cowards. Their dreams told them to turn back. So do not be angry with them any more."

"There is truth in what you say, old man," replied Owl Bear; "I will take your words."

IV

In those days the Piegans were a great tribe. When they travelled, if you were with the head ones, you could not see the last ones, they were so far back. They had more horses than they could count, so they used fresh horses every day and travelled very fast. On the twenty-fourth day they reached the place where Owl Bear had told the Snake they would camp, and put up their lodges along the creek. Soon some young men came in, and said they had seen some fresh horse trails up toward the mountain.

"It must be the Snakes," said the chief; "they have already arrived, although there is yet one night." So he called one of his wives, and getting on their horses they set out to find the Snake camp. They took the trail up over the mountain, and soon came in sight of the lodges. It was a big camp. Every open place in the valley was covered with lodges, and the hills were dotted with horses; for the Snakes had a great many more horses than the Piegans.

Some of the Snakes saw the Piegans coming, and they ran to the chief, saying: "Two strangers are in sight, coming this way. What shall be done?"

"Do not harm them," replied the chief. "They are friends of mine. I have been expecting them." Then the Snakes wondered, for the chief had told them nothing about his war trip.

Now when Owl Bear had come to the camp, he asked in signs for the chiefs lodge, and they pointed him to one in the middle. It was small and old. The Piegan got off his horse, and the Snake chief came out and hugged him and kissed him, and said: "I am glad you have come to-day to my lodge. So are my people. You are tired. Enter my lodge and we will eat." So they went inside and many of the Snakes came in, and they had a great feast.

Then the Snake chief told his people how he had met the Piegan, and how brave he was, and that now they were going to make a great peace; and he sent some men to tell the people, so that they would be ready to move camp in the morning. Evening came. Everywhere people were shouting out for feasts, and the chief took Owl Bear to them. It was very late when they returned. Then the Snake had one of his wives make a bed at the back of the lodge; and when it was ready he said: "Now, my friend, there is your bed. This is now your lodge; also the woman who made the bed, she is now your wife; also everything in this lodge is yours. The parfleches, saddles, food, robes, bowls, everything is yours. I give them to you because you are my friend and a brave man."

"You give me too much," replied Owl Bear. "I am ashamed, but I take your words. I have nothing with me but one wife. She is yours."

Next morning camp was broken early. The horses were driven in, and the Snake chief gave Owl Bear his whole band,—two hundred head, all large, powerful horses.

All were now ready, and the chiefs started ahead. Close behind them were all the warriors, hundreds and hundreds, and last came the women and children, and the young men driving the loose horses. As they came in sight of the Piegan camp, all the warriors started out to meet them, dressed in their war costumes and singing the great war song. There was no wind, and the sound came across the valley and up the hill like the noise of thunder. Then the Snakes began to sing, and thus the two parties advanced.

At last they met. The Piegans turned and rode beside them, and so they came to the camp. Then they got off their horses and kissed each other. Every Piegan asked a Snake into his lodge to eat and rest, and the Snake women put up their lodges beside the Piegan lodges. So the great peace was made.

In Owl Bear's lodge there was a great feast, and when they had finished he said to his people: "Here is the man whose scalp I took. Did I say I killed him? No. I gave him my knife and told him to kill me. He would not do it; and he gave me his knife, but I would not kill him. So we talked together what we should do, and now we have made peace. And now (turning to the Snake) this is your lodge, also all the things in it. My horses, too, I give you. All are yours."

So it was. The Piegan took the Snake's wife, lodge, and horses, and the Snake took the Piegan's, and they camped side by side. All the people camped together, and feasted each other and made presents. So the peace was made.

V

For many days they camped side by side. The young men kept hunting, and the women were always busy drying meat and tanning robes and cowskins. Buffalo were always close, and after a while the people had all the meat and robes they could carry. Then, one day, the Snake chief said to Owl Bear: "Now, my friend, we have camped a long time together, and I am glad we have made peace. We have dug a hole in the ground, and in it we have put our anger and covered it up, so there is no more war between us. And now I think it time to go. To-morrow morning the Snakes break camp and go back south."

"Your words are good," replied Owl Bear. "I too am glad we have made this peace. You say you must go south, and I feel lonesome. I would like you to go with us so we could camp together a long time, but as you say, so it shall be done. To-morrow you will start south. I too shall break camp, for I would be lonesome here without you; and the Piegans will start in the home direction."

The lodges were being taken down and packed. The men sat about the fireplaces, taking a last smoke together. They were now great friends. Many Snakes had married Piegan women, and many Piegans had married Snake women. At last all was ready. The great chiefs mounted their horses and started out, and soon both parties were strung out on the trail.

Some young men, however, stayed behind to gamble a while. It was yet early in the morning, and by riding fast it would not take them long to catch up with their camps. All day they kept playing; and sometimes the Piegans would win, and sometimes the Snakes.

It was now almost sunset. "Let us have one horse race," they said, "and we will stop." Each side had a good horse, and they ran their best; but they came in so close together it could not be told who won. The Snakes claimed that their horse won, and the Piegans would not allow it. So they got angry and began to quarrel, and pretty soon they began to fight and to shoot at each other, and some were killed.

Since that time the Snakes and Piegans have never been at peace.

THE LOST WOMAN
I

A long time ago the Blackfeet were camped on Backfat Creek. There was in the camp a man who had but one wife, and he thought a great deal of her. He never wanted to have two wives. As time passed they had a child, a little girl. Along toward the end of the summer, this man's wife wanted to get some berries, and she asked her husband to take her to a certain place where berries grew, so that she could get some. The man said to his wife: "At this time of the year, I do not like to go to that place to pick berries. There are always Snake or Crow war parties travelling about there." The woman wanted very much to go, and she coaxed her husband about it a great deal; and at last he said he would go, and they started, and many women followed them.

When they came to where the berries grew, the man said to his wife: "There are the berries down in that ravine. You may go down there and pick them, and I will go up on this hill and stand guard. If I see any one coming, I will call out to you, and you must all get on your horses and run." So the women went down to pick berries.

The man went up on the hill and sat down and looked over the country. After a little time, he looked down into another ravine not far off, and saw that it was full of horsemen coming. They started to gallop up towards him, and he called out in a loud voice, "Run, run, the enemy is rushing on us." The women started to run, and he jumped on his horse and followed them. The enemy rushed after them, and he drew his bow and arrows, and got ready to fight and defend the women. After they had gone a little way, the enemy had gained so much that they were shooting at the Blackfeet with their arrows, and the man was riding back and forth behind the women, and whipping up the horses, now of one, now of another, to make them go faster. The enemy kept getting closer, and at last they were so near that they were beginning to thrust at him with their lances, and he was dodging them and throwing himself down, now on one side of his horse, and then on the other.

At length he found that he could no longer defend all the women, so he made up his mind to leave those that had the slowest horses to the mercy of the enemy, while he would go on with those that had the faster ones. When he found that he must leave the women, he was excited and rode on ahead; but as he passed, he heard some one call out to him, "Don't leave me," and he looked to one side, and saw that he was leaving his wife. When he heard his wife call out thus to him, he said to her: "There is no life for me here. You are a fine-looking woman. They will not kill you, but there is no life for me." She answered: "No, take pity on me. Do not leave me. My horse is giving out. Let us both get on one horse and then, if we are caught, we will die together." When he heard this, his heart was touched and he said: "No, wife, I will not leave you. Run up beside my horse and jump on behind me." The enemy were now so near that they had killed or captured some of the women, and they had come up close enough to the man so that they got ready to hit at him with their war clubs. His horse was now wounded in places with arrows, but it was a good, strong, fast horse.

His wife rode up close to him, and jumped on his horse behind him. When he started to run with her, the enemy had come up on either side of him, and some were behind him, but they were afraid to shoot their arrows for fear of hitting their own people, so they struck at the man with their war clubs. But they did not want to kill the woman, and they did not hurt him. They reached out with their hands to try to pull the woman off the horse; but she had put her arms around her husband and held on tight, and they could not get her off, but they tore her clothing off her. As she held her husband, he could not use his arrows, and could not fight to defend himself. His horse was now going very slowly, and all the enemy had caught up to them, and were all around them.

The man said to his wife: "Never mind, let them take you: they will not kill you. You are too handsome a woman for them to kill you." His wife said, "No, it is no harm for us both to die together." When he saw that his wife would not get off the horse and that he could not fight, he said to her: "Here, look out! You are crowding me on to the neck of the horse. Sit further back." He began to edge himself back, and at last, when he got his wife pretty far back on the horse, he gave a great push and shoved her off behind. When she fell off, his horse had more speed and began to run away from the enemy, and he would shoot back his arrows; and now, when they would ride up to strike him with their hatchets, he would shoot them and kill them, and they began to be afraid of him, and to edge away from him. His horse was very long-winded; and now, as he was drawing away from the enemy, there were only two who were yet able to keep up with him. The rest were being left behind, and they stopped, and went back to where the others had killed or captured the women; and now only two men were pursuing.

After a little while, the Blackfoot jumped off his horse to fight on foot, and the two enemies rode up on either side of him, but a long way off, and jumped off their horses. When he saw the two on either side of him, he took a sheaf of arrows in his hand and began to rush, first toward the one on the right, and then toward the one on the left. As he did this, he saw that one of the men, when he ran toward him and threatened to shoot, would draw away from him, while the other would stand still. Then he knew that one of them was a coward and the other a brave man. But all the time they were closing in on him. When he saw that they were closing in on him, he made a rush at the brave man. This one was shooting arrows all the time; but the Blackfoot did not shoot until he got close to him, and then he shot an arrow into him and ran up to him and hit him with his stone axe and killed him. Then he turned to the cowardly one and ran at him. The man turned to run, but the Blackfoot caught him and hit him with his axe and killed him.

After he had killed them, he scalped them and took their arrows, their horses, and the stone knives that they had. Then he went home, and when he rode into the camp he was crying over the loss of his wife. When he came to his lodge and got off his horse, his friends went up to him and asked what was the matter. He told them how all the women had been killed, and how he had been pursued by two enemies, and had fought with them and killed them both, and he showed them the arrows and the horses and the scalps. He told the women's relations that they had all been killed; and all were in great sorrow, and crying over the loss of their friends.

The next morning they held a council, and it was decided that a party should go out and see where the battle had been, and find out what had become of the women. When they got to the place, they found all the women there dead, except this man's wife. Her they could not find. They also found the two Indians that the man had said that he had killed, and, besides, many others that he had killed when he was running away.

II

When he got back to the camp, this Blackfoot picked up his child and put it on his back, and walked round the camp mourning and crying, and the child crying, for four days and four nights, until he was exhausted and worn out, and then he fell asleep. When the rest of the people saw him walking about mourning, and that he would not eat nor drink, their hearts were very sore, and they felt very sorry for him and for the child, for he was a man greatly thought of by the people.

While he lay there asleep, the chief of the camp came to him and woke him, and said: "Well, friend, what have you decided on? What is your mind? What are you going to do?" The man answered: "My child is lonely. It will not eat. It is crying for its mother. It will not notice any one. I am going to look for my wife." The chief said, "I cannot say anything." He went about to all the lodges and told the people that this man was going away to seek his wife.

Now there was in the camp a strong medicine man, who was not married and would not marry at all. He had said, "When I had my dream, it told me that I must never have a wife." The man who had lost his wife had a very beautiful sister, who had never married. She was very proud and very handsome. Many men had wanted to marry her, but she would not have anything to do with any man. The medicine man secretly loved this handsome girl, the sister of the poor man. When he heard of this poor man's misfortune, the medicine man was in great sorrow, and cried over it. He sent word to the poor man, saying: "Go and tell this man that I have promised never to take a wife, but that if he will give me his beautiful sister, he need not go to look for his wife. I will send my secret helper in search of her."

When the young girl heard what this medicine man had said, she sent word to him, saying, "Yes, if you bring my brother's wife home, and I see her sitting here by his side, I will marry you, but not before." But she did not mean what she said. She intended to deceive him in some way, and not to marry him at all. When the girl sent this message to him, the medicine man sent for her and her brother to come to his lodge. When they had come, he spoke to the poor man and said, "If I bring your wife here, are you willing to give me your sister for my wife?" The poor man answered, "Yes." But the young girl kept quiet in his presence, and had nothing to say. Then the medicine man said to them: "Go. To-night in the middle of the night you will hear me sing." He sent everybody out of his lodge, and said to the people: "I will close the door of my lodge, and I do not want any one to come in to-night, nor to look through the door. A spirit will come to me to-night." He made the people know, by a sign put out before the door of his lodge, that no one must enter it, until such time as he was through making his medicine. Then he built a fire, and began to get out all his medicine. He unwrapped his bundle and took out his pipe and his rattles and his other things. After a time, the fire burned down until it was only coals and his lodge was dark, and on the fire he threw sweet-scented herbs, sweet grass, and sweet pine, so as to draw his dream-helper to him.

Now in the middle of the night he was in the lodge singing, when suddenly the people heard a strange voice in the lodge say: "Well, my chief, I have come. What is it?" The medicine man said, "I want you to help me." The voice said, "Yes, I know it, and I know what you want me to do." The medicine man asked, "What is it?" The voice said, "You want me to go and get a woman." The medicine man answered: "That is what I want. I want you to go and get a woman—the lost woman." The voice said to him, "Did I not tell you never to call me, unless you were in great need of my help?" The medicine man answered, "Yes, but that girl that was never going to be married is going to be given to me through your help." Then the voice said, "Oh!" and it was silent for a little while. Then it went on and said: "Well, we have a good feeling for you, and you have been a long time not married; so we will help you to get that girl, and you will have her. Yes, we have great pity on you. We will go and look for this woman, and will try to find her, but I cannot promise you that we will bring her; but we will try. We will go, and in four nights I will be back here again at this same time, and I think that I can bring the woman; but I will not promise. While I am gone, I will let you know how I get on. Now I am going away." And then the people heard in the lodge a sound like a strong wind, and nothing more. He was gone.

Some people went and told the sister what the medicine man and the voice had been saying, and the girl was very down-hearted, and cried over the idea that she must be married, and that she had been forced into it in this way.

III

When the dream person went away, he came late at night to the camp of the Snakes, the enemy. The woman who had been captured was always crying over the loss of her man and her child. She had another husband now. The man who had captured her had taken her for his wife. As she was lying there, in her husband's lodge, crying for sorrow for her loss, the dream person came to her. Her husband was asleep. The dream-helper touched her and pushed her a little, and she looked up and saw a person standing by her side; but she did not know who it was. The person whispered in her ear, "Get up, I want to take you home." She began to edge away from her husband, and at length got up, and all the time the person was moving toward the door. She followed him out, and saw him walk away from the lodge, and she went after. The person kept ahead, and the woman followed him, and they went away, travelling very fast. After they had travelled some distance, she called out to the dream person to stop, for she was getting tired. Then the person stopped, and when he saw the woman sitting, he would sit down, but he would not talk to her.

As they travelled on, the woman, when she got tired, would sit down, and because she was very tired, she would fall asleep; and when she awoke and looked up, she always saw the person walking away from her, and she would get up and follow him. When day came, the shape would be far ahead of her, but at night it would keep closer. When she spoke to this person, the woman would call him "young man." At one time she said to him, "Young man, my moccasins are all worn out, and my feet are getting very sore, and I am very tired and hungry." When she had said this, she sat down and fell asleep, and as she was falling asleep, she saw the person going away from her. He went back to the lodge of the medicine man.

During this night the camp heard the medicine man singing his song, and they knew that the dream person must be back again, or that his chief must be calling him. The medicine man had unwrapped his bundle, and had taken out all his things, and again had a fire of coals, on which he burned sweet pine and sweet grass. Those who were listening heard a voice say: "Well, my chief, I am back again, and I am here to tell you something. I am bringing the woman you sent me after. She is very hungry and has no moccasins. Get me those things, and I will take them back to her." The medicine man went out of the lodge, and called to the poor man, who was mourning for his wife, that he wanted to see him. The man came, carrying the child on his back, to hear what the medicine man had to say. He said to him: "Get some moccasins and something to eat for your wife. I want to send them to her. She is coming." The poor man went to his sister, and told her to give him some moccasins and some pemmican. She made a bundle of these things, and the man took them to the medicine man, who gave them to the dream person; and again he disappeared out of the lodge like a wind.

IV

When the woman awoke in the morning and started to get up, she hit her face against a bundle lying by her, and when she opened it, she found in it moccasins and some pemmican; and she put on the moccasins and ate, and while she was putting on the moccasins and eating, she looked over to where she had last seen the person, and he was sitting there with his back toward her. She could never see his face. When she had finished eating, he got up and went on, and she rose and followed. They went on, and the woman thought, "Now I have travelled two days and two nights with this young man, and I wonder what kind of a man he is. He seems to take no notice of me." So she made up her mind to walk fast and to try to overtake him, and see what sort of a man he was. She started to do so, but however fast she walked, it made no difference. She could not overtake him. Whether she walked fast, or whether she walked slow, he was always the same distance from her. They travelled on until night, and then she lay down again and fell asleep. She dreamed that the young man had left her again.

The dream person had really left her, and had gone back to the medicine man's lodge, and said to him: "Well, my chief, I am back again. I am bringing the woman. You must tell this poor man to get on his horse, and ride back toward Milk River (the Teton). Let him go in among the high hills on this side of the Muddy, and let him wait there until daylight, and look toward the hills of Milk River; and after the sun is up a little way, he will see a band of antelope running toward him, along the trail that the Blackfeet travel. It will be his wife who has frightened these antelope. Let him wait there for a while, and he will see a person coming. This will be his wife. Then let him go to meet her, for she has no moccasins. She will be glad to see him, for she is crying all the time."

The medicine man told the poor man this, and he got on his horse and started, as he had been told. He could not believe that it was true. But he went. At last he got to the place, and a little while after the sun had risen, as he was lying on a hill looking toward the hills of the Milk River, he saw a band of antelope running toward him, as he had been told he would see. He lay there for a long time, but saw nothing else come in sight; and finally he got angry and thought that what had been told him was a lie, and he got up to mount his horse and ride back. Just then he

saw, away down, far off on the prairie, a small black speck, but he
did not think it was moving, it was so far off,—barely to be seen.
He thought maybe it was a rock. He lay down again and took sight
on the speck by a straw of grass in front of him, and looked for a
long time, and after a while he saw the speck pass the straw, and
then he knew it was something. He got on his horse and started to
ride up and find out what it was, riding way around it, through the
hills and ravines, so that he would not be seen. He rode up in a
ravine behind it, pretty near to it, and then he could see it was a
person on foot. He got out his bow and arrows and held them ready
to use, and then started to ride up to it. He rode toward the person,
and at last he got near enough to see that it was his wife. When he
saw this, he could not help crying; and as he rode up, the woman
looked back, and knew first the horse, and then her husband, and
she was so glad that she fell down and knew nothing.

After she had come to herself and they had talked together,
they got on the horse and rode off toward camp. When he came
over the hill in sight of camp, all the people began to say, "Here
comes the man"; and at last they could see from a distance that he
had some one on the horse behind him, and they knew that it must
be his wife, and they were glad to see him bringing her back, for he
was a man thought a great deal of, and everybody liked him and
liked his wife and the way he was kind to her.

Then the handsome girl was given to the medicine man and
became his wife.

ADVENTURES OF BULL TURNS ROUND
I

Once the camp moved, but one lodge stayed. It belonged to Wolf Tail; and Wolf Tail's younger brother, Bull Turns Round, lived with him. Now their father loved both his sons, but he loved the younger one most, and when he went away with the big camp, he said to Wolf Tail: "Take care of your young brother; he is not yet a strong person. Watch him that nothing befall him."

One day Wolf Tail was out hunting, and Bull Turns Round sat in front of the lodge making arrows, and a beautiful strange bird lit on the ground before him. Then cried one of Wolf Tail's wives, "Oh, brother, shoot that little bird." "Don't bother me, sister," he replied, "I am making arrows." Again the woman said, "Oh, brother, shoot that bird for me." Then Bull Turns Round fitted an arrow to his bow and shot the bird, and the woman went and picked it up and stroked her face with it, and her face swelled up so big that her eyes and nose could not be seen. But when Bull Turns Round had shot the bird, he went off hunting and did not know what had happened to the woman's face.

Now when Wolf Tail came home and saw his wife's face, he said, "What is the matter?" and his wife replied: "Your brother has pounded me so that I cannot see. Go now and kill him." But Wolf Tail said, "No, I love my brother; I cannot kill him." Then his wife cried and said: "I know you do not love me; you are glad your brother has beaten me. If you loved me, you would go and kill him."

Then Wolf Tail went out and looked for his brother, and when he had found him, he said: "Come, let us get some feathers. I know where there is an eagle's nest;" and he took him to a high cliff, which overhung the river, and on the edge of this cliff was a dead tree, in the top of which the eagles had built their nest. Then said Wolf Tail, "Climb up, brother, and kill the eagles;" and when Bull Turns Round had climbed nearly to the top, Wolf Tail called out, "I am going to push the tree over the cliff, and you will be killed."

"Oh, brother! oh, brother! pity me; do not kill me," said Bull Turns Round.

"Why did you beat my wife's face so?" said Wolf Tail.

"I didn't," cried the boy; "I don't know what you are talking about."

"You lie," said Wolf Tail, and he pushed the tree over the cliff. He looked over and saw his brother fall into the water, and he did not come up again. Then Wolf Tail went home and took down his lodge, and went to the main camp. When his father saw him coming with only his wives, he said to him, "Where is your young brother?" And Wolf Tail replied: "He went hunting and did not come back. We waited four days for him. I think the bears must have killed him."

II

Now when Bull Turns Round fell into the river, he was stunned, and the water carried him a long way down the stream and finally lodged him on a sand shoal. Near this shoal was a lodge of Under Water People (*Sū'-yē-tŭp'-pi*), an old man, his wife, and two daughters. This old man was very rich: he had great flocks of geese, swans, ducks, and other water-fowl, and a big herd of buffalo which were tame. These buffalo always fed near by, and the old man called them every evening to come and drink. But he and his family ate none of these. Their only food was the bloodsucker.

Now the old man's daughters were swimming about in the evening, and they found Bull Turns Round lying on the shoal, dead, and they went home and told their father, and begged him to bring the person to life, and give him to them for a husband. "Go, my daughters," he said, "and make four sweat lodges, and I will bring the person." He went and got Bull Turns Round, and when the sweat lodges were finished, the old man took him into one of them, and when he had sprinkled water on the hot rocks, he scraped a great quantity of sand off Bull Turns Round. Then he took him into another lodge and did the same thing, and when he had taken him into the fourth sweat lodge and scraped all the sand off him, Bull Turns Round came to life, and the old man led him out and gave him to his daughters. And the old man gave his son-in-law a new lodge and bows and arrows, and many good presents.

Then the women cooked some bloodsuckers, and gave them to their husband, but when he smelled of them he could not eat, and he threw them in the fire. Then his wives asked him what he would eat. "Buffalo," he replied, "is the only meat for men."

"Oh, father!" cried the girls, running to the old man's lodge, "our husband will not eat our food. He says buffalo is the only meat for men."

"Go then, my daughters," said the old man, "and tell your husband to kill a buffalo, but do not take nor break any bones, for I will make it alive again." Then the old man called the buffalo to come and drink, and Bull Turns Round shot a fat cow and took all the meat. And when he had roasted the tongue, he gave each of his wives a small piece of it, and they liked it, and they roasted and ate plenty of the meat.

One day Bull Turns Round went to the old man and said, "I mourn for my father."

"How did you come to be dead on the sand shoal?" asked the old man. Then Bull Turns Round told what his brother had done to him.

"Take this piece of sinew," said the old man. "Go and see your father. When you throw this sinew on the fire, your brother and his wife will roll, and twist up and die." Then the old man gave him a herd of buffalo, and many dogs to pack the lodge, and other things; and Bull Turns Round took his wives, and went to find his father.

One day, just after sunset, they came in sight of the big camp, and they went and pitched the lodge on the top of a very high butte; and the buffalo fed close by, and there were so many of them that they covered the whole hill.

Now the people were starving, and some had died, for they had no buffalo. In the morning, early, a man arose whose son had starved to death, and when he went out and saw this lodge on the top of the hill, and all the buffalo feeding by it, he cried out in a loud voice; and the people all came out and looked at it, and they were afraid, for they thought it was *Stōn'-i-tăp-i*. Then said the man whose son had died: "I am no longer glad to live. I will go up to this lodge, and find out what this is." Now when he said this, all the men grasped their bows and arrows and followed him, and when they went up the hill, the buffalo just moved out of their path and kept on feeding; and just as they came to the lodge, Bull Turns Round came out, and all the people said, "Here is the one whom we thought the bears had killed." Wolf Tail ran up, and said, "Oh, brother, you are not dead. You went to get feathers, but we thought you had been killed." Then Bull Turns Round called his brother into the lodge, and he threw the sinew on the fire; and Wolf Tail, and his wife, who was standing outside, twisted up and died.

Then Bull Turns Round told his father all that had happened to him; and when he learned that the people were starving, he filled his mouth with feathers and blew them out, and the buffalo ran off in every direction, and he said to the people, "There is food, go chase it." Then the people were very glad, and they came each one and gave him a present. They gave him war shirts, bows and arrows, shields, spears, white robes, and many curious things.

KŬT-O´-YIS

Long ago, down where Two Medicine and Badger Creeks come together, there lived an old man. He had but one wife and two daughters. One day there came to his camp a young man who was very brave and a great hunter. The old man said: "Ah! I will have this young man to help me. I will give him my daughters for wives." So he gave him his daughters. He also gave this son-in-law all his wealth, keeping for himself only a little lodge, in which he lived with his old wife. The son-in-law lived in a lodge that was big and fine.

At first the son-in-law was very good to the old people. Whenever he killed anything, he gave them part of the meat, and furnished plenty of robes and skins for their bedding and clothing. But after a while he began to be very mean to them.

Now the son-in-law kept the buffalo hidden under a big log jam in the river. Whenever he wanted to kill anything, he would have the old man go to help him; and the old man would stamp on the log jam and frighten the buffalo, and when they ran out, the young man would shoot one or two, never killing wastefully. But often he gave the old people nothing to eat, and they were hungry all the time, and began to grow thin and weak.

One morning, the young man called his father-in-law to go down to the log jam and hunt with him. They started, and the young man killed a fat buffalo cow. Then he said to the old man, "Hurry back now, and tell your children to get the dogs and carry this meat home, then you can have something to eat." And the old man did as he had been ordered, thinking to himself: "Now, at last, my son-in-law has taken pity on me. He will give me part of this meat." When he returned with the dogs, they skinned the cow, cut up the meat and packed it on the dog travois, and went home. Then the young man had his wives unload it, and told his father-in-law to go home. He did not give him even a piece of liver. Neither would the older daughter give her parents anything to eat, but the younger took pity on the old people and stole a piece of meat, and when she got a chance threw it into the lodge to the old people. The son-in-law told his wives not to give the old people anything to eat. The only way they got food was when the younger woman would throw them a piece of meat unseen by her husband and sister.

Another morning, the son-in-law got up early, and went and kicked on the old man's lodge to wake him, and called him to get up and help him, to go and pound on the log jam to drive out the buffalo, so that he could kill some. When the old man pounded on the jam, a buffalo ran out, and the son-in-law shot it, but only wounded it. It ran away, but at last fell down and died. The old man followed it, and came to where it had lost a big clot of blood from its wound. When he came to where this clot of blood was lying on the ground, he stumbled and fell, and spilled his arrows out of his quiver; and while he was picking them up, he picked up also the clot of blood, and hid it in his quiver. "What are you picking up?" called out the son-in-law. "Nothing," said the old man; "I just fell down and spilled my arrows, and am putting them back." "Curse you, old man," said the son-in-law, "you are lazy and useless. Go back and tell your children to come with the dogs and get this dead buffalo." He also took away his bow and arrows from the old man.

The old man went home and told his daughters, and then went over to his own lodge, and said to his wife: "Hurry now, and put the kettle on the fire. I have brought home something from the butchering." "Ah!" said the old woman, "has our son-in-law been generous, and given us something nice?" "No," answered the old man; "hurry up and put the kettle on." When the water began to boil, the old man tipped his quiver up over the kettle, and immediately there came from the pot a noise as of a child crying, as if it were being hurt, burnt or scalded. They looked in the kettle, and saw there a little boy, and they quickly took it out of the water. They were very much surprised. The old woman made a lashing to put the child in, and then they talked about it. They decided that if the son-in-law knew that it was a boy, he would kill it, so they resolved to tell their daughters that the baby was a girl. Then he would be glad, for he would think that after a while he would have it for a wife. They named the child Kŭt-o´-yis (Clot of Blood).

The son-in-law and his wives came home, and after a while he heard the child crying. He told his youngest wife to go and find out whether that baby was a boy or a girl; if it was a boy, to tell them to kill it. She came back and told them that it was a girl. He did not believe this, and sent his oldest wife to find out the truth of the matter. When she came back and told him the same thing, he believed that it was really a girl. Then he was glad, for he thought that when the child had grown up he would have another wife. He said to his youngest wife, "Take some pemmican over to your mother; not much, just enough so that there will be plenty of milk for the child."

Now on the fourth day the child spoke, and said, "Lash me in turn to each one of these lodge poles, and when I get to the last one, I will fall out of my lashing and be grown up." The old woman did so, and as she lashed him to each lodge pole he could be seen to grow, and finally when they lashed him to the last pole, he was a man. After Kŭt-o´-yis had looked about the inside of the lodge, he looked out through a hole in the lodge covering, and then, turning round, he said to the old people: "How is it there is nothing to eat in this lodge? I see plenty of food over by the other lodge." "Hush up," said the old woman, "you will be heard. That is our son-in-law. He does not give us anything at all to eat." "Well," said Kŭt-o´-yis, "where is your pis´kun?" The old woman said, "It is down by the river. We pound on it and the buffalo come out."

Then the old man told him how his son-in-law abused him. "He has taken my weapons from me, and even my dogs; and for many days we have had nothing to eat, except now and then a small piece of meat our daughter steals for us."

"Father," said Kŭt-o´-yis, "have you no arrows?" "No, my son," he replied; "but I have yet four stone points."

"Go out then and get some wood," said Kŭt-o´-yis. "We will make a bow and arrows. In the morning we will go down and kill something to eat."

Early in the morning Kŭt-o´-yis woke the old man, and said, "Come, we will go down now and kill when the buffalo come out." When they had reached the river, the old man said: "Here is the place to stand and shoot. I will go down and drive them out." As he pounded on the jam, a fat cow ran out, and Kŭt-o´-yis killed it.

Meantime the son-in-law had gone out, and as usual knocked on the old man's lodge, and called to him to get up and go down to help him kill. The old woman called to him that her husband had already gone down. This made the son-in-law very angry. He said: "I have a good mind to kill you right now, old woman. I guess I will by and by."

The son-in-law went on down to the jam, and as he drew near, he saw the old man bending over, skinning a buffalo. "Old man," said he, "stand up and look all around you. Look well, for it will be your last look." Now when he had seen the son-in-law coming, Kŭt-o´-yis had lain down and hidden himself behind the buffalo's carcass. He told the old man to say to his son-in-law, "You had better take your last look, for I am going to kill you, right now." The old man said this. "Ah!" said the son-in-law, "you make me angrier still, by talking back to me." He put an arrow to his bow and shot at the old man, but did not hit him. Kŭt-o´-yis told the old man to pick up the arrow and shoot it back at him, and he did so. Now they shot at each other four times, and then the old man said to Kŭt-o´-yis: "I am afraid now. Get up and help me." So Kŭt-o´-yis got up on his feet and said: "Here, what are you doing? I think you have been badly treating this old man for a long time."

Then the son-in-law smiled pleasantly, for he was afraid of Kŭt-o´-yis. "Oh, no," he said, "no one thinks more of this old man than I do. I have always taken great pity on him."

Then Kŭt-o´-yis said: "You lie. I am going to kill you now." He shot him four times, and the man died. Then Kŭt-o´-yis told the old man to go and bring down the daughter who had acted badly toward him. He did so, and Kŭt-o´-yis killed her. Then he went up to the lodges and said to the younger woman, "Perhaps you loved your husband." "Yes," she said, "I love him." So he killed her, too. Then he said to the old people: "Go over there now, and live in that lodge. There is plenty there to eat, and when it is gone I will kill more. As for myself, I will make a journey around about. Where are there any people? In what direction?" "Well," said the old man, "up above here on Badger Creek and Two Medicine, where the pis´kun is, there are some people."

Kŭt-o´-yis went up to where the pis´kun was, and saw there many lodges of people. In the centre of the camp was a large lodge, with a figure of a bear painted on it. He did not go into this lodge, but went into a very small one near by, where two old women lived; and when he went in, he asked them for something to eat. They set before him some lean dried meat and some belly fat. "How is this?" he asked. "Here is a pis´kun with plenty of fat meat and back fat. Why do you not give me some of that?" "Hush," said the old women. "In that big lodge near by, lives a big bear and his wives and children. He takes all those nice things and leaves us nothing. He is the chief of this place."

Early in the morning, Kŭt-o´-yis told the old women to get their dog travois, and harness it, and go over to the pis´kun, and that he was going to kill for them some fat meat. He reached there just about the time the buffalo were being driven in, and shot a cow, which looked very scabby, but was really very fat. Then he helped the old women to butcher, and when they had taken the meat to camp, he said to them, "Now take all the choice fat pieces, and hang them up so that those who live in the bear lodge will notice them."

They did this, and pretty soon the old chief bear said to his children: "Go out now, and look around. The people have finished killing by this time. See where the nicest pieces are, and bring in some nice back fat." A young bear went out of the lodge, stood up and looked around, and when it saw this meat close by, at the old women's lodge, it went over and began to pull it down. "Hold on there," said Kŭt-o´-yis. "What are you doing here, taking the old women's meat?" and he hit him over the head with a stick that he had. The young bear ran home crying, and said to his father, "A young man has hit me on the head." Then all the bears, the father and mother, and uncles and aunts, and all the relations, were very angry, and all rushed out toward the old women's lodge.

Kŭt-o´-yis killed them all, except one little child bear, a female, which escaped. "Well," said Kŭt-o´-yis, "you can go and breed bears, so there will be more."

Then said Kŭt-o´-yis to the old women: "Now, grandmothers, where are there any more people? I want to travel around and see them." The old women said: "The nearest ones are at the point of rocks (on Sun River). There is a pis´kun there." So Kŭt-o´-yis travelled off toward this place, and when he reached the camp, he entered an old woman's lodge.

The old woman set before him a plate of bad food. "How is this?" he asked. "Have you nothing better than this to set before a stranger? You have a pis´kun down there, and must get plenty of fat meat. Give me some pemmican." "We cannot do that," the old woman replied, "because there is a big snake here, who is chief of the camp. He not only takes the best pieces, but often he eats a handsome young woman, when he sees one." When Kŭt-o´-yis heard this he was angry, and went over and entered the snake's lodge. The women were cooking up some sarvis berries. He picked up the dish, and ate the berries, and threw the dish out of the door. Then he went over to where the snake was lying asleep, pricked him with his knife, and said: "Here, get up. I have come to see you." This made the snake angry. He partly raised himself up and began to rattle, when Kŭt-o´-yis cut him into pieces with his knife. Then he turned around and killed all his wives and children, except one little female snake, which escaped by crawling into a crack in the rocks. "Oh, well," said Kŭt-o´-yis, "you can go and breed young snakes, so there will be more. The people will not be afraid of little snakes." Kŭt-o´-yis said to the old woman, "Now you go into this snake's lodge and take it for yourself, and everything that is in it."

Then he asked them where there were some more people. They told him that there were some people down the river, and some up in the mountains. But they said: "Do not go there, for it is bad, because Ai-sin´-o-ko-ki (Wind Sucker) lives there. He will kill you." It pleased Kŭt-o´-yis to know that there was such a person, and he went to the mountains. When he got to the place where Wind Sucker lived, he looked into his mouth, and could see many dead people there,—some skeletons and some just dead. He went in, and there he saw a fearful sight. The ground was white as snow with the bones of those who had died. There were bodies with flesh on them; some were just dead, and some still living. He spoke to a living person, and asked, "What is that hanging down above us?" The person answered that it was Wind Sucker's heart. Then said Kŭt-o´-yis: "You who still draw a little breath, try to shake your heads (in time to the song), and those who are still able to move, get up and dance. Take courage now, we are going to have the ghost dance." So Kŭt-o´-yis bound his knife, point upward, to the top of his head and began to dance, singing the ghost song, and all the others danced with him; and as he danced up and down, the point of the knife cut Wind Sucker's heart and killed him. Kŭt-o´-yis took his knife and cut through Wind Sucker's ribs, and freed those who were able to crawl out, and said to those who could still travel to go and tell their people that they should come here for the ones who were still alive but unable to walk.

Then he asked some of these people: "Where are there any other people? I want to visit all the people." They said to him: "There is a camp to the westward up the river, but you must not take the left-hand trail going up, because on that trail lives a woman, a handsome woman, who invites men to wrestle with her and then kills them. You must avoid her." This was what Kŭt-o´-yis was looking for. This was his business in the world, to kill off all the bad things. So he asked the people just where this woman lived, and asked where it was best to go to avoid her. He did this, because he did not wish the people to know that he wanted to meet her.

He started on his way, and at length saw this woman standing by the trail. She called out to him, "Come here, young man, come here; I want to wrestle with you." "No," replied the young man, "I am in a hurry. I cannot stop." But the woman called again, "No, no, come now and wrestle once with me." When she had called him four times, Kŭt-o´-yis went up to her. Now on the ground, where this woman wrestled with people, she had placed many broken and sharp flints, partly hiding them by the grass. They seized each other, and began to wrestle over these broken flints, but Kŭt-o´-yis looked at the ground and did not step on them. He watched his chance, and suddenly gave the woman a wrench, and threw her down on a large sharp flint, which cut her in two; and the parts of her body fell asunder.

Then Kŭt-o´-yis went on, and after a while came to where a woman kept a sliding place; and at the far end of it there was a rope, which would trip people up, and when they were tripped, they would fall over a high cliff into deep water, where a great fish would eat them. When this woman saw him coming, she cried out, "Come over here, young man, and slide with me." "No," he replied, "I am in a hurry." She kept calling him, and when she had called the fourth time, he went over to slide with her. "This sliding," said the woman, "is a very pleasant pastime." "Ah!" said Kŭt-o´-yis, "I will look at it." He looked at the place, and, looking carefully, he saw the hidden rope. So he started to slide, and took out his knife, and when he reached the rope, which the woman had raised, he cut it, and when it parted, the woman fell over backward into the water, and was eaten up by the big fish.

Again he went on, and after a while he came to a big camp. This was the place of a man-eater. Kŭt-o´-yis called a little girl he saw near by, and said to her: "Child, I am going into that lodge to let that man-eater kill and eat me. Watch close, therefore, and when you can get hold of one of my bones, take it out and call all the dogs, and when they have all come up to you, throw it down and cry out, 'Kŭt-o´-yis, the dogs are eating your bones!'"

Then Kŭt-o´-yis entered the lodge, and when the man-eater saw him, he cried out, "*O'ki, O'ki*," and seemed glad to see him, for he was a fat young man. The man-eater took a large knife, and went up to Kŭt-o´-yis, and cut his throat, and put him into a great stone kettle to cook. When the meat was cooked, he drew the kettle from the fire, and ate the body, limb by limb, until it was all eaten up.

Then the little girl, who was watching, came up to him, and said, "Pity me, man-eater, my mother is hungry and asks you for those bones." So the old man bunched them up together and handed them to her. She took them out, and called all the dogs to her, and threw the bones down to the dogs, crying out, "Look out, Kŭt-o´-yis; the dogs are eating you!" and when she said that, Kŭt-o´-yis arose from the pile of bones.

Again he went into the lodge, and when the man-eater saw him, he cried out, "How, how, how! the fat young man has survived," and seemed surprised. Again he took his knife and cut Kŭt-o´-yis' throat, and threw him into the kettle. Again, when the meat was cooked, he ate it up, and again the little girl asked for the bones, which he gave her; and, taking them out, she threw them to the dogs, crying, "Kŭt-o´-yis, the dogs are eating you!" and Kŭt-o´-yis again arose from the bones.

When the man-eater had cooked him four times, he again went into the lodge, and, seizing the man-eater, he threw him into the boiling kettle, and his wives and children too, and boiled them to death.

The man-eater was the seventh and last of the bad animals and people who were destroyed by Kŭt-o´-yis.

THE BAD WIFE

I

There was once a man who had but one wife. He was not a chief, but a very brave warrior. He was rich, too, so he could have had plenty of wives if he wished; but he loved his wife very much, and did not want any more. He was very good to this woman. She always wore the best clothes that could be found. If any other woman had a fine buckskin dress, or something very pretty, the man would buy it for her.

It was summer. The berries were ripe, and the woman kept saying to her husband, "Let us go and pick some berries for winter." "No," replied the man. "It is dangerous now. The enemy is travelling all around." But still the woman kept teasing him to go. So one day he told her to get ready. Some other women went, too. They all went on horseback, for the berries were a long way from camp. When they got to the place, the man told the women to keep near their horses all the time. He would go up on a butte near by and watch. "Be careful," he said. "Keep by your horses, and if you see me signal, throw away your berries, get on your horses and ride towards camp as fast as you can."

They had not picked many berries before the man saw a war party coming. He signalled the women, and got on his horse and rode towards them. It happened that this man and his wife both had good horses, but the others, all old women, rode slow old travois horses, and the enemy soon overtook and killed them. Many kept on after the two on good horses, and after a while the woman's horse began to get tired; so she asked her husband to let her ride on his horse with him. The woman got up behind him, and they went on again. The horse was a very powerful one, and for a while went very fast; but two persons make a heavy load, and soon the enemy began to gain on them. The man was now in a bad plight; the enemy were overtaking him, and the woman holding him bound his arms so that he could not use his bow.

"Get off," he said to her. "The enemy will not kill you. You are too young and pretty. Some one of them will take you, and I will get a big party of our people and rescue you."

"No, no," cried the woman; "let us die here together."

"Why die?" cried the man. "We are yet young, and may live a long time together. If you don't get off, they will soon catch us and kill me, and then they will take you anyhow. Get off, and in only a short time I will get you back."

"No, no," again cried the woman; "I will die here with you."

"Crazy person!" cried the man, and with a quick jerk he threw the woman off.

As he said, the enemy did not kill her. The first one who came up counted *coup* and took her. The man, now that his horse was lightened, easily ran away from the war party, and got safe to camp.

II

Then there was great mourning. The relatives of the old women who had been killed, cut their hair and cried. The man, too, cut off his hair and mourned. He knew that his wife was not killed, but he felt very badly because he was separated from her. He painted himself black, and walked all through the camp, crying. His wife had many relations, and some of them went to the man and said: "We pity you very much. We mourn, too, for our sister. But come. Take courage. We will go with you, and try to get her back."

"It is good," replied the man. "I feel as if I should die, stopping uselessly here. Let us start soon."

That evening they got ready, and at daylight started out on foot. There were seven of them in all. The husband, five middle-aged men, the woman's relations, and a young man, her own young brother. He was a very pretty boy. His hair was longer than any other person's in camp.

They soon found the trail of the war party, and followed it for some days. At last they came to the Big River, and there, on the other side, they saw many lodges. They crept down a coulée into the valley, and hid in a small piece of timber just opposite the camp. Toward evening the man said: "*Kyi*, my brothers. To-night I will swim across and look all through the camp for my wife. If I do not find her, I will cache and look again to-morrow evening. But if I do not return before daylight of the second night, then you will know I am killed. Then you will do as you think best. Maybe you will want to take revenge. Maybe you will go right back home. That will be as your hearts feel."

As soon as it was dark, he swam across the river and went all about through the camp, peeping in through the doorways of the lodges, but he did not see his wife. Still, he knew she must be there. He had followed the trail of the party to this place. They had not killed her on the way. He kept looking in at the lodges until it was late, and the people let the fires go out and went to bed. Then the man went down to where the women got their water from the river. Everywhere along the stream was a cut bank, but in one place a path of steps had been made down to the water's edge. Near this path, he dug a hole in the bank and crawled into it, closing up the entrance, except one small hole, through which he could look, and watch the people who came to the river.

As soon as it was daylight, the women began to come for water. *Tum, tum, tum, tum,* he could hear their footsteps as they came down the path, and he looked eagerly at every one. All day long the people came and went,—the young and old; and the children played about near him. He saw many strange people that day. It was now almost sunset, and he began to think that he would not see his wife there. *Tum, tum, tum, tum,* another woman came down the steps, and stopped at the water's edge. Her dress was strange, but he thought he knew the form. She turned her head and looked down the river, and he saw her face. It was his wife. He pushed away the dirt, crawled out, went to her and kissed her. "*Kyi,*" he said, "hurry, and let us swim across the river. Five of your relations and your own young brother are waiting for us in that piece of timber."

"Wait," replied his wife. "These people have given me a great many pretty things. Let me go back. When it is night I will gather them up, steal a horse, and cross over to you."

"No, no," cried the man. "Let the pretty things go; come, let us cross at once."

"Pity me," said the woman. "Let me go and get my things. I will surely come to-night. I speak the truth."

"How do you speak the truth?" asked her husband.

"That my relations there across the river may be safe and live long, I speak the truth."

"Go then," said the man, "and get your things. I will cross the river now." He went up on the bank and walked down the river, keeping his face hidden. No one noticed him, or if they did, they thought he belonged to the camp As soon as he had passed the first bend, he swam across the river, and soon joined his relations.

"I have seen my wife," he said to them. "She will come over as soon as it is dark. I let her go back to get some things that were given her."

"You are crazy," said one of the men, "very crazy. She already loves this new man she has, or she would not have wanted to go back."

"Stop that," said the husband; "do not talk bad of her. She will surely come."

III

The woman went back to her lodge with the water, and, sitting down near the fireplace, she began to act very strangely. She took up pieces of charred wood, dirt, and ashes in her hands and ate them, and made queer noises.

"What is it?" asked the man who had taken her for a wife. "What is the matter with you?" He spoke in signs.

The woman also spoke in signs. She answered him: "The Sun told me that there are seven persons across the river in that piece of timber. Five of them are middle-aged, another is a young boy with very long hair, another is a man who mourns. His hair is cut short."

The Snake did not know what to do, so he called in some chiefs and old men to advise with him. They thought that the woman might be very strong medicine. At all events, it would be a good thing to go and look. So the news was shouted out, and in a short time all the warriors had mounted their best horses, and started across the river. It was then almost dark, so they surrounded the piece of timber, and waited for morning to begin the search.

"*Kyi*," said one of the woman's relations to her husband. "Did I not speak the truth? You see now what that woman has done for us."

At daylight the poor husband strung his bow, took a handful of arrows from his quiver, and said: "This is my fault. I have brought you to this. It is right that I should die first," and he started to go out of the timber.

"Wait," said the eldest relative. "It shall not be so. I am the first to go. I cannot stay back to see my brother die. You shall go out last." So he jumped out of the brush, and began shooting his arrows, but was soon killed.

"My brother is too far on the road alone," cried another relation, and he jumped out and fought, too. What use, one against so many? The Snakes soon had his scalp.

So they went out, one after another, and at last the husband was alone. He rushed out very brave, and shot his arrows as fast as he could. "Hold!" cried the Snake man to his people. "Do not kill him; catch him. This is the one my wife said to bring back alive. See! his hair is cut short." So, when the man had shot away all his arrows, they seized and tied him, and, taking the scalps of the others, returned to camp.

They took the prisoner into the lodge where his wife was. His hands were tied behind his back, and they tied his feet, too. He could not move.

As soon as the man saw his wife, he cried. He was not afraid. He did not care now how soon he died. He cried because he was thinking of all the trouble and death this woman had caused. "What have I done to you," he asked his wife, "that you should treat me this way? Did I not always use you well? I never struck you. I never made you work hard."

"What does he say?" asked the Snake man.

"He says," replied the woman, "that when you are done smoking, you must knock the ashes and fire out of your pipe on his breast."

The Snake was not a bad-hearted man, but he thought now that this woman had strong medicine, that she had Sun power; so he thought that everything must be done as she said. When the man had finished smoking, he emptied the pipe on the Piegan's breast, and the fire burned him badly.

Then the poor man cried again, not from the pain, but to think what a bad heart this woman had. Again he spoke to her. "You cannot be a person," he said. "I think you are some fearful animal, changed to look like a woman."

"What is he saying now?" asked the Snake.

"He wants some boiling water poured on his head," replied the woman.

"It shall be as he says," said the Snake; and he had his women heat some water. When it was ready, one of them poured a little of it here and there on the captive's head and shoulders. Wherever the hot water touched, the hair came out and the skin peeled off. The pain was so bad that the Piegan nearly fainted. When he revived, he said to his wife: "Pity me. I have suffered enough. Let them kill me now. Let me hurry to join those who are already travelling to the Sand Hills."

The woman turned to the Snake chief, and said, "The man says that he wants you to give him to the Sun."

"It is good," said the Snake. "To-morrow we move camp. Before we leave here, we will give him to the Sun."

There was an old woman in this camp who lived all alone, in a little lodge of her own. She had some friends and relations, but she

said she liked to live by herself. She had heard that a Piegan had
been captured, and went to the lodge where he was. When she saw
them pour the boiling water on him, she cried and felt badly. This
old woman had a very good heart. She went home and lay down by
her dog, and kept crying, she felt so sorry for this poor man. Pretty
soon she heard people shouting out the orders of the chief. They
said: "Listen! listen! To-morrow we move camp. Get ready now and
pack up everything. Before we go, the Piegan man will be given to
the Sun."

Then the old woman knew what to do. She tied a piece of
buckskin around her dog's mouth, so he could not bark, and then
she took him way out in the timber and tied him where he could
not be seen. She also filled a small sack with pemmican, dried
meat, and berries, and put it near the dog.

In the morning the people rose early. They smoothed a cotton-
wood tree, by taking off the bark, and painted it black. Then they
stood the Piegan up against it, and fastened him there with a great
many ropes. When they had tied him so he could not move, they
painted his face black, and the chief Snake made a prayer, and
gave him to the Sun.

Every one was now busy getting ready to move camp. This old
woman had lost her dog, and kept calling out for him and looking
all around. "*Tsis'-i!*" she cried. "*Tsis'-i!* Come here. Knock the dog
on the head! Wait till I find him, and I'll break his neck."

The people were now all packed up, and some had already
started on the trail. "Don't wait for me," the old woman said. "Go
on, I'll look again for my dog, and catch up with you."

When all were gone, the old woman went and untied her dog,
and then, going up to where the Piegan was tied, she cut the ropes,
and he was free. But already the man was very weak, and he fell
down on the ground. She rubbed his limbs, and pretty soon he felt
better. The old woman was so sorry for him that she cried again,
and kissed him. Then the man cried, too. He was so glad that some
one pitied him. By and by he ate some of the food the old woman
had given him, and felt strong again. He said to her in signs: "I am
not done. I shall go back home now, but I will come again. I will
bring all the Piegans with me, and we will have revenge."

"You say well," signed the old woman.

"Help me," again said the man. "If, on the road you are
travelling, this camp should separate, mark the trail my wife takes
with a stick. You, too, follow the party she goes with, and always

put your lodge at the far end of the village. When I return with my people, I will enter your lodge, and tell you what to do."

"I take your speech," replied the old woman. "As you say, so it shall be." Then she kissed him again, and started on after her people. The man went to the river, swam across, and started for the North.

IV

Why are the people crying? Why is all this mourning? Ah! the poor man has returned home, and told how those who went with him were killed. He has told them the whole story. They are getting ready for war. Every one able to fight is going with this man back to the Snakes. Only a few will be left to guard the camp. The mother of that bad woman is going, too. She has sharpened her axe, and told what she will do when she sees her daughter. All are ready. The best horses have been caught up and saddled, and the war party has started,—hundreds and hundreds of warriors. They are strung out over the prairie as far as you can see.

When they got to the Missouri River, the poor man showed them where the lodge in which they had tortured him had stood. He took them to see the tree, where he had been bound. The black paint was still on it.

From here, they went slowly. Some young men were sent far ahead to scout. The second day, they came back to the main body, and said they had found a camping place just deserted, and that there the trail forked. The poor man then went ahead, and at the forks he found a willow twig stuck in the ground, pointing to the left hand trail. When the others came up, he said to them: "Take care of my horse now, and travel slowly. I will go ahead on foot and find the camp. It must be close. I will go and see that old woman, and find out how things are."

Some men did not want him to do this; they said that the old woman might tell about him, and then they could not surprise the camp.

"No," replied the man. "It will not be so. That old woman is almost the same as my mother. I know she will help us."

He went ahead carefully, and near sunset saw the camp. When it was dark, he crept near it and entered the old woman's lodge. She had placed it behind, and a little way off from, the others. When he went in the old woman was asleep, but the fire was still burning a little. He touched her, and she jumped up and started to scream; but he put his hand on her mouth, and when she saw who it was she laughed and kissed him. "The Piegans have come," he told her. "We are going to have revenge on this camp to-night. Is my wife here?"

"Still here," replied the old woman. "She is chief now. They think her medicine very strong."

"Tell your friends and relations," said the Piegan, "that you have had a dream, and that they must move into the brush yonder. Have them stay there with you, and they will not be hurt. I am going now to get my people."

It was very late in the night. Most of the Snakes were in bed and asleep. All at once the camp was surrounded with warriors, shouting the war cry and shooting, stabbing, and knocking people on the head as fast as they came out of the lodges.

That Piegan woman cried out: "Don't hurt me. I am a Piegan. Are any of my people here?"

"Many of your relations are here," some one said. "They will protect you."

Some young men seized and tied her, as her husband had said to do. They had hard work to keep her mother from killing her. "*Hai yah!*" the old woman cried. "There is my Snake woman daughter. Let me split her head open."

The fight was soon over. The Piegans killed the people almost as fast as they came out of their lodges. Some few escaped in the darkness. When the fight was over, the young warriors gathered up a great pile of lodge poles and brush, and set fire to it. Then the poor man tore the dress off his bad wife, tied the scalp of her dead Snake man around her neck, and told her to dance the scalp dance in the fire. She cried and hung back, calling out for pity. The people only laughed and pushed her into the fire. She would run through it, and then those on the other side would push her back. So they kept her running through the fire, until she fell down and died.

The old Snake woman had come out of the brush with her relations. Because she had been so good, the Piegans gave her, and those with her, one-half of all the horses and valuable things they had taken. "*Kyi!*" said the Piegan chief. "That is all for you, because you helped this poor man. To-morrow morning we start back North. If your heart is that way, go too and live with us." So these Snakes joined the Piegans and lived with them until they died, and their children married with the Piegans, and at last they were no longer Snake people.

THE LOST CHILDREN

Once a camp of people stopped on the bank of a river. There were but a few lodges of them. One day the little children in the camp crossed the river to play on the other side. For some time they stayed near the bank, and then they went up over a little hill, and found a bed of sand and gravel; and there they played for a long time.

There were eleven of these children. Two of them were daughters of the chief of the camp, and the smaller of these wanted the best of everything. If any child found a pretty stone, she would try to take it for herself. The other children did not like this, and they began to tease the little girl, and to take her things away from her. Then she got angry and began to cry, and the more she cried, the more the children teased her; so at last she and her sister left the others, and went back to the camp.

When they got there, they told their father what the other children had done to them, and this made the chief very angry. He thought for a little while, and then got up and went out of the lodge, and called aloud, so that everybody might hear, saying: "Listen! listen! Your children have teased my child and made her cry. Now we will move away, and leave them behind. If they come back before we get started, they shall be killed. If they follow us and overtake the camp, they shall be killed. If the father and mother of any one of them take them into their lodge, I will kill that father and mother. Hurry now, hurry and pack up, so that we can go. Everybody tear down the lodges, as quickly as you can."

When the people heard this, they felt very sorry, but they had to do as the chief said; so they tore down the lodges, and quickly packed the dog travois, and started off. They packed in such a hurry that they left many little things lying in camp,—knives and awls, bone needles and moccasins.

The little children played about in the sand for a long time, but at last they began to get hungry; and one little girl said to the others, "I will go back to the camp, and get some dried meat and bring it here, so that we may eat." And she started to go to the camp. When she came to the top of the hill and looked across the river, she saw that there were no lodges there, and did not know what to think of it. She called down to the children, and said, "The camp has gone"; but they did not believe her, and went on playing. She kept on calling, and at last some of them came to her, and then all, and saw that it was as she had said. They went down to the river, and crossed it, and went to where the lodges had stood.

When they got there, they saw on the ground the things that had been left out in packing; and as each child saw and knew something that had belonged to its own parents, it cried and sang a little song, saying: "Mother, here is your bone needle; why did you leave your children?" "Father, here is your arrow; why did you leave your children?" It was very mournful, and they all cried.

There was among them a little girl who had on her back her baby brother, whom she loved dearly. He was very young, a nursing child, and already he was hungry and beginning to fret. This little girl said to the others: "We do not know why they have gone, but we know they have gone. We must follow the trail of the camp, and try to catch up with them." So the children started to follow the camp. They travelled on all day; and just at night they saw, near the trail, a little lodge. They had heard the people talk of a bad old woman who killed and ate persons, and some of the children thought that this old woman might live here; and they were afraid to go to the lodge. Others said: "Perhaps some person lives here who has a good heart. We are very tired and very hungry and have nothing to eat and no place to keep warm. Let us go to this lodge."

They went to it; and when they went in, they saw sitting by the fire an old woman. She spoke kindly to them, and asked them where they were travelling; and they told her that the camp had moved on and left them, and that they were trying to find their people, that they had nothing to eat, and were tired and hungry. The old woman fed them, and told them to sleep here to-night, and to-morrow they could go on and find their people. "The camp," she said, "passed here to-day when the sun was low. They have not gone far. To-morrow you will overtake them." She spread some robes on the ground and said: "Now lie here and sleep. Lie side by side with your heads toward the fire, and when morning comes, you can go on your journey." The children lay down and soon slept.

In the middle of the night, the old woman got up, and built a big fire, and put on it a big stone kettle, full of water. Then she took a big knife, and, commencing at one end of the row, began to cut off the heads of the children, and to throw them into the pot. The little girl with the baby brother lay at the other end of the row, and while the old woman was doing this, she awoke and saw what was taking place. When the old woman came near to her, she jumped up and began to beg that she would not kill her. "I am strong," she said. "I will work hard for you. I can bring your wood and water, and tan your skins. Do not kill my little brother and me. Take pity on us and save us alive. Everybody has left us, but do you have pity. You shall see how quickly I will work, how you will always have plenty of wood. I can work quickly and well." The old woman thought for a little while, then she said: "Well, I will let you live for a time, anyhow. You shall sleep safely to-night."

The next day, early, the little girl took her brother on her back, and went out and gathered a big pile of wood, and brought it to the lodge before the old woman was awake. When she got up, she called to the girl, "Go to the river and get a bucket of water." The girl put her brother on her back, and took the bucket to go. The old woman said to her: "Why do you carry that child everywhere? Leave him here." The girl said: "Not so. He is always with me, and if I leave him he will cry and make a great noise, and you will not like that." The old woman grumbled, but the girl went on down to the river.

When she got there, just as she was going to fill her bucket, she saw standing by her a great bull. It was a mountain buffalo, one of those who live in the timber; and the long hair of its head was all full of pine needles and sticks and branches, and matted together. (It was a *Su'ye-stŭ'mik*, a water bull.) When the girl saw him, she prayed him to take her across the river, and so to save her and her little brother from the bad old woman. The bull said, "I will take you across, but first you must take some of the sticks out of my head." The girl begged him to start at once; but the bull said, "No, first take the sticks out of my head." The girl began to do it, but before she had done much, she heard the old woman calling to her to bring the water. The girl called back, "I am trying to get the water clear," and went on fixing the buffalo's head. The old woman called again, saying, "Hurry, hurry with that water." The girl answered, "Wait, I am washing my little brother." Pretty soon the old woman called out, "If you don't bring that water, I will kill you and your brother." By this time the girl had most of the sticks out of the bull's head, and he told her to get on his back, and went into the water and swam with her across the river. As he reached the other bank, the girl could see the old woman coming from her lodge down to the river with a big stick in her hand.

When the bull reached the bank, the girl jumped off his back and started off on the trail of the camp. The bull swam back again to the other side of the river, and there stood the old woman. This bull was a sort of servant of the old woman. She said to him: "Why did you take those children across the river? Take me on your back now and carry me across quickly, so that I can catch them." The bull said, "First take these sticks out of my head." "No," said the old woman; "first take me across, then I will take the sticks out." The bull repeated, "First take the sticks out of my head, then I will take you across." This made the old woman very mad, and she hit him with the stick she had in her hand; but when she saw that he would not go, she began to pull the sticks out of his head very roughly, tearing out great handfuls of hair, and every moment ordering him to go, and threatening what she would do to him when she got back. At last the bull took her on his back, and began to swim across with her, but he did not swim fast enough to please her, so she began to pound him with her club to make him go faster; and when the bull got to the middle of the river, he rolled over on his side, and the old woman slipped off, and was carried down the river and drowned.

The girl followed the trail of the camp for several days, feeding on berries and roots that she dug; and at last one night after dark she overtook the camp. She went into the lodge of an old woman, who was camped off at one side, and the old woman pitied her and gave her some food, and told her where her father's lodge was. The girl went to it, but when she went in, her parents would not receive her. She had tried to overtake them for the sake of her little brother, who was growing thin and weak because he had not nursed; and now her mother was afraid to have her stay with them. She even went and told the chief that her children had come back. Now when the chief heard that these two children had come back, he was angry; and he ordered that the next day they should be tied to a post in the camp, and that the people should move on and leave them here. "Then," he said, "they cannot follow us."

The old woman who had pitied the children, when she heard what the chief had ordered, made up a bundle of dried meat, and hid it in the grass near the camp. Then she called her dog to her,—a little curly dog. She said to the dog:—

"Now listen. To-morrow when we are ready to start, I will call you to come to me, but you must pay no attention to what I say. Run off, and pretend to be chasing squirrels. I will try to catch you, and if I do so, I will pretend to whip you; but do not follow me. Stay behind, and when the camp has passed out of sight, chew off the strings that bind those children; and when you have done this, show them where I have hidden that food. Then you can follow the camp and catch up to us." The dog stood before the old woman, and listened to all that she said, turning his head from side to side, as if paying close attention.

Next morning it was done as the chief had said. The children were tied to the tree with raw hide strings, and the people tore down all the lodges and moved off. The old woman called her dog to follow her, but he was digging at a gopher hole and would not come. Then she went up to him and struck at him hard with her whip, but he dodged and ran away, and then stood looking at her. Then the old woman got very mad and cursed him, but he paid no attention; and finally she left him, and followed the camp. When the people had all passed out of sight, the dog went to the children, and gnawed the strings which tied them, until he had bitten them through. So the children were free.

Then the dog was glad, and danced about and barked and ran round and round. Pretty soon he came up to the little girl, and looked up in her face, and then started away, trotting. Every little while he would stop and look back. The girl thought he wanted her to follow him. She did so, and he took her to where the bundle of dried meat was, and showed it to her. Then, when he had done this, he jumped up on her, and licked the baby's face, and then started off, running as hard as he could along the trail of the camp, never stopping to look back. The girl did not follow him. She now knew that it was no use to go to the camp again. Their parents would not receive them, and the chief would perhaps order them to be killed.

She went on her way, carrying her little brother and the bundle of dried meat. She travelled for many days, and at last came to a place where she thought she would stop. Here she built a little lodge of poles and brush, and stayed there. One night she had a dream, and an old woman came to her in the dream, and said to her, "To-morrow take your little brother, and tie him to one of the lodge poles, and the next day tie him to another, and so every day tie him to one of the poles, until you have gone all around the lodge and have tied him to each pole. Then you will be helped, and will no more have bad luck."

When the girl awoke in the morning, she remembered what the dream had told her, and she bound her little brother to one of the lodge poles; and each day after this she tied him to one of the poles. Each day he grew larger, until, when she had gone all around the lodge, he was grown to be a fine young man.

Now the girl was glad, and proud of her young brother who was so large and noble-looking. He was quiet, not speaking much, and sometimes for days he would not say anything. He seemed to be thinking all the time. One morning he told the girl that he had a dream and that he wished her to help him build a pis´kun. She was afraid to ask him about the dream, for she thought if she asked questions he might not like it. So she just said she was ready to do what he wished. They built the pis´kun, and when it was finished, the boy said to his sister: "The buffalo are to come to us, and you are not to see them. When the time comes, you are to cover your head and to hold your face close to the ground; and do not lift your head nor look, until I throw a piece of kidney to you." The girl said, "It shall be as you say."

When the time came, the boy told her where to go; and she went to the place, a little way from the lodge, not far from the corral, and sat down on the ground, and covered her head, holding her face close to the earth. After she had sat there a little while, she heard the sound of animals running, and she was excited and curious, and raised her head to look; but all she saw was her brother, standing near, looking at her. Before he could speak, she said to him: "I thought I heard buffalo coming, and because I was anxious for food, I forgot my promise and looked. Forgive me this time, and I will try again." Again she bent her face to the ground, and covered her head.

Soon she heard again the sound of animals running, at first a long way off, and then coming nearer and nearer, until at last they seemed close, and she thought they were going to run over her. She sprang up in fright and looked about, but there was nothing to be seen but her brother, looking sadly at her. She went close to him and said: "Pity me. I was afraid, for I thought the buffalo were going to run over me." He said: "This is the last time. If again you look, we will starve; but if you do not look, we will always have plenty, and will never be without meat." The girl looked at him, and said, "I will try hard this time, and even if those animals run right over me, I will not look until you throw the kidney to me." Again she covered her head, pressing her face against the earth and putting her hands against her ears, so that she might not hear. Suddenly, sooner than she thought, she felt the blow from the meat thrown at her, and, springing up, she seized the kidney and began to eat it. Not far away was her brother, bending over a fat cow; and, going up to him, she helped him with the butchering.

After that was done, she kindled a fire and cooked the best parts of the meat, and they ate and were satisfied.

The boy became a great hunter. He made fine arrows that went faster than a bird could fly, and when he was hunting, he watched all the animals and all the birds, and learned their ways, and how to imitate them when they called. While he was hunting, the girl dressed buffalo hides and the skins of deer and other animals. She made a fine new lodge, and the boy painted it with figures of all the birds and the animals he had killed.

One day, when the girl was bringing water, she saw a little way off a person coming. When she went in the lodge, she told her brother, and he went out to meet the stranger. He found that he was friendly and was hunting, but had had bad luck and killed nothing. He was starving and in despair, when he saw this lone lodge and made up his mind to go to it. As he came near it, he began to be afraid, and to wonder if the people who lived there were enemies or ghosts; but he thought, "I may as well die here as starve," so he went boldly to it. The strange person was very much surprised to see this handsome young man with the kind face, who could speak his own language. The boy took him into the lodge, and the girl put food before him. After he had eaten, he told his story, saying that the game had left them, and that many of his people were dying of hunger. As he talked, the girl listened; and at last she remembered the man, and knew that he belonged to her camp.

She asked him questions, and he talked about all the people in the camp, and even spoke of the old woman who owned the dog. The boy advised the stranger, after he had rested, to return to his camp, and tell the people to move up to this place, that here they would find plenty of game. After he had gone, the boy and his sister talked of these things. The girl had often told him what she had suffered, what the chief had said and done, and how their own parents had turned against her, and that the only person whose heart had been good to her was this old woman. As the young man heard all this again, he was angry at his parents and the chief, but he felt great kindness for the old woman and her dog. When he learned that those bad people were living, he made up his mind that they should suffer and die.

When the strange person reached his own camp, he told the people how well he had been treated by these two persons, and that they wished him to bring the whole camp to where they were, and that there they should have plenty. This made great joy in the camp, and all got ready to move. When they reached the lost children's camp, they found everything as the stranger had said. The brother gave a feast; and to those whom he liked he gave many presents, but to the old woman and the dog he gave the best presents of all. To the chief nothing at all was given, and this made him very much ashamed. To the parents no food was given, but the boy tied a bone to the lodge poles above the fire, and told the parents to eat from it without touching it with their hands. They were very hungry, and tried to eat from this bone; and as they were stretching out their necks to reach it—for it was above them—the boy cut off their heads with his knife. This frightened all the people, the chief most of all; but the boy told them how it all was, and how he and his sister had survived.

When he had finished speaking, the chief said he was sorry for what he had done, and he proposed to his people that this young man should be made their chief. They were glad to do this. The boy was made the chief, and lived long to rule the people in that camp.

MIK-A´PI—RED OLD MAN
I

It was in the valley of "It fell on them" Creek, near the mountains, that the Pikŭn´i were camped when Mik-a´pi went to war. It was far back, in the days of stone knives, long before the white people had come. This was the way it happened.

Early in the morning a band of buffalo were seen in the foot-hills of the mountains, and some hunters went out to get meat. Carefully they crawled along up the coulées and drew near to the herd; and, when they had come close to them, they began to shoot, and their arrows pierced many fat cows. But even while they were thus shooting, they were surprised by a war party of Snakes, and they began to run back toward the camp. There was one hunter, named Fox-eye, who was very brave. He called to the others to stop, saying: "They are many and we are few, but the Snakes are not brave. Let us stop and fight them." But the other hunters would not listen. "We have no shields," they said, "nor our war medicine. There are many of the enemy. Why should we foolishly die?"

They hurried on to camp, but Fox-eye would not turn back. He drew his arrows from the quiver, and prepared to fight. But, even as he placed an arrow, a Snake had crawled up by his side, unseen. In the still air, the Piegan heard the sharp twang of a bow string, but, before he could turn his head, the long, fine-pointed arrow pierced him through and through. The bow and arrows dropped from his hands, he swayed, and then fell forward on the grass, dead. But now the warriors came pouring from the camp to aid him. Too late! The Snakes quickly scalped their fallen enemy, scattered up the mountain, and were lost to sight.

Now Fox-eye had two wives, and their father and mother and all their near relations were dead. All Fox-eye's relatives, too, had long since gone to the Sand Hills. So these poor widows had no one to avenge them, and they mourned deeply for the husband so suddenly taken from them. Through the long days they sat on a near hill and mourned, and their mourning was very sad.

There was a young warrior named Mik-a´pi. Every morning he was awakened by the crying of these poor widows, and through the day his heart was touched by their wailing. Even when he went to rest, their mournful cries reached him through the darkness, and he could not sleep. So he sent his mother to them. "Tell them," he said, "that I wish to speak to them." When they had entered, they sat close by the door-way, and covered their heads.

"*Kyi!*" said Mik-a´pi. "For days and nights I have heard your mourning, and I too have silently mourned. My heart has been very sad. Your husband was my near friend, and now he is dead and no relations are left to avenge him. So now, I say, I will take the load from your hearts. I will avenge him. I will go to war and take many scalps, and when I return, they shall be yours. You shall paint your faces black, and we will all rejoice that Fox-eye is avenged."

When the people heard that Mik-a´pi was going to war, many warriors wished to join him, but he refused them; and when he had taken a medicine sweat, and got a medicine-pipe man to make medicine for him during his absence, he started from the camp one evening, just after sunset. It is only the foolish warrior who travels in the day; for other war parties may be out, or some camp-watcher sitting on a hill may see him from far off, and lay plans to destroy him. Mik-a´pi was not one of these. He was brave but cautious, and he had strong medicine. Some say that he was related to the ghosts, and that they helped him. Having now started to war against the Snakes, he travelled in hidden places, and at sunrise would climb a hill and look carefully in all directions, and during the long day would lie there, and watch, and take short sleeps.

Now, when Mik-a´pi had come to the Great Falls (of the Missouri), a heavy rain set in; and, seeing a hole in the rocks, he crawled in and lay down in the farther end to sleep. The rain did not cease, and when night came he could not travel because of the darkness and storm; so he lay down to sleep again. But soon he heard something coming into the cave toward him, and then he felt a hand laid on his breast, and he put out his hand and touched a person. Then Mik-a´pi put the palm of his hand on the person's breast and jerked it to and fro, and then he touched the person with the point of his finger, which, in the sign language, means, "Who are you?"

The strange person then took Mik-a´pi's hand, and made him feel of his own right hand. The thumb and all the fingers were closed except the forefinger, which was extended; and when Mik-a´pi touched it the person moved his hand forward with a zigzag motion, which means "Snake." Then Mik-a´pi was glad. Here had come to him one of the tribe he was seeking. But he thought it best to wait for daylight before attacking him. So, when the Snake in signs asked him who he was, he replied, by making the sign for paddling a canoe, that he was a Pend d'Oreille, or River person. For he knew that the Snakes and the Pend d'Oreilles were at peace.

Then they both lay down to sleep, but Mik-a´pi did not sleep. Through the long night he watched for the first dim light, so that he might kill his enemy. The Snake slept soundly; and just at daybreak Mik-a´pi quietly strung his bow, fitted an arrow, and, taking aim, sent the thin shaft through his enemy's heart. The Snake quivered, half rose up, and with a groan fell back dead. Then Mik-a´pi took his scalp and his bow and arrows, and also his bundle of moccasins; and as daylight had come, he went out of the cave and looked all about. No one was in sight. Probably the Snake, like himself, had gone alone to war. But, ever cautious, he travelled only a short distance, and waited for night before going on. The rain had ceased and the day was warm. He took a piece of dried meat and back fat from his pouch and ate them, and, after drinking from the river, he climbed up on a high rock wall and slept.

Now in his dream he fought with a strange people, and was wounded. He felt blood trickling from his wounds, and when he awoke, he knew that he had been warned to turn back. The signs also were bad. He saw an eagle rising with a snake, which dropped from its claws and escaped. The setting sun, too, was painted,—a sure warning to people that danger is near. But, in spite of all these things, Mik-a´pi determined to go on. He thought of the poor widows mourning and waiting for revenge. He thought of the glad welcome of the people, if he should return with many scalps; and he thought also of two young sisters, whom he wanted to marry. Surely, if he could return and bring the proofs of brave deeds, their parents would be glad to give them to him.

II

It was nearly night. The sun had already disappeared behind the sharp-pointed gray peaks. In the fading light the far-stretching prairie was turning dark. In a valley, sparsely timbered with quaking aspens and cotton-woods, stood a large camp. For a long distance up and down the river rose the smoke of many lodges. Seated on a little hill overlooking the valley, was a single person. With his robe drawn tightly around him, he sat there motionless, looking down on the prairie and valley below.

Slowly and silently something was crawling through the grass toward him. But he heard nothing. Still he gazed eastward, seeking to discover any enemy who might be approaching. Still the dark object crawled slowly onward. Now it was so close to him that it could almost touch him. The person thought he heard a sound, and started to turn round. Too late! Too late! A strong arm grasped him about the neck and covered his mouth. A long jagged knife was thrust into his breast again and again, and he died without a cry. Strange that in all that great camp no one should have seen him killed!

Still extended on the ground, the dark figure removed the scalp. Slowly he crawled back down the hill, and was lost in the gathering darkness. It was Mik-a´pi, and he had another Snake scalp tied to his belt. His heart was glad, yet he was not satisfied. Some nights had passed since the bad signs had warned him, yet he had succeeded. "One more," he said. "One more scalp I must have, and then I will go back." So he went far up on the mountain, and hid in some thick pines and slept. When daylight came, he could see smoke rise as the women started their fires. He also saw many people rush up on the hill, where the dead watcher lay. He was too far off to hear their angry shouts and mournful cries, but he sung to himself a song of war and was happy.

Once more the sun went to his lodge behind the mountains, and as darkness came Mik-a´pi slowly descended the mountain and approached the camp. This was the time of danger. Behind each bush, or hidden in a bunch of the tall rye grass, some person might be watching to warn the camp of an approaching enemy. Slowly and like a snake, he crawled around the outskirts of the camp, listening and looking. He heard a cough and saw a movement of a bush. There was a Snake. Could he kill him and yet escape? He was close to him now. So he sat and waited, considering how to act. For a long time he sat there waiting. The moon rose and travelled high in the sky. The Seven Persons slowly swung around, and pointed downward. It was the middle of the night. Then the person in the bush stood up and stretched out his arms and yawned, for he was tired of watching, and thought that no danger was near; but as he stood thus, an arrow pierced his breast. He gave a loud yell and tried to run, but another arrow struck him and he fell.

At the sound the warriors rushed forth from the lodges and the outskirts of the camp; but as they came, Mik-a´pi tore the scalp from his fallen enemy, and started to run toward the river. Close behind him followed the Snakes. Arrows whizzed about him. One pierced his arm. He plucked it out. Another struck his leg, and he fell. Then a great shout arose from the Snakes. Their enemy was down. Now they would be revenged for two lately taken lives. But where Mik-a'pi fell was the verge of a high rock wall; below rushed the deep river, and even as they shouted, he rolled from the wall, and disappeared in the dark water far below. In vain they searched the shores and bars. They did not find him.

Mik-a'pi had sunk deep in the water. The current was swift, and when at last he rose to the surface, he was far below his pursuers. The arrow in his leg pained him, and with difficulty he crawled out on a sand-bar. Luckily the arrow was lance-shaped instead of barbed, so he managed to draw it out. Near by on the bar was a dry pine log, lodged there by the high spring water. This he managed to roll into the stream; and, partly resting on it, he again drifted down with the current. All night he floated down the river, and when morning came he was far from the camp of the Snakes. Benumbed with cold and stiff from the arrow wounds, he was glad to crawl out on the bank, and lie down in the warm sunshine. Soon he slept.

III

The sun was already in the middle when he awoke. His wounds were swollen and painful; yet he hobbled on for a time, until the pain became so great he could go no further, and he sat down, tired and discouraged.

"True the signs," he said. "How crazy I was to go against them! Useless now my bravery, for here I must stay and die. The widows will still mourn; and in their old age who will take care of my father and my mother? Pity me now, oh Sun! Help me, oh great Above Medicine Person! Look down on your wounded and suffering child. Help me to survive!"

What was that crackling in the brush near by? Was it the Snakes on his trail? Mik-a'pi strung his bow and drew out his arrows. No; it was not a Snake. It was a bear. There he stood, a big grizzly bear, looking down at the wounded man. "What does my brother here?" he said. "Why does he pray to survive?"

"Look at my leg," said Mik-a'pi, "swollen and sore. Look at my wounded arm. I can hardly draw the bow. Far the home of my people, and my strength is gone. Surely here I must die, for I cannot travel and I have no food."

"Now courage, my brother," said the bear. "Now not faint heart, my brother, for I will help you, and you shall survive."

When he had said this, he lifted Mik-a′pi and carried him to a place of thick mud; and here he took great handfuls of the mud and plastered the wounds, and he sung a medicine song while putting on the mud. Then he carried Mik-a′pi to a place where were many sarvis berries, and broke off great branches of the fruit, and gave them to him, saying, "Eat, my brother, eat!" and he broke off more branches, full of large ripe berries, for him; but already Mik-a′pi was satisfied and could eat no more. Then said the bear, "Lie down, now, on my back, and hold tight by my hair, and we will travel on." And when Mik-a′pi had got on and was ready, he started off on a long swinging trot.

All through the night he travelled on without stopping. When morning came, they rested awhile, and ate more berries; and again the bear plastered his wounds with mud. In this way they travelled on, until, on the fourth day, they came close to the lodges of the Pikŭn′i; and the people saw them coming and wondered.

"Get off, my brother, get off," said the bear. "There are your people. I must leave you." And without another word, he turned and went off up the mountain.

All the people came out to meet the warrior, and they carried him to the lodge of his father. He untied the three scalps from his belt and gave them to the widows, saying: "You are revenged. I wipe away your tears." And every one rejoiced. All his female relations went through the camp, shouting his name and singing, and every one prepared for the scalp dance.

First came the widows. Their faces were painted black, and they carried the scalps tied on poles. Then came the medicine men, with their medicine pipes unwrapped; then the bands of the *I-kun-uh′-kah-tsi*, all dressed in war costume; then came the old men; and last the women and children. They all sang the war song and danced. They went all through the village in single file, stopping here and there to dance, and Mik-a′pi sat outside the lodge, and saw all the people dance by him. He forgot his pain and was proud, and although he could not dance, he sang with them.

Soon they made the Medicine Lodge, and, first of all the warriors, Mik-a′pi was chosen to cut the raw-hide which binds the poles, and as he cut the strands, he counted the *coups* he had made. He told of the enemies he had killed, and all the people shouted his name and praised him. The father of those two young sisters gave them to him. He was glad to have such a son-in-law. Long lived Mik-a´pi. Of all the great chiefs who have lived and died, he was the greatest. He did many other great and daring things. It must be true, as the old men have said, that he was helped by the ghosts, for no one can do such things without help from those fearful and unknown persons.

HEAVY COLLAR AND THE GHOST WOMAN

The Blood camp was on Old Man's River, where Fort McLeod now stands. A party of seven men started to war toward the Cypress Hills. Heavy Collar was the leader. They went around the Cypress Mountains, but found no enemies and started back toward their camp. On their homeward way, Heavy Collar used to take the lead. He would go out far ahead on the high hills, and look over the country, acting as scout for the party. At length they came to the south branch of the Saskatchewan River, above Seven Persons' Creek. In those days there were many war parties about, and this party travelled concealed as much as possible in the coulées and low places.

As they were following up the river, they saw at a distance three old bulls lying down close to a cut bank. Heavy Collar left his party, and went out to kill one of these bulls, and when he had come close to them, he shot one and killed it right there. He cut it up, and, as he was hungry, he went down into a ravine below him, to roast a piece of meat; for he had left his party a long way behind, and night was now coming on. As he was roasting the meat, he thought,—for he was very tired,—"It is a pity I did not bring one of my young men with me. He could go up on that hill and get some hair from that bull's head, and I could wipe out my gun." While he sat there thinking this, and talking to himself, a bunch of this hair came over him through the air, and fell on the ground right in front of him. When this happened, it frightened him a little; for he thought that perhaps some of his enemies were close by, and had thrown the bunch of hair at him. After a little while, he took the hair, and cleaned his gun and loaded it, and then sat and watched for a time. He was uneasy, and at length decided that he would go on further up the river, to see what he could discover. He went on, up the stream, until he came to the mouth of the St. Mary's River. It was now very late in the night, and he was very tired, so he crept into a large bunch of rye-grass to hide and sleep for the night.

The summer before this, the Blackfeet (Sik-si-kau) had been camped on this bottom, and a woman had been killed in this same patch of rye-grass where Heavy Collar had lain down to rest. He did not know this, but still he seemed to be troubled that night. He could not sleep. He could always hear something, but what it was he could not make out. He tried to go to sleep, but as soon as he dozed off he kept thinking he heard something in the distance. He spent the night there, and in the morning when it became light, there he saw right beside him the skeleton of the woman who had been killed the summer before.

That morning he went on, following up the stream to Belly River. All day long as he was travelling, he kept thinking about his having slept by this woman's bones. It troubled him. He could not forget it. At the same time he was very tired, because he had walked so far and had slept so little. As night came on, he crossed over to an island, and determined to camp for the night. At the upper end of the island was a large tree that had drifted down and lodged, and in a fork of this tree he built his fire, and got in a crotch of one of the forks, and sat with his back to the fire, warming himself, but all the time he was thinking about the woman he had slept beside the night before. As he sat there, all at once he heard over beyond the tree, on the other side of the fire, a sound as if something were being dragged toward him along the ground. It sounded as if a piece of a lodge were being dragged over the grass. It came closer and closer.

Heavy Collar was scared. He was afraid to turn his head and look back to see what it was that was coming. He heard the noise come up to the tree in which his fire was built, and then it stopped, and all at once he heard some one whistling a tune. He turned around and looked toward the sound, and there, sitting on the other fork of the tree, right opposite to him, was the pile of bones by which he had slept, only now all together in the shape of a skeleton. This ghost had on it a lodge covering. The string, which is tied to the pole, was fastened about the ghost's neck; the wings of the lodge stood out on either side of its head, and behind it the lodge could be seen, stretched out and fading away into the darkness. The ghost sat on the old dead limb and whistled its tune, and as it whistled, it swung its legs in time to the tune.

When Heavy Collar saw this, his heart almost melted away. At length he mustered up courage, and said: "Oh ghost, go away, and do not trouble me. I am very tired; I want to rest." The ghost paid no attention to him, but kept on whistling, swinging its legs in time to the tune. Four times he prayed to her, saying: "Oh ghost, take pity on me! Go away and leave me alone. I am tired; I want to rest." The more he prayed, the more the ghost whistled and seemed pleased, swinging her legs, and turning her head from side to side, sometimes looking down at him, and sometimes up at the stars, and all the time whistling.

When he saw that she took no notice of what he said, Heavy Collar got angry at heart, and said, "Well, ghost, you do not listen to my prayers, and I shall have to shoot you to drive you away." With that he seized his gun, and throwing it to his shoulder, shot right at the ghost. When he shot at her, she fell over backward into the darkness, screaming out: "Oh Heavy Collar, you have shot me, you have killed me! You dog, Heavy Collar! there is no place on this earth where you can go that I will not find you; no place where you can hide that I will not come."

As she fell back and said this, Heavy Collar sprang to his feet, and ran away as fast as he could. She called after him: "I have been killed once, and now you are trying to kill me again. Oh Heavy Collar!" As he ran away, he could still hear her angry words following him, until at last they died away in the distance. He ran all night long, and whenever he stopped to breathe and listen, he seemed to hear in the distance the echoes of her voice. All he could hear was, "Oh Heavy Collar!" and then he would rush away again. He ran until he was all tired out, and by this time it was daylight. He was now quite a long way below Fort McLeod. He was very sleepy, but dared not lie down, for he remembered that the ghost had said that she would follow him. He kept walking on for some time, and then sat down to rest, and at once fell asleep.

Before he had left his party, Heavy Collar had said to his young men: "Now remember, if any one of us should get separated from the party, let him always travel to the Belly River Buttes. There will be our meeting-place." When their leader did not return to them, the party started across the country and went toward the Belly River Buttes. Heavy Collar had followed the river up, and had gone a long distance out of his way; and when he awoke from his sleep he too started straight for the Belly River Buttes, as he had said he would.

When his party reached the Buttes, one of them went up on top of the hill to watch. After a time, as he looked down the river, he saw two persons coming, and as they came nearer, he saw that one of them was Heavy Collar, and by his side was a woman. The watcher called up the rest of the party, and said to them: "Here comes our chief. He has had luck. He is bringing a woman with him. If he brings her into camp, we will take her away from him." And they all laughed. They supposed that he had captured her. They went down to the camp, and sat about the fire, looking at the two people coming, and laughing among themselves at the idea of their chief bringing in a woman. When the two persons had come close, they could see that Heavy Collar was walking fast, and the woman would walk by his side a little way, trying to keep up, and then would fall behind, and then trot along to catch up to him again. Just before the pair reached camp there was a deep ravine that they had to cross. They went down into this side by side, and then Heavy Collar came up out of it alone, and came on into the camp.

When he got there, all the young men began to laugh at him and to call out, "Heavy Collar, where is your woman?" He looked at them for a moment, and then said: "Why, I have no woman. I do not understand what you are talking about." One of them said: "Oh, he has hidden her in that ravine. He was afraid to bring her into camp." Another said, "Where did you capture her, and what tribe does she belong to?" Heavy Collar looked from one to another, and said: "I think you are all crazy. I have taken no woman. What do you mean?" The young man said: "Why, that woman that you had with you just now: where did you get her, and where did you leave her? Is she down in the coulée? We all saw her, and it is no use to deny that she was with you. Come now, where is she?" When they said this, Heavy Collar's heart grew very heavy, for he knew that it must have been the ghost woman; and he told them the story. Some of the young men could not believe this, and they ran down to the ravine, where they had last seen the woman. There they saw in the soft dirt the tracks made by Heavy Collar, when he went down into the ravine, but there were no other tracks near his, where they had seen the woman walking. When they found that it was a ghost that had come along with Heavy Collar, they resolved to go back to their main camp. The party had been out so long that their moccasins were all worn out, and some of them were footsore, so that they could not travel fast, but at last they came to the cut banks, and there found their camp—seven lodges.

That night, after they had reached camp, they were inviting each other to feasts. It was getting pretty late in the night, and the moon was shining brightly, when one of the Bloods called out for Heavy Collar to come and eat with him. Heavy Collar shouted, "Yes, I will be there pretty soon." He got up and went out of the lodge, and went a little way from it, and sat down. While he was sitting there, a big bear walked out of the brush close to him. Heavy Collar felt around him for a stone to throw at the bear, so as to scare it away, for he thought it had not seen him. As he was feeling about, his hand came upon a piece of bone, and he threw this over at the bear, and hit it. Then the bear spoke, and said: "Well, well, well, Heavy Collar; you have killed me once, and now here you are hitting me. Where is there a place in this world where you can hide from me? I will find you, I don't care where you may go." When Heavy Collar heard this, he knew it was the ghost woman, and he jumped up and ran toward his lodge, calling out, "Run, run! a ghost bear is upon us!"

All the people in the camp ran to his lodge, so that it was crowded full of people. There was a big fire in the lodge, and the wind was blowing hard from the west. Men, women, and children were huddled together in the lodge, and were very much afraid of the ghost. They could hear her walking toward the lodge, grumbling, and saying: "I will kill all these dogs. Not one of them shall get away." The sounds kept coming closer and closer, until they were right at the lodge door. Then she said, "I will smoke you to death." And as she said this, she moved the poles, so that the wings of the lodge turned toward the west, and the wind could blow in freely through the smoke hole. All this time she was threatening terrible things against them. The lodge began to get full of smoke, and the children were crying, and all were in great distress—almost suffocating. So they said, "Let us lift one man up here inside, and let him try to fix the ears, so that the lodge will get clear of smoke." They raised a man up, and he was standing on the shoulders of the others, and, blinded and half strangled by the smoke, was trying to turn the wings. While he was doing this, the ghost suddenly hit the lodge a blow, and said, "*Un!*" and this scared the people who were holding the man, and they jumped and let him go, and he fell down. Then the people were in despair, and said, "It is no use; she is resolved to smoke us to death." All the time the smoke was getting thicker in the lodge.

Heavy Collar said: "Is it possible that she can destroy us? Is there no one here who has some strong dream power that can overcome this ghost?"

His mother said: "I will try to do something. I am older than any of you, and I will see what I can do." So she got down her medicine bundle and painted herself, and got out a pipe and filled it and lighted it, and stuck the stem out through the lodge door, and sat there and began to pray to the ghost woman. She said: "Oh ghost, take pity on us, and go away. We have never wronged you, but you are troubling us and frightening our children. Accept what I offer you, and leave us alone."

A voice came from behind the lodge and said: "No, no, no; you dogs, I will not listen to you. Every one of you must die."

The old woman repeated her prayer: "Ghost, take pity on us. Accept this smoke and go away."

Then the ghost said: "How can you expect me to smoke, when I am way back here? Bring that pipe out here. I have no long bill to reach round the lodge." So the old woman went out of the lodge door, and reached out the stem of the pipe as far as she could reach around toward the back of the lodge. The ghost said: "No, I do not wish to go around there to where you have that pipe. If you want me to smoke it, you must bring it here." The old woman went around the lodge toward her, and the ghost woman began to back away, and said, "No, I do not smoke that kind of a pipe." And when the ghost started away, the old woman followed her, and she could not help herself.

She called out, "Oh my children, the ghost is carrying me off!" Heavy Collar rushed out, and called to the others, "Come, and help me take my mother from the ghost." He grasped his mother about the waist and held her, and another man took him by the waist, and another him, until they were all strung out, one behind the other, and all following the old woman, who was following the ghost woman, who was walking away.

All at once the old woman let go of the pipe, and fell over dead. The ghost disappeared, and they were troubled no more by the ghost woman.

THE WOLF-MAN

There was once a man who had two bad wives. They had no shame. The man thought if he moved away where there were no other people, he might teach these women to become good, so he moved his lodge away off on the prairie. Near where they camped was a high butte, and every evening about sundown, the man would go up on top of it, and look all over the country to see where the buffalo were feeding, and if any enemies were approaching. There was a buffalo skull on the hill, which he used to sit on.

"This is very lonesome," said one woman to the other, one day. "We have no one to talk with nor to visit."

"Let us kill our husband," said the other. "Then we will go back to our relations and have a good time."

Early in the morning, the man went out to hunt, and as soon as he was out of sight, his wives went up on top of the butte. There they dug a deep pit, and covered it over with light sticks, grass, and dirt, and placed the buffalo skull on top.

In the afternoon they saw their husband coming home, loaded down with meat he had killed. So they hurried to cook for him. After eating, he went up on the butte and sat down on the skull. The slender sticks gave way, and he fell into the pit. His wives were watching him, and when they saw him disappear, they took down the lodge, packed everything on the dog travois, and moved off, going toward the main camp. When they got near it, so that the people could hear them, they began to cry and mourn.

"Why is this?" they were asked. "Why are you mourning? Where is your husband?"

"He is dead," they replied. "Five days ago he went out to hunt, and he never came back." And they cried and mourned again.

When the man fell into the pit, he was hurt. After a while he tried to get out, but he was so badly bruised he could not climb up. A wolf, travelling along, came to the pit and saw him, and pitied him. *Ah-h-w-o-o-o-o! Ah-h-w-o-o-o-o!* he howled, and when the other wolves heard him they all came running to see what was the matter. There came also many coyotes, badgers, and kit-foxes.

"In this hole," said the wolf, "is my find. Here is a fallen-in man. Let us dig him out, and we will have him for our brother."

They all thought the wolf spoke well, and began to dig. In a little while they had a hole close to the man. Then the wolf who found him said, "Hold on; I want to speak a few words to you." All the animals listening, he continued, "We will all have this man for our brother, but I found him, so I think he ought to live with us big wolves." All the others said that this was well; so the wolf went into the hole, and tearing down the rest of the dirt, dragged the almost dead man out. They gave him a kidney to eat, and when he was able to walk a little, the big wolves took him to their home. Here there was a very old blind wolf, who had powerful medicine. He cured the man, and made his head and hands look like those of a wolf. The rest of his body was not changed.

In those days the people used to make holes in the pis'kun walls and set snares, and when wolves and other animals came to steal meat, they were caught by the neck. One night the wolves all went down to the pis'kun to steal meat, and when they got close to it, the man-wolf said: "Stand here a little while. I will go down and fix the places, so you will not be caught." He went on and sprung all the snares; then he went back and called the wolves and others,—the coyotes, badgers, and foxes,—and they all went in the pis'kun and feasted, and took meat to carry home.

In the morning the people were surprised to find the meat gone, and their nooses all drawn out. They wondered how it could have been done. For many nights the nooses were drawn and the meat stolen; but once, when the wolves went there to steal, they found only the meat of a scabby bull, and the man-wolf was angry, and cried out: "Bad-you-give-us-o-o-o! Bad-you-give-us-o-o-o-o!"

The people heard him, and said: "It is a man-wolf who has done all this. We will catch him." So they put pemmican and nice back fat in the pis'kun, and many hid close by. After dark the wolves came again, and when the man-wolf saw the good food, he ran to it and began eating. Then the people all rushed in and caught him with ropes and took him to a lodge. When they got inside to the light of the fire, they knew at once who it was. They said, "This is the man who was lost."

"No," said the man, "I was not lost. My wives tried to kill me. They dug a deep hole, and I fell into it, and I was hurt so badly that I could not get out; but the wolves took pity on me and helped me, or I would have died there."

When the people heard this, they were angry, and they told the man to do something.

"You say well," he replied. "I give those women to the *I-kun-uh'-kah-tsi;* they know what to do."

After that night the two women were never seen again.

THE FAST RUNNERS

Once, long ago, the antelope and the deer met on the prairie. At this time both of them had galls and both dew claws. They began to talk together, and each was telling the other what he could do. Each one told how fast he could run, and before long they were disputing as to which could run the faster. Neither would allow that the other could beat him, so they agreed that they would have a race to decide which was the swifter, and they bet their galls on the race. When they ran, the antelope proved the faster runner, and beat the deer and took his gall.

Then the deer said: "Yes, you have beaten me on the prairie, but that is not where I live. I only go out there sometimes to feed, or when I am travelling around. We ought to have another race in the timber. That is my home, and there I can run faster than you can."

The antelope felt very big because he had beaten the deer in the race, and he thought wherever they might be, he could run faster than the deer. So he agreed to race in the timber, and on this race they bet their dew claws.

They ran through the thick timber, among the brush and over fallen logs, and this time the antelope ran slowly, because he was not used to this kind of travelling, and the deer easily beat him, and took his dew claws.

Since then the deer has had no gall, and the antelope no dew claws.

TWO WAR TRAILS
I

Many years ago there lived in the Blood camp a boy named
Screech Owl (A´-tsi-tsi). He was rather a lonely boy, and did not
care to go with other boys. He liked better to be by himself. Often
he would go off alone, and stay out all night away from the camp.
He used to pray to all kinds of birds and animals that he saw, and
ask them to take pity on him and help him, saying that he wanted
to be a warrior. He never used paint. He was a fine looking young
man, and he thought it was foolish to use paint to make oneself
good looking.

When Screech Owl was about fourteen years old, a large party
of Blackfeet were starting to war against the Crees and the
Assinaboines. The young man said to his father: "Father, with this
war party many of my cousins are going. I think that now I am old
enough to go to war, and I would like to join them." His father
said, "My son, I am willing; you may go." So he joined the party.

His father gave his son his own war horse, a black horse with
a white spot on its side—a very fast horse. He offered him arms,
but the boy refused them all, except a little trapping axe. He said,
"I think this hatchet will be all that I shall need." Just as they
were about to start, his father gave the boy his own war headdress.
This was not a war bonnet, but a plume made of small feathers,
the feathers of thunder birds, for the thunder bird was his father's
medicine. He said to the boy, "Now, my son, when you go into
battle, put this plume in your head, and wear it as I have worn it."

The party started and travelled north-east, and at length they
came to where Fort Pitt now stands, on the Saskatchewan River.
When they had got down below Fort Pitt, they saw three riders,
going out hunting. These men had not seen the war party. The
Blackfeet started around the men, so as to head them off when
they should run. When they saw the men, the Screech Owl got off
his horse, and took off all his clothes, and put on his father's war
plume, and began to ride around, singing his father's war song.
The older warriors were getting ready for the attack, and when
they saw this young boy acting in this way, they thought he was
making fun of the older men, and they said: "Here, look at this boy!
Has he no shame? He had better stay behind." When they got on
their horses, they told him to stay behind, and they charged the
Crees. But the boy, instead of staying behind, charged with them,
and took the lead, for he had the best horse of all. He, a boy, was
leading the war party, and still singing his war song.

The three Crees began to run, and the boy kept gaining on them. They did not want to separate, they kept together; and as the boy was getting closer and closer, the last one turned in his saddle and shot at the Screech Owl, but missed him. As the Cree fired, the boy whipped up his horse, and rode up beside the Cree and struck him with his little trapping axe, and knocked him off his horse. He paid no attention to the man that he had struck, but rode on to the next Cree. As he came up with him, the Cree raised his gun and fired, but just as he did so, the Blackfoot dropped down on the other side of his horse, and the ball passed over him. He straightened up on his horse, rode up by the Cree, and as he passed, knocked him off his horse with his axe. When he knocked the second Cree off his horse, the Blackfeet, who were following, whooped in triumph and to encourage him, shouting, "*A-wah-heh'*" (Take courage). The boy was still singing his father's war song.

By this time, the main body of the Blackfeet were catching up with him. He whipped his horse on both sides, and rode on after the third Cree, who was also whipping his horse as hard as he could, and trying to get away. Meantime, some of the Blackfeet had stopped to count *coup* on and scalp the two dead Crees, and to catch the two ponies. Screech Owl at last got near to the third Cree, who kept aiming his gun at him. The boy did not want to get too close, until the Cree had fired his gun, but he was gaining a little, and all the time was throwing himself from side to side on his horse, so as to make it harder for the Cree to hit him. When he had nearly overtaken the enemy, the Cree turned, raised his gun and fired; but the boy had thrown himself down behind his horse, and again the ball passed over him. He raised himself up on his horse, and rushed on the Cree, and struck him in the side of the body with his axe, and then again, and with the second blow, he knocked him off his horse.

The boy rode on a little further, stopped, and jumped off his horse, while the rest of the Blackfeet had come up and were killing the fallen man. He stood off to one side and watched them count *coup* on and scalp the dead.

The Blackfeet were much surprised at what the young man had done. After a little while, the leader decided that they would go back to the camp from which they had come. When he had returned from this war journey this young man's name was changed from A'-tsi-tsi to E-kūs'-kini (Low Horn). This was his first war path.

From that time on the name of E-kūs´-kini was often heard as that of one doing some great deed.

E-kūs´-kini started on his last war trail from the Black-foot crossing *(Su-yoh-pah'-wah-ku)*. He led a party of six Sarcees. He was the seventh man.

On the second day out, they came to the Red Deer's River. When they reached this river, they found it very high, so they built a raft to cross on. They camped on the other side. In crossing, most of their powder got wet. The next morning, when they awoke, E-kūs´-kini said: "Well, trouble is coming for us. We had better go back from here. We started on a wrong day. I saw in my sleep our bodies lying on the prairie, dead." Some of the young men said: "Oh well, we have started, we had better go on. Perhaps it is only a mistake. Let us go on and try to take some horses anyhow." E-kūs´-kini said: "Yes, that is very true. To go home is all foolishness; but remember that it is by your wish that we are going on." He wanted to go back, not on his own account, but for the sake of his young men—to save his followers.

From there they went on and made another camp, and the next morning he said to his young men: "Now I am sure. I have seen it for certain. Trouble is before us." They camped two nights at this place and dried some of their powder, but most of it was caked and spoilt. He said to his young men: "Here, let us use some sense about this. We have no ammunition. We cannot defend ourselves. Let us turn back from here." So they started across the country for their camp.

They crossed the Red Deer's River, and there camped again. The next morning E-kūs´-kini said: "I feel very uneasy to-day. Two of you go ahead on the trail and keep a close lookout. I am afraid that to-day we are going to see our enemy." Two of the young men went ahead, and when they had climbed to the top of a ridge and looked over it on to Sarvis Berry (Saskatoon) Creek, they came back and told E-kūs´-kini that they had seen a large camp of people over there, and that they thought it was the Piegans, Bloods, Blackfeet, and Sarcees, who had all moved over there together. Saskatoon Creek was about twenty miles from the Blackfoot camp. He said: "No, it cannot be our people. They said nothing about moving over here; it must be a war party. It is only a few days since we left, and there was then no talk of their leaving that camp. It cannot be they." The two young men said: "Yes, they are our people. There are too many of them for a war party. We think that the whole camp is there." They discussed this for some little time, E-kūs´-kini insisting that it could not be the Blackfoot camp, while the young men felt sure that it was. These two men said, "Well, we are going on into the camp now." Low Horn said: "Well, you may go. Tell my father that I will come into the camp to-night. I do not like to go in in the daytime, when I am not bringing back anything with me."

It was now late in the afternoon, and the two young men went ahead toward the camp, travelling on slowly. A little after sundown, they came down the hill on to the flat of the river, and saw there the camp. They walked down toward it, to the edge of the stream, and there met two women, who had come down after water. The men spoke to them in Sarcee, and said, "Where is the Sarcee camp?" The women did not understand them, so they spoke again, and asked the same question in Blackfoot. Then these two women called out in the Cree language, "Here are two Blackfeet, who have come here and are talking to us." When these men heard the women talk Cree, and saw what a mistake they had made, they turned and ran away up the creek. They ran up above camp a short distance, to a place where a few willow bushes were hanging over the stream, and pushing through these, they hid under the bank, and the willows above concealed them. The people in the camp came rushing out, and men ran up the creek, and down, and looked everywhere for the two enemies, but could find nothing of them.

Now when these people were running in all directions, hunting for these two men, E-kūs´-kini was coming down the valley slowly with the four other Sarcees. He saw some Indians coming toward him, and supposed that they were some of his own people, coming to meet him, with horses for him to ride. At length, when they were close to him, and E-kūs´-kini could see that they were the enemy, and were taking the covers off their guns, he jumped to one side and stood alone and began to sing his war song. He called out, "Children of the Crees, if you have come to try my manhood, do your best." In a moment or two he was surrounded, and they were shooting at him from all directions. He called out again, "People, you can't kill me here, but I will take my body to your camp, and there you shall kill me." So he advanced, fighting his way toward the Cree camp, but before he started, he killed two of the Crees there. His enemies kept coming up and clustering about him: some were on foot and some on horseback. They were thick about him on all sides, and they could not shoot much at him, for fear of killing their own people on the other side.

One of the Sarcees fell. E-kūs´-kini said to his men, *"A-wah-heh´"* (Take courage). "These people cannot kill us here. Where that patch of choke-cherry brush is, in the very centre of their camp, we will go and take our stand." Another Sarcee fell, and now there were only three of them. E-kūs´-kini said to his remaining men: "Go straight to that patch of brush, and I will fight the enemy off in front and at the sides, and so will keep the way open for you. These people cannot kill us here. There are too many of their own people. If we can get to that brush, we will hurt them badly." All this time they were killing enemies, fighting bravely, and singing their war songs. At last they gained the patch of brush, and then with their knives they began to dig holes in the ground, and to throw up a shelter.

In the Cree camp was Kŏm-in'-ă-kūs (Round), the chief of the Crees, who could talk Blackfoot well. He called out: "E-kūs´-kini, there is a little ravine running out of that brush patch, which puts into the hills. Crawl out through that, and try to get away. It is not guarded." E-kūs´-kini replied: "No, Children of the Crees, I will not go. You must remember that it is E-kūs´-kini that you are fighting with—a man who has done much harm to your people. I am glad that I am here. I am sorry for only one thing; that is, that my ammunition is going to run out. To-morrow you may kill me."

All night long the fight was kept up, the enemy shooting all the time, and all night long E-kūs´-kini sang his death song. Kŏm-in'-ă-kūs called to him several times: "E-kūs´-kini, you had better do what I tell you. Try to get away." But he shouted back, "No," and laughed at them. He said: "You have killed all my men. I am here alone, but you cannot kill me." Kŏm-in'-ă-kūs, the chief, said: "Well, if you are there at daylight in the morning, I will go into that brush and will catch you with my hands. I will be the man who will put an end to you." E-kūs´-kini said: "Kŏm-in'-ă-kūs, do not try to do that. If you do, you shall surely die." The patch of brush in which he had hidden had now been all shot away, cut off by the bullets of the enemy.

When day came, E-kūs´-kini called out: "Eh, Kŏm-in'-ă-kūs, it is broad daylight now. I have run out of ammunition. I have not another grain of powder in my horn. Now come and take me in your hands, as you said you would." Kŏm-in'-ă-kūs answered: "Yes,

I said that I was the one who was going to catch you this morning. Now I am coming."

He took off all his clothes, and alone rushed for the breastworks. E-kūs´-kini's ammunition was all gone, but he still had one load in his gun, and his dagger. Kŏm-in'-ă-kūs came on with his gun at his shoulder, and E-kūs´-kini sat there with his gun in his hand, looking at the man who was coming toward him with the cocked gun pointed at him. He was singing his death song. As Kŏm-in'-ă-kūs got up close, and just as he was about to fire, E-kūs´-kini threw up his gun and fired, and the ball knocked off the Cree chiefs forefinger, and going on, entered his right eye and came out at the temple, knocking the eye out. Kŏm-in'-ă-kūs went down, and his gun flew a long way.

When Kŏm-in'-ă-kūs fell, the whole camp shouted the war whoop, and cried out, "This is his last shot," and they all charged on him. They knew that he had no more ammunition.

The head warrior of the Crees was named Bunch of Lodges. He was the first man to jump inside the breastworks. As he sprang inside, E-kūs´-kini met him, and thrust his dagger through him, and killed him on the spot. Then, as the enemy threw themselves on him, and he began to feel the knives stuck into him from all sides, he gave a war whoop and laughed, and said, "Only now I begin to think that I am fighting." All the time he was cutting and stabbing, jumping backward and forward, and all the time laughing. When he was dead, there were fifteen dead Crees lying about the earthworks. E-kūs´-kini body was cut into small pieces and scattered all over the country, so that he might not come to life again.

III

That morning, before it was daylight, the two Sarcees who had hidden in the willows left their hiding-place and made their way to the Blackfoot camp. When they got there, they told that when they had left the Cree camp E-kūs´-kini was surrounded, and the firing was terrible. When E-kūs´-kini's father heard this, he got on his horse and rode through the camp, calling out: "My boy is surrounded; let us turn out and go to help him. I have no doubt they are many tens to one, but he is powerful, and he may be fighting yet." No time was lost in getting ready, and soon a large party started for the Cree camp. When they came to the battle-ground, the camp had been moved a long time. The old man looked about, trying to gather up his son's body, but it was found only in small pieces, and not more than half of it could be gathered up.

After the fight was over, the Crees started on down to go to their own country. One day six Crees were travelling along on foot, scouting far ahead. As they were going down into a little ravine, a grizzly bear jumped up in front of them and ran after them. The bear overtook, and tore up, five of them, one after another. The sixth got away, and came home to camp. The Crees and the Blackfeet believe that this was the spirit of E-kūs´-kini, for thus he comes back. They think that he is still on the earth, but in a different shape.

E-kūs´-kini was killed about forty years ago. When he was killed, he was still a boy, not married, only about twenty-four years old.

STORIES OF ANCIENT TIMES

SCARFACE
ORIGIN OF THE MEDICINE LODGE
I

In the earliest times there was no war. All the tribes were at peace. In those days there was a man who had a daughter, a very beautiful girl. Many young men wanted to marry her, but every time she was asked, she only shook her head and said she did not want a husband.

"How is this?" asked her father. "Some of these young men are rich, handsome, and brave."

"Why should I marry?" replied the girl. "I have a rich father and mother. Our lodge is good. The parfleches are never empty. There are plenty of tanned robes and soft furs for winter. Why worry me, then?"

The Raven Bearers held a dance; they all dressed carefully and wore their ornaments, and each one tried to dance the best. Afterwards some of them asked for this girl, but still she said no. Then the Bulls, the Kit-foxes, and others of the *I-kun-uh´-kah-tsi* held their dances, and all those who were rich, many great warriors, asked this man for his daughter, but to every one of them she said no. Then her father was angry, and said: "Why, now, this way? All the best men have asked for you, and still you say no. I believe you have a secret lover."

"Ah!" said her mother. "What shame for us should a child be born and our daughter still unmarried!" "Father! mother!" replied the girl, "pity me. I have no secret lover, but now hear the truth. That Above Person, the Sun, told me, 'Do not marry any of those men, for you are mine; thus you shall be happy, and live to great age'; and again he said, 'Take heed. You must not marry. You are mine.'"

"Ah!" replied her father. "It must always be as he says." And they talked no more about it.

There was a poor young man, very poor. His father, mother, all his relations, had gone to the Sand Hills. He had no lodge, no wife to tan his robes or sew his moccasins. He stopped in one lodge to-day, and to-morrow he ate and slept in another; thus he lived. He was a good-looking young man, except that on his cheek he had a scar, and his clothes were always old and poor.

After those dances some of the young men met this poor Scarface, and they laughed at him, and said: "Why don't you ask that girl to marry you? You are so rich and handsome!" Scarface did not laugh; he replied: "Ah! I will do as you say. I will go and ask her." All the young men thought this was funny. They laughed a great deal. But Scarface went down by the river. He waited by the river, where the women came to get water, and by and by the girl came along. "Girl," he said, "wait. I want to speak with you. Not as a designing person do I ask you, but openly where the Sun looks down, and all may see."

"Speak then," said the girl.

"I have seen the days," continued the young man "You have refused those who are young, and rich, and brave. Now, to-day, they laughed and said to me, 'Why do you not ask her?' I am poor, very poor. I have no lodge, no food, no clothes, no robes and warm furs. I have no relations; all have gone to the Sand Hills; yet, now, to-day, I ask you, take pity, be my wife."

The girl hid her face in her robe and brushed the ground with the point of her moccasin, back and forth, back and forth; for she was thinking. After a time she said: "True. I have refused all those rich young men, yet now the poor one asks me, and I am glad. I will be your wife, and my people will be happy. You are poor, but it does not matter. My father will give you dogs. My mother will make us a lodge. My people will give us robes and furs. You will be poor no longer."

Then the young man was happy, and he started to kiss her, but she held him back, and said: "Wait! The Sun has spoken to me. He says I may not marry; that I belong to him. He says if I listen to him, I shall live to great age. But now I say: Go to the Sun. Tell him, 'She whom you spoke with heeds your words. She has never done wrong, but now she wants to marry. I want her for my wife.' Ask him to take that scar from your face. That will be his sign. I will know he is pleased. But if he refuses, or if you fail to find his lodge, then do not return to me."

"Oh!" cried the young man, "at first your words were good. I was glad. But now it is dark. My heart is dead. Where is that far-off lodge? where the trail, which no one yet has travelled?"

"Take courage, take courage!" said the girl; and she went to her lodge.

II

Scarface was very sad. He sat down and covered his head with his robe and tried to think what to do. After a while he got up, and went to an old woman who had been kind to him. "Pity me," he said. "I am very poor. I am going away now on a long journey. Make me some moccasins."

"Where are you going?" asked the old woman. "There is no war; we are very peaceful here."

"I do not know where I shall go," replied Scarface. "I am in trouble, but I cannot tell you now what it is."

So the old woman made him some moccasins, seven pairs, with parfleche soles, and also she gave him a sack of food,—pemmican of berries, pounded meat, and dried back fat; for this old woman had a good heart. She liked the young man.

All alone, and with a sad heart, he climbed the bluffs and stopped to take a last look at the camp. He wondered if he would ever see his sweetheart and the people again. " *Hai'-yu!* Pity me, O Sun," he prayed, and turning, he started to find the trail.

For many days he travelled on, over great prairies, along timbered rivers and among the mountains, and every day his sack of food grew lighter; but he saved it as much as he could, and ate berries, and roots, and sometimes he killed an animal of some kind. One night he stopped by the home of a wolf. "*Hai-yah!*" said that one; "what is my brother doing so far from home?"

"Ah!" replied Scarface, "I seek the place where the Sun lives; I am sent to speak with him."

"I have travelled far," said the wolf. "I know all the prairies, the valleys, and the mountains, but I have never seen the Sun's home. Wait; I know one who is very wise. Ask the bear. He may tell you."

The next day the man travelled on again, stopping now and then to pick a few berries, and when night came he arrived at the bear's lodge.

"Where is your home?" asked the bear. "Why are you travelling alone, my brother?"

"Help me! Pity me!" replied the young man; "because of her words I seek the Sun. I go to ask him for her."

"I know not where he stops," replied the bear. "I have travelled by many rivers, and I know the mountains, yet I have never seen his lodge. There is some one beyond, that striped-face, who is very smart. Go and ask him."

The badger was in his hole. Stooping over, the young man shouted: "Oh, cunning striped-face! Oh, generous animal! I wish to speak with you."

"What do you want?" said the badger, poking his head out of the hole.

"I want to find the Sun's home," replied Scarface. "I want to speak with him."

"I do not know where he lives," replied the badger. "I never travel very far. Over there in the timber is a wolverine. He is always travelling around, and is of much knowledge. Maybe he can tell you."

Then Scarface went to the woods and looked all around for the wolverine, but could not find him. So he sat down to rest *"Hai'-yu! Hai'-yu!"* he cried. "Wolverine, take pity on me. My food is gone, my moccasins worn out. Now I must die."

"What is it, my brother?" he heard, and looking around, he saw the animal sitting near.

"She whom I would marry," said Scarface, "belongs to the Sun; I am trying to find where he lives, to ask him for her."

"Ah!" said the wolverine. "I know where he lives. Wait; it is nearly night. To-morrow I will show you the trail to the big water. He lives on the other side of it."

Early in the morning, the wolverine showed him the trail, and Scarface followed it until he came to the water's edge. He looked out over it, and his heart almost stopped. Never before had any one seen such a big water. The other side could not be seen, and there was no end to it. Scarface sat down on the shore. His food was all gone, his moccasins worn out. His heart was sick. "I cannot cross this big water," he said. "I cannot return to the people. Here, by this water, I shall die."

Not so. His Helpers were there. Two swans came swimming up to the shore. "Why have you come here?" they asked him. "What are you doing? It is very far to the place where your people live."

"I am here," replied Scarface, "to die. Far away, in my country, is a beautiful girl. I want to marry her, but she belongs to the Sun. So I started to find him and ask for her. I have travelled many days. My food is gone. I cannot go back. I cannot cross this big water, so I am going to die."

"No," said the swans; "it shall not be so. Across this water is the home of that Above Person. Get on our backs, and we will take you there."

Scarface quickly arose. He felt strong again. He waded out into the water and lay down on the swans' backs, and they started off. Very deep and black is that fearful water. Strange people live there, mighty animals which often seize and drown a person. The swans carried him safely, and took him to the other side. Here was a broad hard trail leading back from the water's edge.

"*Kyi*" said the swans. "You are now close to the Sun's lodge. Follow that trail, and you will soon see it."

III

Scarface started up the trail, and pretty soon he came to some beautiful things, lying in it. There was a war shirt, a shield, and a bow and arrows. He had never seen such pretty weapons; but he did not touch them. He walked carefully around them, and travelled on. A little way further on, he met a young man, the handsomest person he had ever seen. His hair was very long, and he wore clothing made of strange skins. His moccasins were sewn with bright colored feathers. The young man said to him, "Did you see some weapons lying on the trail?"

"Yes," replied Scarface; "I saw them."

"But did you not touch them?" asked the young man.

"No; I thought some one had left them there, so I did not take them." "You are not a thief," said the young man. "What is your name?"

"Scarface."

"Where are you going?"

"To the Sun."

"My name," said the young man, "is A-pi-su´-ahts. The Sun is my father; come, I will take you to our lodge. My father is not now at home, but he will come in at night."

Soon they came to the lodge. It was very large and handsome; strange medicine animals were painted on it. Behind, on a tripod, were strange weapons and beautiful clothes—the Sun's. Scarface was ashamed to go in, but Morning Star said, "Do not be afraid, my friend; we are glad you have come."

They entered. One person was sitting there, Ko-ko-mik´-e-is, the Sun's wife, Morning Star's mother. She spoke to Scarface kindly, and gave him something to eat. "Why have you come so far from your people?" she asked.

Then Scarface told her about the beautiful girl he wanted to marry. "She belongs to the Sun," he said. "I have come to ask him for her."

When it was time for the Sun to come home, the Moon hid Scarface under a pile of robes. As soon as the Sun got to the doorway, he stopped, and said, "I smell a person."

"Yes, father," said Morning Star; "a good young man has come to see you. I know he is good, for he found some of my things on the trail and did not touch them."

Then Scarface came out from under the robes, and the Sun entered and sat down. "I am glad you have come to our lodge," he said. "Stay with us as long as you think best. My son is lonesome sometimes; be his friend."

The next day the Moon called Scarface out of the lodge, and said to him: "Go with Morning Star where you please, but never hunt near that big water; do not let him go there. It is the home of great birds which have long sharp bills; they kill people. I have had many sons, but these birds have killed them all. Morning Star is the only one left."

So Scarface stayed there a long time and hunted with Morning Star. One day they came near the water, and saw the big birds.

"Come," said Morning Star; "let us go and kill those birds."

"No, no!" replied Scarface; "we must not go there. Those are very terrible birds; they will kill us."

Morning Star would not listen. He ran towards the water, and Scarface followed. He knew that he must kill the birds and save the boy. If not, the Sun would be angry and might kill him. He ran ahead and met the birds, which were coming towards him to fight, and killed every one of them with his spear: not one was left. Then the young men cut off their heads, and carried them home. Morning Star's mother was glad when they told her what they had done, and showed her the birds' heads. She cried, and called Scarface "my son." When the Sun came home at night, she told him about it, and he too was glad. "My son," he said to Scarface, "I will not forget what you have this day done for me. Tell me now, what can I do for you?"

"*Hai´-yu*" replied Scarface. "*Hai´-yu*, pity me. I am here to ask you for that girl. I want to marry her. I asked her, and she was glad; but she says you own her, that you told her not to marry."

"What you say is true," said the Sun. "I have watched the days, so I know it. Now, then, I give her to you; she is yours. I am glad she has been wise. I know she has never done wrong. The Sun pities good women. They shall live a long time. So shall their husbands and children. Now you will soon go home. Let me tell you something. Be wise and listen: I am the only chief. Everything is mine. I made the earth, the mountains, prairies, rivers, and forests. I made the people and all the animals. This is why I say I alone am the chief. I can never die. True, the winter makes me old and weak, but every summer I grow young again."

Then said the Sun: "What one of all animals is smartest? The raven is, for he always finds food. He is never hungry. Which one of all the animals is most *Nat-o'-ye*? The buffalo is. Of all animals, I like him best. He is for the people. He is your food and your shelter. What part of his body is sacred? The tongue is. That is mine. What else is sacred? Berries are. They are mine too. Come with me and see the world." He took Scarface to the edge of the sky, and they looked down and saw it. It is round and flat, and all around the edge is the jumping-off place [or walls straight down]. Then said the Sun: "When any man is sick or in danger, his wife may promise to build me a lodge, if he recovers. If the woman is pure and true, then I will be pleased and help the man. But if she is bad, if she lies, then I will be angry. You shall build the lodge like the world, round, with walls, but first you must build a sweat house of a hundred sticks. It shall be like the sky [a hemisphere], and half of it shall be painted red. That is me. The other half you will paint black. That is the night."

Further said the Sun: "Which is the best, the heart or the brain? The brain is. The heart often lies, the brain never." Then he told Scarface everything about making the Medicine Lodge, and when he had finished, he rubbed a powerful medicine on his face, and the scar disappeared. Then he gave him two raven feathers, saying: "These are the sign for the girl, that I give her to you. They must always be worn by the husband of the woman who builds a Medicine Lodge."

The young man was now ready to return home. Morning Star and the Sun gave him many beautiful presents. The Moon cried and kissed him, and called him "my son." Then the Sun showed him the short trail. It was the Wolf Road (Milky Way). He followed it, and soon reached the ground.

IV

It was a very hot day. All the lodge skins were raised, and the people sat in the shade. There was a chief, a very generous man, and all day long people kept coming to his lodge to feast and smoke with him. Early in the morning this chief saw a person sitting out on a butte near by, close wrapped in his robe. The chief's friends came and went, the sun reached the middle, and passed on, down towards the mountains. Still this person did not move. When it was almost night, the chief said: "Why does that person sit there so long? The heat has been strong, but he has never eaten nor drunk. He may be a stranger; go and ask him in."

So some young men went up to him, and said: "Why do you sit here in the great heat all day? Come to the shade of the lodges. The chief asks you to feast with him."

Then the person arose and threw off his robe, and they were surprised. He wore beautiful clothes. His bow, shield, and other weapons were of strange make. But they knew his face, although the scar was gone, and they ran ahead, shouting, "The scarface poor young man has come. He is poor no longer. The scar on his face is gone."

All the people rushed out to see him. "Where have you been?" they asked. "Where did you get all these pretty things?" He did not answer. There in the crowd stood that young woman; and taking the two raven feathers from his head, he gave them to her, and said: "The trail was very long, and I nearly died, but by those Helpers, I found his lodge. He is glad. He sends these feathers to you. They are the sign."

Great was her gladness then. They were married, and made the first Medicine Lodge, as the Sun had said. The Sun was glad. He gave them great age. They were never sick. When they were very old, one morning, their children said: "Awake! Rise and eat." They did not move. In the night, in sleep, without pain, their shadows had departed for the Sand Hills.

ORIGIN OF THE I-KUN-UH´-KAH-TSI
I
THE BULL BAND

The people had built a great pis´kun, very high and strong, so that no buffalo could escape; but somehow the buffalo would not jump over the cliff. When driven toward it, they would run nearly to the edge, and then, swerving to the right or left, they would go down the sloping hills and cross the valley in safety. So the people were hungry, and began to starve.

One morning, early, a young woman went to get water, and she saw a herd of buffalo feeding on the prairie, right on the edge of the cliff above the pis´kun. "Oh!" she cried out, "if you will only jump off into the pis´kun, I will marry one of you." This she said for fun, not meaning it, and great was her wonder when she saw the buffalo come jumping, tumbling, falling over the cliff.

Now the young woman was scared, for a big bull with one bound cleared the pis´kun walls and came toward her. "Come," he said, taking hold of her arm. "No, no!" she replied pulling back. "But you said if the buffalo would jump over, you would marry one; see, the pis´kun is filled." And without more talk he led her up over the bluff, and out on to the prairie.

When the people had finished killing the buffalo and cutting up the meat, they missed this young woman, and her relations were very sad, because they could not find her. Then her father took his bow and quiver, and said, "I will go and find her." And he went up over the bluff and out on the prairie.

After he had travelled some distance he came to a wallow, and a little way off saw a herd of buffalo. While sitting by the wallow,—for he was tired—and thinking what he should do, a magpie came and lit near him. "Ha! *Ma-me-at-si-kim-i*," he said, "you are a beautiful bird; help me. Look everywhere as you travel about, and if you see my daughter, tell her, 'Your father waits by the wallow.'" The magpie flew over by the herd of buffalo, and seeing the young woman, he lit on the ground near her, and commenced picking around, turning his head this way and that way, and, when close to her, he said, "Your father waits by the wallow." "Sh-h-h! sh-h-h!" replied the girl, in a whisper, looking around scared, for her bull husband was sleeping near by. "Don't speak so loud. Go back and tell him to wait."

"Your daughter is over there with the buffalo. She says 'wait!'" said the magpie, when he had flown back to the man.

By and by the bull awoke, and said to his wife, "Go and get me some water." Then the woman was glad, and taking a horn from his head she went to the wallow. "Oh, why did you come?" she said to her father. "You will surely be killed."

"I came to take my daughter home; come, let us hurry."

"No, no!" she replied; "not now. They would chase us and kill us. Wait till he sleeps again, and I will try to get away," and, filling the horn with water, she went back.

The bull drank a swallow of the water. "Ha!" said he, "a person is close by here."

"No one," replied the woman; but her heart rose up.

The bull drank a little more, and then he stood up and bellowed, "*Bu-u-u! m-m-ah-oo!*" Oh, fearful sound! Up rose the bulls, raised their short tails and shook them, tossed their great heads, and bellowed back. Then they pawed the dirt, rushed about here and there, and coming to the wallow, found that poor man. There they trampled him with their great hoofs, hooked him and trampled him again, and soon not even a small piece of his body could be seen.

Then his daughter cried, "*Oh! ah! Ni-nah-ah! Oh! ah! Ni-nah-ah!*" (My father! My father!) "Ah!" said her bull husband, "you mourn for your father. You see now how it is with us. We have seen our mothers, fathers, many of our relations, hurled over the rocky walls, and killed for food by your people. But I will pity you. I will give you one chance. If you can bring your father to life, you and he can go back to your people."

Then the woman said to the magpie: "Pity me. Help me now; go and seek in the trampled mud; try and find a little piece of my father's body, and bring it to me."

The magpie flew to the place. He looked in every hole, and tore up the mud with his sharp nose. At last he found something white; he picked the mud from around it, and then pulling hard, he brought out a joint of the backbone, and flew with it back to the woman.

She placed it on the ground, covered it with her robe, and then sang. Removing the robe, there lay her father's body as if just dead. Once more she covered it with the robe and sang, and when she took away the robe, he was breathing, and then he stood up. The buffalo were surprised; the magpie was glad, and flew round and round, making a great noise.

"We have seen strange things this day," said her bull husband. "He whom we trampled to death, even into small pieces, is alive again. The people's medicine is very strong. Now, before you go, we will teach you our dance and our song. You must not forget them." When the dance was over, the bull said: "Go now to your home, and do not forget what you have seen. Teach it to the people. The medicine shall be a bull's head and a robe. All the persons who are to be 'Bulls' shall wear them when they dance."

Great was the joy of the people, when the man returned with his daughter. He called a council of the chiefs, and told them all that had happened. Then the chiefs chose certain young men, and this man taught them the dance and song of the bulls, and told them what the medicine should be. This was the beginning of the *I-kun-uh´-kah-tsi.*

II
THE OTHER BANDS

For a long time the buffalo had not been seen. The pis´kun was useless, and the hunters could find no food for the people. Then a man who had two wives, a daughter, and two sons, said: "I shall not stop here to die. To-morrow we will move toward the mountains, where we shall perhaps find deer and elk, sheep and antelope, or, if not, at least we shall find plenty of beaver and birds. Thus we shall survive."

When morning came, they packed the travois, lashed them on the dogs, and then moved out. It was yet winter, and they travelled slowly. They were weak, and could go but a little way in a day. The fourth night came, and they sat in their lodge, very tired and hungry. No one spoke, for those who are hungry do not care for words. Suddenly the dogs began to bark, and soon, pushing aside the door-curtain, a young man entered.

"*O´kyi!*" said the old man, and he motioned the stranger to a sitting-place.

They looked at this person with surprise and fear, for there was a black wind which had melted the snow, and covered the prairie with water, yet this person's leggings and moccasins were dry. They sat in silence a long time.

Then said he: "Why is this? Why do you not give me some food?"

"Ah!" replied the old man, "you behold those who are truly poor. We have no food. For many days the buffalo did not come in sight, and we shot deer and other animals which people eat, and when all these had been killed, we began to starve. Then said I, 'We will not stay here to starve to death'; and we started for the mountains. This is the fourth night of our travels."

"Ah!" said the young man. "Then your travels are ended. Close by here, we are camped by our pis´kun. Many buffalo have been run in, and our parfleches are filled with dried meat. Wait; I will go and bring you some."

As soon as he went out, they began to talk about this strange person. They were very much afraid of him, and did not know what to do. The children began to cry, and the women were trying to quiet them, when the young man returned, bringing some meat and three *pis-tsi-ko'-an.*

"*Kyi!*" said he. "To-morrow move over to our lodges. Do not be afraid. No matter what strange things you see, do not fear. All will be your friends. Now, one thing I caution you about. In this be careful. If you should find an arrow lying about, in the pis´kun, or outside, no matter where, do not touch it; neither you, nor your wives nor children." Having said this, he went out.

Then the old man took his pipe and smoked and prayed, saying: "Hear now, Sun! Listen, Above People. Listen, Under Water People. Now you have taken pity. Now you have given us food. We are going to those strange ones, who walk through water with dry moccasins. Protect us among those to-be-feared people. Let us survive. Man, woman, child, give us long life; give us long life!"

Once more the smell of roasting meat. The children played. They talked and laughed who had so long been silent. They ate plenty and lay down and slept.

Early in the morning, as soon as the sun rose, they took down their lodge, packed up, and started for the strange camp. They found it was a wonderful place. There by the pis´kun, and far up and down the valley were the lodges of meat-eaters. They could not see them all, but close by they saw the lodges of the Bear band, the Fox band, and the Badger band. The father of the young man who had given them meat was chief of the Wolf band, and by that band they pitched their lodge. Ah! That was a happy place. Food there was plenty. All day people shouted out for feasts, and everywhere was heard the sound of drums and song and dancing.

The new-comers went to the pis´kun for meat, and one of the children found an arrow lying on the ground. It was a beautiful arrow, the stone point long and sharp, the shaft round and straight. All around the people were busy; no one was looking. The boy picked up the arrow and hid it under his robe. Then there was a fearful noise. All the animals howled and growled, and ran toward him. But the chief Wolf said: "Hold! We will let him go this time; for he is young yet, and not of good sense." So they let him go.

When night came, some one shouted out for a feast, saying: "*Wo´-ka-hit! Wo´-ka-hit! Mah-kwe´-i-ke-tum-ok-ah-wah-hit. Ke-tŭk´-ka-pŭk´-si-pim.*" ("Listen! Listen! Wolf, you are to feast. Enter with your friend.") "We are asked," said the chief Wolf to his new friend, and together they went to the lodge.

Within, the fire burned brightly, and many men were already there, the old and wise of the Raven band. Hanging behind the seats were the writings of many deeds. Food was placed before them,—pemmican of berries and dried back fat; and when they had eaten, a pipe was lighted. Then spoke the Raven chief: "Now, Wolf, I am going to give our new friend a present. What say you?"

"It is as you say," replied the Wolf. "Our new friend will be glad."

Then the Raven chief took from the long parfleche sack a slender stick, beautifully dressed with many colored feathers; and on the end of it was fastened the skin of a raven, head, wings, feet, and all. "We," he said, "are the *Mas-to-pa´-ta-kiks* (Raven carriers, or those who bear the Raven). Of all the above animals, of all the flyers, where is one so smart? None. The Raven's eyes are sharp. His wings are strong. He is a great hunter and never hungry. Far, far off on the prairie he sees his food, and deep hidden in the pines it does not escape his eye. Now the song and the dance."

When he had finished singing and dancing, he gave the stick to the man, and said: "Take it with you, and when you have returned to your people, you shall say: Now there are already the Bulls, and he who is the Raven chief says: 'There shall be more, there shall be the *I-kun-uh´-kah-tsi*, so that the people may survive, and of them shall be the Raven carriers.' You will call a council of the chiefs and wise old men, and they will choose the persons. Teach them the song and the dance, and give them the medicine. It shall be theirs forever."

Soon they heard another person shouting for a feast, and, going, they entered the lodge of the *Sin´-o-pah* chief. Here, too, were the old men assembled. After they had eaten of that set before them, the chief said: "Those among whom you are newly arrived are generous. They do not look at their possessions, but give to the stranger and pity the poor. The Kit-fox is a little animal, but what one is smarter? None. His hair is like the dead prairie grass. His eyes are sharp, his feet noiseless, his brain cunning. His ears receive the far-off sound. Here is our medicine, take it." And he gave the stick. It was long, crooked at one end, wound with fur, and tied here and there to it were eagle feathers. At the end was a fox's skin. Again the chief said: "Hear our song. Do not forget it; and the dance, too, you must remember. When you get home, teach them to the people."

Again they heard the feast shout, and he who called was the Bear chief. Now when they had smoked, the chief said: "What say you, friend Wolf? Shall we give our new friend something?"

"As you say," replied the Wolf. "It is yours to give."

Then said the Bear: "There are many animals, and some of them are powerful. But the Bear is the strongest and bravest of all. He fears nothing, and is always ready to fight." Then he put on a necklace of bear claws, a belt of bear fur, and around his head a band of the fur; and sang and danced. When he had finished, he gave them to the man, saying: "Teach the people our song and dance, and give them this medicine. It is powerful."

It was now very late. The Seven Persons had arrived at midnight, yet again they heard the feast shout from the far end of camp. In this lodge the men were painted with streaks of red and their hair was all brushed to one side. After the feast the chief said: "We are different from all the others here. We are called the *Mūt'-siks* We are death. We know not fear. Even if our enemies are in number like the grass, we do not turn away, but fight and conquer. Bows are good weapons. Spears are better, but our weapon is the knife." Then the chief sang and danced, and afterwards he gave the Wolf's friend the medicine. It was a long knife, and many scalps were tied on the handle. "This," he said, "is for the *I-kun-uh'-kah-tsi.*"

Once more they were called to a feast and entered the Badger chief's lodge. He taught the man the Badger song and dance and gave him the medicine. It was a large rattle, ornamented with beaver claws and bright feathers. They smoked two pipes in the Badger's lodge, and then went home and slept.

Early next day, the man and his family took down their lodge, and prepared to move camp. Many women came and made them presents of dried meat, pemmican, and berries. They were given so much they could not take it all with them. It was many days before they joined the main camp, for the people, too, had moved to the south after buffalo. As soon as the lodge was pitched, the man called all the chiefs to come and feast, and he told them all he had seen, and showed them the medicines. The chiefs chose certain young men for the different bands, and this man taught them the songs and dances, and gave each band their medicine.

ORIGIN OF THE MEDICINE PIPE

Thunder—you have heard him, he is everywhere. He roars in the mountains, he shouts far out on the prairie. He strikes the high rocks, and they fall to pieces. He hits a tree, and it is broken in slivers. He strikes the people, and they die. He is bad. He does not like the towering cliff, the standing tree, or living man. He likes to strike and crush them to the ground. Yes! yes! Of all he is most powerful; he is the one most strong. But I have not told you the worst: he sometimes steals women.

Long ago, almost in the beginning, a man and his wife were sitting in their lodge, when Thunder came and struck them. The man was not killed. At first he was as if dead, but after a while he lived again, and rising looked about him. His wife was not there. "Oh, well," he thought, "she has gone to get some water or wood," and he sat a while; but when the sun had under-disappeared, he went out and inquired about her of the people. No one had seen her. He searched throughout the camp, but did not find her. Then he knew that Thunder had stolen her, and he went out on the hills alone and mourned.

When morning came, he rose and wandered far away, and he asked all the animals he met if they knew where Thunder lived. They laughed, and would not answer. The Wolf said: "Do you think we would seek the home of the only one we fear? He is our only danger. From all others we can run away; but from him there is no running. He strikes, and there we lie. Turn back! go home! Do not look for the dwelling-place of that dreadful one." But the man kept on, and travelled far away. Now he came to a lodge,—a queer lodge, for it was made of stone; just like any other lodge, only it was made of stone. Here lived the Raven chief. The man entered.

"Welcome, my friend," said the chief of Ravens. "Sit down, sit down." And food was placed before him.

Then, when he had finished eating, the Raven said, "Why have you come?"

"Thunder has stolen my wife," replied the man. "I seek his dwelling-place that I may find her."

"Would you dare enter the lodge of that dreadful person?" asked the Raven. "He lives close by here. His lodge is of stone, like this; and hanging there, within, are eyes,—the eyes of those he has killed or stolen. He has taken out their eyes and hung them in his lodge. Now, then, dare you enter there?"

"No," replied the man. "I am afraid. What man could look at such dreadful things and live?"

"No person can," said the Raven. "There is but one old Thunder fears. There is but one he cannot kill. It is I, it is the Ravens. Now I will give you medicine, and he shall not harm you. You shall enter there, and seek among those eyes your wife's; and if you find them, tell that Thunder why you came, and make him give them to you. Here, now, is a raven's wing. Just point it at him, and he will start back quick; but if that fail, take this. It is an arrow, and the shaft is made of elk-horn. Take this, I say, and shoot it through the lodge."

"Why make a fool of me?" the poor man asked. "My heart is sad. I am crying." And he covered his head with his robe, and wept.

"Oh," said the Raven, "you do not believe me. Come out, come out, and I will make you believe." When they stood outside, the Raven asked, "Is the home of your people far?"

"A great distance," said the man.

"Can you tell how many days you have travelled?"

"No," he replied, "my heart is sad. I did not count the days. The berries have grown and ripened since I left."

"Can you see your camp from here?" asked the Raven.

The man did not speak. Then the Raven rubbed some medicine on his eyes and said, "Look!" The man looked, and saw the camp. It was close. He saw the people. He saw the smoke rising from the lodges.

"Now you will believe," said the Raven. "Take now the arrow and the wing, and go and get your wife."

So the man took these things, and went to the Thunder's lodge. He entered and sat down by the door-way. The Thunder sat within and looked at him with awful eyes. But the man looked above, and saw those many pairs of eyes. Among them were those of his wife.

"Why have you come?" said the Thunder in a fearful voice.

"I seek my wife," the man replied, "whom you have stolen. There hang her eyes."

"No man can enter my lodge and live," said the Thunder; and he rose to strike him. Then the man pointed the raven wing at the Thunder, and he fell back on his couch and shivered. But he soon recovered, and rose again. Then the man fitted the elk-horn arrow to his bow, and shot it through the lodge of rock; right through that lodge of rock it pierced a jagged hole, and let the sunlight in.

"Hold," said the Thunder. "Stop; you are the stronger. Yours the great medicine. You shall have your wife. Take down her eyes."

Then the man cut the string that held them, and immediately his wife stood beside him.

"Now," said the Thunder, "you know me. I am of great power. I live here in summer, but when winter comes, I go far south. I go south with the birds. Here is my pipe. It is medicine. Take it, and keep it. Now, when I first come in the spring, you shall fill and light this pipe, and you shall pray to me, you and the people. For I bring the rain which makes the berries large and ripe. I bring the rain which makes all things grow, and for this you shall pray to me, you and all the people."

Thus the people got the first medicine pipe. It was long ago.

THE BEAVER MEDICINE

This story goes back many years, to a time before the Indians went to war against each other. Then there was peace among all the tribes. They met, and did not kill each other. They had no guns and they had no horses. When two tribes met, the head chiefs would take each a stick and touch each other. Each had counted a *coup* on the other, and they then went back to their camps. It was more a friendly than a hostile ceremony.

Oftentimes, when a party of young men had gone to a strange camp, and had done this to those whom they had visited, they would come back to their homes and would tell the girls whom they loved that they had counted a *coup* on this certain tribe of people. After the return of such a party, the young women would have a dance. Each one would wear clothing like that of the man she loved, and as she danced, she would count a *coup*, saying that she herself had done the deed which her young lover had really done. Such was the custom of the people.

There was a chief in a camp who had three wives, all very pretty women. He used to say to these women, whenever a dance was called: "Why do not you go out and dance too? Perhaps you have some one in the camp that you love, and for whom you would like to count a *coup*" Then the women would say, "No, we do not wish to join the dance; we have no lovers."

There was in the camp a poor young man, whose name was Ápi-kŭnni. He had no relations, and no one to tan robes or furs for him, and he was always badly clad and in rags. Whenever he got some clothing, he wore it as long as it would hold together. This young man loved the youngest wife of the chief, and she loved him. But her parents were not rich, and they could not give her to Ápi-kŭnni, and when the chief wanted her for a wife, they gave her to him. Sometimes Ápi-kŭnni and this girl used to meet and talk together, and he used to caution her, saying, "Now be careful that you do not tell any one that you see me." She would say, "No, there is no danger; I will not let it be known."

One evening, a dance was called for the young women to dance, and the chief said to his wives: "Now, women, you had better go to this dance. If any of you have persons whom you love, you might as well go and dance for them." Two of them said: "No, we will not go. There is no one that we love." But the third said, "Well, I think I will go and dance." The chief said to her, "Well, go then; your lover will surely dress you up for the dance."

The girl went to where Ápi-kŭnni as living in an old woman's lodge, very poorly furnished, and told him what she was going to do, and asked him to dress her for the dance. He said to her: "Oh, you have wronged me by coming here, and by going to the dance. I told you to keep it a secret." The girl said: "Well, never mind; no one will know your dress. Fix me up, and I will go and join the dance anyway." "Why," said Api-kŭnni, "I never have been to war. I have never counted any *coups*. You will go and dance and will have nothing to say. The people will laugh at you." But when he found that the girl wanted to go, he painted her forehead with red clay, and tied a goose skin, which he had, about her head, and lent her his badly tanned robe, which in spots was hard like a parfleche. He said to her, "If you will go to the dance, say, when it comes your turn to speak, that when the water in the creeks gets warm, you are going to war, and are going to count a *coup* on some people."

The woman went to the dance, and joined in it. All the people were laughing at her on account of her strange dress,—a goose skin around her head, and a badly tanned robe about her. The people in the dance asked her: "Well, what are you dancing for? What can you tell?" The woman said, "I am dancing here to-day, and when the water in the streams gets warm next spring, I am going to war; and then I will tell you what I have done to any people." The chief was standing present, and when he learned who it was that his young wife loved, he was much ashamed and went to his lodge.

When the dance was over, this young woman went to the lodge of the poor young man to give back his dress to him. Now, while she had been gone, Ápi-kŭnni had been thinking over all these things, and he was very much ashamed. He took his robe and his goose skin and went away. He was so ashamed that he went away at once, travelling off over the prairie, not caring where he went, and crying all the time. As he wandered away, he came to a lake, and at the foot of this lake was a beaver dam, and by the dam a beaver house. He walked out on the dam and on to the beaver house. There he stopped and sat down, and in his shame cried the rest of the day, and at last he fell asleep on the beaver house.

While he slept, he dreamed that a beaver came to him—a very large beaver—and said: "My poor young man, come into my house. I pity you, and will give you something that will help you." So Ápi-kŭnni got up, and followed the beaver into the house. When he was in the house, he awoke, and saw sitting opposite him a large white beaver, almost as big as a man. He thought to himself, "This must be the chief of all the beavers, white because very old." The beaver was singing a song. It was a very strange song, and he sang it a long time. Then he said to Ápi-kŭnni, "My son, why are you mourning?" and the young man told him everything that had happened, and how he had been shamed. Then the beaver said: "My son, stay here this winter with me. I will provide for you. When the time comes, and you have learned our songs and our ways, I will let you go. For a time make this your home." So Ápi-kŭnni stayed there with the beaver, and the beaver taught him many strange things. All this happened in the fall.

Now the chief in the camp missed this poor young man, and he asked the people where he had gone. No one knew. They said that the last that had been seen of him he was travelling toward the lake where the beaver dam was.

Ápi-kŭnni had a friend, another poor young man named Wolf Tail, and after a while, Wolf Tail started out to look for his friend. He went toward this lake, looking everywhere, and calling out his name. When he came to the beaver house, he kicked on the top and called, "Oh, my brother, are you here?" Ápi-kŭnni answered him, and said: "Yes, I am here. I was brought in while I was asleep, and I cannot give you the secret of the door, for I do not know it myself." Wolf Tail said to him, "Brother, when the weather gets warm a party is going to start from camp to war." Ápi-kŭnni said: "Go home and try to get together all the moccasins you can, but do not tell them that I am here. I am ashamed to go back to the camp. When the party starts, come this way and bring me the moccasins, and we two will start from here." He also said: "I am very thin. The beaver food here does not agree with me. We are living on the bark of willows." Wolf Tail went back to the camp and gathered together all the moccasins that he could, as he had been asked to do.

When the spring came, and the grass began to start, the war party set out. At this time the beaver talked to Ápi-kŭnni a long time, and told him many things. He dived down into the water, and brought up a long stick of aspen wood, cut off from it a piece as long as a man's arm, trimmed the twigs off it, and gave it to the young man. "Keep this," the beaver said, "and when you go to war take it with you." The beaver also gave him a little sack of medicine, and told him what he must do.

When the party started out, Wolf Tail came to the beaver house, bringing the moccasins, and his friend came out of the house. They started in the direction the party had taken and travelled with them, but off to one side. When they stopped at night, the two young men camped by themselves.

They travelled for many days, until they came to Bow River, and found that it was very high. On the other side of the river, they saw the lodges of a camp. In this camp a man was making a speech, and Api-kŭnni said to his friend, "Oh, my brother, I am going to kill that man to-day, so that my sweetheart may count *coup* on him." These two were at a little distance from the main party, above them on the river. The people in the camp had seen the Blackfeet, and some had come down to the river. When Api-kunni had said this to Wolf Tail, he took his clothes off and began to sing the song the beaver had taught him. This was the song:—

I am like an island,
For on an island I got my power.
In battle I live
While people fall away from me.

While he sang this, he had in his hand the stick which the beaver had given him. This was his only weapon.

He ran to the bank, jumped in and dived, and came up in the middle of the river, and started to swim across. The rest of the Blackfeet saw one of their number swimming across the river, and they said to each other: "Who is that? Why did not some one stop him?" While he was swimming across, the man who had been making the speech saw him and went down to meet him. He said: "Who can this man be, swimming across the river? He is a stranger. I will go down and meet him, and kill him." As the boy was getting close to the shore, the man waded out in the stream up to his waist, and raised his knife to stab the swimmer. When Ápi-kŭnni got near him, he dived under the water and came up close to the man, and thrust the beaver stick through his body, and the man fell down in the water and died. Ápi-kŭnni caught the body, and dived under the water with it, and came up on the other side where he had left his friend. Then all the Blackfeet set up the war whoop, for they were glad, and they could hear a great crying in the camp. The people there were sorry for the man who was killed.

People in those days never killed one another, and this was the first man ever killed in war.

They dragged the man up on the bank, and Ápi-kŭnni said to his brother, "Cut off those long hairs on the head." The young man did as he was told. He scalped him and counted *coup* on him; and from that time forth, people, when they went to war, killed one another and scalped the dead enemy, as this poor young man had done. Two others of the main party came to the place, and counted *coup* on the dead body, making four who had counted *coup*. From there, the whole party turned about and went back to the village whence they had come.

When they came in sight of the lodges, they sat down in a row facing the camp. The man who had killed the enemy was sitting far in front of the others. Behind him sat his friend, and behind Wolf Tail, sat the two who had counted *coup* on the body. So these four were strung out in front of the others. The chief of the camp was told that some people were sitting on a hill near by, and when he had gone out and looked, he said: "There is some one sitting way in front. Let somebody go out and see about it." A young man ran out to where he could see, and when he had looked, he ran back and said to the chief, "Why, that man in front is the poor young man."

The old chief looked around, and said: "Where is that young woman, my wife? Go and find her." They went to look for her, and found her out gathering rosebuds, for while the young man whom she loved was away, she used to go out and gather rosebuds and dry them for him. When they found her, she had her bosom full of them. When she came to the lodge, the chief said to her: "There is the man you love, who has come. Go and meet him." She made ready quickly and ran out and met him. He said: "Give her that hair of the dead man. Here is his knife. There is the coat he had on, when I killed him. Take these things back to the camp, and tell the people who made fun of you that this is what you promised them at the time of that dance."

The whole party then got up and walked to the camp. The woman took the scalp, knife and coat to the lodge, and gave them to her husband. The chief invited Ápi-kûnni to come to his lodge to visit him. He said: "I see that you have been to war, and that you have done more than any of us have ever done. This is a reason why you should be a chief. Now take my lodge and this woman, and live here. Take my place and rule these people. My two wives will be your servants." When Ápi-kûnni heard this, and saw the young woman sitting there in the lodge, he could not speak. Something seemed to rise up in his throat and choke him.

So this young man lived in the camp and was known as their chief.

After a time, he called his people together in council and told them of the strange things the beaver had taught him, and the power that the beaver had given him. He said: "This will be a benefit to us while we are a people now, and afterward it will be handed down to our children, and if we follow the words of the beaver we will be lucky. This seed the beaver gave me, and told me to plant it every year. When we ask help from the beaver, we will smoke this plant."

This plant was the Indian tobacco, and it is from the beaver that the Blackfeet got it. Many strange things were taught this man by the beaver, which were handed down and are followed till to-day.

THE BUFFALO ROCK

A small stone, which is usually a fossil shell of some kind, is known by the Blackfeet as I-nis´-kim, the buffalo stone. This object is strong medicine, and, as indicated in some of these stories, gives its possessor great power with buffalo. The stone is found on the prairie, and the person who succeeds in obtaining one is regarded as very fortunate. Sometimes a man, who is riding along on the prairie, will hear a peculiar faint chirp, such as a little bird might utter. The sound he knows is made by a buffalo rock. He stops and searches on the ground for the rock, and if he cannot find it, marks the place and very likely returns next day, either alone or with others from the camp, to look for it again. If it is found, there is great rejoicing. How the first buffalo rock was obtained, and its power made known, is told in the following story.

Long ago, in the winter time, the buffalo suddenly disappeared. The snow was so deep that the people could not move in search of them, for in those days they had no horses. So the hunters killed deer, elk, and other small game along the river bottoms, and when these were all killed off or driven away, the people began to starve.

One day, a young married man killed a jack-rabbit. He was so hungry that he ran home as fast as he could, and told one of his wives to hurry and get some water to cook it. While the young woman was going along the path to the river, she heard a beautiful song. It sounded close by, but she looked all around and could see no one. The song seemed to come from a cotton-wood tree near the path. Looking closely at this tree she saw a queer rock jammed in a fork, where the tree was split, and with it a few hairs from a buffalo, which had rubbed there. The woman was frightened and dared not pass the tree. Pretty soon the singing stopped, and the I-nis´-kim [buffalo rock] spoke to the woman and said: "Take me to your lodge, and when it is dark, call in the people and teach them the song you have just heard. Pray, too, that you may not starve, and that the buffalo may come back. Do this, and when day comes, your hearts will be glad."

The woman went on and got some water, and when she came back, took the rock and gave it to her husband, telling him about the song and what the rock had said. As soon as it was dark, the man called the chiefs and old men to his lodge, and his wife taught them this song. They prayed, too, as the rock had said should be done. Before long, they heard a noise far off. It was the tramp of a great herd of buffalo coming. Then they knew that the rock was very powerful, and, ever since that, the people have taken care of it and prayed to it.

[NOTE.—I-nis´-kims are usually small *Ammonites*, or sections of *Baculites,* or sometimes merely oddly shaped nodules of flint. It is said of them that if an I-nis´-kim is wrapped up and left undisturbed for a long time, it will have young ones; two small stones similar in shape to the original one will be found in the package with it.]

ORIGIN OF THE WORM PIPE

There was once a man who was very fond of his wife. After they had been married for some time they had a child, a boy. After that, the woman got sick, and did not get well. The young man did not wish to take a second woman. He loved his wife so much. The woman grew worse and worse. Doctoring did not seem to do her any good. At last she died. The man used to take his baby on his back and travel out, walking over the hills crying. He kept away from the camp. After some time, he said to the little child: "My little boy, you will have to go and live with your grandmother. I am going to try and find your mother, and bring her back." He took the baby to his mother's lodge, and asked her to take care of it, and left it with her. Then he started off, not knowing where he was going nor what he was going to do.

He travelled toward the Sand Hills. The fourth night out he had a dream. He dreamed that he went into a little lodge, in which lived an old woman. This old woman said to him, "Why are you here, my son?" He said: "I am mourning day and night, crying all the while. My little son, who is the only one left me, also mourns." "Well," said the old woman, "for whom are you mourning?" He said: "I am mourning for my wife. She died some time ago. I am looking for her." "Oh!" said the old woman, "I saw her. She passed this way. I myself am not powerful medicine, but over by that far butte lives another old woman. Go to her, and she will give you power to enable you to continue your journey. You could not go there by yourself without help. Beyond the next butte from her lodge, you will find the camp of the ghosts."

The next morning he awoke and went on to the next butte. It took him a long day to get there, but he found no lodge there, so he lay down and went to sleep. Again he dreamed. In his dream, he saw a little lodge, and an old woman came to the door-way and called him. He went in, and she said to him: "My son, you are very poor. I know why you have come this way. You are seeking your wife, who is now in the ghost country. It is a very hard thing for you to get there. You may not be able to get your wife back, but I have great power, and I will do all I can for you. If you do exactly as I tell you, you may succeed." She then spoke to him with wise words, telling him what he should do. Also she gave him a bundle of medicine, which would help him on his journey.

Then she said: "You stay here for a while, and I will go over there [to the ghosts' camp], and try to bring some of your relations; and if I am able to bring them back, you may return with them, but on the way you must shut your eyes. If you should open them and look about you, you would die. Then you would never come back. When you get to the camp, you will pass by a big lodge, and they will say to you, 'Where are you going, and who told you to come here?' You will reply, 'My grandmother, who is standing out here with me, told me to come.' They will try to scare you. They will make fearful noises, and you will see strange and terrible things; but do not be afraid."

Then the old woman went away, and after a time came back with one of the man's relations. He went with this relation to the ghosts' camp. When they came to the big lodge, some one called out and asked the man what he was doing, and he answered as the old woman had told him to do. As he passed on through the camp, the ghosts tried to scare him with all kinds of fearful sights and sounds, but he kept up a brave heart.

He came to another lodge, and the man who owned it came out, and asked him where he was going. He said: "I am looking for my dead wife, I mourn for her so much that I cannot rest. My little boy, too, keeps crying for his mother. They have offered to give me other wives, but I do not want them. I want the one for whom I am searching."

The ghost said to him: "It is a fearful thing that you have come here. It is very likely that you will never go away. There never was a person here before." The ghost asked him to come into the lodge, and he went.

Now this chief ghost said to him: "You will stay here four nights, and you will see your wife; but you must be very careful or you will never go back. You will die right here."

Then the chief went outside and called out for a feast, inviting this man's father-in-law and other relations, who were in the camp, saying, "Your son-in-law invites you to a feast," as if to say that their son-in-law was dead, and had become a ghost, and had arrived at the ghost camp.

Now when these invited people, the relations and some of the principal men of the camp, had reached the lodge, they did not like to go in. They called out, "There is a person here." It seems as if there was something about him that they could not bear the smell of. The ghost chief burned sweet pine in the fire, which took away this smell, and the people came in and sat down. Then the host said to them: "Now pity this son-in-law of yours. He is seeking his wife. Neither the great distance nor the fearful sights that he has seen here have weakened his heart. You can see for yourselves he is tender-hearted. He not only mourns for his wife, but mourns because his little boy is now alone with no mother; so pity him and give him back his wife."

The ghosts consulted among themselves, and one said to the person, "Yes, you will stay here four nights; then we will give you a medicine pipe, the Worm Pipe, and we will give you back your wife, and you may return to your home."

Now, after the third night, the chief ghost called together all the people, and they came, the man's wife with them. One of them came beating a drum; and following him was another ghost, who carried the Worm Pipe, which they gave to him. Then said the chief ghost: "Now, be very careful. Tomorrow you and your wife will start on your homeward journey. Your wife will carry the medicine pipe, and some of your relations are going along with you for four days. During this time, you must not open your eyes, or you will return here and be a ghost forever. You see that your wife is not now a person; but in the middle of the fourth day you will be told to look, and when you have opened your eyes, you will see that your wife has become a person, and that your ghost relations have disappeared."

His father-in-law spoke to him before he went away, and said: "When you get near home, you must not go at once into the camp. Let some of your relations know that you have arrived, and ask them to build a sweat house for you. Go into this sweat house and wash your body thoroughly, leaving no part of it, however small, uncleansed; for if you do you will be nothing [will die]. There is something about us ghosts difficult to remove. It is only by a thorough sweat that you can remove it. Take care, now, that you do as I tell you. Do not whip your wife, nor strike her with a knife, nor hit her with fire; for if you do, she will vanish before your eyes and return to the Sand Hills."

Now they left the ghost country to go home, and on the fourth day, the wife said to her husband, "Open your eyes." He looked about him and saw that those who had been with them had vanished, but he found that they were standing in front of the old woman's lodge by the butte. She came out and said: "Here, give me back those mysterious medicines of mine, which enabled you to accomplish your purpose." He returned them to her, and became then fully a person once more.

Now, when they drew near to the camp, the woman went on ahead, and sat down on a butte. Then some curious persons came out to see who it might be. As they approached, the woman called out to them: "Do not come any nearer. Go tell my mother and my relations to put up a lodge for us, a little way from camp, and to build a sweat house near by it." When this had been done, the man and his wife went in and took a thorough sweat, and then they went into the lodge, and burned sweet grass and purified their clothing and the Worm Pipe; and then their relations and friends came in to see them. The man told them where he had been, and how he had managed to get back his wife, and that the pipe hanging over the door-way was a medicine pipe, the Worm Pipe, presented to him by his ghost father-in-law. That is how the people came to possess the Worm Pipe. This pipe belongs to that band of the Piegans known as *Esk'-sin-i-tŭp'piks,* the Worm People.

Not long after this, in the night, this man told his wife to do something; and when she did not begin at once, he picked up a brand from the fire, not that he intended to strike her with it, but he made as if he would hit her, when all at once she vanished, and was never seen again.

THE GHOSTS' BUFFALO

A long time ago there were four Blackfeet, who went to war against the Crees. They travelled a long way, and at last their horses gave out, and they started back toward their homes. As they were going along they came to the Sand Hills; and while they were passing through them, they saw in the sand a fresh travois trail, where people had been travelling.

One of the men said: "Let us follow this trail until we come up with some of our people. Then we will camp with them." They followed the trail for a long way, and at length one of the Blackfeet, named E-kūs´-kini,—a very powerful person,—said to the others: "Why follow this longer? It is just nothing." The others said: "Not so. These are our people. We will go on and camp with them." They went on, and toward evening, one of them found a stone maul and a dog travois. He said: "Look at these things. I know this maul and this travois. They belonged to my mother, who died. They were buried with her. This is strange." He took the things. When night overtook the men, they camped.

Early in the morning, they heard, all about them, sounds as if a camp of people were there. They heard a young man shouting a sort of war cry, as young men do; women chopping wood; a man calling for a feast, asking people to come to his lodge and smoke,—all the different sounds of the camp. They looked about, but could see nothing; and then they were frightened and covered their heads with their robes. At last they took courage, and started to look around and see what they could learn about this strange thing. For a little while they saw nothing, but pretty soon one of them said: "Look over there. See that pis´kun. Let us go over and look at it." As they were going toward it, one of them picked up a stone pointed arrow. He said: "Look at this. It belonged to my father. This is his place." They started to go on toward the pis´kun, but suddenly they could see no pis´kun. It had disappeared all at once.

A little while after this, one of them spoke up, and said: "Look over there. There is my father running buffalo. There! he has killed. Let us go over to him." They all looked where this man pointed, and they could see a person on a white horse, running buffalo. While they were looking, the person killed the buffalo, and got off his horse to butcher it. They started to go over toward him, and saw him at work butchering, and saw him turn the buffalo over on its back; but before they got to the place where he was, the person got on his horse and rode off, and when they got to where he had been skinning the buffalo, they saw lying on the ground only a dead mouse. There was no buffalo there. By the side of the mouse was a buffalo chip, and lying on it was an arrow painted red. The man said: "That is my father's arrow. That is the way he painted them." He took it up in his hands; and when he held it in his hands, he saw that it was not an arrow but a blade of spear grass. Then he laid it down, and it was an arrow again.

Another Blackfoot found a buffalo rock, I-nis´-kim.

Some time after this, the men got home to their camp. The man who had taken the maul and the dog travois, when he got home and smelled the smoke from the fire, died, and so did his horse. It seems that the shadow of the person who owned the things was angry at him and followed him home. Two others of these Blackfeet have since died, killed in war; but E-kūs´-kini is alive yet. He took a stone and an iron arrow point that had belonged to his father, and always carried them about with him. That is why he has lived so long. The man who took the stone arrow point found near the pis´kun, which had belonged to his father, took it home with him. This was his medicine. After that he was badly wounded in two fights, but he was not killed; he got well.

The one who took the buffalo rock, I-nis´-kim, it afterward made strong to call the buffalo into the pis´kun. He would take the rock and put it in his lodge close to the fire, where he could look at it, and would pray over it and make medicine. Sometimes he would ask for a hundred buffalo to jump into the pis´kun, and the next day a hundred would jump in. He was powerful.

STORIES OF OLD MAN

THE BLACKFOOT GENESIS

All animals of the Plains at one time heard and knew him, and all birds of the air heard and knew him. All things that he had made understood him, when he spoke to them,—the birds, the animals, and the people.

Old Man was travelling about, south of here, making the people. He came from the south, travelling north, making animals and birds as he passed along. He made the mountains, prairies, timber, and brush first. So he went along, travelling northward, making things as he went, putting rivers here and there, and falls on them, putting red paint here and there in the ground,—fixing up the world as we see it to-day. He made the Milk River (the Teton) and crossed it, and, being tired, went up on a little hill and lay down to rest. As he lay on his back, stretched out on the ground, with arms extended, he marked himself out with stones,—the shape of his body, head, legs, arms, and everything. There you can see those rocks to-day. After he had rested, he went on northward, and stumbled over a knoll and fell down on his knees. Then he said, "You are a bad thing to be stumbling against"; so he raised up two large buttes there, and named them the Knees, and they are called so to this day. He went on further north, and with some of the rocks he carried with him he built the Sweet Grass Hills.

Old Man covered the plains with grass for the animals to feed on. He marked off a piece of ground, and in it he made to grow all kinds of roots and berries,—camas, wild carrots, wild turnips, sweet-root, bitter-root, sarvis berries, bull berries, cherries, plums, and rosebuds. He put trees in the ground. He put all kinds of animals on the ground. When he made the bighorn with its big head and horns, he made it out on the prairie. It did not seem to travel easily on the prairie; it was awkward and could not go fast. So he took it by one of its horns, and led it up into the mountains, and turned it loose; and it skipped about among the rocks, and went up fearful places with ease. So he said, "This is the place that suits you; this is what you are fitted for, the rocks and the mountains." While he was in the mountains, he made the antelope out of dirt, and turned it loose, to see how it would go. It ran so fast that it fell over some rocks and hurt itself. He saw that this would not do, and took the antelope down on the prairie, and turned it loose; and it ran away fast and gracefully, and he said, "This is what you are suited to."

One day Old Man determined that he would make a woman and a child; so he formed them both—the woman and the child, her son—of clay. After he had moulded the clay in human shape, he said to the clay, "You must be people," and then he covered it up and left it, and went away. The next morning he went to the place and took the covering off, and saw that the clay shapes had changed a little. The second morning there was still more change, and the third still more. The fourth morning he went to the place, took the covering off, looked at the images, and told them to rise and walk; and they did so. They walked down to the river with their Maker, and then he told them that his name was *Na'pi,* Old Man.

As they were standing by the river, the woman said to him, "How is it? will we always live, will there be no end to it?" He said: "I have never thought of that. We will have to decide it. I will take this buffalo chip and throw it in the river. If it floats, when people die, in four days they will become alive again; they will die for only four days. But if it sinks, there will be an end to them." He threw the chip into the river, and it floated. The woman turned and picked up a stone, and said: "No, I will throw this stone in the river; if it floats we will always live, if it sinks people must die, that they may always be sorry for each other." The woman threw the stone into the water, and it sank. "There," said Old Man, "you have chosen. There will be an end to them."

It was not many nights after, that the woman's child died, and she cried a great deal for it. She said to Old Man: "Let us change this. The law that you first made, let that be a law." He said: "Not so. What is made law must be law. We will undo nothing that we have done. The child is dead, but it cannot be changed. People will have to die."

That is how we came to be people. It is he who made us.

The first people were poor and naked, and did not know how to get a living. Old Man showed them the roots and berries, and told them that they could eat them; that in a certain month of the year they could peel the bark off some trees and eat it, that it was good. He told the people that the animals should be their food, and gave them to the people, saying, "These are your herds." He said: "All these little animals that live in the ground—rats, squirrels, skunks, beavers—are good to eat. You need not fear to eat of their flesh." He made all the birds that fly, and told the people that there was no harm in their flesh, that it could be eaten. The first people that he created he used to take about through the timber and swamps and over the prairies, and show them the different plants. Of a certain plant he would say, "The root of this plant, if gathered in a certain month of the year, is good for a certain sickness." So they learned the power of all herbs.

In those days there were buffalo. Now the people had no arms, but those black animals with long beards were armed; and once, as the people were moving about, the buffalo saw them, and ran after them, and hooked them, and killed and ate them. One day, as the Maker of the people was travelling over the country, he saw some of his children, that he had made, lying dead, torn to pieces and partly eaten by the buffalo. When he saw this he was very sad. He said: "This will not do. I will change this. The people shall eat the buffalo."

He went to some of the people who were left, and said to them, "How is it that you people do nothing to these animals that are killing you?" The people said: "What can we do? We have no way to kill these animals, while they are armed and can kill us." Then said the Maker: "That is not hard. I will make you a weapon that will kill these animals." So he went out, and cut some sarvis berry shoots, and brought them in, and peeled the bark off them. He took a larger piece of wood, and flattened it, and tied a string to it, and made a bow. Now, as he was the master of all birds and could do with them as he wished, he went out and caught one, and took feathers from its wing, and split them, and tied them to the shaft of wood. He tied four feathers along the shaft, and tried the arrow at a mark, and found that it did not fly well. He took these feathers off, and put on three; and when he tried it again, he found that it was good. He went out and began to break sharp pieces off the stones. He tried them, and found that the black flint stones made the best arrow points, and some white flints. Then he taught the people how to use these things.

Then he said: "The next time you go out, take these things with you, and use them as I tell you, and do not run from these animals. When they run at you, as soon as they get pretty close, shoot the arrows at them, as I have taught you; and you will see that they will run from you or will run in a circle around you."

Now, as people became plenty, one day three men went out on to the plain to see the buffalo, but they had no arms. They saw the animals, but when the buffalo saw the men, they ran after them and killed two of them, but one got away. One day after this, the people went on a little hill to look about, and the buffalo saw them, and said, "*Saiyah*, there is some more of our food," and they rushed on them. This time the people did not run. They began to shoot at the buffalo with the bows and arrows *Na'pi* had given them, and the buffalo began to fall; but in the fight a person was killed.

At this time these people had flint knives given them, and they cut up the bodies of the dead buffalo. It is not healthful to eat the meat raw, so Old Man gathered soft dry rotten driftwood and made punk of it, and then got a piece of hard wood, and drilled a hole in it with an arrow point, and gave them a pointed piece of hard wood, and taught them how to make a fire with fire sticks, and to cook the flesh of these animals and eat it.

They got a kind of stone that was in the land, and then took another harder stone and worked one upon the other, and hollowed out the softer one, and made a kettle of it. This was the fashion of their dishes.

Also Old Man said to the people: "Now, if you are overcome, you may go and sleep, and get power. Something will come to you in your dream, that will help you. Whatever these animals tell you to do, you must obey them, as they appear to you in your sleep. Be guided by them. If anybody wants help, if you are alone and travelling, and cry aloud for help, your prayer will be answered. It may be by the eagles, perhaps by the buffalo, or by the bears. Whatever animal answers your prayer, you must listen to him."

That was how the first people got through the world, by the power of their dreams.

After this, Old Man kept on, travelling north. Many of the animals that he had made followed him as he went. The animals understood him when he spoke to them, and he used them as his servants. When he got to the north point of the Porcupine Mountains, there he made some more mud images of people, and blew breath upon them, and they became people. He made men and women. They asked him, "What are we to eat?" He made many images of clay, in the form of buffalo. Then he blew breath on these, and they stood up; and when he made signs to them, they started to run. Then he said to the people, "Those are your food." They said to him, "Well, now, we have those animals; how are we to kill them?" "I will show you," he said. He took them to the cliff, and made them build rock piles like this, >; and he made the people hide behind these piles of rock, and said, "When I lead the buffalo this way, as I bring them opposite to you, rise up."

After he had told them how to act, he started on toward a herd of buffalo. He began to call them, and the buffalo started to run toward him, and they followed him until they were inside the lines. Then he dropped back; and as the people rose up, the buffalo ran in a straight line and jumped over the cliff. He told the people to go and take the flesh of those animals. They tried to tear the limbs apart, but they could not. They tried to bite pieces out, and could not. So Old Man went to the edge of the cliff, and broke some pieces of stone with sharp edges, and told them to cut the flesh with these. When they had taken the skins from these animals, they set up some poles and put the hides on them, and so made a shelter to sleep under. There were some of these buffalo that went over the cliff that were not dead. Their legs were broken, but they were still alive. The people cut strips of green hide, and tied stones in the middle, and made large mauls, and broke in the skulls of the buffalo, and killed them.

After he had taught those people these things, he started off again, travelling north, until he came to where Bow and Elbow rivers meet. There he made some more people, and taught them the same things. From here he again went on northward. When he had come nearly to the Red Deer's River, he reached the hill where the Old Man sleeps. There he lay down and rested himself. The form of his body is to be seen there yet.

When he awoke from his sleep, he travelled further northward and came to a fine high hill. He climbed to the top of it, and there sat down to rest. He looked over the country below him, and it pleased him. Before him the hill was steep, and he said to himself, "Well, this is a fine place for sliding; I will have some fun," and he began to slide down the hill. The marks where he slid down are to be seen yet, and the place is known to all people as the "Old Man's Sliding Ground."

This is as far as the Blackfeet followed Old Man. The Crees know what he did further north.

In later times once, *Na'pi* said, "Here I will mark you off a piece of ground," and he did so. Then he said: "There is your land, and it is full of all kinds of animals, and many things grow in this land. Let no other people come into it. This is for you five tribes (Blackfeet, Bloods, Piegans, Gros Ventres, Sarcees). When people come to cross the line, take your bows and arrows, your lances and your battle axes, and give them battle and keep them out. If they gain a footing, trouble will come to you."

Our forefathers gave battle to all people who came to cross these lines, and kept them out. Of late years we have let our friends, the white people, come in, and you know the result. We, his children, have failed to obey his laws.

THE DOG AND THE STICK

This happened long ago. In those days the people were hungry. No buffalo nor antelope were seen on the prairie. The deer and the elk trails were covered with grass and leaves; not even a rabbit could be found in the brush. Then the people prayed, saying: "Oh, Old Man, help us now, or we shall die. The buffalo and deer are gone. Uselessly we kindle the morning fires; useless are our arrows; our knives stick fast in the sheaths."

Then Old Man started out to find the game, and he took with him a young man, the son of a chief. For many days they travelled the prairies and ate nothing but berries and roots. One day they climbed a high ridge, and when they had reached the top, they saw, far off by a stream, a single lodge.

"What kind of a person can it be," said the young man, "who camps there all alone, far from friends?"

"That," said Old Man, "is the one who has hidden all the buffalo and deer from the people. He has a wife and a little son."

Then they went close to the lodge, and Old Man changed himself into a little dog, and he said, "That is I." Then the young man changed himself into a root-digger, and he said, "That is I."

Now the little boy, playing about, found the dog, and he carried it to his father, saying, "Look! See what a pretty little dog I have found."

"Throw it away," said his father; "it is not a dog." And the little boy cried, but his father made him carry the dog away. Then the boy found the root-digger; and, again picking up the dog, he carried them both to the lodge, saying, "Look, mother! see the pretty root-digger I have found!"

"Throw them both away," said his father; "that is not a stick, that is not a dog."

"I want that stick," said the woman; "let our son have the little dog."

"Very well," said her husband, "but remember, if trouble comes, you bring it on yourself and on our son." Then he sent his wife and son off to pick berries; and when they were out of sight, he went out and killed a buffalo cow, and brought the meat into the lodge and covered it up, and the bones, skin and offal he threw in the creek. When his wife returned, he gave her some of the meat to roast; and while they were eating, the little boy fed the dog three times, and when he gave it more, his father took the meat away, saying, "That is not a dog, you shall not feed it more."

In the night, when all were asleep, Old Man and the young man arose in their right shapes, and ate of the meat. "You were right," said the young man; "this is surely the person who has hidden the buffalo from us." "Wait," said Old Man; and when they had finished eating, they changed themselves back into the stick and the dog.

In the morning the man sent his wife and son to dig roots, and the woman took the stick with her. The dog followed the little boy. Now, as they travelled along in search of roots, they came near a cave, and at its mouth stood a buffalo cow. Then the dog ran into the cave, and the stick, slipping from the woman's hand, followed, gliding along like a snake. In this cave they found all the buffalo and other game, and they began to drive them out; and soon the prairie was covered with buffalo and deer. Never before were seen so many.

Pretty soon the man came running up, and he said to his wife, "Who now drives out my animals?" and she replied, "The dog and the stick are now in there." "Did I not tell you," said he, "that those were not what they looked like? See now the trouble you have brought upon us," and he put an arrow on his bow and waited for them to come out. But they were cunning, for when the last animal—a big bull—was about to go out, the stick grasped him by the hair under his neck, and coiled up in it, and the dog held on by the hair beneath, until they were far out on the prairie, when they changed into their true shapes, and drove the buffalo toward camp.

When the people saw the buffalo coming, they drove a big band of them to the pis'kun; but just as the leaders were about to jump off, a raven came and flapped its wings in front of them and croaked, and they turned off another way. Every time a band of buffalo was driven near the pis'kun, this raven frightened them away. Then Old Man knew that the raven was the one who had kept the buffalo cached.

So he went and changed himself into a beaver, and lay stretched out on the bank of the river, as if dead; and the raven, which was very hungry, flew down and began to pick at him. Then Old Man caught it by the legs and ran with it to camp, and all the chiefs came together to decide what should be done with it. Some said to kill it, but Old Man said, "No! I will punish it," and he tied it over the lodge, right in the smoke hole.

As the days went by, the raven grew poor and weak, and his eyes were blurred with the thick smoke, and he cried continually to Old Man to pity him. One day Old Man untied him, and told him to take his right shape, saying: "Why have you tried to fool Old Man? Look at me! I cannot die. Look at me! Of all peoples and tribes I am the chief. I cannot die. I made the mountains. They are standing yet. I made the prairies and the rocks. You see them yet. Go home, then, to your wife and your child, and when you are hungry hunt like any one else, or you shall die."

THE BEARS

Now Old Man was walking along, and far off he saw many wolves; and when he came closer, he saw there the chief of the wolves, a very old one, and sitting around him were all his children.

Old Man said, "Pity me, Wolf Chief; make me into a wolf, that I may live your way and catch deer and everything that runs fast."

"Come near then," said the Wolf Chief, "that I may rub your body with my hands, so that hair will cover you."

"Hold," said Old Man; "do not cover my body with hair. On my head, arms, and legs only, put hair."

When the Chief Wolf had done so, he said to Old Man: "You shall have three companions to help you, one is a very swift runner, another a good runner, and the last is not very fast. Take them with you now, and others of my younger children who are learning to hunt, but do not go where the wind blows; keep in the shelter, or the young ones will freeze to death." Then they went hunting, and Old Man led them on the high buttes, where it was very cold.

At night, they lay down to sleep, and Old Man nearly froze; and he said to the wolves, "Cover me with your tails." So all the wolves lay down around him, and covered his body with their tails, and he soon got warm and slept. Before long he awoke and said angrily, "Take off those tails," and the wolves moved away; but after a little time he again became cold, and cried out, "Oh my young brothers, cover me with your tails or I shall freeze." So they lay down by him again and covered his body with their tails.

When it was daylight, they all rose and hunted. They saw some moose, and, chasing them, killed three. Now, when they were about to eat, the Chief Wolf came along with many of his children, and one wolf said, "Let us make pemmican of those moose"; and every one was glad. Then said the one who made pemmican, "No one must look, everybody shut his eyes, while I make the pemmican"; but Old Man looked, and the pemmican-maker threw a round bone and hit him on the nose, and it hurt. Then Old Man said, "Let me make the pemmican." So all the wolves shut their eyes, and Old Man took the round bone and killed the wolf who had hit him. Then the Chief Wolf was angry, and he said, "Why did you kill your brother?" "I didn't mean to," replied Old Man. "He looked and I threw the round bone at him, but I only meant to hurt him a little." Then said the Chief Wolf: "You cannot live with us any longer. Take one of your companions, and go off by yourselves and hunt." So Old Man took the swift runner, and they went and lived by themselves a long time; and they killed all the elk, and deer, and antelope, and moose they wanted.

One morning they awoke, and Old Man said: "Oh my young brother, I have had a bad dream. Hereafter, when you chase anything, if it jumps a stream, you must not follow it. Even a little spring you must not jump." And the wolf promised not to jump over water.

Now one day the wolf was chasing a moose, and it ran on to an island. The stream about it was very small; so the wolf thought: "This is such a little stream that I must jump it. That moose is very tired, and I don't think it will leave the island." So he jumped on to the island, and as soon as he entered the brush, a bear caught him, for the island was the home of the Chief Bear and his two brothers.

Old Man waited a long time for the wolf to come back, and then went to look for him. He asked all the birds he met if they had seen him, but they all said they had not.

At last he saw a kingfisher, who was sitting on a limb overhanging the water. "Why do you sit there, my young brother?" said Old Man. "Because," replied the kingfisher, "the Chief Bear and his brothers have killed your wolf; they have eaten the meat and thrown the fat into the river, and whenever I see a piece come floating along, I fly down and get it." Then said Old Man, "Do the Bear Chief and his brothers often come out? and where do they live?" "They come out every morning to play," said the kingfisher; "and they live upon that island."

Old Man went up there and saw their tracks on the sand, where they had been playing, and he turned himself into a rotten tree. By and by the bears came out, and when they saw the tree, the Chief Bear said: "Look at that rotten tree. It is Old Man. Go, brothers, and see if it is not." So the two brothers went over to the tree, and clawed it; and they said, "No, brother, it is only a tree." Then the Chief Bear went over and clawed and bit the tree, and although it hurt Old Man, he never moved. Then the Bear Chief was sure it was only a tree, and he began to play with his brothers. Now while they were playing, and all were on their backs, Old Man leaned over and shot an arrow into each one of them; and they cried out loudly and ran back on the island. Then Old Man changed into himself, and walked down along the river. Pretty soon he saw a frog jumping along, and every time it jumped it would say, "*Ni'-nah O-kyai'-yu!*" And sometimes it would stop and sing:—

"*Ni'-nah*	*O-kyai'-yu!*	*Ni'-nah*	*O-kyai'-yu!*
Chief	Bear!	Chief	Bear!
Nap'-i	*I-nit'-si-wah*	*Ni'-nah*	*O-kyai'-yu!*"
Old Man	kill him	Chief	Bear!

"What do you say?" cried Old Man. The frog repeated what he had said.

"Ah!" exclaimed Old Man, "tell me all about it."

"The Chief Bear and his brothers," replied the frog, "were playing on the sand, when Old Man shot arrows into them. They are not dead, but the arrows are very near their hearts; if you should shove ever so little on them, the points would cut their hearts. I am going after medicine now to cure them."

Then Old Man killed the frog and skinned her, and put the hide on himself and swam back to the island, and hopped up toward the bears, crying at every step, "*Ni'-nah O-kyai'-yu!*" just as the frog had done.

"Hurry," cried the Chief Bear.

"Yes," replied Old Man, and he went up and shoved the arrow into his heart.

"I cured him; he is asleep now," he cried, and he went up and shoved the arrow into the biggest brother's heart. "I cured them; they are asleep now"; and he went up and shoved the arrow into the other bear's heart. Then he built a big fire and skinned the bears, and tried out the fat and poured it into a hollow in the ground; and he called all the animals to come and roll in it, that they might be fat. And all the animals came and rolled in it. The bears came first and rolled in it, that is the reason they get so fat. Last of all came the rabbits, and the grease was almost all gone; but they filled their paws with it and rubbed it on their backs and between their hind legs. That is the reason why rabbits have two such large layers of fat on their backs, and that is what makes them so fat between the hind legs.

[NOTE.—The four preceding stories show the serious side of Old Man's character. Those which follow represent him as malicious, foolish, and impotent.]

THE WONDERFUL BIRD

One day, as Old Man was walking about in the woods, he saw something very queer. A bird was sitting on the limb of a tree making a strange noise, and every time it made this noise, its eyes would go out of its head and fasten on the tree; then it would make another kind of a noise, and its eyes would come back to their places.

"Little Brother," cried Old Man, "teach me how to do that."

"If I show you how to do that," replied the bird, "you must not let your eyes go out of your head more than three times a day. If you do, you will be sorry."

"Just as you say, Little Brother. The trick is yours, and I will listen to you."

When the bird had taught Old Man how to do it, he was very glad, and did it three times right away. Then he stopped. "That bird has no sense," he said. "Why did he tell me to do it only three times? I will do it again, anyhow." So he made his eyes go out a fourth time; but now he could not call them back. Then he called to the bird, "Oh Little Brother, come help me get back my eyes." The little bird did not answer him. It had flown away. Then Old Man felt all over the trees with his hands, but he could not find his eyes; and he wandered about for a long time, crying and calling the animals to help him.

A wolf had much fun with him. The wolf had found a dead buffalo, and taking a piece of the meat which smelled bad, he would hold it close to Old Man. "I smell something dead," Old Man would say. "I wish I could find it; I am nearly starved to death." And he would feel all around for it. Once, when the wolf was doing this, Old Man caught him, and, plucking out one of his eyes, he put it in his own head. Then he could see, and was able to find his own eyes; but he could never again do the trick the little bird had taught him.

THE RACE

Once Old Man was travelling around, when he heard some very queer singing. He had never heard anything like this before, and looked all around to see who it was. At last he saw it was the cottontail rabbits, singing and making medicine. They had built a fire, and got a lot of hot ashes, and they would lie down in these ashes and sing while one covered them up. They would stay there only a short time though, for the ashes were very hot.

"Little Brothers," said Old Man, "that is very wonderful, how you lie in those hot ashes and coals without burning. I wish you would teach me how to do it."

"Come on, Old Man," said the rabbits, "we will show you how to do it. You must sing our song, and only stay in the ashes a short time." So Old Man began to sing, and he lay down, and they covered him with coals and ashes, and they did not burn him at all.

"That is very nice," he said. "You have powerful medicine. Now I want to know it all, so you lie down and let me cover you up."

So the rabbits all lay down in the ashes, and Old Man covered them up, and then he put the whole fire over them. One old rabbit got out, and Old Man was about to put her back when she said, "Pity me, my children are about to be born."

"All right," replied Old Man. "I will let you go, so there will be some more rabbits; but I will roast these nicely and have a feast." And he put more wood on the fire. When the rabbits were cooked, he cut some red willow brush and laid them on it to cool. The grease soaked into these branches, so, even to-day if you hold red willow over a fire, you will see the grease on the bark. You can see, too, that ever since, the rabbits have a burnt place on their backs, where the one that got away was singed.

Old Man sat down, and was waiting for the rabbits to cool a little, when a coyote came along, limping very badly. "Pity me, Old Man," he said, "you have lots of cooked rabbits; give me one of them."

"Go away," exclaimed Old Man. "If you are too lazy to catch your food, I will not help you."

"My leg is broken," said the coyote. "I can't catch anything, and I am starving. Just give me half a rabbit."

"I don't care if you die," replied Old Man. "I worked hard to cook all these rabbits, and I will not give any away. But I will tell you what we will do. We will run a race to that butte, way out there, and if you beat me you can have a rabbit."

"All right," said the coyote. So they started. Old Man ran very fast, and the coyote limped along behind, but close to him, until they got near to the butte. Then the coyote turned round and ran back very fast, for he was not lame at all. It took Old Man a long time to go back, and just before he got to the fire, the coyote swallowed the last rabbit, and trotted off over the prairie.

THE BAD WEAPONS

Once Old Man was fording a river, when the current carried him down stream, and he lost his weapons. He was very hungry, so he took the first wood he could find, and made a bow and arrows, and a handle for his knife and spear. When he had finished them, he started up a mountain. Pretty soon he saw a bear digging roots, and he thought he would have some fun, so he hid behind a log and called out, "No-tail animal, what are you doing?" The bear looked up, but, seeing no one, kept on digging.

Then Old Man called out again, "Hi! you dirt-eater!" and then he dodged back out of sight. Then the bear sat up again, and this time he saw Old Man and ran after him.

Old Man began shooting arrows at him, but the points only stuck in the skin, for the shafts were rotten and snapped off. Then he threw his spear, but that too was rotten, and broke. He tried to stab the bear, but his knife handle was also rotten and broke, so he turned and ran; and the bear pursued him. As he ran, he looked about for some weapon, but there was none, not even a rock. He called out to the animals to help him, but none came. His breath was almost gone, and the bear was very close to him, when he saw a bull's horn lying on the ground. He picked it up, placed it on his head, and, turning around, bellowed so loudly that the bear was scared and ran away.

THE ELK

Old Man was very hungry. He had been a long time without food, and was thinking how he could get something to eat, when he saw a band of elk on a ridge. So he went up to them and said, "Oh, my brothers, I am lonesome because I have no one to follow me."

"Go on, Old Man," said the elk, "we will follow you." Old Man led them about a long time, and when it was dark, he came near a high-cut bank. He ran around to one side where there was a slope, and he went down and then stood right under the steep bluff, and called out, "Come on, that is a nice jump, you will laugh."

So the elk jumped off, all but one cow, and were killed.

"Come on," said Old Man, "they have all jumped but you, it is nice."

"Take pity on me," replied the cow. "My child is about to be born, and I am very heavy. I am afraid to jump."

"Go on, then," answered Old Man; "go and live; then there will be plenty of elk again some day."

Now Old Man built a fire and cooked some ribs, and then he skinned all the elk, cut up the meat to dry, and hung the tongues up on a pole.

Next day he went off, and did not come back until night, when he was very hungry again. "I'll roast some ribs," he said, "and a tongue, and I'll stuff a marrow gut and cook that. I guess that will be enough for to-night." But when he got to the place, the meat was all gone. The wolves had eaten it. "I was smart to hang up those tongues," he said, "or I would not have had anything to eat." But the tongues were all hollow. The mice had eaten the meat out, leaving only the skin. So Old Man starved again.

OLD MAN DOCTORS

A pis´kun had been built, and many buffalo had been run in and killed. The camp was full of meat. Great sheets of it hung in the lodges and on the racks outside; and now the women, having cut up all the meat, were working on the hides, preparing some for robes, and scraping the hair from others, to make leather.

About this time, Old Man came along. He had come from far and was very tired, so he entered the first lodge he came to and sat down. Now this lodge belonged to three old women. Their husbands had died or been killed in war, and they had no relations to help them, so they were very poor. After Old Man had rested a little, they set a dish of food before him. It was dried bull meat, very tough, and some pieces of belly fat.

"*Hai'-yah ho!*" cried Old Man, after he had tasted a piece. "You treat me badly. A whole pis´kun of fat buffalo just killed; the camp red with meat, and here these old women give me tough bull meat and belly fat to eat. Hurry now! roast me some ribs and a piece of back fat."

"Alas!" exclaimed one old woman. "We have no good food. All our helpers are dead, and we take what others leave. Bulls and poor cows are all the people leave us."

"Ah!" said Old Man, "how poor! you are very poor. Take courage now. I will help you. To-morrow they will run another band into the pis´kun. I will be there. I will kill the fattest cow, and you can have it all."

Then the old women were glad. They talked to one another, saying, "Very good heart, Old Man. He helps the poor. Now we will live. We will have marrow guts and liver. We will have paunch and fat kidneys."

Old Man said nothing more. He ate the tough meat and belly fat, and rolled up in his robe and went to sleep.

Morning came. The people climbed the bluffs and went out on to the prairie, where they hid behind the piles of rock and bushes, which reached far out from the cliff in lines which were always further and further apart. After a while, he who leads the buffalo was seen coming, bringing a large band after him. Soon they were inside the lines. The people began to rise up behind them, shouting and waving their robes. Now they reached the edge of the bluff. The leaders tried to stop and turn, but those behind kept pushing on, and nearly the whole band dashed down over the rocks, only a few of the last ones turning aside and escaping.

The lodges were now deserted. All the people were gone to the pis´kun to kill the buffalo and butcher them. Where was Old Man? Did he take his bow and arrows and go to the pis´kun to kill a fat cow for the poor old women? No. He was sneaking around, lifting the door-ways of the lodges and looking in. Bad person, Old Man. In the chiefs lodge he saw a little child, a girl, asleep. Outside was a buffalo's gall, and taking a long stick he dipped the end of it in the gall; and then, reaching carefully into the lodge, he drew it across the lips of the child asleep. Then he threw the stick away, and went in and sat down. Soon the girl awoke and began to cry. The gall was very bitter and burned her lips.

"Pity me, Old Man," she said. "Take this fearful thing from my lips."

"I do not doctor unless I am paid," he replied. Then said the girl: "See all my father's Weapons hanging there His shield, war head-dress, scalps, and knife. Cure me now, and I will give you some of them."

"I have more of such things than I want," he replied. (What a liar! he had none at all.)

Again said the girl, "Pity me, help me now, and I will give you my father's white buffalo robe."

"I have plenty of white robes," replied Old Man. (Again he lied, for he never had one.)

"Old Man," again said the girl, "in this lodge lives a widow woman, my father's relation. Remove this fearful thing from my lips, and I will have my father give her to you."

"Now you speak well," replied Old Man. "I am a little glad. I have many wives" (he had none), "but I would just as soon have another one."

So he went close to the child and pretended to doctor her, but instead of that, he killed her and ran out. He went to the old women's lodge, and wrapped a strip of cowskin about his head, and commenced to groan, as if he was very sick.

Now the people began to come from the pis´kun, carrying great loads of meat. This dead girl's mother came, and when she saw her child lying dead, and blood on the ground, she ran back crying out: "My daughter has been killed! My daughter has been killed!"

Then all the people began to shout out and run around, and the warriors and young men looked in the lodges, and up and down the creek in the brush, but they could find no one who might have killed the child.

Then said the father of the dead girl: "Now, to-day, we will find out who killed this child. Every man in this camp—every young man, every old man—must come and jump across the creek; and if any one does not jump across, if he falls in the water, that man is the one who did the killing."

All heard this, and they began to gather at the creek, one behind another; and the women and children went to look on, for they wanted to see the person who had killed the little child. Now they were ready. They were about to jump, when some one cried out, "Old Man is not here."

"True," said the chief, looking around, "Old Man is not here." And he sent two young men to bring him.

"Old Man!" they cried out, when they came to the lodge, "a child has been killed. We have all got to jump to find out who did it. The chief has sent for you. You will have to jump, too."

"*Ki'-yo!*" exclaimed the old women. "Old Man is very sick. Go off, and let him alone. He is so sick he could not kill meat for us to-day."

"It can't be helped," the young men replied. "The chief says every one must jump."

So Old Man went out toward the creek very slowly, and very much scared. He did not know what to do. As he was going along he saw a *ni'-po-muk-i* and he said: "Oh my little brother, pity me. Give me some of your power to jump the creek, and here is my necklace. See how pretty it is. I will give it to you."

So they traded; Old Man took some of the bird's power, and the bird took Old Man's necklace and put it on.

Now they jump. *Wo'-ka-hi!* they jump way across and far on to the ground. Now they jump; another! another! another! Now it comes Old Man's turn. He runs, he jumps, he goes high, and strikes the ground far beyond any other person's jump. Now comes the *ni'-po-muk-i*. "*Wo'-ka-hi!*" the men shout. "*Ki'-yo!*" cry the women, "the bird has fallen in the creek." The warriors are running to kill him. "Wait! Hold on!" cries the bird. "Let me speak a few words. Every one knows I am a good jumper. I can jump further than any one; but Old Man asked me for some of my power, and I gave it to him, and he gave me this necklace. It is very heavy and pulled me down. That is why I fell into the creek."

Then the people began to shout and talk again, some saying to kill the bird, and some not, when Old Man shouted out: "Wait, listen to me. What's the use of quarrelling or killing anybody? Let us go back, and I will doctor the child alive."

Good words. The people were glad. So they went back, and got ready for the doctoring. First, Old Man ordered a large fire built in the lodge where the dead girl was lying. Two old men were placed at the back of the lodge, facing each other. They had spears, which they held above their heads and were to thrust back and forth at each other in time to the singing. Near the door-way were placed two old women, facing each other. Each one held a *puk'-sah-tchis,*—a maul,—with which she was to beat time to the singing. The other seats in the lodge were taken by people who were to sing. Now Old Man hung a big roll of belly fat close over the fire, so that the hot grease began to drip, and everything was ready, and the singing began. This was Old Man's song:—

Ahk-sa´-kē-wah,   Ahk-sa´-kē-wah,   Ahk-sa´-kē-wah, etc.

I don't care,   I don't care,   I don't care.

And so they sung for a long time, the old men jabbing their spears at each other, and the old women pretending to hit each other with their mauls.

After a while they rested, and Old Man said: "Now I want every one to shut their eyes. No one can look. I am going to begin the real doctoring." So the people shut their eyes, and the singing began again. Then Old Man took the dripping hot fat from the fire, gave it a mighty swing around the circle in front of the people's faces, jumped out the door-way, and ran off. Every one was burned. The two old men wounded each other with their spears. The old women knocked each other on the head with their mauls. The people cried and groaned, wiped their burned faces, and rushed out the door; but Old Man was gone. They saw him no more.

THE ROCK

Once Old Man was travelling, and becoming tired he sat down on a rock to rest. After a while he started to go on, and because the sun was hot he threw his robe over the rock, saying: "Here, I give you my robe, because you are poor and have let me rest on you. Always keep it."

He had not gone very far, when it began to rain, and meeting a coyote he said: "Little brother, run back to that rock, and ask him to lend me his robe. We will cover ourselves with it and keep dry." So the coyote ran back to the rock, but returned without the robe. "Where is the robe?" asked Old Man. "*Sai-yah!*" replied the coyote. "The rock said you gave him the robe, and he was going to keep it."

Then Old Man was very angry, and went back to the rock and jerked the robe off it, saying: "I only wanted to borrow this robe until the rain was over, but now that you have acted so mean about it, I will keep it. You don't need a robe anyhow. You have been out in the rain and snow all your life, and it will not hurt you to live so always."

With the coyote he went off into a coulée, and sat down. The rain was falling, and they covered themselves with the robe and were very comfortable. Pretty soon they heard a loud noise, and Old Man told the coyote to go up on the hill and see what it was. Soon he came running back, saying, "Run! run! the big rock is coming"; and they both ran away as fast as they could. The coyote tried to crawl into a badger hole, but it was too small for him and he stuck fast, and before he could get out, the rock rolled over him and crushed his hind parts. Old Man was scared, and as he ran he threw off his robe and what clothes he could, so that he might run faster. The rock kept gaining on him all the time.

Not far off was a band of buffalo bulls, and Old Man cried out to them, saying, "Oh my brothers, help me, help me. Stop that rock." The bulls ran and tried to stop it, but it crushed their heads. Some deer and antelope tried to help Old Man, but they were killed, too. A lot of rattlesnakes formed themselves into a lariat, and tried to catch it; but those at the noose end were all cut to pieces. The rock was now close to Old Man, so close that it began to hit his heels; and he was about to give up, when he saw a flock of bull bats circling over his head. "Oh my little brothers," he cried, "help me. I am almost dead." Then the bull bats flew down, one after another, against the rock; and every time one of them hit it he chipped off a piece, and at last one hit it fair in the middle and broke it into two pieces.

Then Old Man was very glad. He went to where there was a nest of bull bats, and made the young ones' mouths very wide and pinched off their bills, to make them pretty and queer looking. That is the reason they look so to-day.

THE THEFT FROM THE SUN

Once Old Man was travelling around, when he came to the Sun's lodge, and the Sun asked him to stay a while. Old Man was very glad to do so.

One day the meat was all gone, and the Sun said, "*Kyi!* Old Man, what say you if we go and kill some deer?"

"You speak well," replied Old Man. "I like deer meat."

The Sun took down a bag and pulled out a beautiful pair of leggings. They were embroidered with porcupine quills and bright feathers. "These," said the Sun, "are my hunting leggings. They are great medicine. All I have to do is to put them on and walk around a patch of brush, when the leggings set it on fire and drive the deer out so that I can shoot them."

"*Hai-yah!*" exclaimed Old Man. "How wonderful!" He made up his mind he would have those leggings, if he had to steal them.

They went out to hunt, and the first patch of brush they came to, the Sun set on fire with his hunting leggings. A lot of white-tail deer ran out, and they each shot one.

That night, when they went to bed, the Sun pulled off his leggings and placed them to one side. Old Man saw where he put them, and in the middle of the night, when every one was asleep, he stole them and went off. He travelled a long time, until he had gone far and was very tired, and then, making a pillow of the leggings, lay down and slept. In the morning, he heard some one talking. The Sun was saying, "Old Man, why are my leggings under your head?" He looked around, and saw he was in the Sun's lodge, and thought he must have wandered around and got lost, and returned there. Again the Sun spoke and said, "What are you doing with my leggings?" "Oh," replied Old Man, "I couldn't find anything for a pillow, so I just put these under my head."

Night came again, and again Old Man stole the leggings and ran off. This time he did not walk at all; he just kept running until pretty near morning, and then lay down and slept. You see what a fool he was. He did not know that the whole world is the Sun's lodge. He did not know that, no matter how far he ran, he could not get out of the Sun's sight. When morning came, he found himself still in the Sun's lodge. But this time the Sun said: "Old Man, since you like my leggings so much, I will give them to you. Keep them." Then Old Man was very glad and went away.

One day his food was all gone, so he put on the medicine leggings and set fire to a piece of brush. He was just going to kill some deer that were running out, when he saw that the fire was getting close to him. He ran away as fast as he could, but the fire gained on him and began to burn his legs. His leggings were all on fire. He came to a river and jumped in, and pulled off the leggings as soon as he could. They were burned to pieces.

Perhaps the Sun did this to him because he tried to steal the leggings.

THE FOX

One day Old Man went out hunting and took the fox with him. They hunted for several days, but killed nothing. It was nice warm weather in the late fall. After they had become very hungry, as they were going along one day, Old Man went up over a ridge and on the other side he saw four big buffalo bulls lying down; but there was no way by which they could get near them. He dodged back out of sight and told the fox what he had seen, and they thought for a long time, to see if there was no way by which these bulls might be killed.

At last Old Man said to the fox: "My little brother, I can think of only one way to get these bulls. This is my plan, if you agree to it. I will pluck all the fur off you except one tuft on the end of your tail. Then you go over the hill and walk up and down in sight of the bulls, and you will seem so funny to them that they will laugh themselves to death."

The fox did not like to do this, but he could think of nothing better, so he agreed to what Old Man proposed. Old Man plucked him perfectly bare, except the end of his tail, and the fox went over the ridge and walked up and down. When he had come close to the bulls, he played around and walked on his hind legs and went through all sorts of antics. When the bulls first saw him, they got up on their feet, and looked at him. They did not know what to make of him. Then they began to laugh, and the more they looked at him, the more they laughed, until at last one by one they fell down exhausted and died. Then Old Man came over the hill, and went down to the bulls, and began to butcher them. By this time it had grown a little colder.

"Ah, little brother," said Old Man to the fox, "you did splendidly. I do not wonder that the bulls laughed themselves to death. I nearly died myself as I watched you from the hill. You looked very funny." While he was saying this, he was working away skinning off the hides and getting the meat ready to carry to camp, all the time talking to the fox, who stood about, his back humped up and his teeth chattering with the cold. Now a wind sprang up from the north and a few snowflakes were flying in the air. It was growing colder and colder. Old Man kept on talking, and every now and then he would say something to the fox, who was sitting behind him perfectly still, with his jaw shoved out and his teeth shining.

At last Old Man had the bulls all skinned and the meat cut up, and as he rose up he said: "It is getting pretty cold, isn't it? Well, we do not care for the cold. We have got all our winter's meat, and we will have nothing to do but feast and dance and sing until spring." The fox made no answer. Then Old Man got angry, and called out: "Why don't you answer me? Don't you hear me talking to you?" The fox said nothing. Then Old Man was mad, and he said, "Can't you speak?" and stepped up to the fox and gave him a push with his foot, and the fox fell over. He was dead, frozen stiff with the cold.

OLD MAN AND THE LYNX

Old Man was travelling round over the prairie, when he saw a lot of prairie-dogs sitting in a circle. They had built a fire, and were sitting around it. Old Man went toward them, and when he got near them, he began to cry, and said, "Let me, too, sit by that fire." The prairie-dogs said: "All right, Old Man. Don't cry. Come and sit by the fire." Old Man sat down, and saw that the prairie-dogs were playing a game. They would put one of their number in the fire and cover him up with the hot ashes; and then, after he had been there a little while, he would say *sk, sk*, and they would push the ashes off him, and pull him out.

Old Man said, "Teach me how to do that"; and they told him what to do, and put him in the fire, and covered him up with the ashes, and after a little while he said *sk, sk*, like a prairie-dog, and they pulled him out again. Then he did it to the prairie-dogs. At first he put them in one at a time, but there were many of them, and pretty soon he got tired, and said, "Come, I will put you all in at once." They said, "Very well, Old Man," and all got in the ashes; but just as Old Man was about to cover them up, one of them, a female heavy with young, said, "Do not cover me up; the heat may hurt my children, which are about to be born." Old Man said: "Very well. If you do not want to be covered up, you can sit over by the fire and watch the rest." Then he covered up all the others.

At length the prairie-dogs said *sk, sk*, but Old Man did not sweep the ashes off and pull them out of the fire. He let them stay there and die. The old she one ran off to a hole and, as she went down in it, said *sk, sk*. Old Man chased her, but he got to the hole too late to catch her. So he said: "Oh, well, you can go. There will be more prairie-dogs by and by."

When the prairie-dogs were roasted, Old Man cut a lot of red willow brush to lay them on, and then sat down and began to eat. He ate until he was full, and then felt sleepy. He said to his nose: "I am going to sleep now. Watch for me and wake me up in case anything comes near." Then Old Man slept. Pretty soon his nose snored, and he woke up and said, "What is it?" The nose said, "A raven is flying over there." Old Man said, "That is nothing," and went to sleep again. Soon his nose snored again. Old Man said, "What is it now?" The nose said, "There is a coyote over there, coming this way." Old Man said, "A coyote is nothing," and again went to sleep. Presently his nose snored again, but Old Man did not wake up. Again it snored, and called out, "Wake up, a bob-cat is coming." Old Man paid no attention. He slept on.

The bob-cat crept up to where the fire was, and ate up all the roast prairie-dogs, and then went off and lay down on a flat rock, and went to sleep. All this time the nose kept trying to wake Old Man up, and at last he awoke, and the nose said: "A bob-cat is over there on that flat rock. He has eaten all your food." Then Old Man called out loud, he was so angry. He went softly over to where the bob-cat lay, and seized it, before it could wake up to bite or scratch him. The bob-cat cried out, "Hold on, let me speak a word or two." But Old Man would not listen; he said, "I will teach you to steal my food." He pulled off the lynx's tail, pounded his head against the rock so as to make his face flat, pulled him out long, so as to make him small-bellied, and then threw him away into the brush. As he went sneaking off, Old Man said, "There, that is the way you bob-cats shall always be." That is the reason the lynxes look so today.

Old Man went back to the fire, and looked at the red willow sticks where his food had been, and it made him mad at his nose. He said, "You fool, why did you not wake me?" He took the willow sticks and thrust them in the coals, and when they took fire, he burned his nose. This pained him greatly, and he ran up on a hill and held his nose to the wind, and called on it to blow hard and cool him. A hard wind came, and it blew him away down to Birch Creek. As he was flying along, he caught at the weeds and brush to try to stop himself, but nothing was strong enough to hold him. At last he seized a birch tree. He held on to this, and it did not give way. Although the wind whipped him about, this way and that, and tumbled him up and down, the tree held him. He kept calling to the wind to blow gently, and finally it listened to him and went down.

So he said: "This is a beautiful tree. It has kept me from being blown away and knocked all to pieces. I will ornament it and it shall always be like that." So he gashed it across with his stone knife, as you see it to-day.

THE STORY OF THE THREE TRIBES

THE PAST AND THE PRESENT

Fifty years ago the name Blackfoot was one of terrible meaning to the white traveller who passed across that desolate buffalo-trodden waste which lay to the north of the Yellowstone River and east of the Rocky Mountains. This was the Blackfoot land, the undisputed home of a people which is said to have numbered in one of its tribes—the Pi-kŭn´-i—8000 lodges, or 40,000 persons. Besides these, there were the Blackfeet and the Bloods, three tribes of one nation, speaking the same language, having the same customs, and holding the same religious faith.

But this land had not always been the home of the Blackfeet. Long ago, before the coming of the white men, they had lived in another country far to the north and east, about Lesser Slave Lake, ranging between Peace River and the Saskatchewan, and having for their neighbors on the north the Beaver Indians. Then the Blackfeet were a timber people. It is said that about two hundred years ago the Chippeweyans from the east invaded this country and drove them south and west. Whether or no this is true, it is quite certain that not many generations back the Blackfeet lived on the North Saskatchewan River and to the north of that stream. Gradually working their way westward, they at length reached the Rocky Mountains, and, finding game abundant, remained there until they obtained horses, in the very earliest years of the present century. When they secured horses and guns, they took courage and began to venture out on to the plains and to go to war. From this time on, the Blackfeet made constant war on their neighbors to the south, and in a few years controlled the whole country between the Saskatchewan on the north and the Yellowstone on the south.

It was, indeed, a glorious country which the Blackfeet had wrested from their southern enemies. Here nature has reared great mountains and spread out broad prairies. Along the western border of this region, the Rocky Mountains lift their snow-clad peaks above the clouds. Here and there, from north to south, and from east to west, lie minor ranges, black with pine forests if seen near at hand, or in the distance mere gray silhouettes against a sky of blue. Between these mountain ranges lies everywhere the great prairie; a monotonous waste to the stranger's eye, but not without its charm. It is brown and bare; for, except during a few short weeks in spring, the sparse bunch-grass is sear and yellow, and the silver gray of the wormwood lends an added dreariness to the landscape. Yet this seemingly desert waste has a beauty of its own. At intervals it is marked with green winding river valleys, and everywhere it is gashed with deep ravines, their sides painted in strange colors of red and gray and brown, and their perpendicular walls crowned with fantastic columns and figures of stone or clay, carved out by the winds and the rains of ages. Here and there, rising out of the plain, are curious sharp ridges, or square-topped buttes with vertical sides, sometimes bare, and sometimes dotted with pines,—short, sturdy trees, whose gnarled trunks and thick, knotted branches have been twisted and wrung into curious forms by the winds which blow unceasingly, hour after hour, day after day, and month after month, over mountain range and prairie, through gorge and coulée.

These prairies now seem bare of life, but it was not always so. Not very long ago, they were trodden by multitudinous herds of buffalo and antelope; then, along the wooded river valleys and on the pine-clad slopes of the mountains, elk, deer, and wild sheep fed in great numbers. They are all gone now. The winter's wind still whistles over Montana prairies, but nature's shaggy-headed wild cattle no longer feel its biting blasts. Where once the scorching breath of summer stirred only the short stems of the buffalo-grass, it now billows the fields of the white man's grain. Half-hidden by the scanty herbage, a few bleached skeletons alone remain to tell us of the buffalo; and the broad, deep trails, over which the dark herds passed by thousands, are now grass-grown and fast disappearing under the effacing hand of time. The buffalo have disappeared, and the fate of the buffalo has almost overtaken the Blackfeet.

As known to the whites, the Blackfeet were true prairie Indians, seldom venturing into the mountains, except when they crossed them to war with the Kutenais, the Flatheads, or the Snakes. They subsisted almost wholly on the flesh of the buffalo. They were hardy, untiring, brave, ferocious. Swift to move, whether on foot or horseback, they made long journeys to war, and with telling force struck their enemies. They had conquered and driven out from the territory which they occupied the tribes who once inhabited it, and maintained a desultory and successful warfare against all invaders, fighting with the Crees on the north, the Assinaboines on the east, the Crows on the south, and the

Snakes, Kalispels, and Kutenais on the southwest and west. In those days the Blackfeet were rich and powerful. The buffalo fed and clothed them, and they needed nothing beyond what nature supplied. This was their time of success and happiness.

Crowded into a little corner of the great territory which they once dominated, and holding this corner by an uncertain tenure, a few Blackfeet still exist, the pitiful remnant of a once mighty people. Huddled together about their agencies, they are facing the problem before them, striving, helplessly but bravely, to accommodate themselves to the new order of things; trying in the face of adverse surroundings to wrench themselves loose from their accustomed ways of life; to give up inherited habits and form new ones; to break away from all that is natural to them, from all that they have been taught—to reverse their whole mode of existence. They are striving to earn their living, as the white man earns his, by toil. The struggle is hard and slow, and in carrying it on they are wasting away and growing fewer in numbers. But though unused to labor, ignorant of agriculture, unacquainted with tools or seeds or soils, knowing nothing of the ways of life in permanent houses or of the laws of health, scantily fed, often utterly discouraged by failure, they are still making a noble fight for existence.

Only within a few years—since the buffalo disappeared—has this change been going on; so recently has it come that the old order and the new meet face to face. In the trees along the river valleys, still quietly resting on their aerial sepulchres, sleep the forms of the ancient hunter-warrior who conquered and held this broad land; while, not far away, Blackfoot farmers now rudely cultivate their little crops, and gather scanty harvests from narrow fields.

It is the meeting of the past and the present, of savagery and civilization. The issue cannot be doubtful. Old methods must pass away. The Blackfeet will become civilized, but at a terrible cost. To me there is an interest, profound and pathetic, in watching the progress of the struggle.

DAILY LIFE AND CUSTOMS

Indians are usually represented as being a silent, sullen race, seldom speaking, and never laughing nor joking. However true this may be in regard to some tribes, it certainly was not the case with most of those who lived upon the great Plains. These people were generally talkative, merry, and light-hearted; they delighted in fun, and were a race of jokers. It is true that, in the presence of strangers, they were grave, silent, and reserved, but this is nothing more than the shyness and embarrassment felt by a child in the presence of strangers. As the Indian becomes acquainted, this reserve wears off; he is at his ease again and appears in his true colors, a light-hearted child. Certainly the Blackfeet never were a taciturn and gloomy people. Before the disappearance of the buffalo, they were happy and cheerful. Why should they not have been? Food and clothing were to be had for the killing and tanning. All fur animals were abundant, and thus the people were rich. Meat, really the only food they cared for, was plenty and cost nothing. Their robes and furs were exchanged with the traders for bright-colored blankets and finery. So they wanted nothing.

It is but nine years since the buffalo disappeared from the land. Only nine years have passed since these people gave up that wild, free life which was natural to them, and ah! how dear! Let us go back in memory to those happy days and see how they passed the time.

The sun is just rising. Thin columns of smoke are creeping from the smoke holes of the lodges, and ascending in the still morning air. Everywhere the women are busy, carrying water and wood, and preparing the simple meal. And now we see the men come out, and start for the river. Some are followed by their children; some are even carrying those too small to walk. They have reached the water's edge. Off drop their blankets, and with a plunge and a shivering *ah-h-h* they dash into the icy waters. Winter and summer, storm or shine, this was their daily custom. They said it made them tough and healthy, and enabled them to endure the bitter cold while hunting on the bare bleak prairie. By the time they have returned to the lodges, the women have prepared the early meal. A dish of boiled meat—some three or four pounds—is set before each man; the children are served as much as they can eat, and the wives take the rest. The horses are now seen coming in, hundreds and thousands of them, driven by boys and young men who started out after them at daylight. If buffalo are close at hand, and it has been decided to make a run, each hunter catches his favorite buffalo horse, and they all start out together; they are followed by women, on the travois or pack horses, who will do most of the butchering, and transport the meat and hides to camp. If there is no band of buffalo near by, they go off, singly or by twos and threes, to still-hunt scattering buffalo, or deer, or elk, or such other game as may be found. The women remaining in camp are not idle. All day long they tan robes, dry meat, sew moccasins, and perform a thousand and one other tasks. The young men who have stayed at home carefully comb and braid their hair, paint their faces, and, if the weather is pleasant, ride or walk around the camp so that the young women may look at them and see how pretty they are.

Feasting began early in the morning, and will be carried on far into the night. A man who gives a feast has his wives cook the choicest food they have, and when all is ready, he goes outside the lodge and shouts the invitation, calling out each guest's name three times, saying that he is invited to eat, and concludes by announcing that a certain number of pipes—generally three—will be smoked. The guests having assembled, each one is served with a dish of food. Be the quantity large or small, it is all that he will get. If he does not eat it all, he may carry home what remains. The host does not eat with his guests. He cuts up some tobacco, and carefully mixes it with *l'herbe*, and when all have finished eating, he fills and lights a pipe, which is smoked and passed from one to another, beginning with the first man on his left. When the last person on the left of the host has smoked, the pipe is passed back around the circle to the one on the right of the door, and smoked to the left again. The guests do not all talk at once. When a person begins to speak, he expects every one to listen, and is never interrupted. During the day the topics for conversation are about the hunting, war, stories of strange adventures, besides a good deal of good-natured joking and chaffing. When the third and last pipeful of tobacco has been smoked, the host ostentatiously knocks out the ashes and says *"Kyi"* whereupon all the guests rise and file out. Seldom a day passed but each lodge-owner in camp gave from one to three feasts. In fact almost all a man did, when in camp, was to go from one of these gatherings to another.

A favorite pastime in the day was gambling with a small wheel called *it-se´-wah*. This wheel was about four inches in diameter, and had five spokes, on which were strung different-colored beads, made of bone or horn. A level, smooth piece of ground was selected, at each end of which was placed a log. At each end of the course were two men, who gambled against each other. A crowd always surrounded them, betting on the sides. The wheel was rolled along the course, and each man at the end whence it started, darted an arrow at it. The cast was made just before the wheel reached the log at the opposite end of the track, and points were counted according as the arrow passed between the spokes, or when the wheel, stopped by the log, was in contact with the arrow, the position and nearness of the different beads to the arrow representing a certain number of points. The player who first scored ten points won. It was a very difficult game, and one had to be very skilful to win.

Another popular game was what with more southern tribes is called "hands"; it is like "Button, button, who's got the button?" Two small, oblong bones were used, one of which had a black ring around it. Those who participated in this game, numbering from two to a dozen, were divided into two equal parties, ranged on either side of the lodge. Wagers were made, each person betting with the one directly opposite him. Then a man took the bones, and, by skilfully moving his hands and changing the objects from one to the other, sought to make it impossible for the person opposite him to decide which hand held the marked one. Ten points were the game, counted by sticks, and the side which first got the number took the stakes. A song always accompanied this game, a weird, unearthly air,—if it can be so called,—but when heard at a little distance, very pleasant and soothing. At first a scarcely audible murmur, like the gentle soughing of an evening breeze, it gradually increased in volume and reached a very high pitch, sank quickly to a low bass sound, rose and fell, and gradually died away, to be again repeated. The person concealing the bones swayed his body, arms, and hands in time to the air, and went through all manner of graceful and intricate movements for the purpose of confusing the guesser. The stakes were sometimes very high, two or three horses or more, and men have been known to lose everything they possessed, even to their clothing.

The children, at least the boys, played about and did as they pleased. Not so with the girls. Their duties began at a very early age. They carried wood and water for their mothers, sewed moccasins, and as soon as they were strong enough, were taught to tan robes and furs, make lodges, travois, and do all other woman's—and so menial—work. The boys played at mimic warfare, hunted around in the brush with their bows and arrows, made mud images of animals, and in summer spent about half their time in the water. In winter, they spun tops on the ice, slid down hill on a contrivance made of buffalo ribs, and hunted rabbits.

Shortly after noon, the hunters began to return, bringing in deer, antelope, buffalo, elk, occasionally bear, and, sometimes, beaver which they had trapped. The camp began to be more lively. In all directions persons could be heard shouting out invitations to feasts. Here a man was lying back on his couch singing and drumming; there a group of young men were holding a war dance; everywhere the people were eating, singing, talking, and joking. As the light faded from the western sky and darkness spread over the camp, the noise and laughter increased. In many lodges, the people held social dances, the women, dressed in their best gowns, ranged on one side, the men on the other; all sung, and three or four drummers furnished an accompaniment; the music was lively if somewhat jerky. At intervals the people rose and danced, the "step" being a bending of the knees and swinging of the body, the women holding their arms and hands in various graceful positions.

With the night came the rehearsal of the wondrous doings of the gods. These tales may not be told in the daytime. Old Man would not like that, and would cause any one who narrated them while it was light to become blind. All Indians are natural orators, but some far exceed others in their powers of expression. Their attitudes, gestures, and signs are so suggestive that they alone would enable one to understand the stories they relate. I have seen these story-tellers so much in earnest, so entirely carried away by the tale they were relating, that they fairly trembled with excitement. They held their little audiences spell-bound. The women dropped their half-sewn moccasin from their listless hands, and the men let the pipe go out. These stories for the most part were about the ancient gods and their miraculous doings. They were generally related by the old men, warriors who had seen their best days. Many of them are recorded in this book. They are the explanations of the phenomena of life, and contain many a moral for the instruction of youth.

The *I-kŭn-ŭh'-kah-tsi* contributed not a little to the entertainment of every-day life. Frequent dances were held by the different bands of the society, and the whole camp always turned out to see them. The animal-head masks, brightly painted bodies, and queer performances were dear to the Indian heart.

Such was the every-day life of the Blackfeet in the buffalo days. When the camp moved, the women packed up their possessions, tore down the lodges, and loaded everything on the backs of the ponies or on the travois. Meantime the chiefs had started on, and the soldiers—the Brave band of the *I-kun-uh´-kah-tsi*—followed after them. After these leaders had gone a short distance, a halt was made to allow the column to close up. The women, children, horses, and dogs of the camp marched in a disorderly, straggling fashion, often strung out in a line a mile or two long. Many of the men rode at a considerable distance ahead, and on each side of the marching column, hunting for any game that might be found, or looking over the country for signs of enemies.

Before the Blackfeet obtained horses in the very first years of the present century, and when their only beasts of burden were dogs, their possessions were transported by these animals or on men's backs. We may imagine that in those days the journeys made were short ones, the camp travelling but a few miles.

In moving the camp in ancient days, the heaviest and bulkiest things to be transported were the lodges. These were sometimes very large, often consisting of thirty cow-skins, and, when set up, containing two or three fires like this or in ground plan like this. The skins of these large lodges were sewn together in strips, of which there would be sometimes as many as four; and, when the lodge was set up, these strips were pinned together as the front of a common lodge is pinned to-day. The dogs carried the provisions, tools, and utensils, sometimes the lodge strips, if these were small enough, or anything that was heavy, and yet could be packed in small compass; for since dogs are small animals, and low standing, they cannot carry bulky burdens. Still, some of the dogs were large enough to carry a load of one hundred pounds. Dogs also hauled the travois, on which were bundles and sometimes babies. This was not always a safe means of transportation for infants, as is indicated by an incident related by John Monroe's mother as having occurred in her father's time. The camp, on foot of course, was crossing a strip of open prairie lying between two pieces of timber, when a herd of buffalo, stampeding, rushed through the marching column. The loaded dogs rushed after the buffalo, dragging the travois after them and scattering their loads over the prairie. Among the lost chattels were two babies, dropped off somewhere in the long grass, which were never found.

There were certain special customs and beliefs which were a part of the every-day life of the people.

In passing the pipe when smoking, it goes from the host, who takes the first smoke, to the left, passing from hand to hand to the door. It may not be passed across the door to the man on the other side, but must come back,—no one smoking,—pass the host, and go round to the man across the door from the last smoker. This man smokes and passes it to the one on his left, and so it goes on until it reaches the host again. A person entering a lodge where people are smoking must not pass in front of them, that is, between the smokers and the fire.

A solemn form of affirmation, the equivalent of the civilized oath, is connected with smoking, which, as is well known, is with many tribes of Indians a sacred ceremony. If a man sitting in a lodge tells his companions some very improbable story, something that they find it very hard to believe, and they want to test him, to see if he is really telling the truth, the pipe is given to a medicine man, who paints the stem red and prays over it, asking that if the man's story is true he may have long life, but if it is false his life may end in a short time. The pipe is then filled and lighted, and passed to the man, who has seen and overheard what has been done and said. The medicine man says to him: "Accept this pipe, but remember that, if you smoke, your story must be as sure as that there is a hole through this pipe, and as straight as the hole through this stem. So your life shall be long and you shall survive, but if you have spoken falsely your days are counted." The man may refuse the pipe, saying, "I have told you the truth; it is useless to smoke this pipe." If he declines to smoke, no one believes what he has said; he is looked upon as having lied. If, however, he takes the pipe and smokes, every one believes him. It is the most solemn form of oath. The Blackfoot pipes are usually made of black or green slate or sandstone.

The Blackfeet do not whip their children, but still they are not without some training. Children must be taught, or they will not know anything; if they do not know anything, they will have no sense; and if they have no sense they will not know how to act. They are instructed in manners, as well as in other more general and more important matters.

If a number of boys were in a lodge where older people were sitting, very likely the young people would be talking and laughing about their own concerns, and making so much noise that the elders could say nothing. If this continued too long, one of the older men would be likely to get up and go out and get a long stick and bring it in with him. When he had seated himself, he would hold it up, so that the children could see it and would repeat a cautionary formula, "I will give you gum!" This was a warning to them to make less noise, and was always heeded—for a time. After a little, however, the boys might forget and begin to chatter again, and presently the man, without further warning, would reach over and rap one of them on the head with the stick, when quiet would again be had for a time.

In the same way, in winter, when the lodge was full of old and young people, and through lack of attention the fire died down, some older person would call out, "Look out for the skunk!" which would be a warning to the boys to put some sticks on the fire. If this was not done at once, the man who had called out might throw a stick of wood across the lodge into the group of children, hitting and hurting one or more of them. It was taught also that, if, when young and old were in the lodge and the fire had burned low, an older person were to lay the unburned ends of the sticks upon the fire, all the children in the lodge would have the scab, or itch. So, at the call "Look out for the scab!" some child would always jump to the fire, and lay up the sticks.

There were various ways of teaching and training the children. Men would make long speeches to groups of boys, playing in the camps, telling them what they ought to do to be successful in life. They would point out to them that to accomplish anything they must be brave and untiring in war; that long life was not desirable; that the old people always had a hard time, were given the worst side of the lodge and generally neglected; that when the camp was moved they suffered from cold; that their sight was dim, so that they could not see far; that their teeth were gone, so that they could not chew their food. Only discomfort and misery await the old. Much better, while the body is strong and in its prime, while the sight is clear, the teeth sound, and the hair still black and long, to die in battle fighting bravely. The example of successful warriors would be held up to them, and the boys urged to emulate their brave deeds. To such advice some boys would listen, while others would not heed it.

The girls also were instructed. All Indians like to see women more or less sober and serious-minded, not giggling all the time, not silly. A Blackfoot man who had two or three girls would, as they grew large, often talk to them and give them good advice. After watching them, and taking the measure of their characters, he would one day get a buffalo's front foot and ornament it fantastically with feathers. When the time came, he would call one of his daughters to him and say to her: "Now I wish you to stand here in front of me and look me straight in the eye without laughing. No matter what I may do, do not laugh." Then he would sing a funny song, shaking the foot in the girl's face in time to the song, and looking her steadily in the eye. Very likely before he had finished, she would begin to giggle. If she did this, the father would stop singing and tell her to finish laughing; and when she was serious again, he would again warn her not to laugh, and then would repeat his song. This time perhaps she would not laugh while he was singing. He would go through with this same performance before all his daughters. To such as seemed to have the steadiest characters, he would give good advice. He would talk to each girl of the duties of a woman's life and warn her against the dangers which she might expect to meet.

At the time of the Medicine Lodge, he would take her to the lodge and point out to her the Medicine Lodge woman. He would say: "There is a good woman. She has built this Medicine Lodge, and is greatly honored and respected by all the people. Once she was a girl just like you; and you, if you are good and live a pure life, may some day be as great as she is now. Remember this, and try to live a worthy life."

At the time of the Medicine Lodge, the boys in the camp also gathered to see the young men count their *coups*. A man would get up, holding in one hand a bundle of small sticks, and, taking one stick from the bundle, he would recount some brave deed, throwing away a stick as he completed the narrative of each *coup*, until the sticks were all gone, when he sat down, and another man stood up to begin his recital. As the boys saw and heard all this, and saw how respected those men were who had done the most and bravest things, they said to themselves, "That man was once a boy like us, and we, if we have strong hearts, may do as much as he has done." So even the very small boys used often to steal off from the camp, and follow war parties. Often they went without the knowledge of their parents, and poorly provided, without food or extra moccasins. They would get to the enemy's camp, watch the ways of the young men, and so learn about going to war, how to act when on the war trail so as to be successful. Also they came to know the country.

The Blackfeet men often went off by themselves to fast and dream for power. By no means every one did this, and, of those who attempted it, only a few endured to the end,—that is, fasted the whole four days,—and obtained the help sought. The attempt was not usually made by young boys before they had gone on their first war journey. It was often undertaken by men who were quite mature. Those who underwent this suffering were obliged to abstain from food or drink for four days and four nights, resting for two nights on the right side, and for two nights on the left. It was deemed essential that the place to which a man resorted for this purpose should be unfrequented, where few or no persons had walked; and it must also be a place that tried the nerve, where there was some danger. Such situations were mountain peaks; or narrow ledges on cut cliffs, where a careless movement might cause a man to fall to his death on the rocks below; or islands in lakes, which could only be reached by means of a raft, and where there was danger that a person might be seized and carried off by the Sū'-yē tŭp'-pi, or Under Water People; or places where the dead had been buried, and where there was much danger from ghosts. Or a man might lie in a well-worn buffalo trail, where the animals were frequently passing, and so he might be trodden on by a travelling band of buffalo; or he might choose a locality where bears were abundant and dangerous. Wherever he went, the man built himself a little lodge of brush, moss, and leaves, to keep off the rain; and, after making his prayers to the sun and singing his sacred songs, he crept into the hut and began his fast. He was not allowed to take any covering with him, nor to roof over his shelter with skins. He always had with him a pipe, and this lay by him, filled, so that, when the spirit, or dream, came, it could smoke. They did not appeal to any special class of helpers, but prayed to all alike. Often by the end of the fourth day, a secret helper—usually, but by no means always, in the form of some animal—appeared to the man in a dream, and talked with him, advising him, marking out his course through life, and giving him its power. There were some, however, on whom the power would not work, and a much greater number who gave up the fast, discouraged, before the prescribed time had been completed, either not being able to endure the lack of food and water, or being frightened by the strangeness or loneliness of their surroundings, or by something that they thought they saw or heard. It was no disgrace to fail, nor was the failure necessarily known, for the seeker after power did not always, nor perhaps often, tell any one what he was going to do.

Three modes of burial were practised by the Blackfeet. They buried their dead on platforms placed in trees, on platforms in lodges, and on the ground in lodges. If a man dies in a lodge, it is never used again. The people would be afraid of the man's ghost. The lodge is often used to wrap the body in, or perhaps the man may be buried in it.

As soon as a person is dead, be it man, woman, or child, the body is immediately prepared for burial, by the nearest female relations. Until recently, the corpse was wrapped in a number of robes, then in a lodge covering, laced with rawhide ropes, and placed on a platform of lodge poles, arranged on the branches of some convenient tree. Some times the outer wrapping—the lodge covering—was omitted. If the deceased was a man, his weapons, and often his medicine, were buried with him. With women a few cooking utensils and implements for tanning robes were placed on the scaffolds. When a man was buried on a platform in a lodge, the platform was usually suspended from the lodge poles.

Sometimes, when a great chief or noted warrior died, his lodge would be moved some little distance from the camp, and set up in a patch of brush. It would be carefully pegged down all around, and stones piled on the edges to make it additionally firm. For still greater security, a rope fastened to the lodge poles, where they come together at the smoke hole, came down, and was securely tied to a peg in the ground in the centre of the lodge, where the fireplace would ordinarily be. Then the beds were made up all around the lodge, and on one of them was placed the corpse, lying as if asleep. The man's weapons, pipe, war clothing, and medicine were placed near him, and the door then closed. No one ever again entered such a lodge. Outside the lodge, a number of his horses, often twenty or more, were killed, so that he might have plenty to ride on his journey to the Sand Hills, and to use after arriving there. If a man had a favorite horse, he might order it to be killed at his grave, and his order was always carried out. In ancient times, it is said, dogs were killed at the grave.

Women mourn for deceased relations by cutting their hair short. For the loss of a husband or son (but not a daughter), they not only cut their hair, but often take off one or more joints of their fingers, and always scarify the calves of their legs. Besides this, for a month or so, they daily repair to some place near camp, generally a hill or little rise of ground, and there cry and lament, calling the name of the deceased over and over again. This may be called a chant or song, for there is a certain tune to it. It is in a minor key and very doleful. Any one hearing it for the first time, even though wholly unacquainted with Indian customs, would at once know that it was a mourning song, or at least was the utterance of one in deep distress. There is no fixed period for the length of time one must mourn. Some keep up this daily lament for a few weeks only, and others much longer. I once came across an old wrinkled woman, who was crouched in the sage brush, crying and lamenting for some one, as if her heart would break. On inquiring if any one had lately died, I was told she was mourning for a son she had lost more than twenty years before.

Men mourn by cutting a little of their hair, going without leggings, and for the loss of a son, sometimes scarify their legs. This last, however, is never done for the loss of a wife, daughter, or any relative except a son.

Many Blackfeet change their names every season. Whenever a Blackfoot counts a new *coup*, he is entitled to a new name. A Blackfoot will never tell his name if he can avoid it. He believes that if he should speak his name, he would be unfortunate in all his undertakings.

It was considered a gross breach of propriety for a man to meet his mother-in-law, and if by any mischance he did so, or what was worse, if he spoke to her, she demanded a very heavy payment, which he was obliged to make. The mother-in-law was equally anxious to avoid meeting or speaking to her son-in-law.

HOW THE BLACKFOOT LIVED

The primitive clothing of the Blackfeet was made of the dressed skins of certain animals. Women seldom wore a head covering. Men, however, in winter generally used a cap made of the skin of some small animal, such as the antelope, wolf, badger, or coyote. As the skin from the head of these animals often formed part of the cap, the ears being left on, it made a very odd-looking head-dress. Sometimes a cap was made of the skin of some large bird, such as the sage-hen, duck, owl, or swan.

The ancient dress of the women was a shirt of cowskin, with long sleeves tied at the wrist, a skirt reaching half-way from knees to ankles, and leggings tied above the knees, with sometimes a supporting string running from the belt to the leggings. In more modern times, this was modified, and a woman's dress consisted of a gown or smock, reaching from the neck to below the knees. There were no sleeves, the armholes being provided with top coverings, a sort of cape or flap, which reached to the elbows. Leggings were of course still worn. They reached to the knee, and were generally made, as was the gown, of the tanned skins of elk, deer, sheep, or antelope. Moccasins for winter use were made of buffalo robe, and of tanned buffalo cowskin for summer wear. The latter were always made with parfleche soles, which greatly increased their durability, and were often ornamented over the instep or toes with a three-pronged figure, worked in porcupine quills or beads, the three prongs representing, it is said, the three divisions or tribes of the nation. The men wore a shirt, breech-clout, leggings which reached to the thighs, and moccasins. In winter both men and women wore a robe of tanned buffalo skin, and sometimes of beaver. In summer a lighter robe was worn, made of cowskin or buckskin, from which the hair had been removed. Both sexes wore belts, which supported and confined the clothing, and to which were attached knife-sheaths and other useful articles.

Necklaces and ear-rings were worn by all, and were made of shells, bone, wood, and the teeth and claws of animals. Elk tushes were highly prized, and were used for ornamenting women's dresses. A gown profusely decorated with them was worth two good horses. Eagle feathers were used by the men to make head-dresses and to ornament shields and also weapons. Small bunches of owl or grouse feathers were sometimes tied to the scalp locks. It is doubtful if the women ever took particular care of their hair. The men, however, spent a great deal of time brushing, braiding, and ornamenting their scalp locks. Their hair was usually worn in two braids, one on each side of the head. Less frequently, four braids were made, one behind and in front of each ear. Sometimes, the hair of the forehead was cut off square, and brushed straight up; and not infrequently it was made into a huge topknot and wound with otter fur. Often a slender lock, wound with brass wire or braided, hung down from one side of the forehead over the face.

As a rule, the men are tall, straight, and well formed. Their features are regular, the eyes being large and well set, and the nose generally moderately large, straight, and thin. Their chests are splendidly developed. The women are quite tall for their sex, but, as a rule, not so good-looking as the men. Their hands are large, coarse, and knotted by hard labor; and they early become wrinkled and careworn. They generally have splendid constitutions. I have known them to resume work a day after childbirth; and once, when travelling, I knew a woman to halt, give birth to a child, and catch up with the camp inside of four hours.

As a rule, children are hardy and vigorous. They are allowed to do about as they please from the time they are able to walk. I have often seen them playing in winter in the snow, and spinning tops on the ice, barefooted and half-naked. Under such conditions, those which have feeble constitutions soon die. Only the hardiest reach maturity and old age.

It is said that very long ago the people made houses of mud, sticks, and stones. It is not known what was their size or shape, and no traces of them are known to have been found. For a very long time, the lodge seems to have been their only dwelling. In ancient times, before they had knives of metal, stones were used to hold down the edges of the lodge, to keep it from being blown away. These varied in size from six inches to a foot or more in diameter. Everywhere on the prairie, one may now see circles of these stones, and, within these circles, the smaller ones, which surrounded the fireplace. Some of them have lain so long that only the tops now project above the turf, and undoubtedly many of them are buried out of sight.

Lodges were always made of tanned cowskin, nicely cut and sewn together, so as to form an almost perfect cone. At the top were two large flaps, called ears, which were kept extended or closed, according to the direction and strength of the wind, to create a draft and keep the lodge free from smoke. The lodge covering was supported by light, straight pine or spruce poles, about eighteen of which were required. Twelve cowskins made a lodge about fourteen feet in diameter at the base, and ten feet high. I have heard of a modern one which contained forty skins. It was over thirty feet in diameter, and was so heavy that the skins were sewn in two pieces which buttoned together.

An average-sized dwelling of this kind contained eighteen skins and was about sixteen feet in diameter. The lower edge of the lodge proper was fastened, by wooden pegs, to within an inch or two of the ground. Inside, a lining, made of brightly painted cowskin, reached from the ground to a height of five or six feet. An air space of the thickness of the lodge poles—two or three inches—was thus left between the lining and the lodge covering, and the cold air, rushing up through it from the outside, made a draft, which aided the ears in freeing the lodge of smoke. The door was three or four feet high and was covered by a flap of skin, which hung down on the outside. Thus made, with plenty of buffalo robes for seats and bedding, and a good stock of firewood, a lodge was very comfortable, even in the coldest weather.

It was not uncommon to decorate the outside of the lodge with buffalo tails and brightly painted pictures of animals. Inside, the space around was partitioned off into couches, or seats, each about six feet in length. At the foot and head of every couch, a mat, made of straight, peeled willow twigs, fastened side by side, was suspended on a tripod at an angle of forty-five degrees, so that between the couches spaces were left like an inverted V, making convenient places to store articles which were not in use. The owner of the lodge always occupied the seat or couch at the back of the lodge, directly opposite the door-way, the places on his right being occupied by his wives and daughters; though sometimes a Blackfoot had so many wives that they occupied the whole lodge. The places on his left were reserved for his sons and visitors. When a visitor entered a lodge, he was assigned a seat according to his rank,—the nearer to the host, the greater the honor.

Bows were generally made of ash wood, which grows east of the mountains toward the Sand Hills. When for any reason they could not obtain ash, they used the wood of the choke-cherry tree, but this had not strength nor spring enough to be of much service. I have been told also that sometimes they used hazle wood for bows.

Arrows were made of shoots of the sarvis berry wood, which was straight, very heavy, and not brittle. They were smoothed and straightened by a stone implement. The grooves were made by pushing the shafts through a rib or other flat bone in which had been made a hole, circular except for one or two projections on the inside. These projections worked out the groove. The object of these grooves is said to have been to allow the blood to flow freely. Each man marked his arrows by painting them, or by some special combination of colored feathers. The arrow heads were of two kinds,—barbed slender points for war, and barbless for hunting. Knives were originally made of stone, as were also war clubs, mauls, and some of the scrapers for fleshing and graining hides. Some of the flint knives were long, others short. A stick was fitted to them, forming a wooden handle. The handles of mauls and war clubs were usually made of green sticks fitted as closely as possible into a groove made in the stone, the whole being bound together by a covering of hide put on green, tightly fitted and strongly sewed. This, as it shrunk in drying, bound the different parts of the implement together in the strongest possible manner. Short, heavy spears were used, the points being of stone or bone, barbed.

I have heard no explanation among the Blackfeet of the origin of fire. In ancient times, it was obtained by means of fire sticks, as described elsewhere. The starting of the spark with these sticks is said to have been hard work. At almost their first meeting with the whites, they obtained flints and steels, and learned how to use them.

In ancient times,—in the days of fire sticks and even later, within the memory of men now living,—fire used to be carried from place to place in a "fire horn." This was a buffalo horn slung by a string over the shoulder like a powder horn. The horn was lined with moist, rotten wood, and the open end had a wooden stopper or plug fitted to it. On leaving camp in the morning, the man who carried the horn took from the fire a small live coal and put it in the horn, and on this coal placed a piece of punk, and then plugged up the horn with the stopper. The punk smouldered in this almost air-tight chamber, and, in the course of two or three hours, the man looked at it, and if it was nearly consumed, put another piece of punk in the horn. The first young men who reached the appointed camping ground would gather two or three large piles of wood in different places, and as soon as some one who carried a fire horn reached camp, he turned out his spark at one of these piles of wood, and a little blowing and nursing gave a blaze which started the fire. The other fires were kindled from this first one, and when the women reached camp and had put the lodges up, they went to these fires, and got coals with which to start those in their lodges. This custom of borrowing coals persisted up to the last days of the buffalo, and indeed may even be noticed still.

The punk here mentioned is a fungus, which grows on the birch tree. The Indians used to gather this in large quantities and dry it. It was very abundant at the Touchwood Hills (whence the name) on Beaver Creek, a tributary of the Saskatchewan from the south.

The Blackfeet made buckets, cups, basins, and dishes from the lining of the buffalo's paunch. This was torn off in large pieces, and was stretched over a flattened willow or cherry hoop at the bottom and top. These hoops were sometimes inside and sometimes outside the bucket or dish. In the latter case, the hoop at the bottom was often sewed to the paunch, which came down over it, double on the outside, the needle holes being pitched with gum or tallow. The hoop at the upper edge was also sewed to the paunch, and a rawhide bail passed under it, to carry it by.

These buckets were shaped somewhat like our wooden ones, and were of different sizes, some of them holding four or five gallons. They were more or less flexible, and when carried in a pack, they could be flattened down like a crush hat, and so took up but little room. If set on the ground when full, they would stand up for a while, but as they soon softened and fell down, they were usually hung up by the bail on a little tripod. Cups were made in the same way as buckets, but on a smaller scale and without the bail. Of course, nothing hot could be placed in these vessels.

It is doubtful if the Blackfeet ever made any pottery or basket ware. They, however, made bowls and kettles of stone. There is an ancient children's song which consists of a series of questions asked an elk, and its replies to the same. In one place, the questioner sings, "Elk, what is your bowl (or dish)?" and the elk answers, "*Ok-wi-tok-so-ka*," stone bowl. On this point, Wolf Calf, a very old man, states that in early days the Blackfeet sometimes boiled their meat in a stone bowl made out of a hard clayey rock. Choosing a fragment of the right size and shape, they would pound it with another heavier rock, dealing light blows until a hollow had been made in the top. This hollow was made deeper by pounding and grinding; and when it was deep enough, they put water in it, and set it on the fire, and the water would boil. These pots were strong and would last a long time. I do not remember that any other tribe of Plains Indians made such stone bowls or mortars, though, of course, they were commonly made, and in singular perfection, by the Pacific Coast tribes; and I have known of rare cases in which basalt mortars and small soapstone ollas have been found on the central plateau of the continent in southern Wyoming. These articles, however, had no doubt been obtained by trade from Western tribes.

Serviceable ladles and spoons were made of wood and of buffalo and mountain sheep horn. Basins or flat dishes were sometimes made of mountain sheep horn, boiled, split, and flattened, and also of split buffalo horn, fitted and sewn together with sinew, making a flaring, saucer-shaped dish. These were used as plates or eating dishes. Of course, they leaked a little, for the joints were not tight. Wooden bowls and dishes were made from knots and protuberances of trees, dug out and smoothed by fire and the knife or by the latter alone.

It is not known that these people ever made spears, hooks, or other implements for capturing fish. They appear never to have used boats of any kind, not even "bull boats." Their highest idea of navigation was to lash together a few sticks or logs, on which to transport their possessions across a river.

Red, brown, yellow, and white paints were made by burning clays of these colors, which were then pulverized and mixed with a little grease. Black paint was made of charred wood.

Bags and sacks were made of parfleche, usually ornamented with buckskin fringe, and painted with various designs in bright colors. Figures having sharp angles are most common.

The diet of the Blackfeet was more varied than one would think. Large quantities of sarvis berries (*Amelanchier alnifolia*) were gathered whenever there was a crop (which occurs every other year), dried, and stored for future use. These were gathered by women, who collected the branches laden with ripe fruit, and beat them over a robe spread upon the ground. Choke-cherries were also gathered when ripe, and pounded up, stones and all. A bushel of the fruit, after being pounded up and dried, was reduced to a very small quantity. This food was sometimes eaten by itself, but more often was used to flavor soups and to mix with pemmican. Bull berries (*Shepherdia argentea*) were a favorite fruit, and were gathered in large quantities, as was also the white berry of the red willow. This last is an exceedingly bitter, acrid fruit, and to the taste of most white men wholly unpleasant and repugnant. The Blackfeet, however, are very fond of it; perhaps because it contains some property necessary to the nourishment of the body, which is lacking in their every-day food.

The camas root, which grows abundantly in certain localities on the east slope of the Rockies, was also dug, cooked, and dried. The bulbs were roasted in pits, as by the Indians on the west side of the Rocky Mountains, the Kalispels, and others. It is gathered while in the bloom—June 15 to July 15. A large pit is dug in which a hot fire is built, the bottom being first lined with flat stones. After keeping up this fire for several hours, until the stones and earth are thoroughly heated, the coals and ashes are removed. The pit is then lined with grass, and is filled almost to the top with camas bulbs. Over these, grass is laid, then twigs, and then earth to a depth of four inches. On this a fire is built, which is kept up for from one to three days, according to the quantity of the bulbs in the pit.

When the pit is opened, the small children gather about it to suck the syrup, which has collected on the twigs and grass, and which is very sweet. The fresh-roasted camas tastes something like a roasted chestnut, with a little of the flavor of the sweet potato. After being cooked, the roots are spread out in the sun to dry, and are then put in sacks to be stored away. Sometimes a few are pounded up with sarvis berries, and dried.

Bitter-root is gathered, dried, and boiled with a little sugar. It is a slender root, an inch or two long and as thick as a goose quill, white in color, and looking like short lengths of spaghetti. It is very starchy.

In the spring, a certain root called *mats* was eaten in great quantities. This plant was known to the early French employees of the Hudson's Bay and American Fur Companies as *pomme blanche* (*Psoralea esculenta*).

All parts of such animals as the buffalo, elk, deer, etc., were eaten, save only the lungs, gall, and one or two other organs. A favorite way of eating the paunch or stomach was in the raw state. Liver, too, was sometimes eaten raw. The unborn calf of a fresh-killed animal, especially buffalo, was considered a great delicacy. The meat of this, when boiled, is white, tasteless, and insipid. The small intestines of the buffalo were sometimes dried, but more often were stuffed with long, thin strips of meat. During the stuffing process, the entrail was turned inside out, thus confining with the meat the sweet white fat that covers the intestine. The next step was to roast it a little, after which the ends were tied to prevent the escape of the juices, and it was thoroughly boiled in water. This is a very great delicacy, and when properly prepared is equally appreciated by whites and Indians.

As a rule, there were but two ways of cooking meat,—boiling and roasting. If roasted, it was thoroughly cooked; but if boiled, it was only left in the water long enough to lose the red color, say five or ten minutes. Before they got kettles from the whites, the Blackfeet often boiled meat in a green hide. A hole was dug in the ground, and the skin, flesh side up, was laid in it, being supported about the edges of the hole by pegs. The meat and water having been placed in this hollow, red-hot stones were dropped in the water until it became hot and the meat was cooked.

In time of plenty, great quantities of dried meat were prepared for use when fresh meat could not be obtained. In making dried meat, the thicker parts of an animal were cut in large, thin sheets and hung in the sun to dry. If the weather was not fine, the meat was often hung up on lines or scaffolds in the upper part of the lodge. When properly cured and if of good quality, the sheets were about one-fourth of an inch thick and very brittle. The back fat of the buffalo was also dried, and eaten with the meat as we eat butter with bread. Pemmican was made of the flesh of the buffalo. The meat was dried in the usual way; and, for this use, only lean meat, such as the hams, loin, and shoulders, was chosen. When the time came for making the pemmican, two large fires were built of dry quaking aspen wood, and these were allowed to burn down to red coals. The old women brought the dried meat to these fires, and the sheets of meat were thrown on the coals of one of them, allowed to heat through, turned to keep them from burning, and then thrown on the flesh side of a dry hide, that lay on the ground near by. After a time, the roasting of this dried meat caused a smoke to rise from the fire in use, which gave the meat a bitter taste, if cooked in it. They then turned to the other fire, and used that until the first one had burned clear again. After enough of the roasted meat had been thrown on the hide, it was flailed out with sticks, and being very brittle was easily broken up, and made small. It was constantly stirred and pounded until it was all fine. Meantime, the tallow of the buffalo had been melted in a large kettle, and the pemmican bags prepared. These were made of bull's hide, and were in two pieces, cut oblong, and with the corners rounded off. Two such pieces sewed together made a bag which would hold one hundred pounds. The pounded meat and tallow—the latter just beginning to cool—were put in a trough made of bull's hide, a wooden spade being used to stir the mixture. After it was thoroughly mixed, it was shovelled into one of the sacks, held open, and rammed down and packed tight with a big stick, every effort being made to expel all the air. When the bag was full and packed as tight as possible, it was sewn up. It was then put on the ground, and the women jumped on it to make it still more tight and solid. It was then laid away in the sun to cool and dry. It usually took the meat of two cows to make a bag of one hundred pounds; a very large bull might make a sack of from eighty to one hundred pounds.

A much finer grade of pemmican was made from the choicest parts of the buffalo with marrow fat. To this dried berries and pounded choke-cherries were added, making a delicious food, which was extremely nutritious. Pemmican was eaten either dry as it came from the sack, or stewed with water.

In the spring, the people had great feasts of the eggs of ducks and other water-fowl. A large quantity having been gathered, a hole was dug in the ground, and a little water put in it. At short intervals above the water, platforms of sticks were built, on which the eggs were laid. A smaller hole was dug at one side of the large hole, slanting into the bottom of it. When all was ready, the top of the larger hole was covered with mud, laid upon cross sticks, and red-hot stones were dropped into the slant, when they rolled down into the water, heating it, and so cooking the eggs by steam.

Fish were seldom eaten by these people in early days, but now they seem very fond of them. Turtles, frogs, and lizards are considered creatures of evil, and are never eaten. Dogs, considered a great delicacy by the Crees, Gros Ventres, Sioux, Assinaboines, and other surrounding tribes, were never eaten by the Blackfeet. No religious motive is assigned for this abstinence. I once heard a Piegan say that it was wrong to eat dogs. "They are our true friends," he said. "Men say they are our friends and then turn against us, but our dogs are always true. They mourn when we are absent, and are always glad when we return. They keep watch for us in the night when we sleep. So pity the poor dogs."

Snakes, grasshoppers, worms, and other insects were never eaten. Salt was an unknown condiment. Many are now very fond of it, but I know a number, especially old people, who never eat it.

SOCIAL ORGANIZATION

The social organization of the Blackfeet is very simple. The three tribes acknowledged a blood relationship with each other, and, while distinct, still considered themselves a nation. In this confederation, it was understood that there should be no war against each other. However, between 1860 and 1870, when the whiskey trade was in its height, the three tribes were several times at swords' points on account of drunken brawls. Once, about sixty or seventy years ago, the Bloods and Piegans had a quarrel so serious that men were killed on both sides and horses stolen; yet this was hardly a real war, for only a part of each tribe was involved, and the trouble was not of long duration.

Each one of the Blackfoot tribes is subdivided into gentes, a gens being a body of consanguineal kindred in the male line. It is noteworthy that the Blackfeet, although Algonquins, have this system of subdivision, and it may be that among them the gentes are of comparatively recent date. No special duties are assigned to any one gens, nor has any gens, so far as I know, any special "medicine" or "totem."

Below is a list of the gentes of each tribe.

BLACKFEET *(Sik'-si-kau)*

Gentes:

Puh-ksi-nah'-mah-yiks	Flat Bows.
Mo-tah'-tos-iks	Many Medicines.
Siks-in'-o-kaks	Black Elks.
E'-mi-tah-pahk-sai-yiks	Dogs Naked.
Sa'-yiks	Liars.
Ai-sik'-stuk-iks	Biters.
Tsin-ik-tsis'-tso-yiks	Early Finished Eating.
Ap'-i-kai-yiks	Skunks.

BLOODS (*Kai'-nah*)

Siksin'-o-kaks	Black Elks.
Ah-kwo'-nis-tsists	Many Lodge Poles.
Ap-ut'-o-si'kai-nah	North Bloods.
Is-ts'-kai-nah	Woods Bloods.
In-uhk'-so-yi-stam-iks	Long Tail Lodge Poles.
Nit'-ik-skiks	Lone Fighters.
Siks-ah'-pun-iks	Blackblood.
Ah-kaik'-sum-iks	
I-sis'-o-kas-im-iks	Hair Shirts.
Ak-kai'-po-kaks	Many Children.
Sak-si-nah'-mah-yiks	Short Bows.
Ap'-i-kai-yiks	Skunks.
Ahk-o'-tash-iks	Many Horses.

PIEGANS (*Pi-kun'-i*)

Ah'-pai-tup-iks	Blood People.
Ah-kai-yi-ko-ka'-kin-iks	White Breasts.
Ki'yis	Dried Meat.
Sik-ut'-si-pum-aiks	Black Patched Moccasins.
Sik-o-pok'-si-maiks	Blackfat Roasters.
Tsin-ik-sis'-tso-yiks	Early Finished Eating.
Kut'-ai-im-iks	They Don't Laugh.

I'-pok-si-maiks	Fat Roasters.
Sik'-o-kit-sim-iks	Black Doors.
Ni-taw'-yiks	Lone Eaters.
Ap'-i-kai-yiks	Skunks.
Mi-ah-wah'-pit-siks	Seldom Lonesome.
Nit'-ak-os-kit-si-pup-iks	Obstinate.
Nit'-ik-skiks	Lone Fighters.
I-nuks'-iks	Small Robes.
Mi-aw'-kin-ai-yiks	Big Topknots.
Esk'-sin-ai-tup-iks	Worm People.
I-nuk-si'-kah-ko-pwa-iks	Small Brittle Fat.
Kah'-mi-taiks	Buffalo Dung.
Kut-ai-sot'-si-man	No Parfleche.
Ni-tot'-si-ksis-stan-iks	Kill Close By.
Mo-twai'-naiks	All Chiefs.
Mo-kum'-iks	Red Round Robes.
Mo-tah'-tos-iks	Many Medicines.

It will be readily seen from the translations of the above that each gens takes its name from some peculiarity or habit it is supposed to possess. It will also be noticed that each tribe has a few gentes common to one or both of the other tribes. This is caused by persons leaving their own tribe to live with another one, but, instead of uniting with some gens of the adopted tribe, they have preserved the name of their ancestral gens for themselves and their descendants.

The Blackfoot terms of relationship will be found interesting. The principal family names are as follows:—

My father	*Ni'-nah.*
My mother	*Ni-kis'-ta.*
My elder brother	*Nis'-ah*
My younger brother	*Nis-kun'.*
My older sister	*Nin'-sta.*
My younger sister	*Ni-sis'-ah.*
My uncle	*Nis'-ah.*
My aunt	*Ni-kis'-ta.*
My cousin, male	Same as brother.
My cousin, female	Same as sister.
My grandfather	*Na-ahks'.*
My grandmother	*Na-ahks'.*
My father-in-law	*Na-ahks'.*
My mother-in-law	*Na-ahks'.*
My son	*No-ko'-i.*
My daughter	*Ni-tun'.*
My son-in-law	*Nis'-ah.*

My daughter-in-law	*Ni-tot´-o-ke-man.*
My brother-in-law older than self	*Nis-tum-o´.*
My brother-in-law younger than self	*Nis-tum-o´-kun.*
My sister-in-law	*Ni-tot´-o-ke-man.*
My second cousin	*Nimp´-sa.*
My wife	*Nit-o-ke´-man.*
My husband	*No´-ma.*

As the members of a gens were all considered as relatives, however remote, there was a law prohibiting a man from marrying within his gens. Originally this law was strictly enforced, but like many of the ancient customs it is no longer observed. Lately, within the last forty or fifty years, it has become not uncommon for a man and his family, or even two or three families, on account of some quarrel or some personal dislike of the chief of their own gens, to leave it and join another band. Thus the gentes often received outsiders, who were not related by blood to the gens; and such people or their descendants could marry within the gens. Ancestry became no longer necessary to membership.

As a rule, before a young man could marry, he was required to have made some successful expeditions to war against the enemy, thereby proving himself a brave man, and at the same time acquiring a number of horses and other property, which would enable him to buy the woman of his choice, and afterwards to support her.

Marriages usually took place at the instance of the parents, though often those of the young man were prompted by him. Sometimes the father of the girl, if he desired to have a particular man for a son-in-law, would propose to the father of the latter for the young man as a husband for his daughter.

The marriage in the old days was arranged after this wise: The chief of one of the bands may have a marriageable daughter, and he may know of a young man, the son of a chief of another band, who is a brave warrior, of good character, sober-minded, steadfast, and trustworthy, who he thinks will make a good husband for his daughter and a good son-in-law. After he has made up his mind about this, he is very likely to call in a few of his close relations, the principal men among them, and state to them his conclusions, so as to get their opinions about it. If nothing is said to change his mind, he sends to the father of the boy a messenger to state his own views, and ask how the father feels about the matter.

On receiving this word, the boy's father probably calls together his close relations, discusses the matter with them, and, if the match is satisfactory to him, sends back word to that effect. When this message is received, the relations of the girl proceed to fit her out with the very best that they can provide. If she is the daughter of well-to-do or wealthy people, she already has many of the things that are needed, but what she may lack is soon supplied. Her mother makes her a new cowskin lodge, complete, with new lodge poles, lining, and back rests. A chiefs daughter would already have plenty of good clothing, but if the girl lacks anything, it is furnished. Her dress is made of antelope skin, white as snow, and perhaps ornamented with two or three hundred elk tushes. Her leggings are of deer skin, heavily beaded and nicely fringed, and often adorned with bells and brass buttons. Her summer blanket or sheet is an elk skin, well tanned, without the hair and with the dew-claws left on. Her moccasins are of deer skin, with parfleche soles and worked with porcupine quills. The marriage takes place as soon as these things can be provided.

During the days which intervene between the proposal and the marriage, the young woman each day selects the choicest parts of the meat brought to the lodge,—the tongue, "boss ribs," some choice berry pemmican or what not,—cooks these things in the best style, and, either alone, or in company with a young sister, or a young friend, goes over to the lodge where the young man lives, and places the food before him. He eats some of it, little or much, and if he leaves anything, the girl offers it to his mother, who may eat of it. Then the girl takes the dishes and returns to her father's lodge. In this way she provides him with three meals a day, morning, noon, and night, until the marriage takes place. Every one in camp who sees the girl carrying the food in a covered dish to the young man's lodge, knows that a marriage is to take place; and the girl is watched by idle persons as she passes to and fro, so that the task is quite a trying one for people as shy and bashful as

Indians are. When the time for the marriage has come,—in other words, when the girl's parents are ready,—the girl, her mother assisting her, packs the new lodge and her own things on the horses, and moves out into the middle of the circle—about which all the lodges of the tribe are arranged—and there the new lodge is unpacked and set up. In front of the lodge are tied, let us say, fifteen horses, the girl's dowry given by her father. Very likely, too, the father has sent over to the young man his own war clothing and arms, a lance, a fine shield, a bow and arrows in otter-skin case, his war bonnet, war shirt, and war leggings ornamented with scalps,—his complete equipment. This is set up on a tripod in front of the lodge. The gift of these things is an evidence of the great respect felt by the girl's father for his son-in-law. As soon as the young man has seen the preparations being made for setting up the girl's lodge in the centre of the circle, he sends over to his father-in-law's lodge just twice the number of horses that the girl brought with her,—in this supposed case, thirty.

As soon as this lodge is set up, and the girl's mother has taken her departure and gone back to her own lodge, the young man, who, until he saw these preparations, had no knowledge of when the marriage was to take place, leaves his father's lodge, and, going over to the newly erected one, enters and takes his place at the back of it. Probably during the day he will order his wife to take down the lodge, and either move away from the camp, or at least move into the circle of lodges; for he will not want to remain with his young wife in the most conspicuous place in the camp. Often, on the same day, he will send for six or eight of his friends, and, after feasting them, will announce his intention of going to war, and will start off the same night. If he does so, and is successful, returning with horses or scalps, or both, he at once, on arrival at the camp, proceeds to his father-in-law's lodge and leaves there everything he has brought back, returning to his own lodge on foot, as poor as he left it.

We have supposed the proposal in this case to come from the father of the girl, but if a boy desires a particular girl for his wife, the proposal will come from his father; otherwise matters are managed in the same way.

This ceremony of moving into the middle of the circle was only performed in the case of important people. The custom was observed in what might be called a fashionable wedding among the Blackfeet. Poorer, less important people married more quietly. If the girl had reached marriageable age without having been asked for as a wife, she might tell her mother that she would like to marry a certain young man, that he was a man she could love and respect. The mother communicates this to the father of the girl, who invites the young man to the lodge to a feast, and proposes the match. The young man returns no answer at the time, but, going back to his father's lodge, tells him of the offer, and expresses his feelings about it. If he is inclined to accept, the relations are summoned, and the matter talked over. A favorable answer being returned, a certain number of horses—what the young man or his father, or both together, can spare—are sent over to the girl's father. They send as many as they can, for the more they send, the more they are thought of and looked up to. The girl, unless her parents are very poor, has her outfit, a saddle horse and pack horse with saddle and pack saddle, parfleches, etc. If the people are very poor, she may have only a riding horse. Her relations get together, and do all in their power to give her a good fitting out, and the father, if he can possibly do so, is sure to pay them back what they have given. If he cannot do so, the things are still presented; for, in the case of a marriage, the relations on both sides are anxious to do all that they can to give the young people a good start in life. When all is ready, the girl goes to the lodge where her husband lives, and goes in. If this lodge is too crowded to receive the couple, the young man will make arrangements for space in the lodge of a brother, cousin, or uncle, where there is more room. These are all his close relations, and he is welcome in any of their lodges, and has rights there.

Sometimes, if two young people are fond of each other, and there is no prospect of their being married, they may take riding horses and a pack horse, and elope at night, going to some other camp for a while. This makes the girl's father angry, for he feels that he has been defrauded of his payments. The young man knows that his father-in-law bears him a grudge, and if he afterwards goes to war and is successful, returning with six or seven horses, he will send them all to the camp where his father-in-law lives, to be tied in front of his lodge. This at once heals the breach, and the couple may return. Even if he has not been successful in war and brought horses, which of course he does not always accomplish, he from time to time sends the old man a present, the best he can. Notwithstanding these efforts at conciliation, the parents feel very bitterly against him. The girl has been stolen. The union is no marriage at all. The old people are ashamed and disgraced for their daughter. Until the father has been pacified by satisfactory payments, there is no marriage. Moreover, unless the young man had made a payment, or at least had endeavored to do so, he would be little thought of among his fellows, and looked down on as a poor creature without any sense of honor.

The Blackfeet take as many wives as they wish; but these ceremonies are only carried out in the case of the first wife, the "sits-beside-him" woman. In the case of subsequent marriages, if the man had proved a good, kind husband to his first wife, other men, who thought a good deal of their daughters, might propose to give them to him, so that they would be well treated. The man sent over the horses to the new father-in-law's lodge, and the girl returned to his, bringing her things with her. Or if the man saw a girl he liked, he would propose for her to her father.

Among the Blackfeet, there was apparently no form of courtship, such as prevails among our southern Indians. Young men seldom spoke to young girls who were not relations, and the girls were carefully guarded. They never went out of the lodge after dark, and never went out during the day, except with the mother or some other old woman. The girl, therefore, had very little choice in the selection of a husband. If a girl was told she must marry a certain man, she had to obey. She might cry, but her father's will was law, and she might be beaten or even killed by him, if she did not do as she was ordered. As a consequence of this severity, suicide was quite common among the Blackfoot girls. A girl ordered to marry a man whom she did not like would often watch her chance, and go out in the brush and hang herself. The girl who could not marry the man she wanted to was likely to do the same thing.

The man had absolute power over his wife. Her life was in his hands, and if he had made a payment for her, he could do with her about as he pleased. On the whole, however, women who behaved themselves were well treated and received a good deal of consideration. Those who were light-headed, or foolish, or obstinate and stubborn were sometimes badly beaten. Those who were unfaithful to their husbands usually had their noses or ears, or both, cut off for the first offence, and were killed either by the husband or some relation, or by the *I-kun-uh'-kah-tsi* for the second. Many of the doctors of the highest reputation in the tribe were women.

It is a common belief among some of those who have investigated the subject that the wife in Indian marriage was actually purchased, and became the absolute property of her husband. Though I have a great respect for some of the opinions which have been expressed on this subject, I am obliged to take an entirely different view of the matter. I have talked this subject over many times with young men and old men of a number of tribes, and I cannot learn from them, or in any other way, that in primitive times the woman was purchased from her father. The husband did not have property rights in his wife. She was not a chattel that he could trade away. He had all personal rights, could beat his wife, or, for cause, kill her, but he could not sell her to another man.

All the younger sisters of a man's wife were regarded as his potential wives. If he was not disposed to marry them, they could not be disposed of to any other man without his consent.

Not infrequently, a man having a marriageable daughter formally gave her to some young man who had proved himself brave in war, successful in taking horses, and, above all, of a generous disposition. This was most often done by men who had no sons to support them in their old age.

It is said that in the old days, before they had horses, young men did not expect to marry until they had almost reached middle life,—from thirty-five to forty years of age. This statement is made by Wolf Calf, who is now very old, almost one hundred years, he believes, and can remember back nearly or quite to the time when the Blackfeet obtained their first horses. In those days, young women did not marry until they were grown up, while of late years fathers not infrequently sell their daughters as wives when they are only children.

The first woman a man marries is called his sits-beside-him wife. She is invested with authority over all the other wives, and does little except to direct the others in their work, and look after the comfort of her husband. Her place in the lodge is on his right-hand side, while the others have their places or seats near the door-way. This wife is even allowed at informal gatherings to take a whiff at the pipe, as it is passed around the circle, and to participate in the conversation.

In the old days, it was a very poor man who did not have three wives. Many had six, eight, and some more than a dozen. I have heard of one who had sixteen. In those times, provided a man had a good-sized band of horses, the more wives he had, the richer he was. He could always find young men to hunt for him, if he furnished the mounts, and, of course, the more wives he had, the more robes and furs they would tan for him.

If, for any cause, a man wished to divorce himself from a woman, he had but to send her back to her parents and demand the price paid for her, and the matter was accomplished. The woman was then free to marry again, provided her parents were willing.

When a man dies, his wives become the potential wives of his oldest brother. Unless, during his life, he has given them outright horses and other property, at his death they are entitled to none of his possessions. If he has sons, the property is divided among them, except a few horses, which are given to his brothers. If he has no sons, all the property goes to his brothers, and if there are no brothers, it goes to the nearest male relatives on the father's side.

The Blackfeet cannot be said to have been slave-holders. It is true that the Crees call the Blackfeet women "Little Slaves." But this, as elsewhere suggested, may refer to the region whence they originally came, though it is often explained that it is on account of the manner in which the Blackfeet treat their women, killing them or mutilating their features for adultery and other serious offences.

Although a woman, all her life, was subject to some one's orders, either parent, relative, or husband, a man from his earliest childhood was free and independent. His father would not punish him for any misconduct, his mother dared not. At an early age he was taught to ride and shoot, and horses were given to him. By the time he was twelve, he had probably been on a war expedition or two. As a rule in later times, young men married when they were seventeen or eighteen years of age; and often they resided for several years with their fathers, until the family became so large that there was not room for them all in the lodge.

There were always in the camp a number of boys, orphans, who became the servants of wealthy men for a consideration; that is, they looked after their patron's horses and hunted, and in return they were provided with suitable food and clothing.

Among the Blackfeet, all men were free and equal, and office was not hereditary. Formerly each gens was governed by a chief, who was entitled to his office by virtue of his bravery and generosity. The head chief was chosen by the chiefs of the gentes from their own number, and was usually the one who could show the best record in war, as proved at the Medicine Lodge, at which time he was elected; and for the ensuing year he was invested with the supreme power. But no matter how brave a man might have been, or how successful in war, he could not hope to be the chief either of a gens or of the tribe, unless he was kind-hearted, and willing to share his prosperity with the poor. For this reason, a chief was never a wealthy man, for what he acquired with one hand he gave away with the other. It was he who decided when the people should move camp, and where they should go. But in this, as in all other important affairs, he generally asked the advice of the minor chiefs.

The *I-kun-uh'-kah-tsi* (All Comrades) were directly under the authority of the head chief, and when any one was to be punished, or anything else was to be done which came within their province as the tribal police, it was he who issued the orders. The following were the crimes which the Blackfeet considered sufficiently serious to merit punishment, and the penalties which attached to them.

Murder: A life for a life, or a heavy payment by the murderer or his relatives at the option of the murdered man's relatives. This payment was often so heavy as absolutely to strip the murderer of all property.

Theft: Simply the restoration of the property.

Adultery: For the first offence the husband generally cut off the offending wife's nose or ears; for the second offence she was killed by the All Comrades. Often the woman, if her husband complained of her, would be killed by her brothers or first cousins, and this was more usual than death at the hands of the All Comrades. However, the husband could have her put to death for the first offence, if he chose.

Treachery (that is, when a member of the tribe went over to the enemy or gave them any aid whatever): Death at sight.

Cowardice: A man who would not fight was obliged to wear woman's dress, and was not allowed to marry.

If a man left camp to hunt buffalo by himself, thereby driving away the game, the All Comrades were sent after him, and not only brought him back by main force, but often whipped him, tore his lodge to shreds, broke his travois, and often took away his store of dried meat, pemmican, and other food.

The tradition of the origin of the *I-kun-uh'-kah-tsi* has elsewhere been given. This association of the All Comrades consisted of a dozen or more secret societies, graded according to age, the whole constituting an association which was in part benevolent and helpful, and in part military, but whose main function was to punish offences against society at large. All these societies were really law and order associations. The Mŭt'-sĭks, or Braves, was the chief society, but the others helped the Braves.

A number of the societies which made up the *I-kun-uh'-kah-tsi* have been abandoned in recent years, but several of them still exist. Among the Pi-kun'-i, the list—so far as I have it—is as follows, the societies being named in order from those of boyhood to old age:—

SOCIETIES OF THE ALL COMRADES

Tsĭ-stīks',	Little Birds, includes boys from 15 to 20 years old.
Kŭk-kūīcks',	Pigeons, men who have been to war several times.
Tŭis-kĭs-tīks,	Mosquitoes, men who are constantly going to war
Mŭt'-sĭks,	Braves, tried warriors
Knăts-o-mi'-ta,	All Crazy Dogs, about forty years old.
Ma-stoh'-pa-ta-kīks	Raven Bearers.
E'-mi-taks,	Dogs, old men, Dogs and Tails are different societies, but they dress alike and dance together and alike.
Is'-sui,	Tails,

Ĕts-āi´-nah,	Horns, Bloods, obsolete among the Piegans, but still exists with Bloods.
Sin´-o-pah,	Kit-foxes, Piegans,
Ĕ-ĭn´-a-ke,	Catchers or Soldiers, obsolete for 25-30 years, perhaps longer.
Stŭ´mīks,	Bulls, obsolete for 50 years.

There may be other societies of the All Comrades, but these are the only ones that I know of at present. The Mūt'-sĭks, Braves, and the Knats-o-mi'-ta, All Crazy Dogs, still exist, but many of the others are being forgotten. Since the necessity for their existence has passed, they are no longer kept up. They were a part of the old wild life, and when the buffalo disappeared, and the Blackfeet came to live about an agency, and to try to work for a subsistence, the societies soon lost their importance.

The societies known as Little Birds, Mosquitoes, and Doves are not really bands of the All Comrades, but are societies among the boys and young men in imitation of the I-kun-uh´-kah-tsi, but of comparatively recent origin. Men not more than fifty years old can remember when these societies came into existence. Of all the societies of the I-kun-uh´-kah-tsi, the Sin'-o-pah, or Kit-fox band, has the strongest medicine. This corresponds to the Horns society among the Bloods. They are the same band with different names. They have certain peculiar secret and sacred ceremonies, not to be described here.

The society of the Stum´-īks, or Bulls, became obsolete more than fifty years ago. Their dress was very fine,—bulls' heads and robes.

The members of the younger society purchased individually, from the next older one, its rights and privileges, paying horses for them. For example, each member of the Mosquitoes would purchase from some member of the Braves his right of membership in the latter society. The man who has sold his rights is then a member of no society, and if he wishes to belong to one, must buy into the one next higher. Each of these societies kept some old men as members, and these old men acted as messengers, orators, and so on.

The change of membership from one society to another was made in the spring, after the grass had started. Two, three, or more lodge coverings were stretched over poles, making one very large lodge, and in this the ceremonies accompanying the changes took place.

In later times, the Braves were the most important and best known of any of the All Comrades societies. The members of this band were soldiers or police. They were the constables of the camp, and it was their duty to preserve order, and to punish offenders. Sometimes young men would skylark in camp at night, making a great noise when people wanted to sleep, and would play rough practical jokes, that were not at all relished by those who suffered from them. One of the forms which their high spirits took was to lead and push a young colt up to the door of a lodge, after people were asleep, and then, lifting the door, to shove the animal inside and close the door again. Of course the colt, in its efforts to get out to its mother, would run round and round the lodge, trampling over the sleepers and roughly awakening them, knocking things down and creating the utmost confusion, while the mare would be whinnying outside the lodge, and the people within, bewildered and confused, did not know what the disturbance was all about.

The Braves would punish the young men who did such things,—if they could catch them,—tearing up their blankets, taking away their property, and sometimes whipping them severely. They were the peace officers of the camp, like the *lari pūk'ūs* among the Pawnees.

Among the property of the Brave society were two stone-pointed arrows, one "shield you don't sit down with," and one rattle. The man who carried this rattle was known as Brave Dog, and if it passed from one member of the society to another, the new owner became known as Brave Dog. The man who received the shield could not sit down for the next four days and four nights, but for all that time was obliged to run about the camp, or over the prairie, whistling like a rabbit.

The societies known as Soldiers and Bulls had passed out of existence before the time of men now of middle age. The pipe of the Soldier society is still in existence, in the hands of Double Runner. The bull's head war bonnet, which was the insignia of the Bulls society, was formerly in the possession of Young Bear Chief, at present chief of the Don't Laugh band of the Piegans. He gave it to White Calf, who presented it to a recent agent.

In the old days, and, indeed, down to the time of the disappearance of the buffalo, the camp was always arranged in the form of a circle, the lodges standing at intervals around the circumference, and in the wide inner space there was another circle of lodges occupied by the chief of certain bands of the *I-kun-uh´-kah-tsi*. When all the gentes of the tribe were present, each had its special position in the circle, and always occupied it. The lodge of the chief of the gens stood just within the circle, and about it his people camped. The order indicated in the accompanying diagram represents the Piegan camp as it used to stand thirty-five or forty years ago. A number of the gentes are now extinct, and it is not altogether certain just what the position of those should be; for while all the older men agree on the position to be assigned to certain of the gentes, there are others about which there are differences of opinion or much uncertainty. It is stated that the gentes known as Seldom Lonesome, Dried Meat, and No Parfleche belong to that section of the tribe known as North Piegans, which, at the time of the first treaty, separated from the Pi-kun'-i, and elected to live under British rule.

The lodges of the chiefs of the *I-kun-uh´-kah-tsi* which were within the circle served as lounging and eating places for such members of the bands as were on duty, and were council lodges or places for idling, as the occasion demanded.

When the camp moved, the Blood gens moved first and was followed by the White Breast gens, and so on around the circle to number 24. On camping, the Bloods camped first, and the others after them in the order indicated, number 24 camping last and closing up the circle.

HUNTING

The Blackfoot country probably contained more game and in greater variety than any other part of the continent. Theirs was a land whose physical characteristics presented sharp contrasts. There were far-stretching grassy prairies, affording rich pasturage for the buffalo and the antelope; rough breaks and bad lands for the climbing mountain sheep; wooded buttes, loved by the mule deer; timbered river bottoms, where the white-tailed deer and the elk could browse and hide; narrow, swampy valleys for the moose; and snow-patched, glittering pinnacles of rock, over which the sure-footed white goat took his deliberate way. The climate varied from arid to humid; the game of the prairie, the timber, and the rocks, found places suited to their habits. Fur-bearing animals abounded. Noisy hordes of wild fowl passed north and south in their migrations, and many stopped here to breed.

The Blackfoot country is especially favored by the warm chinook winds, which insure mild winters with but little snow; and although on the plains there is usually little rain in summer, the short prairie grasses are sweet and rich. All over this vast domain, the buffalo were found in countless herds. Elk, deer, antelope, mountain sheep, and bear without number were there. In those days, sheep were to be found on every ridge, and along the rough bad lands far from the mountains. Now, except a few in the "breaks" of the Missouri, they occur only on the highest and most inaccessible mountains, along with the white goats, which, although pre-eminently mountain animals, were in early days sometimes found far out on the prairie.

BUFFALO

The Blackfeet were a race of meat-eaters, and, while they killed large quantities of other game, they still depended for subsistence on the buffalo. This animal provided them with almost all that they needed in the way of food, clothing, and shelter, and when they had an abundance of the buffalo they lived in comfort.

Almost every part of the beast was utilized. The skin, dressed with the hair on, protected them from the winter's cold; freed from the hair, it was used for a summer sheet or blanket, for moccasins, leggings, shirts, and women's dresses. The tanned cowskins made their lodges, the warmest and most comfortable portable shelters ever devised. From the rawhide, the hair having been shaved off, were made parfleches, or trunks, in which to pack small articles. The tough, thick hide of the bull's neck, spread out and allowed to shrink smooth, made a shield for war which would stop an arrow, and turn a lance thrust or the ball from an old-fashioned, smooth-bore gun. The green hide served as a kettle, in which to boil meat. The skin of the hind leg, cut off above the pastern and again some distance above the hock, was sometimes used as a moccasin or boot, the lower opening being sewed up for the toe. A variety of small articles, such as cradles, gun covers, whips, mittens, quivers, bow cases, knife-sheaths, etc., were made from the hide. Braided strands of hide furnished them with ropes and lines. The hair was used to stuff cushions and, later, saddles, and parts of the long black flowing beard to ornament wearing apparel and implements of war, such as shields and quivers. The horns gave them spoons and ladles—sometimes used as small dishes—and ornamented their war bonnets. From the hoofs they made a glue, which they used in fastening the heads and feathers on their arrows, and the sinew backs on their bows. The sinews which lie along the back and on the belly were used as thread and string, and as backing for bows to give them elasticity and strength. From the ribs were made scrapers used in dressing hides, and runners for small sledges drawn by dogs; and they were employed by the children in coasting down hill on snow or ice. The shoulder-blades, lashed to a wooden handle, formed axes, hoes, and fleshers. From the cannon bones (metatarsals and metacarpals) were made scrapers for dressing hides. The skin of the tail, fitted on a stick, was used as a fly brush. These are but a few of the uses to which the product of the buffalo was put. As has been said, almost every part of the flesh was eaten.

Now it must be remembered that in early days the hunting weapons of this people consisted only of stone-pointed arrows, and with such armament the capture of game of the larger sorts must have been a matter of some uncertainty. To drive a rude stone-headed arrow through the tough hide and into the vitals of the buffalo, could not have been—even under the most favorable circumstances—other than a difficult matter; and although we may assume that, in those days, it was easy to steal up to within a few yards of the unsuspicious animals, we can readily conceive that many arrows must have been shot without effect, for one that brought down the game.

Certain ingenious methods were therefore devised to insure the taking of game in large numbers at one time. This was especially the case with the buffalo, which were the food and raiment of the people. One of these contrivances was called pis´kun, deep-kettle; or, since the termination of the word seems to indicate the last syllable of the word *ah'-pun,* blood, it is more likely deep-blood-kettle. This was a large corral, or enclosure, built out from the foot of a perpendicular cliff or bluff, and formed of natural banks, rocks, and logs or brush,—anything in fact to make a close, high barrier. In some places the enclosure might be only a fence of brush, but even here the buffalo did not break it down, for they did not push against it, but ran round and round within, looking for a clear space through which they might pass. From the top of the bluff, directly over the pis´kun, two long lines of rock piles and brush extended far out on the prairie, ever diverging from each other like the arms of the letter V, the opening over the pis´kun being at the angle.

In the evening of the day preceding a drive of buffalo into the pis´kun a medicine man, usually one who was the possessor of a buffalo rock, In-is'-kim, unrolled his pipe, and prayed to the Sun for success. Next morning the man who was to call the buffalo arose very early, and told his wives that they must not leave the lodge, nor even look out, until he returned; that they should keep burning sweet grass, and should pray to the Sun for his success and safety. Without eating or drinking, he then went up on the prairie, and the people followed him, and concealed themselves behind the rocks and bushes which formed the V, or chute. The medicine man put on a head-dress made of the head of a buffalo, and a robe, and then started out to approach the animals. When he had come near to the herd, he moved about until he had attracted the attention of some of the buffalo, and when they began to look at him, he walked slowly away toward the entrance of the chute. Usually the buffalo followed, and, as they did so, he gradually increased his pace. The buffalo followed more rapidly, and the man continually went a little faster. Finally, when the buffalo were fairly within the chute, the people began to rise up from behind the rock piles which the herd had passed, and to shout and wave their robes. This frightened the hinder-most buffalo, which pushed forward on the others, and before long the whole herd was running at headlong speed toward the precipice, the rock piles directing them to the point over the enclosure. When they reached it, most of the animals were pushed over, and usually even the last of the band plunged blindly down into the pis´kun. Many were killed outright by the fall; others had broken legs or broken backs, while some perhaps were uninjured. The barricade, however, prevented them from escaping, and all were soon killed by the arrows of the Indians.

It is said that there was another way to get the buffalo into this chute. A man who was very skilful in arousing the buffalo's curiosity, might go out without disguise, and by wheeling round and round in front of the herd, appearing and disappearing, would induce them to move toward him, when it was easy to entice them into the chute. Once there, the people began to rise up behind them, shouting and waving their robes, and the now terror-stricken animals rushed ahead, and were driven over the cliff into the pis′kun, where all were quickly killed and divided among the people, the chiefs and the leading warrior getting the best and fattest animals.

The pis′kun was in use up to within thirty-five or forty years, and many men are still living who have seen the buffalo driven over the cliff. Such men even now speak with enthusiasm of the plenty that successful drives brought to the camp.

The pis′kuns of the Sik'-si-kau, or Blackfoot tribe, differed in some particulars from those constructed by the Bloods and the Piegans, who live further to the south, nearer to the mountains, and so in a country which is rougher and more broken. The Sik'-si-kau built their pis′kuns like the Crees, on level ground and usually near timber. A large pen or corral was made of heavy logs about eight feet high. On the side where the wings of the chute come together, a bridge, or causeway, was built, sloping gently up from the prairie to the walls of the corral, which at this point were cut away to the height of the bridge above the ground,—here about four feet,—so that the animals running up the causeway could jump down into the corral. The causeway was fenced in on either side by logs, so that the buffalo could not run off it. After they had been lured within the wings of the chute, they were driven toward the corral as already described. When they reached the end of the >, they ran up the bridge, and jumped down into the pen. When it was full, or all had entered, Indians, who had lain hidden near by, ran upon the bridge, and placed poles, prepared beforehand, across the opening through which the animals had entered, and over these poles hung robes, so as entirely to close the opening. The buffalo will not dash themselves against a barrier which is entirely closed, even though it be very frail; but if they can see through it to the outside, they will rush against it, and their great weight and strength make it easy for them to break down any but a heavy wall. Mr. Hugh Monroe tells me that he has seen a pis'kun built of willow brush; and the Cheyennes have stated to me that their buffalo corrals were often built of brush. Sometimes, if the walls of the pis'kun were not high, the buffalo tried to jump or climb over them, and, in doing this, might break them down, and some or all escape. As soon, however, as the animals were in the corral, the people—women and children included—ran up and showed themselves all about the walls, and by their cries kept the buffalo from pressing against the walls. The animals ran round and round within, and the men standing on the walls shot them down as they passed. The butchering was done in the pis'kun, and after this was over, the place was cleaned out, the heads, feet, and least perishable offal being removed. Wolves, foxes, badgers, and other small carnivorous animals visited the pis'kun, and soon made away with the entrails.

In winter, when the snow was on the ground, and the buffalo were to be led to the pis'kun, the following method was adopted to keep the herd travelling in the desired direction after they had got between the wings of the chute. A line of buffalo chips, each one supported on three small sticks, so that it stood a few inches above the snow, was carried from the mouth of the pis'kun straight out toward the prairie. The chips were about thirty feet apart, and ran midway between the wings of the chute. This line was, of course, conspicuous against the white snow, and when the buffalo were running down the chute, they always followed it, never turning to the right nor to the left. In the latter days of the pis'kun, the man who led the buffalo was often mounted on a white horse.

Often, when they drove the buffalo over a high vertical cliff, no corral was built beneath. Most of those driven over were killed or disabled by the fall, and only a few got away. The pis'kuns, as a rule, were built under low-cut bluffs, and sometimes the buffalo were driven in by moonlight.

In connection with the subject of leading or decoying the buffalo, another matter not generally known may be mentioned. Sometimes, as a matter of convenience, a herd was brought from a long distance close up to the camp. This was usually done in the spring of the year, when the horses were thin in flesh and not in condition to stand a long chase. I myself have never seen this; but my friend, William Jackson, was once present at such a drive by the Red River half-breeds, and has described to me the way in which it was done.

The camp was on Box Elder Creek near the Musselshell River. It was in the spring of 1881, and the horses were all pretty well run down and thin, so that their owners wished to spare them as much as possible. The buffalo were seven or eight miles distant, and two men were sent out to bring them to the camp. Other men, leading fresh horses, went with them, and hid themselves among the hills at different points along the course that the buffalo were expected to take, at intervals of a mile and a half. They watched the herd, and were on hand to supply the fresh horses to the men who were bringing it.

The buffalo were on a wide flat, and the men rode over the hill and advanced toward the herd at a walk. At length the buffalo noticed them, and began to huddle up together and to walk about, and at length to walk away. Then the men turned, and rode along parallel to the buffalo's course, and at the same gait that these were taking. When the buffalo began to trot, the men trotted, and when the herd began to lope, the men loped, and at length they were all running pretty fast. The men kept about half a mile from the herd, and up even with the leaders. As they ran, the herd kept constantly edging a little toward the riders, as if trying to cross in front of them. This inclination toward the men was least when they were far off, and greatest when they drew nearer to them. At no time were the men nearer to the herd than four hundred yards. If the buffalo edged too much toward the riders, so that the course they were taking would lead them away from camp, the men would drop back and cross over behind the herd to the other side, and then, pushing their horses hard, would come up with the leaders,—but still at a distance from them,—and then the buffalo would begin to edge toward them, and the herd would be brought back again to the desired course. If necessary, this was repeated, and so the buffalo were kept travelling in a course approximately straight.

By the time the buffalo had got pretty near to the camp, they were pretty well winded, and the tongues of many of them were hanging out. This herd was led up among the rolling hills about a mile from the camp, and there the people were waiting for them, and charged them, when the herd broke up, the animals running in every direction.

Occasionally it would happen that for a long time the buffalo would not be found in a place favorable for driving over the cliff or into a pen. In such cases, the Indians would steal out on foot, and, on a day when there was no wind, would stealthily surround the herd. Then they would startle the buffalo, and yet would keep them from breaking through the circle. The buffalo would "mill" around until exhausted, and at length, when worn out, would be shot down by the Indians. This corresponds almost exactly with one of the methods employed in killing buffalo by the Pawnees in early days before they had horses. In those days the Pi-kŭn´-i were very numerous, and sometimes when a lot of buffalo were found in a favorable position, and there was no wind, the people would surround them, and set up their lodges about them, thus practically building a corral of lodges. After all preparations had been made, they would frighten the buffalo, which, being afraid to pass through between the lodges, would run round and round in a great circle, and when they were exhausted the people would kill them.

Then they always had plenty of buffalo—if not fresh meat, that which they had dried. For in winter they would kill large numbers of buffalo, and would prepare great stores of dried meat. As spring opened, the buffalo would move down to the more flat prairie country away from the pis´kuns. Then the Blackfeet would also move away. As winter drew near, the buffalo would again move up close to the mountains, and the Indians, as food began to become scarce, would follow them toward the pis´kuns. In the last of the summer and early autumn, they always had runners out, looking for the buffalo, to find where they were, and which way they were moving. In the early autumn, all the pis´kuns were repaired and strengthened, so as to be in good order for winter.

In the days before they had horses, and even in later times when the ground was of such a character as to prevent running the buffalo, an ingenious method of still-hunting them was practised. A story told by Hugh Monroe illustrates it. He said: "I was often detailed by the Hudson's Bay Company to go out in charge of a number of men, to kill meat for the fort. When the ground was full of holes and wash-outs, so that running was dangerous, I used to put on a big timber wolf's skin, which I carried for the purpose, tying it at my neck and waist, and then to sneak up to the buffalo. I used a bow and arrows, and generally shot a number without alarming them. If one looked suspiciously at me, I would howl like a wolf. Sometimes the smell of the blood from the wounded and dying would set the bulls crazy. They would run up and lick the blood, and sometimes toss the dead ones clear from the ground. Then they would bellow and fight each other, sometimes goring one another so badly that they died. The great bulls, their tongues covered with blood, their eyes flashing, and tails sticking out straight, roaring and fighting, were terrible to see; and it was a little dangerous for me, because the commotion would attract buffalo from all directions to see what was going on. At such times, I would signal to my men, and they would ride up and scare the buffalo away."

In more modern times, the height of pleasure to a Blackfoot was to ride a good horse and run buffalo. When bows and arrows, and, later, muzzle-loading "fukes" were the only weapons, no more buffalo were killed than could actually be utilized. But after the Winchester repeater came in use, it seemed as if the different tribes vied with each other in wanton slaughter. Provided with one of these weapons and a couple of belts of cartridges, the hunters would run as long as their horses could keep up with the band, and literally cover the prairie with carcasses, many of which were never even skinned.

ANTELOPE

It is said that once in early times the men determined that they would use antelope skins for their women's dresses, instead of cowskins. So they found a place where antelope were plenty, and set up on the prairie long lines of rock piles, or of bushes, so as to form a chute like a >. Near the point where the lines joined, they dug deep pits, which they roofed with slender poles, and covered these with grass and a little dirt. Then the people scattered out, and while most of them hid behind the rock piles and bushes, a few started the antelope toward the mouth of the chute. As they ran by them, the people showed themselves and yelled, and the antelope ran down the chute and finally reached the pits, and falling into them were taken, when they were killed and divided among the hunters. Afterward, this was the common method of securing antelopes up to the coming of the whites.

EAGLES

Before the whites came to the Blackfoot country, the Indian standard of value was eagle tail-feathers. They were used to make war head-dresses, to tie on the head, and to ornament shields, lances, and other weapons. Besides this, the wings were used for fans, and the body feathers for arrow-making. Always a wary bird, the eagle could seldom be approached near enough for killing with the bow and arrow; and, in fact, it seems as if it was considered improper to kill it in that way. The capture of these birds appears to have had about it something of a sacred nature, and, as was always the case among wild Indians when anything important was to be undertaken, it was invariably preceded by earnest prayers to the Deity for help and for success.

There are still living many men who have caught eagles in the ancient method, and, from several of these, accounts have been received, which, while essentially similar, yet differ in certain particulars, especially in the explanations of certain features of the ceremony.

Wolf Calf's account of this ceremony is as follows:—

"A man who started out to catch eagles moved his lodge and his family away from the main camp, to some place where the birds were abundant. A spot was chosen on top of a mound or butte within a few miles of his lodge, and here he dug a pit in the ground as long as his body and somewhat deeper. The earth removed was carried away to a distance, and scattered about so as to make no show. When the pit had been made large enough, it was roofed over with small willow sticks, on which grass was scattered, and over the grass a little earth and stones were laid, so as to give the place a natural look, like the prairie all about it.

"The bait was a piece of bloody neck of a buffalo. This, of course, could be seen a long way off, and by the meat a stuffed wolf skin was often placed, standing up, as if the animal were eating. To the piece of neck was tied a rope, which passed down through the roof of the pit and was held in the watcher's hand.

"After all had been made ready, the next day the man rose very early, before it was light, and, after smoking and praying, left his camp, telling his wives and children not to use an awl while he was gone. He endeavored to reach the pit early in the morning, before it became light, and lay down in it, taking with him a slender stick about six feet long, a human skull, and a little pemmican. Then he waited.

"When the morning came, and the eagles were flying, one of them would see the meat and descend to take it away from the wolf. Finding it held fast by the rope, the bird began to feed on it;

and while it was pecking at the bait, the watcher seized it by the legs, and drew it into the pit, where he killed it, either by twisting its neck, or by crushing it with his knees. Then he laid it to one side, first opening the bill and putting a little piece of pemmican in its mouth. This was done to make the other eagles hungry. While he was in the pit, the man neither ate, drank, nor slept. He had a sleeping-place not far off, to which he repaired each night after dark, and there he ate and drank.

"The reason for taking the skull into the hole with the catcher was, in part, for his protection. It was believed that the ghost of the person to whom the skull had belonged would protect the watcher against harm from the eagle, and besides that, the skull, or ghost, would make the watcher invisible, like a ghost. The eagle would not see him.

"The stick was used to poke or drive away smaller birds, such as magpies, crows, and ravens, which might alight on the roof of the pit, and try to feed on the bait. It was used, also, to drive away the white-headed eagle, which they did not care to catch. These are powerful birds; they could almost kill a person.

"There are two sacred things connected with the catching of eagles,—two things which must be observed if the eagle-catcher is to have good luck. The man who is watching must not eat rosebuds. If he does, the eagle, when he comes down and alights by the bait, will begin to scratch himself and will not attack the bait. The rosebuds will make him itch. Neither the man nor his wife must use an awl while he is absent from his lodge, and is trying to catch the birds. If this is done, the eagles will scratch the catcher. Sometimes one man would catch a great many eagles."

In his day, John Monroe was a famous eagle-catcher, and he has given me the following account of the method as he has practised it. The pit is dug, six feet long, three wide, and four deep, on top of the highest knoll that can be found near a stream. The earth taken out is carried a long way off. Over the pit they put two long poles, one on each side, running lengthwise of the pit, and other smaller sticks are laid across, resting on the poles. The smaller sticks are covered with juniper twigs and long grass. The skin of a wolf, coyote, or fox, is stuffed with grass, and made to look as natural as possible. A hole is cut in the wolf skin and a rope is passed through it, one end being tied to a large piece of meat which lies by the skin, and the other passing through the roof down into the pit. The bait is now covered with grass, and the man returns to his lodge for the night.

During the night, he sings his eagle songs and burns sweet grass for the eagles, rubbing the smoke over his own body to purify himself, so that on the morrow he will give out no scent. Before day he leaves his lodge without eating or drinking, goes to the pit and lies down in it. He uncovers the bait, arranges the roof, and sits there all day holding the rope. Crows and other birds alight by the bait and peck at it, but he pays no attention to them.

The eagle, sailing about high in air, sees the bait, and settles down slowly. It takes it a long time to make up its mind to come to the bait. In the pit, the man can hear the sound of the eagle coming. When the bird settles on the ground, it does not alight on the bait, but at one side of it, striking the ground with a thud—heavily. The man never mistakes anything else for that sound. The eagle walks toward the bait, and all the other birds fly away. It walks on to the roof; and, through the crevices that have been left between the sticks, the man can see in which direction the bird's head is. He carefully pushes the stick aside and, reaching out, grasps the eagle by the two feet. The bird does not struggle much. It is drawn down into the pit, and the man wrings its neck. Then the opening is closed, and the roof arranged as before. So the man waits and catches the eagles that come through the day. Sometimes he sits all day and gets nothing; again he may get eight or ten in a day.

When darkness comes, the man leaves his hiding-place, takes his eagles, and goes home. He carries the birds to a special lodge, prepared outside of the camp, which is called the eagles' lodge. He places them on the ground in a row, and raises their heads, resting them on a stick laid in front of the row. In the mouth of each one is put a piece of pemmican, so that they may not be afraid of the people. The object of feeding the eagles is that their spirits may tell other eagles how they are being treated—that they are being fed by the people. In the lodge is a human skull, and they pray to it, asking the ghost to help them get the eagles.

It is said that in one pit, once, forty eagles were killed in a day. The larger hawks were caught, as well as eagles, though the latter were the most highly valued. Five eagles used to be worth a good horse, a valuation which shows that, in the Blackfoot country, eagles were more plenty, or horses more valuable, than farther south, where, in old times, two eagles would purchase a horse.

OTHER GAME

They had no special means of capturing deer in any numbers. These were usually killed singly. The hunters used to creep up on elk and deer in the brush, and when they had come close to them, they could drive even their stone-pointed arrows deep in the flesh. Often their game was killed dead on the spot, but if not, they left it alone until the next day, when, on going back to the place, it was usually found near by, either dead or so desperately wounded that they could secure it.

Deadfalls were used to catch wolves, foxes, and other fur animals, and small apertures in the pis´kun walls were provided with nooses and snares for the same purpose.

Another way to catch wolves and coyotes was to set heavy stakes in the ground in a circle, about the carcasses of one or two dead buffalo. The stakes were placed at an angle of about forty-five degrees, a few inches apart, and all pointing toward the centre of the circle. At one place, dirt was piled up against the stakes from the outside, and the wolves, climbing up on this, jumped down into the enclosure, but were unable to jump out. Hugh Monroe tells me that, about thirty years ago, he and his sons made a trap like this, and in one night caught eighty-three wolves and coyotes.

In early times, beaver were very abundant and very tame, and were shot with bows and arrows.

The Blackfeet were splendid prairie hunters. They had no superiors in the art of stalking and killing such wary animals as the antelope. Sometimes they wore hats made of the skin and horns of an antelope head, which were very useful when approaching the game. Although the prairie was pre-eminently their hunting-ground, they were also skilful in climbing mountains and killing sheep and goats. On the other hand, the northern Crees, who also are a prairie people, are poor mountain hunters.

THE BLACKFOOT IN WAR

The Blackfeet were a warlike people. How it may have been in the old days, before the coming of the white men, we do not know. Very likely, in early times, they were usually at peace with neighboring tribes, or, if quarrels took place, battles were fought, and men killed, this was only in angry dispute over what each party considered its rights. Their wars were probably not general, nor could they have been very bloody. When, however, horses came into the possession of the Indians, all this must have soon become changed. Hitherto there had really been no incentive to war. From time to time expeditions may have gone out to kill enemies,—for glory, or to take revenge for some injury,—but war had not yet been made desirable by the hope of plunder, for none of their neighbors—any more than themselves—had property which was worth capturing and taking away. Primitive arms, dogs, clothing, and dried meat were common to all the tribes, and were their only possessions, and usually each tribe had an abundance of all these. It was not worth any man's while to make long journeys and to run into danger merely to increase his store of such property, when his present possessions were more than sufficient to meet all his wants. Even if such things had seemed desirable plunder, the amount of it which could be carried away was limited, since—for a war party—the only means of transporting captured articles from place to place was on men's backs, nor could men burdened with loads either run or fight. But when horses became known, and the Indians began to realize what a change the possession of these animals was working in their mode of life, when they saw that, by enormously increasing the transporting power of each family, horses made far greater possessions practicable, that they insured the food supply, rendered the moving of the camp easier and more rapid, made possible long journeys with a minimum of effort, and that they had a value for trading, the Blackfoot mind received a new idea, the idea that it was desirable to accumulate property. The Blackfoot saw that, since horses could be exchanged for everything that was worth having, no one had as many horses as he needed. A pretty wife, a handsome war bonnet, a strong bow, a finely ornamented woman's dress,—any or all of these things a man might obtain, if he had horses to trade for them. The gambler at "hands," or at the ring game, could bet horses. The man who was devoted to his last married wife could give her a horse as an evidence of his affection.

We can readily understand what a change the advent of the horse must have worked in the minds of a people like the Blackfeet, and how this changed mental attitude would react on the Blackfoot way of living. At first, there were but few horses among them, but they knew that their neighbors to the west and south—across the mountains and on the great plains beyond the Missouri and the Yellowstone—had plenty of them; that the Kūtenais, the Kalispels, the Snakes, the Crows, and the Sioux were well provided. They soon learned that horses were easily driven off, and that, even if followed by those whose property they had taken, the pursued had a great advantage over the pursuers; and we may feel sure that it was not long before the idea of capturing horses from the enemy entered some Blackfoot head and was put into practice.

Now began a systematic sending forth of war parties against neighboring tribes for the purpose of capturing horses, which continued for about seventy-five or eighty years, and has only been abandoned within the last six or seven, and since the settlement of the country by the whites made it impossible for the Blackfeet longer to pass backward and forward through it on their raiding expeditions. Horse-taking at once became what might be called an established industry among the Blackfeet. Success brought wealth and fame, and there was a pleasing excitement about the war journey. Except during the bitterest weather of the winter, war parties of Blackfeet were constantly out, searching for camps of their enemies, from whom they might capture horses. Usually the only object of such an expedition was to secure plunder, but often enemies were killed, and sometimes the party set out with the distinct intention of taking both scalps and horses.

Until some time after they had obtained guns, the Blackfeet were on excellent terms with the northern Crees, but later the Chippeways from the east made war on the Blackfeet, and this brought about general hostilities against all Crees, which have continued up to within a few years. If I recollect aright, the last fight which occurred between the Pi-kun'-i and the Crees took place in 1886. In this skirmish, which followed an attempt by the Crees to capture some Piegan horses, my friend, Tail-feathers-coming-in-sight-over-the-Hill, killed and counted *coup* on a Cree whose scalp he afterward sent me, as an evidence of his prowess.

The Gros Ventres of the prairie, of Arapaho stock, known to the Blackfeet as *At-séna,* or Gut People, had been friends and allies of the Blackfeet from the time they first came into the country, early in this century, up to about the year 1862, when, according to Clark, peace was broken through a mistake. A war party of Snakes had gone to a Gros Ventres camp near the Bear Paw Mountains and there killed two Gros Ventres and taken a white pony, which they subsequently gave to a party of Piegans whom they met, and with whom they made peace. The Gros Ventres afterward saw this horse in the Piegan camp and supposed that the latter had killed their tribesman, and this led to a long war. In the year 1867, the Piegans defeated the allied Crows and Gros Ventres in a great battle near the Cypress Mountains, in which about 450 of the enemy are said to have been killed.

An expression often used in these pages, and which is so familiar to one who has lived much with Indians as to need no explanation, is the phrase to count *coup*. Like many of the terms common in the Northwest, this one comes down to us from the old French trappers and traders, and a *coup* is, of course, a blow. As commonly used, the expression is almost a direct translation of the Indian phrase to strike the enemy, which is in ordinary use among all tribes. This striking is the literal inflicting a blow on an individual, and does not mean merely the attack on a body of enemies.

The most creditable act that an Indian can perform is to show that he is brave, to prove, by some daring deed, his physical courage, his lack of fear. In practice, this courage is shown by approaching near enough to an enemy to strike or touch him with something that is held in the hand—to come up within arm's length of him. To kill an enemy is praiseworthy, and the act of scalping him may be so under certain circumstances, but neither of these approaches in bravery the hitting or touching him with something held in the hand. This is counting *coup*.

The man who does this shows himself without fear and is respected accordingly. With certain tribes, as the Pawnees, Cheyennes, and others, it was not very uncommon for a warrior to dash up to an enemy and strike him before making any attempt to injure him, the effort to kill being secondary to the *coup*. The blow might be struck with anything held in the hand,—a whip, coupstick, club, lance, the muzzle of a gun, a bow, or what not. It did not necessarily follow that the person on whom the *coup* had been counted would be injured. The act was performed in the case of a woman, who might be captured, or even on a child, who was being made prisoner.

Often the dealing the *coup* showed a very high degree of courage. As already implied, it might be counted on a man who was defending himself most desperately, and was trying his best to kill the approaching enemy, or, even if the attempt was being made on a foe who had fallen, it was never certain that he was beyond the power of inflicting injury. He might be only wounded, and, just when the enemy had come close to him, and was about to strike, he might have strength enough left to raise himself up and shoot him dead. In their old wars, the Indians rarely took men captive. The warrior never expected quarter nor gave it, and usually men fought to the death, and died mute, defending themselves to the last—to the last, striving to inflict some injury on the enemy.

The striking the blow was an important event in a man's life, and he who performed this feat remembered it. He counted it. It was a proud day for the young warrior when he counted his first *coup*, and each subsequent one was remembered and numbered in the warrior's mind, just as an American of to-day remembers the number of times he has been elected to Congress. At certain dances and religious ceremonies, like that of the Medicine Lodge, the warriors counted—or rather re-counted—their *coups*.

While the *coup* was primarily, and usually, a blow with something held in the hand, other acts in warfare which involved great danger to him who performed them were also reckoned *coups* by some tribes. Thus, for a horseman to ride over and knock down an enemy, who was on foot, was regarded among the Blackfeet as a *coup*, for the horseman might be shot at close quarters, or might receive a lance thrust. It was the same to ride one's horse violently against a mounted foe. An old Pawnee told me of a *coup* that he had counted by running up to a fallen enemy and jumping on him with both feet. Sometimes the taking of horses counted a *coup*, but this was not always the case.

As suggested by what has been already stated, each tribe of the Plains Indians held its own view as to what constituted a *coup*. The Pawnees were very strict in their interpretation of the term, and with them an act of daring was not in itself deemed a *coup*. This was counted only when the person of an enemy was actually touched. One or two incidents which have occurred among the Pawnees will serve to illustrate their notions on this point.

In the year 1867, the Pawnee scouts had been sent up to Ogallalla, Nebraska, to guard the graders who were working on the Union Pacific railroad. While they were there, some Sioux came down from the hills and ran off a few mules, taking them across the North Platte. Major North took twenty men and started after them. Crossing the river, and following it up on the north bank, he headed them off, and before long came in sight of them.

The six Sioux, when they found that they were pursued, left the mules that they had taken, and ran; and the Pawnees, after chasing them eight or ten miles, caught up with one of them, a brother of the well-known chief Spotted Tail. Baptiste Bahele, a half-breed Skidi, had a very fast horse, and was riding ahead of the other Pawnees, and shooting arrows at the Sioux, who was shooting back at him. At length Baptiste shot the enemy's horse in the hip, and the Indian dismounted and ran on foot toward a ravine. Baptiste shot at him again, and this time sent an arrow nearly through his body, so that the point projected in front. The Sioux caught the arrow by the point, pulled it through his body, and shot it back at his pursuer, and came very near hitting him. About that time, a ball from a carbine hit the Sioux and knocked him down.

Then there was a race between Baptiste and the Pawnee next behind him, to see which should count *coup* on the fallen man. Baptiste was nearest to him and reached him first, but just as he got to him, and was leaning over from his horse, to strike the dead man, the animal shied at the body, swerving to one side, and he failed to touch it. The horse ridden by the other Pawnee ran right over the Sioux, and his rider leaned down and touched him.

Baptiste claimed the *coup*—although acknowledging that he had not actually touched the man—on the ground that he had exposed himself to all the danger, and would have hit the man if his horse had not swerved as it did from the body; but the Pawnees would not allow it, and all gave the credit of the *coup* to the other boy, because he had actually touched the enemy.

On another occasion three or four young men started on the warpath from the Pawnee village. When they came near to Spotted Tail's camp on the Platte River, they crossed the stream, took some horses, and got them safely across the river. Then one of the boys recrossed, went back to the camp, and cut loose another horse. He had almost got this one out of the camp, when an Indian came out of a lodge near by, and sat down. The Pawnee shot the Sioux, counted *coup* on him, scalped him, and then hurried across the river with the whole Sioux camp in pursuit. When the party returned to the Pawnee village, this boy was the only one who received credit for a *coup*.

Among the Blackfeet the capture of a shield, bow, gun, war bonnet, war shirt, or medicine pipe was deemed a *coup*.

Nothing gave a man a higher place in the estimation of the people than the counting of *coups*, for, I repeat, personal bravery is of all qualities the most highly respected by Indians. On special occasions, as has been said, men counted over again in public their *coups*. This served to gratify personal vanity, and also to incite the young men to the performance of similar brave deeds. Besides this, they often made a more enduring record of these acts, by reproducing them pictographically on robes, cowskins, and other hides. There is now in my possession an illuminated cowskin, presented to me by Mr. J. Kipp, which contains the record of the *coups* and the most striking events in the life of Red Crane, a Blackfoot warrior, painted by himself. These pictographs are very rude and are drawn after the style common among Plains Indians, but no doubt they were sufficiently lifelike to call up to the mind of the artist each detail of the stirring events which they record.

The Indian warrior who stood up to relate some brave deed which he had performed was almost always in a position to prove the truth of his statements. Either he had the enemy's scalp, or some trophy captured from him, to produce as evidence, or else he had a witness of his feat in some companion. A man seldom boasted of any deed unless he was able to prove his story, and false statements about exploits against the enemy were most unusual. Temporary peace was often made between tribes usually at war, and, at the friendly meetings which took place during such times of peace, former battles were talked over, the performances of various individuals discussed, and the acts of particular men in the different rights commented on. In this way, if any man had falsely claimed to have done brave deeds, he would be detected.

An example of this occurred many years ago among the Cheyennes. At that time, there was a celebrated chief of the Skidi tribe of the Pawnee Nation whose name was Big Eagle. He was very brave, and the Cheyennes greatly feared him, and it was agreed among them that the man who could count *coup* on Big Eagle should be made war chief of the Cheyennes. After a fight on the Loup River, a Cheyenne warrior claimed to have counted *coup* on Big Eagle by thrusting a lance through his buttocks. On the strength of the claim, this man was made war chief of the Cheyennes. Some years later, during a friendly visit made by the Pawnees to the Cheyennes, this incident was mentioned. Big Eagle was present at the time, and, after inquiring into the matter, he rose in council, denied that he had ever been struck as claimed, and, throwing aside his robe, called on the Cheyennes present to examine his body and to point out the scars left by the lance. None were found. It was seen that Big Eagle spoke the truth; and the lying Cheyenne, from the proud position of war chief, sank to a point where he was an object of contempt to the meanest Indian in his tribe.

Among the Blackfeet a war party usually, or often, had its origin in a dream. Some man who has a dream, after he awakes tells of it. Perhaps he may say: "I dreamed that on a certain stream is a herd of horses that have been given to me, and that I am going away to get. I am going to war. I shall go to that place and get my band of horses." Then the men who know him, who believe that his medicine is strong and that he will have good luck, make up their minds to follow him. As soon as he has stated what he intends to do, his women and his female relations begin to make moccasins for him, and the old men among his relations begin to give him arrows and powder and ball to fit him out for war. The relations of those who are going with him do the same for them.

The leader notifies the young men who are going with him on what day and at what hour he intends to start. He determines the time for himself, but does not let the whole camp know it in advance. Of late years, large war parties have not been desirable. They have preferred to go out in small bodies.

Just before a war party sets out, its members get together and sing the "peeling a stick song," which is a wolf song. Then they build a sweat lodge and go into it, and with them goes in an old man, a medicine-pipe man, who has been a good warrior. They fill the pipe and ask him to pray for them, that they may have good luck, and may accomplish what they desire. The medicine-pipe man prays and sings and pours water on the hot stones, and the warriors with their knives slice bits of skin and flesh from their bodies,—their arms and breasts and sometimes from the tip of the tongue,—which they offer to the Sun. Then, after the ceremony is over, all dripping with perspiration from their vapor bath, the men go down to the river and plunge in.

In starting out, a war party often marches in the daytime, but sometimes they travel at night from the beginning. Often they may make an all night march across a wide prairie, in passing over which they might be seen if they travelled in the day. They journey on foot, always. The older men carry their arms, while the boys bear the moccasins, the ropes, and the food, which usually consists of dried meat or pemmican. They carry also coats and blankets and their war bonnets and otter skin medicine. The leader has but little physical labor to perform. His mind is occupied in planning the movements of his party. He is treated with the greatest respect. The others mend his moccasins, and give him the best of the food which they carry.

After they get away from the main camp, the leader selects the strongest of the young men, and sends him ahead to some designated butte, saying, "Go to that place, and look carefully over the country, and if you see nothing, make signals to us to come on." This scout goes on ahead, travelling in the ravines and coulées, and keeps himself well hidden. After he has reconnoitred and made signs that he sees nothing, the party proceeds straight toward him.

The party usually starts early in the morning and travels all day, making camp at sundown. During the day, if they happen to come upon an antelope or a buffalo, they kill it, if possible, and take some of the meat with them. They try in every way to economize their pemmican. They always endeavor to make camp in the thick timber, where they cannot be seen; and here, when it is necessary, on account of bad weather or for other reasons, they build a war lodge. Taking four young cotton-woods or aspens, on which the leaves are left, and lashing them together like lodge poles, but with the butts up, about these they place other similar trees, also butts up and untrimmed. The leaves keep the rain off, and prevent the light of the fire which is built in the lodge from showing through. Sometimes, when on the prairie, where there is no wood, in stormy weather they will build a shelter of rocks. When the party has come close to the enemy, or into a country where the enemy are likely to be found, they build no more fires, but eat their food uncooked.

When they see fresh tracks of people, or signs that enemies are in the country, they stop travelling in the daytime and move altogether by night, until they come to some good place for hiding, and here they stop and sleep. When day comes, the leader sends out young men to the different buttes, to look over the country and see if they can discover the enemy. If some one of the scouts reports that he has seen a camp, and that the enemy have been found, the leader directs his men to paint themselves and put on their war bonnets. This last is a figure of speech, since the war bonnets, having of late years been usually ornamented with brass bells, could not be worn in a secret attack, on account of the noise they would make. Before painting themselves, therefore, they untie their war bonnets, and spread them out on the ground, as if they were about to be worn, and then when they have finished painting themselves, tie them up again. When it begins to get dark, they start on the run for the enemy's camp. They leave their food in camp, but carry their ropes slung over the shoulder and under the arm, whips stuck in belts, guns and blankets.

After they have crept up close to the lodges, the leader chooses certain men that have strong hearts, and takes them with him into the camp to cut loose the horses. The rest of the party remain outside the camp, and look about its outskirts, driving in any horses that may be feeding about, not tied up. Of those who have gone into the camp, some cut loose one horse, while others cut all that may be tied about a lodge. Some go only once into the camp, and some go twice to get the horses. When they have secured the horses, they drive them off a little way from the camp, at first going slowly, and then mount and ride off fast. Generally, they travel two nights and one day before sleeping.

This is the usual method of procedure of an ordinary expedition to capture horses, and I have given it very nearly in the language of the men who explained it to me.

In their hostile encounters, the Blackfeet have much that is common to many Plains tribes, and also some customs that are peculiar to themselves. Like most Indians, they are subject to sudden, apparently causeless, panics, while at other times they display a courage that is heroic. They are firm believers in luck, and will follow a leader who is fortunate in his expeditions into almost any danger. On the other hand, if the leader of a war party loses his young men, or any of them, the people in the camp think that he is unlucky, and does not know how to lead a war party. Young men will not follow him as a leader, and he is obliged to go as a servant or scout under another leader. He is likely never again to lead a war party, having learned to distrust his luck.

If a war party meets the enemy, and kills several of them, losing in the battle one of its own number, it is likely, as the phrase is, to "cover" the slain Blackfoot with all the dead enemies save one, and to have a scalp dance over that remaining one. If a party had killed six of the enemy and lost a man, it might "cover" the slain Blackfoot with five of the enemy. In other words, the five dead enemies would pay for the one which the war party had lost. So far, matters would be even, and they would feel at liberty to rejoice over the victory gained over the one that is left.

The Blackfeet sometimes cut to pieces an enemy killed in battle. If a Blackfoot had a relation killed by a member of another tribe, and afterward killed one of this tribe, he was likely to cut him all to pieces "to get even," that is, to gratify his spite—to obtain revenge. Sometimes, after they had killed an enemy, they dragged his body into camp, so as to give the children an opportunity to count *coup* on it. Often they cut the feet and hands off the dead, and took them away and danced over them for a long time. Sometimes they cut off an arm or a leg, and often the head, and danced and rejoiced over this trophy.

Women and children of hostile tribes were often captured, and adopted into the Blackfoot tribes with all the rights and privileges of indigenous members. Men were rarely captured. When they were taken, they were sometimes killed in cold blood, especially if they had made a desperate resistance before being captured. At other times, the captive would be kept for a time, and then the chief would take him off away from the camp, and give him provisions, clothing, arms, and a horse, and let him go. The captive man always had a hard time at first. When he was brought into the camp, the women and children threw dirt on him and counted *coups* on him, pounding him with sticks and clubs. He was rarely tied, but was always watched. Often the man who had taken him prisoner had great trouble to keep his tribesmen from killing him.

In the very early days of this century, war parties used commonly to start out in the spring, going south to the land where horses were abundant, being absent all summer and the next winter, and returning the following summer or autumn, with great bands of horses. Sometimes they were gone two years. They say that on such journeys they used to go to *Spai'yu ksah'ku*, which means the Spanish lands—*Spai'yu* being a recently made word, no doubt from the French *espagnol*. That they did get as far as Mexico, or at least New Mexico, is indicated by the fact that they brought back branded horses and a few branded mules; for in these early days there was no stock upon the Plains, and animals bearing brands were found only in the Spanish American settlements. The Blackfeet did not know what these marks meant. From their raids into these distant lands, they sometimes brought back arms of strange make, lances, axes, and swords, of a form unlike any that they had seen. The lances had broad heads; some of the axes, as described, were evidently the old "T. Gray" trade axes of the southwest. A sword, described as having a long, slender, straight blade, inlaid with a flower pattern of yellow metal along the back, was probably an old Spanish rapier.

In telling of these journeys to Spanish lands, they say of the very long reeds which grow there, that they are very large at the butt, are jointed, very hard, and very tall; they grow in marshy places; and the water there has a strange, mouldy smell.

It is said, too, that there have been war parties who have crossed the mountains and gone so far to the west that they have seen the big salt water which lies beyond, or west of, the Great Salt Lake. Journeys as far south as Salt Lake were not uncommon, and Hugh Monroe has told me of a war party he accompanied which went as far as this.

RELIGION

In ancient times the chief god of the Blackfeet—their Creator—was *Na'pi* (Old Man). This is the word used to indicate any old man, though its meaning is often loosely given as white. An analysis of the word *Na'pi*, however, shows it to be compounded of the word *Ni'nah*, man, and the particle *a'pi*, which expresses a color, and which is never used by itself, but always in combination with some other word. The Blackfoot word for white is *Ksik-si-num'* while *a'pi*, though also conveying the idea of whiteness, really describes the tint seen in the early morning light when it first appears in the east—the dawn—not a pure white, but that color combined with a faint cast of yellow. *Na'pi*, therefore, would seem to mean dawn-light-color-man, or man-yellowish-white. It is easy to see why old men should be called by this latter name, for it describes precisely the color of their hair.

Dr. Brinton, in his valuable work, American Hero Myths, has suggested a more profound reason why such a name should be given to the Creator. He says: "The most important of all things to life is light. This the primitive savage felt, and personifying it, he made light his chief god. The beginning of day served, by analogy, for the beginning of the world. Light comes before the Sun, brings it forth, creates it, as it were. Hence the Light god is not the Sun god but his antecedent and Creator."

It would be absurd to attribute to the Blackfoot of to-day any such abstract conception of the name of the Creator as that expressed in the foregoing quotation. The statement that Old Man was merely light personified would be beyond his comprehension, and if he did understand what was meant, he would laugh at it, and aver that *Na'pi* was a real man, a flesh and blood person like himself.

The character of Old Man, as depicted in the stories told of him by the Blackfeet, is a curious mixture of opposite attributes. In the serious tales, such as those of the creation, he is spoken of respectfully, and there is no hint of the impish qualities which characterize him in other stories, in which he is powerful, but also at times impotent; full of all wisdom, yet at times so helpless that he has to ask aid from the animals. Sometimes he sympathizes with the people, and at others, out of pure spitefulness, he plays them malicious tricks that are worthy of a demon. He is a combination of strength, weakness, wisdom, folly, childishness, and malice.

Under various names Old Man is known to the Crees, Chippeways, and other Algonquins, and many of the stories that are current among the Blackfeet are told of him among those tribes. The more southern of these tribes do not venerate him as of old, but the Plains and Timber Crees of the north, and the north Chippeways, are said still to be firm believers in Old Man. He was their Creator, and is still their chief god. He is believed in less by the younger generation than the older. The Crees are regarded by the Indians of the Northwest as having very powerful medicine, and this all comes from Old Man.

Old Man can never die. Long ago he left the Blackfeet and went away to the West, disappearing in the mountains. Before his departure he told them that he would always take care of them, and some day would return. Even now, many of the old people believe that he spoke the truth, and that some day he will come back, and will bring with him the buffalo, which they believe the white men havehidden. It is sometimes said, however, that when he left them he told them also that, when he returned, he would find them changed—a different people and living in a different way from that which they practised when he went away. Sometimes, also, it is said that when he disappeared he went to the East.

It is generally believed that Old Man is no longer the principal god of the Blackfeet, that the Sun has taken his place. There is some reason to suspect, however, that the Sun and Old Man are one, that *Nātōs´* is only another name for *Na´pi*, for I have been told by two or three old men that "the Sun is the person whom we call Old Man." However this may be, it is certain that *Na´pi*—even if he no longer occupies the chief place in the Blackfoot religious system—is still reverenced, and is still addressed in prayer. Now, however, every good thing, success in war, in the chase, health, long life, all happiness, come by the special favor of the Sun.

The Sun is a man, the supreme chief of the world. The flat, circular earth in fact is his home, the floor of his lodge, and the over-arching sky is its covering. The moon, *Kō-kō-mik´-ē-ĭs,* night light, is the Sun's wife. The pair have had a number of children, all but one of whom were killed by pelicans. The survivor is the morning star, *A-pi-su-ahts*—early riser.

In attributes the Sun is very unlike Old Man. He is a beneficent person, of great wisdom and kindness, good to those who do right. As a special means of obtaining his favor, sacrifices must be made. These are often presents of clothing, fine robes, or furs, and in extreme cases, when the prayer is for life itself, the offering of a finger, or—still dearer—a lock of hair. If a white buffalo was killed, the robe was always given to the Sun. It belonged to him. Of the buffalo, the tongue—regarded as the greatest delicacy of the whole animal—was especially sacred to the Sun. The sufferings undergone by men in the Medicine Lodge each year were sacrifices to the Sun. This torture was an actual penance, like the sitting for years on top of a pillar, the wearing of a hair shirt, or fasting in Lent. It was undergone for no other purpose than that of pleasing God—as a propitiation or in fulfilment of vows made to him. Just as the priests of Baal slashed themselves with knives to induce their god to help them, so, and for the same reason, the Blackfoot men surged on and tore out the ropes tied to their skins. It is merely the carrying out of a religious idea that is as old as history and as widespread as the globe, and is closely akin to the motive which to-day, in our own centres of enlightened civilization, prompts acts of self-denial and penance by many thousands of intelligent cultivated people. And yet we are horrified at hearing described the tortures of the Medicine Lodge.

Besides the Sun and Old Man, the Blackfoot religious system includes a number of minor deities or rather natural qualities and forces, which are personified and given shape. These are included in the general terms Above Persons, Ground Persons, and Under Water Persons. Of the former class, Thunder is one of the most important, and is worshipped as is elsewhere shown. He brings the rain. He is represented sometimes as a bird, or, more vaguely, as in one of the stories, merely as a fearful person. Wind Maker is an example of an Under Water Person, and it is related that he has been seen, and his form is described. It is believed by some that he lives under the water at the head of the Upper St. Mary's Lake. Those who believe this say that when he wants the wind to blow, he makes the waves roll, and that these cause the wind to blow,—another example of mistaking effect for cause, so common among the Indians. The Ground Man is another below person. He lives under the ground, and perhaps typifies the power of the earth, which is highly respected by all Indians of the west. The Cheyennes also have a Ground Man whom they call The Lower One, or Below Person (*Pun'-ŏ-tsĭ-hyo*). The cold and snow are brought by Cold Maker (*Ai'-so-yim-stan*). He is a man, white in color, with white hair, and clad in white apparel, who rides on a white horse. He brings the storm with him. They pray to him to bring, or not to bring, the storm.

Many of the animals are regarded as typifying some form of wisdom or craft. They are not gods, yet they have power, which, perhaps, is given them by the Sun or by Old Man. Examples of this are shown in some of the stories.

Among the animals especially respected and supposed to have great power, are the buffalo, the bear, the raven, the wolf, the beaver, and the kit-fox. Geese too, are credited with great wisdom and with foreknowledge of the weather. They are led by chiefs. As is quite natural among a people like the Blackfeet, the buffalo stood very high among the animals which they reverenced. It symbolized food and shelter, and was *Nato'yĕ* (of the Sun), sacred. Not a few considered it a medicine animal, and had it for their dream, or secret helper. It was the most powerful of all the animal helpers. Its importance is indicated by the fact that buffalo skulls were placed on the sweat houses built in connection with the Medicine Lodge. A similar respect for the buffalo exists among many Plains tribes, which were formerly dependent on it for food and raiment. A reverence for the bear appears to be common to all North American tribes, and is based not upon anything that the animal's body yields, but perhaps on the fact that it is the largest carnivorous mammal of the continent, the most difficult to kill and extremely keen in all its senses. The Blackfeet believe it to be part brute and part human, portions of its body, particularly the ribs and feet, being like those of a man. The raven is cunning. The wolf has great endurance and much craft. He can steal close to one without being seen. In the stories given in the earlier pages of this book, many of the attributes of the different animals are clearly set forth.

There were various powers and signs connected with these animals so held in high esteem by the Blackfeet, to which the people gave strict heed. Thus the raven has the power of giving people far sight. It was also useful in another way. Often, in going to war, a man would get a raven's skin and stuff the head and neck, and tie it to the hair of the head behind. If a man wearing such a skin got near the enemy without knowing it, the skin would give him warning by tapping him on the back of the head with its bill. Then he would know that the enemy was near, and would hide. If a raven flew over a lodge, or a number of lodges, and cried, and then was joined by other ravens, all flying over the camp and crying, it was a sure sign that during the day some one would come and tell the news from far off. The ravens often told the people that game was near, calling to the hunter and then flying a little way, and then coming back, and again calling and flying toward the game.

The wolves are the people's great friends; they travel with the wolves. If, as they are travelling along, they pass close to some wolves, these will bark at the people, talking to them. Some man will call to them, "No, I will not give you my body to eat, but I will give you the body of some one else, if you will go along with us." This applies both to wolves and coyotes. If a man goes away from the camp at night, and meets a coyote, and it barks at him, he goes back to the camp, and says to the people: "Look out now; be smart. A coyote barked at me to-night." Then the people look out, and are careful, for it is a sure sign that something bad is going to happen. Perhaps some one will be shot; perhaps the enemy will charge the camp.

If a person is hungry and sings a wolf song, he is likely to find food. Men going on a hunting trip sing these songs, which bring them good luck.

The bear has very powerful medicine. Sometimes he takes pity on people and helps them, as in the story of Mik´-api.

Some Piegans, if they wish to travel on a certain day, have the power of insuring good weather on that day. It is supposed that they do this by singing a powerful song. Some of the enemy can cause bad weather, when they want to steal into the camp.

People who belonged to the *Sin'-o-pah* band of the *I-kun-uh'-kah-tsi,* if they were at war in summer and wanted a storm to come up, would take some dirt and water and rub it on the kit-fox skin, and this would cause a rain-storm to come up. In winter, snow and dirt would be rubbed on the skin and this would bring up a snow-storm.

Certain places and inanimate objects are also greatly reverenced by the Blackfeet, and presents are made to them.

The smallest of the three buttes of the Sweet Grass Hills is regarded as sacred. "All the Indians are afraid to go there," Four Bears once told me. Presents are sometimes thrown into the Missouri River, though these are not offerings made directly to the stream, but are given to the Under Water People, who live in it.

Mention has already been made of the buffalo rock, which gives its owner the power to call the buffalo.

Another sacred object is the medicine rock of the Marias. It is a huge boulder of reddish sandstone, two-thirds the way up a steep hill on the north bank of the Marias River, about five miles from Fort Conrad. Formerly, this rock rested on the top of the bluff, but, as the soil about it is worn away by the wind and the rain, it is slowly moving down the hill. The Indians believe it to be alive, and make presents to it. When I first visited it, the ground about it was strewn with decaying remnants of offerings that had been made to it in the past. Among these I noticed, besides fragments of clothing, eagle feathers, a steel finger ring, brass ear-rings, and a little bottle made of two copper cartridge cases.

Down on Milk River, east of the Sweet Grass Hills, is another medicine rock. It is shaped something like a man's body, and looks like a person sitting on top of the bluff. Whenever the Blackfeet pass this rock, they make presents to it. Sometimes, when they give it an article of clothing, they put it on the rock, "and then," as one of them once said to me, "when you look at it, it seems more than ever like a person." Down in the big bend of the Milk River, opposite the eastern end of the Little Rocky Mountains, lying on the prairie, is a great gray boulder, which is shaped like a buffalo bull lying down. This is greatly reverenced by all Plains Indians, Blackfeet included, and they make presents to it. Many other examples of similar character might be given.

The Blackfeet make daily prayers to the Sun and to Old Man, and nothing of importance is undertaken without asking for divine assistance. They are firm believers in dreams. These, they say, are sent by the Sun to enable us to look ahead, to tell what is going to happen. A dream, especially if it is a strong one,—that is, if the dream is very clear and vivid,—is almost always obeyed. As dreams start them on the war path, so, if a dream threatening bad luck comes to a member of a war party, even if in the enemy's country and just about to make an attack on a camp, the party is likely to turn about and go home without making any hostile demonstrations. The animal or object which appears to the boy, or man, who is trying to dream for power, is, as has been said, regarded thereafter as his secret helper, his medicine, and is usually called his dream (Nits-o'-kan).

The most important religious occasion of the year is the ceremony of the Medicine Lodge. This is a sacrifice, which, among the Blackfeet, is offered invariably by women. If a woman has a son or husband away at war, and is anxious about him, or if she has a dangerously sick child, she may make to the Sun a vow in the following words:—

"Listen, Sun. Pity me. You have seen my life. You know that I am pure. I have never committed adultery with any man. Now, therefore, I ask you to pity me. I will build you a lodge. Let my son survive. Bring him back to health, so that I may build this lodge for you."

The vow to build the Medicine Lodge is repeated in a loud voice, outside her lodge, so that all the people may hear it, and if any man can impeach the woman, he is obliged to speak out, in which case she could be punished according to the law. The Medicine Lodge is always built in summer, at the season of the ripening of the sarvis berries, and if, before this time, the person for whom the vow is made dies, the woman is not obliged to fulfil her vow. She is regarded with suspicion, and it is generally believed that she has been guilty of the crime she disavowed. As this cannot be proved, however, she is not punished.

When the time approaches for the building of the lodge, a suitable locality is selected, and all the people move to it, putting up their lodges in a circle about it. In the meantime, at least a hundred buffalo tongues have been collected, cut, and dried by the woman who may be called the Medicine Lodge woman. No one but she is allowed to take part in this work.

Before the tongues are cut and dried, they are laid in a pile in the medicine woman's lodge. She then gives a feast to the old men, and one of them, noted for his honesty, and well liked by all, repeats a very long prayer, asking in substance that the coming Medicine Lodge may be acceptable to the Sun, and that he will look with favor on the people, and will give them good health, plenty of food, and success in war. A hundred songs are then sung, each one different from the others. The feast and singing of these songs lasts a day and a half.

Before the Medicine Lodge is erected, four large sweat lodges are built, all in a line, fronting to the east or toward the rising sun. Two stand in front of the Medicine Lodge, and two behind it. The two nearest the Medicine Lodge are built one day, and the others on the day following. The sticks for the framework of these lodges are cut only by renowned warriors, each warrior cutting one, and, as he brings it in and lays it down, he counts a *coup*, which must be of some especially brave deed. The old men then take the sticks and erect the lodges, placing on top of each a buffalo skull, one half of which is painted red, the other black, to represent day and night, or rather the sun and the moon. When the lodges are finished and the stones heated, the warriors go in to sweat, and with them the medicine pipe men, who offer up prayers.

While this is going on, the young men cut the centre post for the Medicine Lodge, and all the other material for its construction. The women then pack out the post and the poles on horses, followed by the men shouting, singing, and shooting.

In the morning of this day the medicine woman begins a fast, which must last four days and four nights, with only one intermission, as will shortly appear. During that time she may not go out of doors, except between sunset and sunrise. During the whole ceremony her face, hands, and clothing are covered with the sacred red paint.

When all the material has been brought to the spot where the lodge is to be erected, that warrior who, during the previous year, has done the most cutting and stabbing in battle is selected to cut the rawhide to bind it, and while he cuts the strings he counts three *coups*.

The centre post is now placed on the ground, surrounded by the poles and other smaller posts; and two bands of the *I-kun-uh´-kah-tsi*, the Braves, and the All Crazy Dogs approach. Each band sings four songs, and then they raise the lodge amid the shouting of the people. It is said that, in old times, all the bands of the *I-kun-uh´-kah-tsi* took part in this ceremony. For raising the centre post, which is very heavy, lodge poles are tied in pairs, with rawhide, so as to form "shears," each pair being handled by two men. If one of the ropes binding the shears breaks, the men who hold the pair are said to be unlucky; it is thought that they are soon to die. As soon as the centre post is up, the wall posts are erected, and the roof of poles put on, the whole structure being covered with brush. The door-way faces east or southeast, and the lodge is circular in shape, about forty feet in diameter, with walls about seven feet high.

Inside the Medicine Lodge, at the back, or west side, in the principal place in the lodge, is now built a little box-shaped house, about seven feet high, six feet long, and four wide. It is made of brush, so tightly woven that one cannot see inside of it. This is built by a medicine man, the high priest of this ceremony, who, for four days, the duration of the ceremony, neither eats nor goes out of it in the daytime. The people come to him, two at a time, and he paints them with black, and makes for them an earnest prayer to the Sun, that they may have good health, long lives, and good food and shelter. This man is supposed to have power over the rain. As rain would interfere with the ceremonies, he must stop it, if it threatens.

In the meantime, the sacred dried tongues have been placed in the Medicine Lodge. The next morning, the Medicine Lodge woman leaves her own lodge, and, walking very slowly with bowed head, and praying at every step, she enters the Medicine Lodge, and, standing by the pile of tongues, she cuts up one of them and holds it toward heaven, offering it to the Sun; then she eats a part of it and buries the rest in the dirt, praying to the Ground Man, and calling him to bear witness that she has not defiled his body by committing adultery. She then proceeds to cut up the tongues, giving a very small piece to every person, man, woman, or child. Each one first holds it up to the Sun, and then prays to the Sun, Na´-pi, and the Ground Man for long life, concluding by depositing a part of the morsel of tongue on the ground, saying, "I give you this sacred tongue to eat." And now, during the four days, outside the lodge, goes on the counting of the *coups*. Each warrior in turn recounts his success in war,—his battles or his horse-takings. With a number of friends to help him, he goes through a pantomime of all these encounters, showing how he killed this enemy, took a gun from that one, or cut horses loose from the lodge of another. When he has concluded, an old man offers a prayer, and ends by giving him a new name, saying that he hopes he will live well and long under it.

Inside the lodge, rawhide ropes are suspended from the centre post, and here the men fulfil the vows that they have made during the previous year. Some have been sick, or in great danger at war, and they then vowed that if they were permitted to live, or escape, they would swing at the Medicine Lodge. Slits are cut in the skin of their breast, ropes passed through and secured by wooden skewers, and then the men swing and surge until the skin gives way and tears out. This is very painful, and some fairly shriek with agony as they do it, but they never give up, for they believe that if they should fail to fulfil their vow, they would soon die.

On the fourth day every one has been prayed for, every one has made to the Sun his or her present, which is tied to the centre post, the sacred tongues have all been consumed, and the ceremony ends, every one feeling better, assured of long life and plenty.

Most persons have an entirely erroneous idea of the purpose of this annual ceremony. It has been supposed that it was for the purpose of making warriors. This is not true. It was essentially a religious festival, undertaken for the bodily and spiritual welfare of the people according to their beliefs. Incidentally, it furnished an opportunity for the rehearsal of daring deeds. But among no tribes who practised it were warriors made by it. The swinging by the breast and other self-torturings were but the fulfilment of vows, sacred promises made in time of danger, penances performed, and not, as many believe, an occasion for young men to test their courage.

From the Indians of the tribe, the Medicine Lodge woman receives a very high measure of respect and consideration. Blackfoot men have said to me, "We look on the Medicine Lodge woman as you white people do on the Roman Catholic sisters." Not only is she virtuous in deed, but she must be serious and clean-minded. Her conversation must be sober.

Before the coming of the whites, the Blackfeet used to smoke the leaves of a plant which they call *na-wuh'-to-ski*, and which is said to have been received long, long ago from a medicine beaver. It was used unmixed with any other plant. The story of how this came to the tribe is told elsewhere. This tobacco is no longer planted by the Piegans, nor by the Bloods, though it is said that an old Blackfoot each year still goes through the ceremony, and raises a little. The plant grows about ten inches high and has a long seed stalk growing from the centre. White Calf, the chief of the Piegans, has the secrets of the tobacco and is perhaps the only person in the tribe who knows them. From him I have received the following account of the ceremonies connected with it:—

Early in the spring, after the last snow-storm, when the flowers begin to bud (early in the month of May), the women and children go into the timber and prepare a large bed, clearing away the underbrush, weeds and grass and leaves and sticks, raking the ground till the earth is thoroughly pulverized. Elk, deer, and mountain sheep droppings are collected, pounded fine, and mixed with the seed which is to be sown.

On the appointed day all the men gather at the bed. Each one holds in his hand a short, sharp-pointed stick, with which to make a hole in the ground. The men stand in a row extending across the bed. At a signal they make the holes in the ground, and drop in some seed, with some sacred sarvis berries. The tobacco song is sung by the medicine men, all take a short step forward, make another hole, a foot in front of the last, and then drop in it some more seed. Another song is sung, another step taken, and seed is again planted; and this continues until the line of men has moved all the way across the bed, and the planting is completed. The tobacco dance follows the planting.

After the seed has been planted, they leave it and go off after the buffalo. While away during the summer, some important man—one of the medicine men who had taken part in the planting—announces to the people his purpose to go back to look after the crop. He starts, and after he has reached the place, he builds a little fire in the bed, and offers a prayer for the crop, asking that it may survive and do well. Then he pulls up one of the plants, which he takes back with him and shows to the people, so that all may see how the crop is growing. He may thus visit the place three or four times in the course of the summer.

From time to time, while they are absent from the tobacco patch in summer, moving about after the buffalo, the men gather in some lodge to perform a special ceremony for the protection of the crop. Each man holds in his hand a little stick. They sing and pray to the Sun and Old Man, asking that the grasshoppers and other insects may not eat their plants. At the end of each song they strike the ground with their sticks, as if killing grasshoppers and worms. It has sometimes happened that a young man has said that he does not believe that these prayers and songs protect the plants, that the Sun does not send messengers to destroy the worms. To such a one a medicine man will say, "Well, you can go to the place and see for yourself." The young man gets on his horse and travels to the place. When he comes to the edge of the patch and looks out on it, he sees many small children at work there, killing worms. He has not believed in this before, but now he goes back convinced. Such a young man does not live very long.

At length the season comes for gathering the crop, and, at a time appointed, all the camps begin to move back toward the tobacco patch, timing their marches so that all may reach it on the same day. When they get there, they camp near it, but no one visits it except the head man of the medicine men who took charge of the planting. This man goes to the bed, gathers a little of the plant, and returns to the camp.

A small boy, six or eight years old, is selected to carry this plant to the centre of the circle. The man who gathered the tobacco ties it to a little stick, and, under the tobacco, to the stick he ties a baby's moccasin. The little boy carries this stick to the centre of the camp, and stands it in the ground in the middle of the circle, the old man accompanying him and showing him where to put it. It is left there all night. The next day there is a great feast, and the kettles of food are all brought to the centre of the camp. The people all gather there, and a prayer is made. Then they sing the four songs which belong especially to this festival. The first and fourth are merely airs without words; the second has words, the purport of which is, "The sun goes with us." The third song says, "Hear your children's prayer." After the ceremony is over, every one is at liberty to go and gather the tobacco. It is dried and put in sacks for use during the year. The seed is collected for the next planting. When they reach the patch, if the crop is good, every one is glad. After the gathering, they all move away again after the buffalo.

Sometimes a man who was lazy, and had planted no tobacco, would go secretly to the patch, and pull a number of plants belonging to some one else, and hide them for his own use. Now, in these prayers that they offer, they do not ask for mercy for thieves. A man who had thus taken what did not belong to him would have a lizard appear to him in a dream, and then he would fall sick and die. The medicine men would know of all this, but they would not do anything. They would just let him die.

This tobacco was given us by the one who made us.

The Blackfoot cosmology is imperfect and vague, and I have been able to obtain nothing like a complete account of it, for I have found no one who appeared to know the story of the beginning of all things.

Some of the Blackfeet now say that originally there was a great womb, in which were conceived the progenitors of all animals now on earth. Among these was Old Man. As the time for their birth drew near, the animals used to quarrel as to which should be the first to be born, and one day, in a fierce struggle about this, the womb burst, and Old Man jumped first to the ground. For this reason, he named all the animals Nis-kum´-iks, Young Brothers; and they, because he was the first-born, called him Old Man.

There are several different accounts of the creation of the people by Old Man. One is that he married a female dog, and that their progeny were the first people. Others, and the ones most often told, have been given in the Old Man stories already related.

There is an account of the creation which is essentially an Algonquin myth, and is told by most of the tribes of this stock from the Atlantic to the Rocky Mountains, though the hero is variously named. Here is the Blackfoot version of it:—

In the beginning, all the land was covered with water, and Old Man and all the animals were floating around on a large raft. One day Old Man told the beaver to dive and try to bring up a little mud. The beaver went down, and was gone a long time, but could not reach the bottom. Then the loon tried, and the otter, but the water was too deep for them. At last the muskrat dived, and he was gone so long that they thought he had drowned, but he finally came up, almost dead, and when they pulled him on to the raft, they found, in one of his paws, a little mud. With this, Old Man formed the world, and afterwards he made the people.

This myth, while often related by the Blackfoot tribe, is seldom heard among the Bloods or Piegans. It is uncertain whether all three tribes used to know it, but have forgotten it, or whether it has been learned in comparatively modern times by the Blackfeet from the Crees, with whom they have always had more frequent intercourse and a closer connection than the other two tribes.

There is also another version of the origin of death. When Old Man made the first people, he gave them very strong bodies, and for a long time no one was sick. At last, a little child fell ill. Each day it grew weaker and weaker, and at last it fainted. Then the mother went to Old Man, and prayed him to do something for it.

"This," said Old Man, "will be the first time it has happened to the people. You have seen the buffalo fall to the ground when struck with an arrow. Their hearts stop beating, they do not breathe, and soon their bodies become cold. They are then dead. Now, woman, it shall be for you to decide whether death shall come to the people as well as to the other animals, or whether they shall live forever. Come now with me to the river."

When they reached the water's edge, Old Man picked up from the ground a dry buffalo chip and a stone. "Now, woman," he said, "you will tell me which one of these to throw into the water. If what I throw floats, your child shall live; the people shall live forever. If it sinks, then your child shall die, and all the people shall die, each one when his time comes."

The woman stood still a long time, looking from the stone to the buffalo chip, and from the chip to the stone. At last she said, "Throw the stone." Then Old Man tossed it into the river, and it sank to the bottom. "Woman," he cried, "go home; your child is dead." Thus, on account of a foolish woman, we all must die.

The shadow of a person, the Blackfeet say, is his soul. Northeast of the Sweet Grass Hills, near the international boundary line, is a bleak, sandy country called the Sand Hills, and there all the shadows of the deceased good Blackfeet are congregated. The shadows of those who in this world led wicked lives are not allowed to go there. After death, these wicked persons take the shape of ghosts (*Sta-au*), and are compelled ever after to remain near the place where they died. Unhappy themselves, they envy those who are happy, and continually prowl about the lodges of the living, seeking to do them some injury. Sometimes they tap on the lodge skins and whistle down the smoke hole, but if the fire is burning within they will not enter.

Outside in the dark they do much harm, especially the ghosts of enemies who have been killed in battle. These sometimes shoot invisible arrows into persons, causing sickness and death. They have hit people on the head, causing them to become crazy. They have paralyzed people's limbs, and drawn their faces out of shape, and done much other harm.

Ghosts walk above the ground, not on it. An example of this peculiarity is seen in the case of the young man who visited the lodge of the starving family, in the story entitled Origin of the *I-kun-uh'-kah-tsi*.

Ghosts sometimes speak to people. An instance of this is the following, which occurred to my friend Young Bear Chief, and which he related to me. He said: "I once went to war, and took my wife with me. I went to Buffalo Lip Butte, east of the Cypress Mountains; a little creek runs by it. I took eighteen horses from an Assinaboine camp one night, when it was very foggy. I found sixteen horses feeding on the hills, and went into the camp and cut loose two more. Then we went off with the horses. When we started, it was so foggy that I could not see the stars, and I did not know which way to run. I kept travelling in what I supposed was the direction toward home, but I did not know where I was going. After we had gone a long way, I stopped and got off my horse to fix my belt. My wife did not dismount, but sat there waiting for me to mount and ride on.

"I spoke to my wife, and said to her, 'We don't know which way to go.' A voice spoke up right behind me and said: 'It is well; you go ahead. You are going right.' When I heard the voice, the top of my head seemed to lift up and felt as if a lot of needles were sticking into it. My wife, who was right in front of me, was so frightened that she fainted and fell off her horse, and it was a long time before she came to. When she got so she could ride, we went on, and when morning came I found that we were going straight, and were on the west side of the West Butte of the Sweet Grass Hills. We got home all right. This must have been a ghost."

Now and then among the Blackfeet, we find evidences of a belief that the soul of a dead person may take up its abode in the body of an animal. An example of this is seen in the story of E-kūs´-kini, Owls are thought to be the ghosts of medicine men.

The Blackfeet do not consider the Sand Hills a happy hunting ground. There the dead, who are themselves shadows, live in shadow lodges, hunt shadow buffalo, go to war against shadow enemies, and in every way lead an existence which is but a mimicry of this life. In this respect the Blackfeet are almost alone. I know of scarcely any other American tribe, certainly none east of the Rocky Mountains, who are wholly without a belief in a happy future state. The Blackfeet do not especially say that this future life is an unhappy one, but, from the way in which they speak of it, it is clear that for them it promises nothing desirable. It is a monotonous, never ending, and altogether unsatisfying existence,—a life as barren and desolate as the country which the ghosts inhabit. These people are as much attached to life as we are. Notwithstanding the unhappy days which have befallen them of late years,—days of privation and hunger,—they cling to life. Yet they seem to have no fear of death. When their time comes, they accept their fate without a murmur, and tranquilly, quietly pass away.

MEDICINE PIPES AND HEALING

The person whom the whites term "medicine man" is called by the Blackfeet *Ni-namp'-skan.* Mr. Schultz believes this word to be compounded of *nin'nah*, man, and *namp'-ski*, horned toad (*Phrynosoma*), and in this he is supported by Mr. Thomas Bird, a very intelligent half-breed, who has translated a part of the Bible into the Blackfoot language for the Rev. S. Trivett, a Church of England missionary. These gentlemen conclude that the word means "all-face man." The horned toad is called *namp'-ski*, all-face; and as the medicine man, with his hair done up in a huge topknot, bore a certain resemblance to this creature, he was so named. No one among the Blackfeet appears to have any idea as to what the word means.

The medicine pipes are really only pipe stems, very long, and beautifully decorated with bright-colored feathers and the fur of the weasel and other animals. It is claimed that these stems were given to the people long, long ago, by the Sun, and that those who own them are regarded by him with special favor.

Formerly these stems were valued at from fifteen to thirty head of horses, and were bought and sold like any other property. When not in use, they were kept rolled up in many thicknesses of fine tanned fur, and with them were invariably a quantity of tobacco, a sacred whistle, two sacred rattles, and some dried sweet grass, and sweet pine needles.

In the daytime, in pleasant weather, these sacred bundles were hung out of doors behind the owners' lodges, on tripods. At night they were suspended within, above the owners' seat It was said that if at any time a person should walk completely around the lodge of a medicine man, some bad luck would befall him. Inside the lodge, no one was allowed to pass between the fireplace and the pipe stem. No one but a medicine man and his head wife could move or unroll the bundle. The man and his wife were obliged always to keep their faces, hands, and clothing painted with *nits'-i-san,* a dull red paint, made by burning a certain clay found in the bad lands.

The *Ni-namp'-skan* appears to be a priest of the Sun, and prayers offered through him are thought to be specially favored. So the sacred stem is frequently unrolled for the benefit of the sick, for those who are about to undertake a dangerous expedition, such as a party departing to war, for prayers for the general health and prosperity of the people, and for a bountiful supply of food. At the present time these ancient ceremonies have largely fallen into disuse. In fact, since the disappearance of the buffalo, most of the old customs are dying out.

The thunder is believed to bring the rain in spring, and the rain makes the berries grow. It is a rule that after the first thunder is heard in the spring, every medicine man must give a feast and offer prayers for a large berry crop. I have never seen this ceremony, but Mr. Schultz was once permitted to attend one, and has given me the following account of it. He said: "When I entered the lodge with the other guests, the pipe stem had already been unrolled. Before the fire were two huge kettles of cooked sarvis berries, a large bowlful of which was soon set before each guest. Each one, before eating, took a few of the berries and rubbed them into the ground, saying, 'Take pity on us, all Above People, and give us good.'

"When all had finished eating, a large black stone pipe bowl was filled and fitted to the medicine stem, and the medicine man held it aloft and said: 'Listen, Sun! Listen, Thunder! Listen, Old Man! All Above Animals, all Above People, listen. Pity us! You will smoke. We fill the sacred pipe. Let us not starve. Give us rain during this summer. Make the berries large and sweet. Cover the bushes with them. Look down on us all and pity us. Look at the women and the little children; look at us all. Let us reach old age. Let our lives be complete. Let us destroy our enemies. Help the young men in battle. Man, woman, child, we all pray to you; pity us and give us good. Let us survive.'

"He then danced the pipe dance, to be described further on. At this time, another storm had come up, and the thunder crashed directly over our heads.

"'Listen,' said the medicine man. 'It hears us. We are not doing this uselessly'; and he raised his face, animated with enthusiasm, toward the sky, his whole body trembling with excitement; and, holding the pipe aloft, repeated his prayer. All the rest of the people were excited, and repeatedly clasped their arms over their breasts, saying: 'Pity us; good give us; good give us. Let us survive.'

"After this, the pipe was handed to a man on the right of the semi-circle. Another warrior took a lighted brand from the fire, and counted four *coups*, at the end of each *coup* touching the pipe bowl with the brand. When he had counted the fourth *coup*, the pipe was lighted. It was then smoked in turn around the circle, each one, as he received it, repeating a short prayer before he put the stem to his lips. When it was smoked out, a hole was dug in the ground, the ashes were knocked into it and carefully covered over, and the thunder ceremony was ended."

In the year 1885, I was present at the unwrapping of the medicine pipe by Red Eagle, an aged *Ni-namp'-skan* since dead. On this occasion prayers were made for the success of a party of Piegans who had started in pursuit of some Crows who had taken a large band of horses from the Piegans the day before. The ceremony was a very impressive one, and prayers were offered not only for the success of this war party, but also for the general good, as well as for the welfare of special individuals, who were mentioned by name. The concluding words of the general prayer were as follows: "May all people have full life. Give to all heavy bodies. Let the young people grow; increase their flesh. Let all men, women, and children have full life. Harden the bodies of the old people so that they may reach great age."

In 1879, Mr. Schultz saw a sacred pipe unwrapped for the benefit of a sick woman, and on various occasions since he has been present at this ceremony. All accounts of what takes place agree so closely with what I saw that I give only one of them. Mr. Schultz wrote me of the first occasion: "When I entered the lodge, it was already well filled with men who had been invited to participate in the ceremony. The medicine man was aged and gray-headed, and his feeble limbs could scarcely support his body. Between him and his wife was the bundle which contained the medicine pipe, as yet unwrapped, lying on a carefully folded buffalo robe. Plates of food were placed before each guest, and after all had finished eating, and a common pipe had been lighted to be smoked around the circle, the ceremony began.

"With wooden tongs, the woman took a large coal from the fire, and laid it on the ground in front of the sacred stem. Then, while every one joined in singing a chant, a song of the buffalo (without words), she took a bunch of dried sweet grass, and, raising and lowering her hand in time to the music, finally placed the grass on the burning coals. As the thin column of perfumed smoke rose from the burning herb, both she and the medicine man grasped handfuls of it and rubbed it over their persons, to purify themselves before touching the sacred roll. They also took each a small piece of some root from a little pouch, and ate it, signifying that they purified themselves without and within.

"The man and woman now faced each other and again began the buffalo song, keeping time by touching with the clenched hands—the right and left alternately—the wrappings of the pipe, occasionally making the sign for buffalo. Now, too, one could occasionally hear the word *Nai-ai'* in the song. After singing this song for about ten minutes, it was changed to the antelope song, and, instead of touching the roll with the clenched hands, which represented the heavy tread of buffalo, they closed the hands, leaving the index finger extended and the thumbs partly open, and in time to the music, as in the previous song, alternately touched the wrappers with the tips of the left and right forefinger, the motions being quick and firm, and occasionally brought the hands to the side of the head, making the sign for antelope, and at the same time uttering a loud '*Kuh*' to represent the whistling or snorting of that animal.

"At the conclusion of this song, the woman put another bunch of sweet grass on a coal, and carefully undid the wrappings of the pipe, holding each one over the smoke to keep it pure. When the last wrapping was removed, the man gently grasped the stem and, every one beginning the pipe song, he raised and lowered it several times, shaking it as he did so, until every feather and bit of fur and scalp hung loose and could be plainly seen.

"At this moment the sick woman entered the lodge, and with great difficulty, for she was very weak, walked over to the medicine woman and knelt down before her. The medicine woman then produced a small bag of red paint, and painted a broad band across the sick woman's forehead, a stripe down the nose, and a number of round dots on each cheek. Then picking up the pipe stem, which the man had laid down, she held it up toward the sky and prayed, saying, 'Listen, Sun, pity us! Listen, Old Man, pity us! Above People, pity us! Under Water People, pity us! Listen, Sun! Listen, Sun! Let us survive, pity us! Let us survive. Look down on our sick daughter this day. Pity her and give her a complete life.' At the conclusion of this short prayer, all the people uttered a loud *m-m-m-h*, signifying that they took the words to their hearts. Every one now commenced the pipe song, and the medicine woman passed the stem over different parts of the sick woman's body, after which she rose and left the lodge.

"The medicine man now took a common pipe which had been lighted, and blew four whiffs of smoke toward the sky, four toward the ground, and four on the medicine pipe stem, and prayed to the

Sun, Old Man, and all medicine animals, to pity the people and give them long life. The drums were then produced, the war song commenced, and the old man, with a rattle in each hand, danced four times to the door-way and back. He stooped slightly, kept all his limbs very rigid, extending his arms like one giving a benediction, and danced in time to the drumming and singing with quick, sudden steps. This is the medicine pipe dance, which no one but a pipe-owner is allowed to perform. Afterward, he picked up the pipe stem, and, holding it aloft in front of him, went through the same performance. At the conclusion of the dance, the pipe stem was passed from one to another of the guests, and each one in turn held it aloft and repeated a short prayer. The man on my right prayed for the health of his children, the one on my left for success in a proposed war expedition. This concluded the ceremony."

Disease among the Blackfeet is supposed to be caused by evil spirits, usually the spirits or ghosts of enemies slain in battle. These spirits are said to wander about at night, and whenever opportunity offers, they shoot invisible arrows into persons. These cause various internal troubles, such as consumption, hemorrhages, and diseases of the digestive organs. Mice, frogs, snakes, and tailed batrachians are said to cause much disease among women, and hence should be shunned, and on no account handled.

Less important external ailments and hurts, such as ulcers, boils, sprains, and so on, are treated by applying various lotions or poultices, compounded by boiling or macerating certain roots or herbs, known only to the person supplying them. Rheumatic pains are treated in several ways. Sometimes the sweat lodge is used, or hot rocks are applied over the place where the pain is most severe, or actual cautery is practised, by inserting prickly pear thorns in the flesh, and setting fire to them, when they burn to the very point.

The sweat lodge, so often referred to, is used as a curative agent, as well as in religious ceremonies, and is considered very beneficial in illness of all kinds. The sweat lodge is built in the shape of a rough hemisphere, three or four feet high and six or eight in diameter. The frame is usually of willow branches, and is covered with cow-skins and robes. In the centre of the floor, a small hole is dug out, in which are to be placed red hot stones. Everything being ready, those who are to take the sweat remove their clothing and crowd into the lodge. The hot rocks are then handed in from the fire outside, and the cowskins pulled down to the ground to exclude any cold air. If a medicine pipe man is not at hand, the oldest person present begins to pray to the Sun, and at the same time sprinkles water on the hot rocks, and a dense steam rises, making the perspiration fairly drip from the body. Occasionally, if the heat becomes too intense, the covering is raised for a few minutes to admit a little air. The sweat bath lasts for a long time, often an hour or more, during which many prayers are offered, religious songs chanted, and several pipes smoked to the Sun. As has been said, the sweat lodge is built to represent the Sun's own lodge or home, that is, the world. The ground inside the lodge stands for its surface, which, according to Blackfoot philosophy, is flat and round. The framework represents the sky, which far off, on the horizon, reaches down to and touches the world.

As soon as the sweat is over, the men rush out, and plunge into the stream to cool off. This is invariably done, even in winter, when the ice has to be broken to make a hole large enough to bathe in. It is said that, when the small-pox was raging among these Indians, they used the sweat lodge daily, and that hundreds of them, sick with the disease, were unable to get out of the river, after taking the bath succeeding a sweat, and were carried down stream by the current and drowned.

It is said that wolves, which in former days were extremely numerous, sometimes went crazy, and bit every animal they met with, sometimes even coming into camps and biting dogs, horses, and people. Persons bitten by a mad wolf generally went mad, too. They trembled and their limbs jerked, they made their jaws work and foamed at the mouth, often trying to bite other people. When any one acted in this way, his relations tied him hand and foot with ropes, and, having killed a buffalo, they rolled him up in the green hide, and then built a fire on and around him, leaving him in the fire until the hide began to dry and burn. Then they pulled him out and removed the buffalo hide, and he was cured. While in the fire, the great heat caused him to sweat profusely, so much water coming out of his body that none was left in it, and with the water the disease went out, too. All the old people tell me that they have seen individuals cured in this manner of a mad wolf's bite.

Whenever a person is really sick, a doctor is sent for. Custom requires that he shall be paid for his services before rendering them. So when he is called, the messenger says to him, "A——presents to you a horse, and asks you to come and doctor him." Sometimes the fee may be several horses, and sometimes a gun, saddle, or some article of wearing-apparel. This fee pays only for one visit, but the duration of the visit is seldom less than twelve hours, and sometimes exceeds forty-eight. If, after the expiration of the visit, the patient feels that he has been benefited, he will probably send for the doctor again, but if, on the other hand, he continues to grow worse, he is likely to send for another. Not infrequently two or more doctors may be present at the same time, taking turns with the patient. In early days, if a man fell sick, and remained so for three weeks or a month, he had to start anew in life when he recovered; for, unless very wealthy, all his possessions had gone to pay doctor's fees. Often the last horse, and even the lodge, weapons, and extra clothing were so parted with. Of late years, however, since the disappearance of the buffalo, the doctors' fees are much more moderate.

The doctor is named *I-so-kin'-ŭh-kin,* a word difficult to translate. The nearest English meaning of the word seems to be "heavy singer for the sick." As a rule all doctors sing while endeavoring to work their cures, and, as helpers, a number of women are always present. Disease being caused by evil spirits, prayers, exhortations, and certain mysterious methods must be observed to rid the patient of their influence. No two doctors have the same methods or songs. Herbs are sometimes used, but not always. One of their medicines is a great yellow fungus which grows on the pine trees. This is dried and powdered, and administered either dry or in an infusion. It is a purgative. As a rule, these doctors, while practising their rites, will not allow any one in the lodge, except the immediate members of the sick man's family. Mr. Schultz, who on more than one occasion has been present at a doctoring, gives the following account of one of the performances.

"The patient was a man in the last stages of consumption. When the doctor entered the lodge, he handed the sick man a strip of buckskin, and told him to tie it around his chest. The patient then reclined on a couch, stripped to the waist, and the doctor kneeled on the floor beside him. Having cleared a little space of the loose dirt and dust, the doctor took two coals from the fire, laid them in this place, and put a pinch of dried sweet grass on each of them. As the smoke arose from the burning grass, he held his drum over it, turning it from side to side, and round and round. This was supposed to purify it. Laying aside the drum, he held his hands in the smoke, and rubbed his arms and body with it. Then, picking up the drum, he began to tap it rapidly, and prayed, saying: 'Listen, my dream. This you told me should be done. This you said should be the way. You said it would cure the sick. Help me now. Do not lie to me. Help me, Sun person. Help me to cure this sick man.'

"He then began to sing, and as soon as the women had caught the air, he handed the drum to one of them to beat, and, still singing himself, took an eagle's wing and dipped the tip of it in a cup of 'medicine.' It was a clear liquid, and looked as if it might be simply water. Placing the tip of the wing in his mouth, he seemed to bite off the end of it, and, chewing it a little, spat it out on the patient's breast. Then, in time to the singing, he brushed it gently off, beginning at the throat and ending at the lower ribs. This was repeated three times. Next he took the bandage from the patient, dipped it in the cup of medicine, and, wringing it out, placed it on the sick man's chest, and rubbed it up and down, and back and forth, after which he again brushed the breast with the eagle wing. Finally, he lighted a pipe, and, placing the bowl in his mouth, blew the smoke through the stem all over the patient's breast, shoulders, neck, and arms, and finished the ceremony by again brushing with the wing. At intervals of two or three hours, the whole ceremony was repeated. The doctor arrived at the lodge of the sick man about noon, and left the next morning, having received for his services a saddle and two blankets."

"Listen, my dream—" This is the key to most of the Blackfoot medicine practices. These doctors for the most part effect their cures by prayer. Each one has his dream, or secret helper, to whom he prays for aid, and it is by this help that he expects to restore his patient to health. No doubt the doctors have the fullest confidence that their practices are beneficial, and in some cases they undoubtedly do good because of the implicit confidence felt in them by the patient.

Often, when a person is sick, he will ask some medicine man to unroll his pipe. If able to dance, he will take part in the ceremony, but if not, the medicine man paints him with the sacred symbols. In any case a fervent prayer is offered by the medicine man for the sick person's recovery. The medicine man administers no remedies; the ceremony is purely religious. Being a priest of the Sun, it is thought that god will be more likely to listen to him than he would to an ordinary man.

Although the majority of Blackfoot doctors are men, there are also many women in the guild, and some of them are quite noted for their success. Such a woman, named Wood Chief Woman, is now alive on the Blackfoot reservation. She has effected many wonderful cures. Two Bear Woman is a good doctor, and there are many others.

In the case of gunshot wounds a man's "dream," or "medicine," often acts directly and speedily. Many cases are cited in which this charm, often the stuffed skin of some bird or animal, belonging to the wounded man, becomes alive, and by its power effects a cure. Many examples of this might be given but for lack of space. Entirely honest Indians and white men have seen such cures and believe in them.

THE BLACKFOOT OF TO-DAY

In the olden times the Blackfeet were very numerous, and it is said that then they were a strong and hardy people, and few of them were ever sick. Most of the men who died were killed in battle, or died of old age. We may well enough believe that this was the case, because the conditions of their life in those primitive times were such that the weakly and those predisposed to any constitutional trouble would not survive early childhood. Only the strongest of the children would grow up to become the parents of the next generation. Thus a process of selection was constantly going on, the effect of which was no doubt seen in the general health of the people.

With the advent of the whites, came new conditions. Various special diseases were introduced and swept off large numbers of the people. An important agent in their destruction was alcohol.

In the year 1845, the Blackfeet were decimated by the small-pox. This disease appears to have travelled up the Missouri River; and in the early years, between 1840 and 1850, it swept away hosts of Mandans, Rees, Sioux, Crows, and other tribes camped along the great river. I have been told, by a man who was employed at Fort Union in 1842-43, that the Indians died there in such numbers that the men of the fort were kept constantly at work digging trenches in which to bury them, and when winter came, and the ground froze so hard that it was no longer practicable to bury the dead, their bodies were stacked up like cord wood in great piles to await the coming of spring. The disease spread from tribe to tribe, and finally reached the Blackfeet. It is said by whites who were in the country at the time, that this small-pox almost swept the Plains bare of Indians.

In the winter of 1857-58, small-pox again carried off great numbers, but the mortality was not to be compared with that of 1845. In 1864, measles ran through all the Blackfoot camps, and was very fatal, and again in 1869 they had the small-pox.

Between the years 1860 and 1875, a great deal of whiskey was traded to the Blackfeet. Having once experienced the delights of intoxication, the Indians were eager for liquor, and the traders found that robes and furs could be bought to better advantage for whiskey than for anything else. To be sure, the personal risk to the trader was considerably increased by the sale of whiskey, for when drunk the Indians fought like demons among themselves or with the traders. But, on the other hand, whiskey for trading to Indians cost but a trifle, and could be worked up, and then diluted, so that a little would go a long way.

As a measure of partial self-protection, the traders used to deal out the liquor from the keg or barrel in a tin scoop so constructed that it would not stand on a flat surface, so that an Indian, who was drinking, had to keep the vessel in his hand until the liquor was consumed, or else it would be spilled and lost. This lessened the danger of any shooting or stabbing while the Indian was drinking, and an effort was usually made to get him out of the store as soon as he had finished. Nevertheless, drunken fights in the trading-stores were of common occurrence, and the life of a whiskey-trader was one of constant peril. I have talked with many men who were engaged in this traffic, and some of the stories they tell are thrilling. It was a common thing in winter for the man who unbarred and opened the store in the morning to have a dead Indian fall into his arms as the door swung open. To prop up against the door a companion who had been killed or frozen to death during the night seems to have been regarded by the Indians as rather a delicate bit of humor, in the nature of a joke on the trader. Long histories of the doings of these whiskey trading days have been related to me, but the details are too repulsive to be set down. The traffic was very fatal to the Indians.

The United States has laws which prohibit, under severe penalties, the sale of intoxicants to Indians, but these laws are seldom enforced. To the north of the boundary line, however, in the Northwest Territories, the Canadian Mounted Police have of late years made whiskey-trading perilous business. Of Major Steell's good work in putting down the whiskey traffic on the Blackfoot agency in Montana, I shall speak further on, and to-day there is not very much whiskey sold to the Blackfeet. Constant vigilance is needed, however, to keep traders from the borders of the reservation.

In the winter of 1883-84 more than a quarter of the Piegan tribe of the Blackfeet, which then numbered about twenty-five or twenty-six hundred, died from starvation. It had been reported to the Indian Bureau that the Blackfeet were practically self-supporting and needed few supplies. As a consequence of this report, appropriations for them were small. The statement was entirely and fatally misleading. The Blackfeet had then never done anything toward self-support, except to kill buffalo. But just before this, in the year 1883, the buffalo had been exterminated from the

Blackfoot country. In a moment, and without warning, the people had been deprived of the food supply on which they had depended. At once they had turned their attention to the smaller game, and, hunting faithfully the river bottoms, the brush along the small streams, and the sides of the mountains, had killed off all the deer, elk, and antelope; and at the beginning of the winter found themselves without their usual stores of dried meat, and with nothing to depend on, except the scanty supplies in the government storehouse. These were ridiculously inadequate to the wants of twenty-five hundred people, and food could be issued to them only in driblets quite insufficient to sustain life. The men devoted themselves with the utmost faithfulness to hunting, killing birds, rabbits, prairie-dogs, rats, anything that had life; but do the best they might, the people began to starve. The very old and the very young were the first to perish; after that, those who were weak and sickly, and at last some even among the strong and hardy. News of this suffering was sent East, and Congress ordered appropriations to relieve the distress; but the supplies had to be freighted in wagons for one hundred and fifty or two hundred miles before they were available. If the Blackfeet had been obliged to depend on the supplies authorized by the Indian Bureau, the whole tribe might have perished, for the red tape methods of the Government are not adapted to prompt and efficient action in times of emergency. Happily, help was nearer at hand. The noble people of Montana, and the army officers stationed at Fort Shaw, did all they could to get supplies to the sufferers. One or two Montana contractors sent on flour and bacon, on the personal assurance of the newly appointed agent that he would try to have them paid. But it took a long time to get even these supplies to the agency, over roads sometimes hub deep in mud, or again rough with great masses of frozen clay; and all the time the people were dying.

During the winter, Major Allen had been appointed agent for the Blackfeet, and he reached the agency in the midst of the worst suffering, and before any effort had been made to relieve it. He has told me a heart-rending story of the frightful suffering which he found among these helpless people.

In his efforts to learn exactly what was their condition, Major Allen one day went into twenty-three houses and lodges to see for himself just what the Indians had to eat. In only two of these homes did he find anything in the shape of food. In one house a rabbit was boiling in a pot. The man had killed it that morning, and it was being cooked for a starving child. In another lodge, the hoof of a steer was cooking,—only the hoof,—to make soup for the family. Twenty-three lodges Major Allen visited that day, and the little rabbit and the steer's hoof were all the food he found. "And then," he told me, with tears in his eyes, "I broke down. I could go no further. To see so much misery, and feel myself utterly powerless to relieve it, was more than I could stand."

Major Allen had calculated with exactest care the supplies on hand, and at this time was issuing one-seventh rations. The Indians crowded around the agency buildings and begged for food. Mothers came to the windows and held up their starving babies that the sight of their dull, pallid faces, their shrunken limbs, and their little bones sticking through their skins might move some heart to pity. Women brought their young daughters to the white men in the neighborhood, and said, "Here, you may have her, if you will feed her; I want nothing for myself; only let her have enough to eat, that she may not die." One day, a deputation of the chiefs came to Major Allen, and asked him to give them what he had in his storehouses. He explained to them that it must be some time before the supplies could get there, and that only by dealing out what he had with the greatest care could the people be kept alive until provisions came. But they said: "Our women and children are hungry, and we are hungry. Give us what you have, and let us eat once and be filled. Then we will die content; we will not beg any more." He took them into the storehouse, and showed them just what food he had,—how much flour, how much bacon, how much rice, coffee, sugar, and so on through the list—and then told them that if this was issued all at once, there was no hope for them, they would surely die, but that he expected supplies by a certain day. "And," said he, "if they do not come by that time, you shall come in here and help yourselves. That I promise you." They went away satisfied.

Meanwhile, the supplies were drawing near. The officer in command of Fort Shaw had supplied fast teams to hurry on a few loads to the agency, but the roads were so bad that the wagon trains moved with appalling slowness. At length, however, they had advanced so far that it was possible to send out light teams, to meet the heavily laden ones, and bring in a few sacks of flour and bacon; and every little helped. Gradually the suffering was relieved, but the memory of that awful season of famine will never pass from the minds of those who witnessed it.

There is a record of between four and five hundred Indians who died of hunger at this time, and this includes only those who were buried in the immediate neighborhood of the agency and for whom coffins were made. It is probable that nearly as many more died in the camps on other creeks, but this is mere conjecture. It is no exaggeration to say, however, that from one-quarter to one-third of the Piegan tribe starved to death during that winter and the following spring.

The change from living in portable and more or less open lodges to permanent dwellings has been followed by a great deal of illness, and at present the people appear to be sickly, though not so much so as some other tribes I have known, living under similar conditions further south.

Like other Indians, the Blackfeet have been several times a prey to bad agents,—men careless of their welfare, who thought only about drawing their own pay, or, worse, who used their positions simply for their own enrichment, and stole from the government and Indians alike everything upon which they could lay hands. It was with great satisfaction that I secured the discharge of one such man a few years ago, and I only regret that it was not in my power to have carried the matter so far that he might have spent a few years in prison.

The present agent of the Blackfeet, Major George Steell, is an old-timer in the country and understands Indians very thoroughly. In one respect, he has done more for this people than any other man who has ever had charge of them, for he has been an uncompromising enemy of the whiskey traffic, and has relentlessly pursued the white men who always gather about an agency to sell whiskey to the Indians, and thus not only rob them of their possessions, but degrade them as well. The prison doors of Deer Lodge have more than once opened to receive men sent there through the energy of Major Steell. For the good work he has done in this respect, this gentleman deserves the highest credit, and he is a shining example among Indian agents.

As recently as 1887 it was rather unusual to see a Blackfoot Indian clad in white men's clothing; the only men who wore coats and trousers were the police and a few of the chiefs; to-day it is quite as unusual to see an Indian wearing a blanket. Not less striking than this difference in their way of life, is the change which has taken place in the spirit of the tribe.

I was passing through their reservation in 1888, when the chiefs asked me to meet them in council and listen to what they had to say.

I learned that they wished to have a message taken to the Great Father in the East, and, after satisfying myself that their complaint was well grounded, I promised to do for them what I could. I accomplished what they desired, and since that time I have taken much active interest in this people, and my experience with them has shown me very clearly how much may be accomplished by the unaided efforts of a single individual who thoroughly understands the needs of a tribe of Indians. During my annual visits to the Blackfeet reservation, which have extended over two, three, or four months each season, I see a great many of the men and have long conversations with them. They bring their troubles to me, asking what they shall do, and how their condition may be improved. They tell me what things they want, and why they think they ought to have them. I listen, and talk to them just as if they were so many children. If their requests are unreasonable, I try to explain to them, step by step, why it is not best that what they desire should be done, or tell them that other things which they ask for seem proper, and that I will do what I can to have them granted. If one will only take the pains necessary to make things clear to him, the adult Indian is a reasonable being, but it requires patience to make him understand matters which to a white man would need no explanation. As an example, let me give the substance of a conversation had last autumn with a leading man of the Piegans who lives on Cut Bank River, about twenty-five miles from the agency. He said to me:—

"We ought to have a storehouse over here on Cut Bank, so that we will not be obliged each week to go over to the agency to get our food. It takes us a day to go, and a day to come, and a day there; nearly three days out of every week to get our food. When we are at work cutting hay, we cannot afford to spend so much time travelling back and forth. We want to get our crops in, and not to be travelling about all the time. It would be a good thing, too, to have a blacksmith shop here, so that when our wagons break down, we will not have to go to the agency to get them mended."

This is merely the substance of a much longer speech, to which I replied by a series of questions, something like the following:—

"Do you remember talking to me last year, and telling me on this same spot that you ought to have beef issued to you here, and ought not to have to make the long journey to the agency for your meat?" "Yes."

"And that I told you I agreed with you, and believed that some of the steers could just as well be killed here by the agency herder and issued to those Indians living near here?" "Yes."

"That change has been made, has it not? You now get your beef here, don't you?" "Yes."

"You know that the Piegans have a certain amount of money coming to them every year, don't you?" "Yes."

"And that some of that money goes to pay the expenses of the agency, some for food, some to pay clerks and blacksmiths, some to buy mowing-machines, wagons, harness, and rakes, and some to buy the cattle which have been issued to you?" "Yes."

"Now, if a government storehouse were to be built over here, clerks hired to manage it, a blacksmith shop built and another blacksmith hired, that would all cost money, wouldn't it?" "Yes."

"And that money would be taken out of the money coming next year to the Piegans, wouldn't it?" "Yes."

"And if that money were spent for those things, the people would have just so many fewer wagons, mowing-machines, rakes, and cattle issued to them next year, wouldn't they?" "Yes."

"Well, which would be best for the tribe, which would you rather have, a store and a blacksmith shop here on Cut Bank, or the money which those things would cost in cows and farming implements?"

"I would prefer that we should have the cattle and the tools."

"I think you are right. It would save trouble to each man, if the government would build a storehouse for him right next his house, but it would be a waste of money. Many white men have to drive ten, twenty, or thirty miles to the store, and you ought not to complain if you have to do so."

After this conversation the man saw clearly that his request was an unreasonable one, but if I had merely told him that he was a fool to want a store on Cut Bank, he would never have been satisfied, for his experiences were so limited that he could not have reasoned the thing out for himself.

In my talks with these people, I praise those who have worked hard and lived well during the past year, while to those who have been idle or drunken or have committed crimes, I explain how foolish their course has been and try to show them how impossible it is for a man to be successful if he acts like a child, and shows that he is a person of no sense. A little quiet talk will usually demonstrate to them that they have been unwise, and they make fresh resolutions and promise amendment. Of course the only argument I use is to tell them that one course will be for their material advancement, and is the way a white man would act, while the other will tend to keep them always poor.

Some years ago, the Blackfeet made a new treaty, by which they sold to the government a large portion of their lands. By this treaty, which was ratified by Congress in May, 1887, they are to receive $150,000 annually for a period of ten years, when government support is to be withdrawn. This sum is a good deal more than is required for their subsistence, and, by the terms of the treaty, the surplus over what is required for their food and clothing is to be used in furnishing to the Indians farming implements, seed, live stock, and such other things as will help them to become self-supporting.

The country which the Blackfeet inhabit lies just south of the parallel of 49°, close to the foot of the Rocky Mountains, and is very cold and dry. Crops can be grown there successfully not more than once in four or five years, and the sole products to be depended on are oats and potatoes, which are raised only by means of irrigation. It is evident, therefore, that the Piegan tribe of the Blackfeet can never become an agricultural people. Their reservation, however, is well adapted to stock-raising, and in past years the cattlemen from far and from near have driven their herds on to the reservation to eat the Blackfoot grass; and the remonstrances of the Indians have been entirely disregarded. Some years ago, I came to the conclusion that the proper occupation for these Indians was stock-raising. Horses they already had in some numbers, but horses are not so good for them as cattle, because horses are more readily sold than cattle, and an Indian is likely to trade his horse for whiskey and other useless things. Cattle they are much less likely to part with, and besides this, require more attention than horses, and so are likely to keep the Indians busy and to encourage them to work.

Within the past three or four years, I have succeeded in inducing the Indian Bureau to employ a part of the treaty money coming to the Blackfeet in purchasing for them cattle.

It was impressed upon them that they must care for the cattle, not kill and eat any of them, but keep them for breeding purposes. It was represented to them that, if properly cared for, the cattle would increase each year, until a time might come when each Indian would be the possessor of a herd, and would then be rich like the white cattlemen.

The severe lesson of starvation some years before had not failed to make an impression, and it was perhaps owing to this terrible experience that the Piegans did not eat the cows as soon as they got them, as other Indian tribes have so often done. Instead of this, each man took the utmost care of the two or three heifers he received. Little shelters and barns were built to protect them during the winter.

Indians who had never worked before, now tried to borrow a mowing-machine, so as to put up some hay for their animals. The tribe seemed at once to have imbibed the idea of property, and each man was as fearful lest some accident should happen to his cows as any white man might have been. Another issue of cattle was made, and the result is that now there is hardly an individual in the tribe who is not the possessor of one or more cows. Scarcely any of the issued cattle have been eaten; there has been almost no loss from lack of care; the original stock has increased and multiplied, and now the Piegans have a pretty fair start in cattle.

This material advancement is important and encouraging. But richer still is the promise for the future. A few years ago, the Blackfeet were all paupers, dependent on the bounty of the government and the caprice of the agent. Now, they feel themselves men, are learning self-help and self-reliance, and are looking forward to a time when they shall be self-supporting. If their improvement should be as rapid for the next five years as it has been for the five preceding 1892, a considerable portion of the tribe will be self-supporting at the date of expiration of the treaty.

It is commonly believed that the Indian is hopelessly lazy, and that he will do no work whatever. This misleading notion has been fostered by the writings of many ignorant people, extending over a long period of time. The error had its origin in the fact that the work which the savage Indian does is quite different from that performed by the white laborer. But it is certain that no men ever worked harder than Indians on a journey to war, during which they would march on foot hundreds of miles, carrying heavy loads on their backs, then have their fight, or take their horses, and perhaps ride for several days at a stretch, scarcely stopping to eat or rest. That they did not labor regularly is of course true, but when they did work, their toil was very much harder than that ever performed by the white man.

The Blackfeet now are willing to work in the same way that the white man works. They appreciate, as well as any one, the fact that old things have passed away, and that they must now adapt themselves to new surroundings. Therefore, they work in the hay fields, tend stock, chop logs in the mountains, haul firewood, drive freighting teams, build houses and fences, and, in short, do pretty much all the work that would be done by an ordinary ranchman. They do not perform it so well as white men would; they are much more careless in their handling of tools, wagons, mowing-machines, or other implements, but they are learning all the time, even if their progress is slow.

The advance toward civilization within the past five years is very remarkable and shows, as well as anything could show, the adaptability of the Indian. At the same time, I believe that if it had not been for that fateful experience known as "the starvation winter," the progress made by the Blackfeet would have been very much less than it has been. The Indian requires a bitter lesson to make him remember.

But besides this lesson, which at so terrible a cost demonstrated to him the necessity of working, there has been another factor in the progress of the Blackfoot. If he has learned the lesson of privation and suffering, the record given in these pages has shown that he is not less ready to respond to encouragement, not less quickened and sustained by friendly sympathy. Without such encouragement he will not persevere. If his crops fail him this year, he has no heart to plant the next. A single failure brings despair. Yet if he is cheered and helped, he will make other efforts. The Blackfeet have been thus sustained; they have felt that there was an inducement for them to do well, for some one whom they trusted was interested in their welfare, was watching their progress, and was trying to help them. They knew that this person had no private interest to serve, but wished to do the best that he could for his people. Having an exaggerated idea of his power to aid them, they have tried to follow his advice, so as to obtain his good-will and secure his aid with the government. Thus they have had always before them a definite object to strive for.

The Blackfoot of to-day is a working man. He has a little property which he is trying to care for and wishes to add to. With a little help, with instruction, and with encouragement to persevere, he will become in the next few years self-supporting, and a good citizen.

TRUTH OF A HOPI

Stories Relating to the Origin, Myths and Clan Histories of the Hopi
Edmund Nequatewa

This is one of the rarest types of ethnographic documents, one actually written by a native American. Mr. Nequatewa ably relates some of the mythological stories also covered by Voth. However, the bulk of this book—by far the most valuable section—covers the historical legends of the Hopi, from a Hopi viewpoint. The Hopi 'theory' (Nequatewa's word) was that the 'Bahana' (the white people) emerged from the under-world alongside the Hopi, and went off in search of the truth. Someday they would return and live in harmony with the Hopi, bringing wisdom and great abundance.

So what is the truth of a Hopi? The return of the Bahana didn't work out quite that way. The Hopi resisted enculturation, sometimes through armed resistance, at other times through nonviolent resistance (as when they hide the children from the policeman coming to take them to the boarding schools). However, all the while they apparently kept their good natured belief that someday their ironic 'theory' of the inherent goodness of the whites would work out.

Throughout, Nequatewa relates incidents and characterizations of Hopis that go far beyond the 'Noble Savage' sterotypes of brave warriors and laconic wisemen. The Hopi who occupy these pages are all too human, and that alone is a drop of truth that is missing from accounts of the Hopi, even to the present day. —J.B. Hare

Table of Contents

FOREWORD

The stories related in this little book represent the origin, myths and history of a group of Hopi clans. They carry us from the very beginning of things down to modern times. One might say that they are the "Old Testament" of these people. They tell of their origin, their sacred beliefs, their wanderings and their trials. The first story is one recounted only by the Priests of the "One Horned Fraternity" in the village of Shung-opovi. Edmund Nequatewa, a Shung-opovi man who recorded this story, is of the Sun Forehead Clan and is a member of the One Horned Fraternity. Clan stories are not supposed to be told by the members of unrelated clans but members of the powerful One Horned Fraternity may tell all the clan stories belonging to the clans of their village. Each society has its own group of stories and sacred songs which it may give, but no other society is supposed to know these or to relate them.

The clans concerned in this particular story are the following: the Bear Clan, *Hona-wungwa*; the Strap Clan, *Bia-quois-wungwa*; the Blue Bird Clan, *Chosh-wungwa*; the Spider Clan, *Koking-wungwa*; the Gopher Clan (extinct), *Mui-wungwa*; and the "Greasy Eye Cavities of the Skull Clan," *Wikurs-wungwa* (now extinct). Other clan stories are included in this book.

The Crow, *Ungwish-wungwa*, or Kachina Clan story is closely connected with the first story, the "Truth of a Hopi," and their later history forms a part of our tale. These people came to the Hopi towns after the arrival of the Strap Clan and the Parrot Clan, Gash-wungwa (Zuni Clan from Awatovi).

The Legend of Palotquopi is the story of the Cloud or Water Clan group; these were the last to arrive. Several of these clans are mentioned in our main story. The Cloud, *Omow-wungwa*, or Water Clan (nicknamed Flood Clan) was originally the Corn Clan, *Ka-eu-wungwa*. After the disaster at Palotquopi this clan split and three others were formed, the Snow Clan, *Nuva-wungwa*, the Wilted Corn Clan, *Pikas-wungwa*, and the Rabbit Bush Clan, *Sivaf-wungwa* (now extinct). With these clans came the Eagle Clan, *Qua-wungwa*, the Tobacco Clan, *Bif-wungwa*, the Rabbit Clan, *Taf-wungwa*, the Sand Clan, *Teu-wungwa*, the Bamboo or Reed Clan, *Wuko-bacab-wungwa*, the Sun Forehead Clan, *Kala-wungwa*, originally the Eagle Clan, and the Sun Clan, *Tawa-wungwa*. When this group arrived, the Crow Clan was already settled at Mishongnovi by the Corn Rock.

The clans mentioned above, with which the three stories deal, represent all the clans in the village of Shung-opovi, with the exception of the following group: Badger Clan, *Honan-wungwa*, Butterfly Clan, *Poval-wungwa*, Tansy Mustard Clan, *As-wungwa*, and the Parrot Clan, *Gash-wungwa*, said to be a Zuni Clan. These clans came from Awatovi, after the destruction of that village.

As the North American Indian never developed a written language, all traditions are passed down by "word of mouth." Boys were initiated into the sacred societies when they reached early maturity, and were then taught the traditions and history of their people. Since the intrusion of the White Man and the development of his school system, there has been a consequent breaking down of the ancient customs. Although the young men are still initiated into the societies, it is usually at a much later period and often even after marriage. The old men complain of the careless inattention of the younger generation and are fearful that their history and traditions may fall into confusion and be forever lost to the coming generations. And so, today we find many of the more thoughtful men anxious to have these precious records permanently recorded in writing.

In the following pages the author's style remains practically unchanged, only slight alterations having been made here and there by the editor for the sake of clarifying the meaning. Historic events have been checked by the editor and many explanatory footnotes added.

The author and the editor are greatly indebted to Dr. Harold S. Colton, Miss Katharine Bartlett, Mr. Lyndon Hargrave, and various Hopi informants for their kind cooperation and assistance in compiling this little book.

MARY-RUSSELL F. COLTON, *Editor.*

Flagstaff, Arizona,
September 1, 1936

CHAPTER I

HOW THE PEOPLE CAME OUT OF THE UNDERWORLD

ALAIKSAI!—Attention. Before anybody's memory the Hopi lived in the underworld, which was the original place of all human life. Here, in the beginning, all life and everything was good in peace and happy. The people were governed by the chiefs (*Mongwi*), village criers (*Chakmongwi*), priests (*Momwit*), and high priests and all their religious rites were ruled by the high priests. The people were classed as common, middle, and first class.

The time came when the common and middle class of people grew wise to the doings of the priests and the high priests. All the days of their lives these poor people had been cheated of their family rights by the upper classes of the people. At times the wives of the lower class were visited by these men and by the priests and high priests, while the poor husbands of the women were away. Now all this kept on from bad to worse.

By this time the wives of the priests and the higher class of men also grew wise to what had been going on for all these years, and they were greatly troubled. Then, gossip, quarreling and fighting started between the men and women. Some priests said that it was a joy to cheat and steal another man's wife and that they would pray hard and earnest for prosperity. The women in return said, "If this is so and true, would it be more joyful to you men if we did the same to you as you have done to us? Would you then pray harder still for prosperity?"

This question was, of course, asked by decent women brought up before guilty men and at this, every heart was troubled. The women turned their husbands away. They had no place to go but to their gathering places, called kivas, which were the underground houses—meeting places at times of ceremonies. In these kivas some hearts were sad and some did not seem to care so very much. They were all waiting and watching to see who would leave the kiva first to go to their houses to see if their wives would refuse to let them in. Some women had declared that they would not let their husbands in, so they put their belongings outside of their doors.

The men left the kiva one by one, going to their homes to try their wives, but finding their things outside, they had to go to the homes of their relatives. Even there, they were not welcomed and were not invited to cat, so they were forced to take two or three ears of corn to the kiva to roast. That was all they had for their meal on that day. The night came on. What were they going to do?

This was the question. Some said they would stay in the kivas and live on roasted corn as long as they could, thinking that the women might get over this trouble and their anger.

While the wives were still feeling strong against their men, they called a council. Every woman was present. At this council it was decided that the men would be falsely forgiven and would be taken back by every wife. All this was followed out and the husbands were made happy. But knowing all this, the chief, Yai-hiwa, and village crier, and their families, were greatly troubled and were sad. A thought came to the chief's mind of what he should do and how he must punish his people. Now with all this he was troubled in mind. About this time, when the men had been falsely forgiven, the women were going around and running wild after the unmarried boys, so that they might break the hearts of their husbands and so be revenged. Their families were neglected and their fires and cookings were left unattended. Among both men and women there was not a soul who could be happy in such sinful days, for there was murder, suicide, and every other wicked thing that made the days darker and darker.

All this worry and sorrow was on the chief. What could be done? Nobody knew. So he went calling on his wise men (*Posi-wiwaimkum*) personally, and broken hearted as he was, he could not help but shed tears at every call. These wise men were named Kotiwa, Tani, Sootiwa, Komay, Seytiwa, Nawiki, and Kowisa, and they were the best of all wise men, with high ideals. But everything was for the chief to say in those days, so he asked every wise man to come to his counsel on the fourth day, out at a distant place away from the people.

The day came and the chief was out early that morning. With his bag of tobacco and pipes he was waiting for his wise men to come to the appointed place. One by one they came, each with his bag of tobacco and his pipe. The village crier was the last to arrive, and now everyone had come who was expected. Here they kindled a fire and being weary and sad they were rather quiet, sitting around their fire. The chief filled up his pipe with tobacco, lit it and smoked, then passed it to Yai-owa, the village crier. He puffed the smoke four times, then looked up to the chief, saying, "Father." In return the chief said, "My son." The pipe was passed on around in the same manner to every man. After the chief's pipe was all smoked out, every man filled his own pipe. Every pipe was first handed to the chief. Here they had their fatherly and brotherly smoke.

When the smoking was done the chief said, "My dear fellowmen, I pray in hopes that the gods, our fathers, get the smell of our smoking that they may have mercy upon us. With their power, I pray we will succeed and win because of what I have planned to do. My dear fellowmen, it is this. We must find a new place somewhere and we must find some way to get out of this sinful land, either below or above. I am in hopes to save some of you people if you only could realize this and feel as grieved as I do, about the trouble we are having this very day. I pray you to help me." Everybody was silent, arms folded, heads down over their knees while the chief was speaking. Every word was heard.

Then they said, "Our father, our chief, we pray with all our hearts and we are ready to help you. We will stand with you. We will walk in your path and whatever you ask of us we will do."

"Very well," he said, "be watchful and look ahead in my path that I may not mislead you. I pray you all and hope that the words you have spoken are from the very hearts of you and are true."

"We pray you, chief, that the words we speak are from every heart, and they are true."

"Very well, my fellowmen, I thank you. We will get busy at once. Tomorrow we will make *pahos* (prayer offerings) for our gods asking for the mercy and blessings that they bring upon us. I, the chief, Yai-hiwa, again thank you all. Be here earlier tomorrow."

The men went to their homes with the hope of success in their hearts, for they were true, honest men and were loyal to their chief.

The next morning being the second day of the meeting, the chief and all his wise men came to the same place where they had met the day before and here they smoked, as usual. Every man had brought his material with which to make pahos, or prayer sticks.

"Now," said the chief, "my dear fellowmen, let us start our work, and let every heart be in earnest. Let no soul be discouraged for we must work till we succeed."

"Our father and chief, we are strong in heart to be with you. There is no thought in us to forsake you."

"Very well, I thank you all," said the chief.

So here they made their prayer sticks all the forenoon and part of the afternoon. The chief had done his cutting of the pahos first, then the rest had copied after his, for he knew every sort of cut for a certain god. All this was well done."

When they had finished their paho making, every man, with his tray or plaque full of prayer sticks held in front of him, again circled around the fire and filled his pipe with tobacco to smoke. With a Hopi, smoking a pipe is the most true and earnest way of showing himself in prayer. Here they let the smoke pass from their mouths onto the trays of their prayer offerings to let the gods know they were earnest. With the Hopi, the smell of the smoke is the most sincere message to the gods, and for this reason much smoking is done at the times of all ceremonies. Now the work was well done for that day, so the chief said, "This will be all for today, and tomorrow we will see again what we can do. Let us all leave our pahos here and four of you will stay to guard our things, while the rest of us will go home and get something to eat. Then we will all come back and will bring you something to eat, and from now on we will camp here to the finish."

This was the third day of their session. The four men stayed to watch, so that nothing would harm their prayer offerings, for they afraid that the witches and the wizards might send a spy to find out what was going on, for it has always been believed by the Hopi that the witches and wizards could change their form into anything—into wild animals or birds of any kind. The men who had gone home all came back and brought food for the rest that had stayed. Now they were to take turns that night in watching, so that nothing could come close enough to see what kind of pahos they had made. They did this and at last morning came and the watchmen had done well.

Then the chief called his men to come together and take their places in a circle, and their smoking started, asking for mercy and the blessings of the gods, and all this was done. And again the chief looked up and said, "My dear fellowmen, our work is done so far, but we must have someone—we must call somebody who is wiser than we are to do the rest, or to finish the work for us. So let us now sing the calling song." With this song they called the mocking bird, *Yapa*. Now when he came he asked them, "Why do you want me? What can I do for you?"

The chief said, "We are in great need of you for you are so much wiser than us all, and you know all the songs of our gods. We need your help. We want to be sure that we make no mistakes. This is why we have called for you to come, and so we did make some pahos for you."

The chief handed him a tray of pahos, and the mocking bird was very glad to receive the prayer offerings. This was the fourth day when the mocking bird was called.

After receiving the prayer sticks the mocking bird said, "Yes, I am called a wise bird and one that knows everything, and of the songs I know all. But there is still somebody higher than I and he is above me, and this one is the canary bird, *Si-katsi*. Make no mistakes, call him. If he comes and says for me to help you, then I will, for he is still the wisest of all and his advice we must follow. Now I must go and hide for I do not want him to know and grow jealous because I came first."

The mocking bird left and was gone. Then again they sang their calling song for the canary bird and he came and sat on a nearby bush.

"Welcome," said the men, and he flew and sat down right in the center of them.

"Why do you call me?" he asked. "Why do you want me here?"

"Yes," said the chief, "we called you because we are in trouble and you being the wisest of all, we need your help. With all my heart, truly and honestly I pray you to help us."

"You are right," said the bird, "I am always in all prayer offerings. My feathers are always first. The trouble you are having I know all about. I wondered why you have waited so long to call me."

"My dear bird," said the chief, "it is like this. Our minds are full; we are almost insane and cannot think right, so do not think we mean to pass you by."

"I understand you," said the bird, "so I am here to help you. But I cannot do everything alone. I cannot perform my ceremony without the magic songs. The mocking bird must be with us. Call him at once. We need him."

Again the Hopis sang their calling song and soon the mocking bird was in sight. As he came near everybody said, "Welcome."

"Yes, here I am," said the bird, "Why do you want me?"

"It is I," said the canary. "Without you and your magic songs nothing could be done."

"Certainly, being noted for my songs I feel that it is my duty to be here and help you," said the mocking bird.

Before getting things ready for the ceremony, the two birds flew back around the rocks and there they changed their form into human beings. When they came back, the Hopis saw that they were handsome tall men with long straight black hair.

Now all this time the men were getting the things ready with which the Birdmen were to work and perform their ceremony. In laying the altar they spread out the sand in a small square and in the center they placed a sacred water bowl and for each direction an ear of corn was placed. Each ear of corn was of a different color- yellow for the north, blue for the west, red for the south, and white for the east.

When the altar was set up, they were ready for the mocking bird to take the lead in singing. The first songs were for making up the medicine water in the sacred water bowl. After the medicine water was :made, the calling songs were to be next, but the questions arose: who would they call first? Who would have the courage and strength to go out to find a place for these Hopis to go, where they might rest and live in peace? The two Birdmen knowing all things, the Hopis left everything to them that there might be no more trouble. So they first called the eagle, *Kwa-hu.* At the end of every song the sacred water was sprinkled to each direction.

As they were singing the eagle came and sat in the midst of them and said, "Why do you call me? Why do you want me?"

"Welcome," said the men. "You being strong on the wing that is why we call you. We want you to help us. We think that you might find a place for us that we may be saved, and we pray that you will."

"Even though being a bird of the air and strong on the wing it is a hard undertaking. But with all my heart I am willing to help you, so let us hope for the best and pray our gods that I may come back to you alive. To be sure, which way must I go?" asked the eagle.

"We wish you would go up into the skies. There may be an opening and another world up there," said the men.

When the eagle was ready to fly and the prayer feathers were tied around his neck and upon each foot, the eagle said, "Pray that I may find a place up there and bring good news." Then off he went up into the skies. He circled round and round above these men and they watched him as he went up, till he was no more to be seen. At last it was getting late in the day and the people felt rather uneasy about him, but finally he was seen coming down, and now it was very late. It seemed as though he was just dropping down, and sure enough he was. He was hardly alive when he came and dropped in front of them all, exhausted, and they rushed to him and rubbed him till he came to. Soon he was quite well and had come to himself again. Then he was ready to tell the news.

"I know you are anxious to hear how far I have gone and what I have seen. Well, my dear good men," he said, "to tell you the truth, the way up there is rather discouraging. When I left here and kept going higher and higher, not a living thing was to be seen above the clouds. As I went on going higher I began to wonder where I would rest, but there was nothing to light on and nowhere to get a rest. When I looked up, it seems as though there is an opening up there, but I was getting very tired already, and if I didn't start to come back I might not be able to return here alive and tell you this news."

After hearing all this they were very much troubled and deep in sadness,, and they wondered what else must be done. The eagle then received his prize of many prayer offerings and was asked to stay with them to the finish, and, of course, he was glad to be with them.

By this time the two leaders—canary and mocking bird—thought of someone else to call. Again they were singing the calling song, and in singing the song it was mentioned who they wanted. Before the fourth song was half sung, a hawk, *Ki-sa* came and circled above once and sat down in the midst of them and said, "Why do you call me? Why do you want me?"

"We call you because we are in trouble and we need your help," said the men.

"Yes, I do know that you are in trouble," said the hawk. "All who have a heart wish to help and save you, and I am willing to do whatever you will ask of me."

"Very well," said the Hopis, "we want you to search the skies for us . You are strong on the wing and can fly high, so we feel that you might be able to find a way out of this wicked world."

"Very well," said he, "I will try."

So they made ready for the hawk to fly and put prayer feathers on him as was done to the eagle—around his neck and on his feet.

When he was all ready, he said, "Pray with all your hearts that I may find a place for you and bring you good news."

"We will," said the men, "for we want to save our families and many others who have good hearts, so may our gods take care of you while you are on the journey."

Up the hawk went and circled round and round overhead, as the eagle had done. For a long time he could be seen up in the air till he was gone above the clouds. All this time the men were singing prayer and luck songs that nothing would happen to the hawk.

It was getting late and everybody was rather uneasy again, and they kept watching for him very anxiously. Finally, he was seen again, but he did not seem to be alive and the eagle did not wait to be asked but went right up to meet him. Then every heart was troubled because they thought that he was surely dead. Now, before the eagle knew, the hawk had dropped past him, and then he just dived for the hawk, to catch him, and when the eagle did catch him his mouth was wide open but his heart was still beating a little. When the eagle came down with him in his claws he laid him down on a white robe and every eye was full of tears. Soon one of the men started to rub him, while the mocking bird sang the "life returning song." When he came to he was quite weak, and earnest prayers were shown by smoking many pipes for the hawk. Now by this time he was ready to tell his story.

"I know," said the hawk, "you are all anxious to hear what I have found out for you up in the skies. When I left here, the first part about going up is the same as what brother eagle had seen and told you. I had gone as far as he did, then I took the courage upon myself and went on up as far as I could see up there. I am quite sure that there is an opening up there, but I was tired out and was not able to go any further before I knew that I was dropping down. I tried to turn myself over, but could not make it, for I was exhausted. Finally I felt something hurting me on my sides. I opened my eyes and found myself in the sharp claws of brother eagle. Then, I do not know how we got here, but now I thank the gods and you all that I am alive again. But let us not be discouraged, we might find someone that will make it up there and find out for us all about what is up there. I know every heart is in trouble. My heart is in trouble too because of you."

After hearing this story of the hawk, there was very little light in the hearts of the men. But the thoughts with the men were still very deep of what is to be done next, or who would be the third to try the skies for these Hopis. Everything and everybody was very still and quiet—prayers were being said by the smoking of many pipes.

The next morning being the fifth day of their ceremony, the wise Birdmen—canary and mocking bird—called the men to attention, to come around the altar and fill up their pipes by which to say their prayers again to the gods. After this was said and done, they started singing the calling ceremony again, but they did not know who they were calling this time. Before long something came and just went "whip," sounding like a whip over their heads many times and then sat down in the midst of them, and he was a swallow, *Powvowkiaya*.

He said, "Here I am."

"Welcome," said the men.

"Why do you call me? Why do you want me?" said the bird.

"Yes," said they, "we need you. We want you to help us out of the troubles we are having. We want to be saved."

"I know you do," said the swallow. "I was anxious and longed to be called, but I know your minds are full and of course I know the way things have happened, so I have no envy against those who were called first, because I may not be able to equal what they have already done, but do understand that I am willing to help you."

"Yes," they said, "you being strong and swift on the wing, we pray in hopes that you will make it up through the skies to find a place for us, and here we have these prayer feathers made for you to wear on the way."

"Thank you," said he, "I would be happy to have them, but all those might be in the way so I will go without them."

"Very well," said the Hopis, "you know best of how you go in the air. May our gods bless us and have mercy upon us so that nothing will happen to you and we pray that our gods may take care of you on your journey and bring you back safely to us, so pray that no heart may be discouraged."

"You have all said well. I thank you all," said he.

Then he went off and in a little while he was out of sight. The men filled their pipes and were smoking. Those who were not smoking were singing the prayer songs of good luck. Again it was getting late in the day and the men were still strong with smoking and singing, while the eagle and the hawk were looking up into the skies with their sharp eyes. Finally they saw that the swallow was coming and they hesitated not, but flew right up to meet him.

When they reached him he was nearly done and with a faint voice he said, "Catch me." They made a dive for him and did catch him and brought him down and right away they gave him some water and started to rub him up till he had come to himself. While he was resting the gift of prayer feathers was given to him.

When the chief handed all this to him, he said, "This is our gift to you, from us all. We are glad that you have returned to us again."

"Yes," said the swallow bird, "and I know you would like to hear what I have seen and done. It is too high up there. What these two brothers and I have seen is too great and wonderful, and to anybody without wings it is dangerous because the wind is strong up there. Going into the opening I got scared of the wind and was afraid to go any higher for fear I may not be able to come back. If I did I might not be alive to tell you this. What all I did see I could not begin to tell you all about it."

Now the Hopis were wondering who would be the next one to fly into the skies for them, so rather hopelessly they filled their pipes again to smoke and to pray some more, and of course they were very silent.

Finally the canary bird spoke up and said, "My dear fellowmen, we will make our last try so we will call brother shrike, *Si-katsi* and see what he can do for us. He is pretty wise too, so cheerfully come to the altar and we will sing again."

They all moved up around the altar and took up a little more courage, hoping down in their hearts for success. Before many calling songs were ended someone came flying very close to the ground and sat down on top of a nearby bush and from there into the midst of them.

"Welcome," said the Hopis.

"Yes, yes, here I am," he said. "Why do you want me in such a hurry?"

"Yes," said the mocking bird. "Here we are in trouble. Brother canary and I have been working here with these Hopis trying and hoping to find a place and a way to save them from this sinful land. These three brothers here have done their best up in the skies and they all seem to be very certain about an opening somewhere up there. This is why we wanted and called you, hoping that you can find another world and save us."

"With all my heart," said the shrike, "I am here to help you. I know and feel that it must be a hard undertaking because these three brothers were not able to make it. But to be sure, you must all tell me if you are all earnest in the hope to be saved. Somebody's heart must be bad here and he is the one that is holding you back and keeping you working so hard. Every heart must be true and honest. Let us all be one if we really want to be saved."

The chief of course was most troubled to think of all that time he had spent and had not yet accomplished anything, for he, himself, had good faith in his men and trusted them. Anyway, he asked the people then if there is any one of them with a false heart and who is intending to forsake them and they declared themselves to their chief and father to be all true men.

"No fault having been found in you, it gives me courage to go on and take the trip," said the shrike, "so pray for the best while I am away." He went off on a slow flight and as he went higher, he kept going faster. Soon he was no more to be seen. The men then took their pipes, filled them up and smoked with all their hearts, while the canary and the mocking bird were singing their prayer songs. The eagle and hawk were keeping their sharp eyes looking up into the skies.

Praying for many days with their pipes, every tongue was burning with the taste of the tobacco, but their courage was still strong for they were hoping for good news with all their anxious hearts. The day seemed very long.

It was very late when the shrike was seen high up in the sky and he was very slowly coming down. The eagle and the hawk saw that he was still strong so they did not go up to meet him for his little wings were still holding him up. As he was coming down nearer everybody was asked to hold their heads down with high hopes that he may land safely. As he landed they felt that their prayers were answered and they were filled with much joy. The shrike was asked to be seated in the center of them and be resting while the men joined in prayer by smoking their pipes.

When this was done the chief said to the bird, "I am more than glad and happy to see you come back to us again and it is not only I, but everybody here who is anxious to hear the news of what you have for us, so let us hear you."

"It is the same story," said the shrike, "from here on up to where these others had gotten to. When I passed that, I could see the opening and from there on the passage looked rather narrow. As I went on higher into the narrow passage, in there I found many a projecting rock on which I could light and rest myself. Then, at last, up through the opening which is just like a kiva you have down here. The light and sunshine is much better than here, but there is no sign of human life, only the animals and birds of all kinds. Now the question is, how are we going to get you up there? Because even the strongest birds carrying you one by one could not get you all up through there."

"So it is," said the chief, "that is another hard proposition, but let no heart be discouraged. Let us all be strong and we will succeed and leave our troubles behind here in this sinful world for I am more than glad and happy to know that there is another and better world up above, so if there is anyone present to give us advice of what is to be done next, I would like to hear him."

"It is I, who am called Kochoilaftiyo (the poker boy) said a boy who was sitting way in the back. They did not even know that he was with them all this time, for he was ranked and considered as of the low class people.

"Come forward to my side," said the chief.

And he was seated on the left side of him. Being only a poor boy it was rather doubtful to the others that he would know of any advice to give, but he was treated like the others and so they smoked their pipes together. When this was done, the chief asked him of what he had in mind.

"It is not much of anything," said the boy. "But I am with you and with all my heart I wish to help you. You know and everybody knows that I am not recognized nor respected half as much as the others."

"You have spoken the truth, but you must forget that now," said the chief. "You who are with me here, I refuse no one."

"I thank you," said the boy with eyes full of tears. "I know a little creature, *kuna* (chipmunk), who lives on the nuts of the pines. I think he knows how to plant and grow those pines and he may have some seeds. If he would come and plant and grow us one of those tall trees it might reach the sky so that we may climb up on it. He lives in the rocks and pines."

"Very well," said the chief, "let us call him." At this he turned to the mocking bird and asked him to sing his calling song for the chipmunk. At the altar the mocking bird picked up his rattle and started to sing. It was not very long before the chipmunk appeared over the rocks with his usual chip-chip voice, and when he did come up he ran in front of the altar.

"Why do you call me, and why do you want me?" he asked.

"It is because we are in trouble. We need your help."

"I am ready," he said.

"As you are noted for your tree planting and know how to make them grow so fast we would like you to plant one for us that will reach up to the sky and into the new world. We have been here many days trying to find out how we can get up there."

"Yes," said the chipmunk, "I do know how to plant trees, but I cannot be very sure and promise you that I could make it grow up to reach the sky, but for your sake I will try, so let us pray to our gods who really have power."

They filled up their pipes and smoked again, to carry their earnest prayers to the gods. After this was done, the little chipmunk reached into his bag for his tree seeds. "This," he said, "is a spruce. We will try it first." He put it in his mouth and sang four of his magic songs. Then he took it out and set it in the ground in front of him, watching it very closely. Again he reached into his little bag and drew out his little rattle of sea shells with which he sang over his planted seed. Soon the tree began to grow out of the ground, and when it was about three inches high, he spit all over it and around the roots. With that it began to grow faster. Now, he kept this up as he was singing and his mouth began to get awfully dry so he asked for some water to increase the moisture in himself. Finally the tree was as high as a man stood and when it got this high he would run up on it and with his little paws would pull it upward at the very top. With songs and pulling it up, the tree was growing very fast indeed. The little creature kept this up till it had grown to its full height, but it did not reach the sky.

"I have done my best," said the chipmunk. "The tree will grow no more."

The high hopes of the chief sank again because the tree did not reach the opening up in the sky.

"Being called to help you," said the chipmunk, "I will try again, so keep your hopes and do not be discouraged. I think it has weakened this tree making it grow too fast, so this time it will be a little slower."

And he reached into his little bag for another seed which was a fir-pine. This he planted, with the same performance as the first time. Again, the little tree began to grow and the chipmunk repeated his same songs with new and strong hopes that he might make it reach the hole in the sky. Going up on this tree he would take his sacred meal and at the very top, with his prayer, he would throw this meal upward as high as he could, hoping that this would make it grow up through the opening.

While he was busy growing his tree every man was smoking his pipe and they were making their earnest prayers from their very hearts. Finally the chipmunk came back down to the ground again and said, "My tree has stopped growing again, although it has passed the first one by four men's height, but be not discouraged, I will try again. First, I must have prayer."

He reached into his bag and out he brought his little pipe and smoked. While he was smoking he kept a seed in his mouth which was a long-needle pine. When he had finished he set the seed in the ground again, and started his performance in the same manner with all the hopes of making it reach the sky, but this was also in vain, though it did pass the two first trees.

Now not only the chipmunk, but all the rest of the people were very much troubled and crying in their hearts to think that the trees had failed to reach the opening in the sky. The chipmunk, with a broken heart, filled up his little pipe and smoked, thinking very hard of what he could do next, because he thought himself powerless and knew that only his gods had unlimited power so with his smoking he prayed the gods for more wisdom. He could see that every heart was sad for the men were sitting around with their heads down upon their folded arms over their knees.

A thought came to him now, so he slowly raised his head and said, "We are all very sad but I will try again, so I wish to ask you from your very hearts if there is someone here who is not very willing to go and hates to leave behind the ones he loves or there may be some of you that still have evil thoughts in your hearts. All this work and many sleepless nights are getting heavy on our father, our chief. We must confess ourselves to him and to our gods that we will do right and will try to live the right kind of life in the upper world."

"We are all true," said they, "If we were not true we would not have stayed to this day with our chief."

The chipmunk left them and went to a place where the bamboo tree grows." Here he took a little shoot of a bamboo plant and with this he brought a tiny piñon shell full of water. These he set on a small basket tray and smoked his pipe over it, which was his earnest prayer. Others followed in the same manner. When this was done he put the piñon shell of water in the ground, at an arm length deep and on top of it he planted the bamboo shoot and he covered it up. He took his sacred corn meal in his right hand and stood over the plant and said his prayers in silence. Then he threw the meal high up toward the sky. Then the others followed one by one.

"Now," he said, "this being the last plant I know that will grow high we must give all our hearts to our gods that they may believe and answer our prayers and make this tree grow up through the opening in the sky.

When all their preparations were made and their sacred corn meal was thrown up toward the sky, the two birdmen started to sing their magic songs and the rest all joined with them because by that time, they knew the songs so that they could follow along with them. After the songs were ended, the little chipmunk ran up the tree and when he got to the top he pulled on it and he ran back four times up into that tree. Then he came down and filled up his pipe and started smoking.

He was always keeping time with the singing and he knew just when to run up the tree, and he just kept this performance up till the tree was high enough, and still they were singing and then, while they were singing, they asked the four other birds that had made their attempt to go up into the sky to find the opening, to fly up and see how high the tree had gone up, because by that time, the little chipmunk was tired, he couldn't run up the high tree again.

Now these birds, that is, the eagle and the hawk and the swallow bird and the shrike, made their trip up into the sky to the top of this tree four times and each time, when they came back they told the people that it was coming nearer to the opening. Toward the last, it was only the shrike that could go up and he made this trip up four times. But the last trip he made he stayed up on the top limb, and with him on the top limb the tree went through the opening. Of course, the old shrike felt very safe because he knew he could come back down, resting on the limbs of the tree.

When he came down he told the people that the tree had gone through the opening. Now the chipmunk was very glad that it had gone through, and of course you know that he was overjoyed. Then the chipmunk told them that it would be rather impossible to climb up on the tree. He told them that this tree was hollow inside and he started to gnawing on the bottom of the tree to cut an opening into it. While he was gnawing away all the men circled around the little fire and started their prayers again by smoking. After all this was done the chief said that as it was rather late in the day they would start their prayers and songs for the people at dawn. Now they were all very anxious to see the morning come and before it did come the chief had appointed two birds—the eagle and the swallow, to be on the look-out, so that no wicked people might pass.

Now on this day, before they started out, the chief said to the wise men that they must give an order for some kind of a guard that would hold back the bad people and the witches and wizards that would try to steal their way into the reed with the rest of the people. So the chief told the wise men to make their pahos for each four directions. These were to represent the closing of all the different trails from all directions. When these were made he sent out the One Horned Society or priests who were supposed to guard the North and West, and the Two Horned priests to guard the South and East. When they got to the four directions they made four lines out of sacred corn meal about six feet long and on both ends of the lines they set a paho falling backward—not toward the bamboo. Whoever steals their way into the bamboo and crosses this line will perish, which means that they will drop dead. Of course, many people tried to cross from different directions and were found dead.

This is how two of the societies or religions were started; *Kwakant* (One Horned Society) and *A-alt* (Two Horned Society), which are still in existence today. Whoever came to the bamboo by the set path came safely to the chief, to join in going to the Upper World.

The time came for them to sing their calling songs and before they started to sing they renewed their altar on which they had laid their prayer offerings. They made four of these prayer offerings and set them up on four sides of the tree to hold it up. These prayer offerings were about the span of a man's hand. When they started to sing they had to sing around the altar and the two birds were watching the opening at the bottom of the tree so in case the wicked people should start to come through they could drive them away. The two birds were appointed because they had sharp claws. When they started to sing their calling song, being a magic song, it took effect and they found the names of men who were in this ceremony following one another because the calling song as it began, named all the wise men who were serving in the ceremony. Before long the people were coming up one after another—that is, one family after another family.

When the people were gathered there, the chief had his prayer offering ready and at the foot of the tree he set this little prayer offering down in front of it. Then with his sacred corn meal he made a line pointing into it and then he walked in and his family followed and the rest of the royal families came after him, like the family of the village crier and the families of the others who had a high position, such as the high priest.

As they were going up through the tree the shrike started outside, because he was rather light and he could rest on the limbs. They didn't know how far they were going up. It took them quite a long while and the chief was rather anxious to get up to the top and after a long time they finally came up to the opening. When the chief got up there the shrike was waiting for him and when he crawled out of the tree the rest followed and as some of these people came out they started to sing the same songs that they were singing down at the bottom. These songs were limited and they were only to be sung four times, because they were awfully long songs. In a ceremony like this everybody was so anxious to get to the top it didn't seem so long and before all the people were through, the songs were ended and there were still some more people gathered around the tree. Then everywhere there was trouble down below, for those who hadn't been able to get up while the songs were being sung had to stay at the bottom, because the ceremony couldn't be sung any more.

Then the One Horned Priests who remained below had to cut the tree down for fear that someone might steal their way up, so they cut down the tree and this tree still had some people in it, so that is why the bamboo is jointed—because the people in there stuck in the tree and the tree kind of shrunk in between them.

CHAPTER II
MASAUWU

Now the chief was pleased to be on top, but of course, he was rather kind of suspicious for fear that some witches or wizards might have come through. They found that there was sunshine and birds and rather a prosperous looking world—sun, grass, flowers, trees and everything else up above.

When they had been up a few days, the chief asked his people if any of them had brought up anything with them to eat, or seeds of any kind. They searched one another and they found some corn and of course it was rather late in the season to plant anything now, so they didn't plant, they lived on game and wild fruit and seeds of the different kinds of plants.

Before very long there was a little girl who took sick and died suddenly. When this little girl died the chief held a council to find out if they had brought up any witches with them. Finally one of the girls had to admit that she was one of them. Of course they were very much troubled over her and got ahold of her and tied her up and were ready to throw her back into the underworld. The girl didn't want to be thrown back into the underworld so she told them not to be troubled because after death you went back into that underworld and were safe, that you returned to your own people down there again.

They asked her to prove it. "Well," she said, "I can easily prove it if you come to the kiva (opening). We can look down and see the little dead girl playing around down there just as happy as she can be."

And so they went to the kiva hole and looked down and saw this little girl playing around with the rest of the children below. When the witch girl had proved this to the people the chief had to permit her to stay.

On the fourth night after they came up to the world on top, they saw a fire a little distance away and they wondered who it could be, so the next morning the chief sent his braves to see where the fire had been. No sign of fire was to be found, only huge footprints of a big man or a giant, for these footprints were larger than any living man's. The braves came back to the chief and told of what big footprints they had seen, and they were all very much frightened. The chief thought the only thing to do was to have a ceremony of prayer offerings or paho making and offer these to their neighbor, the giant, for fear that he might be a man of some power, who might do them harm someday.

The village crier was called to announce the day for this ceremony. When the people came to the chief they found him to be sad of heart and they all knew why he was so sad. The chief told his fellow men what he thought it was best they should do, that they might make these prayer offerings to the fire or whoever it was that had the fire. As usual they all smoked their pipes before they set to work to make their pahos. When all was done they put these offerings together on one plaque, which received their earnest prayers as they smoked their pipes, and all this was done before it was taken to their strange neighbors.

Before it was taken over, the chief called for volunteers, to see who would step forward to take these prayer offerings to the being at the fire. They were to be taken at night and someone would have to carry it who was very brave. Four young men offered themselves and said they would take the offering over to the fire for among the Hopi four was the limit, and they were permitted to go.

Going over with the tray of prayer offerings they saw at first in the distance only a faint light and they were very much afraid. Coming closer, they could see someone sitting by the fire and facing away from them and they could only see the back of his head. This head was of rather a great size, like the biggest squash, and there was no hair on it. As they came closer they were more and more frightened, but at last they got to him. He would not turn his face toward the fire, so they called to him and asked him who he was, but he would not answer. They called to him a second time and he ref used again to answer them. They called to him a third time, and again they received no answer. They called again, a fourth time, and asked him if he had some other language and did not understand them. Then he answered and said he was surprised to see that they had come to his fire because no one had ever gotten so near to him before.

When he said this he turned around toward the light and his face was all bloody and he had a mask on; his head was big and his mask was terrible looking. These four men were very much frightened and all felt something creeping back of their heads. Finally they got over their spell and told him what they had brought him, which the chief had sent over with his wishes that he would be their good friend and neighbor and not try to make them any trouble. They handed him the tray of pahos which he gladly received and was very much pleased with them, and he said that he prized them very highly.

Then he told these young men who he was. He was their god—the god of the Upper World, and it all belonged to him. Although being the god of the Upper World, he could not walk about in the day time, but only at night by the light of the fire. So he told these young men to tell their chief who he was—that he was now his god, who walked in the dark and is called the Masauwu. He was the god of death and life. He told the young men to tell the chief not to be afraid, that he being the god of death, whoever died would go to him first and he would show him back to the underworld by way of the kiva, through which they had come out.

When the young men went back to the chief, they told him the man at the fire received his offering and prized it very highly as it had been a long time since he had received any offering of pahos like that. This was the first time they had ever seen this man who said he was their god and ever since he has been worshipped by the Hopi. Since he told the people he was the god of death, they always go to him when they go on the warpath and ask him to paralyze their enemies with fear so that they may be victorious.

CHAPTER III
HOW THE MOCKING BIRD GAVE THE PEOPLE MANY LANGUAGES

AFTER awhile the chief said that they must move away from the kiva for fear that some of his people might become discouraged in some way, or lose courage and want to go back. They might die or want to die, so he didn't like to be near the kiva for fear the people might be going back and looking down toward their old home.

Even though the Chief had decided to move the people away from the kiva he was very much troubled and wondered how the kiva should be regarded by them, whether it should be thought of with apprehension and fear. So the chief called his wise men together to consult them on his ideas regarding this matter, but none of these men could give him any help or find him an answer. They could only ask him what he had in mind, saying that whatever the chief wished, their gods may consent to fulfill. "Very well," said their chief, "let us make some pahos and with these offerings we will ask the big waters to come and cover up the kiva and that will make it impossible for anyone to go back there."

When all these were made the young men were asked to take them to the southwest, toward *Patuwakachi* (the ocean) and at a good distance away from the kiva these pahos were set with the wishes and prayers of the chief that the waters may only come as far as the spot where the offerings were placed. Now every day, for four days the young men were sent back to this place where they had put these pahos to see if there were any signs of moisture or the coming of *Paso* (the roaring waters). Now every day the water was seen to be creeping up on these pahos and at the end of the fourth day the people began to feel the damp air. Then the big wind came and it kept up for many days and at last *Paso* had come and it had covered up all the land around the kiva so that no one could reach it. This was, of course, a very fearful thing to all the people.

Of course, no one knows how long they lived around that place, but after a great many years they increased and they started to have more trouble among themselves. The chief was afraid that something might happen again so he had a council with his men once more, and he asked them what should be done. One of the men said that the only thing that he thought of was, if they only could speak different languages and learn to eat different kinds of food from one another, they might start away or become parted in many divisions.

"Why," said the chief, "how could we do this?"

Someone said, "Well, don't we have the mocking bird who knows many songs and why shouldn't he give us many different languages?"

"Well," said the chief, "I think that is a very good idea."

Then he asked the men to come the next day so that they could make their prayer offerings for the mocking bird. So the next day the men came over with their trays and some materials with which to make their prayer offerings. They started work that morning and kept on until late in the afternoon. When all their prayer offerings were finished, the crier called out for the men to bring him their presents of food for them all to eat. After they finished their meal they started singing the calling songs for the mocking bird, and at the end of four songs the mocking bird came.

When he came he asked them why he was being so anxiously called. The chief answered him and said, "It is because we are in trouble and we wish to have some changes made, if it would be possible." Then the mocking bird asked what kind of changes.

"Well," said the chief, "would it be possible that we, living here as one people, could be given different languages'?"

The mocking bird said, "It can be done."

The chief asked, "How soon can you do it?"

The mocking bird said that it would take overnight to give them different languages. The mocking bird asked the chief if he would like to speak some other different language, but the chief said he would rather keep his own language.

Well, that night it was only the chief and the mocking bird who stayed up to see how this thing would work out. During the night the mocking bird went from camp to camp and at each camp he would take something out of the fireplace and then turn right around and bury something in the fireplace again. He had a sort of buckskin pouch and whatever he took out of the fireplace he put into this pouch and he was holding on tight to this pouch for fear that something would escape out of there. Just about dawn the mocking bird finished his job. He took his buckskin pouch to the chief and told the chief to dig a hole in the ground. The chief did this and the mocking bird told him to put the pouch in the hole and bury it there and build a fire over it. Now when the morning came, the people woke up with different languages and they couldn't understand one another.

They were very much troubled because they couldn't understand one another and they came up to the chief and the chief couldn't make them understand. The mocking bird was the only one that could understand, so he was the interpreter.

"Well," said the chief, "you are a pretty wise bird. Now you and I will travel the same direction toward the rising sun and the sun may be our god, great and wise. With its light we can see and walk. Wherever this place is where the sun rises, I would like to see who will get there first for there we may learn who is our true god. If not, the sun itself is our god for there must be some spirit, somewhere, that really does look after us. If either you or I should get to the sun first, the great star will appear and many other stars will fall from the heavens, by which those who are still on the journey will know that one of us has reached the journey's end. Then the one who has arrived with his people must settle down and look forward to meeting his brother when he comes with wisdom and truth that he may teach the true religion of god."

CHAPTER IV
THE HOPI DECIDE TO SEEK A NEW HOME. HOW CERTAIN CLANS RECEIVED THEIR NAMES

ALL THIS time while the people were together, they learned to eat some of the wild seeds besides corn and different kinds of fruit and wheat. The mocking bird asked the chief to get all the different kinds of foodstuffs together and call the people to come and gather there, and decide and choose their food, or the chief food, that they wished to live on as they traveled along. Of course in those days the chief had charge of all the foodstuffs.

So he asked the people to gather all this food together and when they had gotten all they could collect he sent word out for no more people to come. When everything was gathered in, the chief sent word for the people to come together. Of course, all this time the mocking bird was still with them, because they could not go without him.

When the people came the chief asked them to look this foodstuff over and choose what they would like to take along in case they wanted to separate and travel along in different directions. Now that the mocking bird had given the people different languages and they couldn't understand each other they thought it would be best to separate.

After he had said all this the men shook hands to show that they were brothers and they started out on the race for the same point, as they were both anxious to learn and to find out who is the true God. Before they parted they said they would start out on their journey on the fourth day from that time, but during these three days the people of these two men and the women folk were getting ready the foodstuff for them to take along. Of course each of them had quite a number of people besides just their families.

On the fourth day all the tribes came together—Navajo, Supai, Paiute, Apache, Zuni, Utes and the Bahana. When they came up, the chief had all the different kinds of seeds of corn and grain, of melon and fruit, laid out for them to choose. Then he asked the different tribes to step forward and take their choice.

The Navajo slipped forward hurriedly and picked out the largest ear of corn, which he thought was the wise thing to do. But the chief and the others knew that the long ear of corn could not last long and was not easily raised. Afterward the rest of the tribes took their choice in turn.

The Hopi took the shortest ear of corn and also squash and beans. The Apache didn't take any, for they said they would rather live on game. Supai took some peaches—he preferred the fruit most. The Zuni took corn and wheat. Paiute didn't take any, he too said he would rather live on wild game and fruit. Utes didn't take any either. The Bahana (White man) took his choice last and was rather slow and considered well and finally he took some wheat which was not so heavy and he could carry more of it than the corn.

When they started out, for a few days they were kind of looking out for one another and keeping track of the time. They travelled on for many days and it got so that it was rather discouraging for they never had thought that the sun rose so far away; they thought that the sun rose only a short distance off. Finally they got so they didn't count the days any more.

As they traveled along, the first party came on a dead bear. They thought that they would name themselves the "Bear Clan" (*Hona-wunga*) and by this they could be recognized. They took the paws off the bear and took the flesh and bones out of them and stuffed them up with grass.

The second band came along and they too, found the dead bear. They had so many things to carry that they thought they needed some straps, so they took the hide off the bear and made straps of it. Then they thought they would take the name of "Strap Clan" (*Biaquoiswungwa*) by which they would be known.

Then it was many days before the third band came along. When they came to the dead bear it was all bones and the ribs were sticking up in the air and the bluebirds were sitting on them. Well, seeing the bluebirds there they thought they would call themselves the "Bluebird Clan", *Chosh-wunga*, by which name they would recognize each other. Then they went on, following the rest who were ahead of them. They must have known in some way that the two other clans were ahead of them.

Not very long after the "Bluebird Clan" had left this place, another band came along and they too found the dead bear. Inside of the skeleton of the bear was a spider web. Seeing the spider, they thought they would call themselves the "Spider Clan", *Koking-wungwa*.

Then the next band came along not very far behind them, and they too came to the same spot. They found gopher mounds around the skeleton of the bear so they thought they would call themselves the "Gopher Clan", *Mui-wunga*.

Maybe a few years later, another band came up and they too came to the same place and found that the skeleton of the bear was all in pieces. They found the skull with the greasy eye cavities, and they thought they would call themselves the *Wikurswungwa* Clan, "The greasy eye cavities of the skull." (Clan now extinct.)

These groups were all going eastward, toward the rising sun and of course, the man who was to be the Bahana, went on and got ahead.

As they were following one another, of course they all had it in mind to see the Eastern Star. Their brother, Bahana, had gone on and they thought he might be held up somewhere and they hoped to get ahead of him for they all hoped they would reach the rising sun first. Of course, out of all these clans the Bear Clan was ahead. Each clan wished to get ahead. One day the Spider Clan came upon a spider lying outside of its hole, and of course the leaders stopped and wondered if this spider could speak to them. So the chief called his people and they all gathered around the spider, wondering at it. Finally the Spider Woman spoke to them.

She called them her children and grandchildren. Then she said that if they needed to be helped she could help them. They said they would like to be helped, because they rather thought they were getting away behind the rest of the people. So the Spider Woman said that they would have to stay with her a few days and that she would get them something to travel with so they could go on faster. They said they would like to travel faster because on account of the children they were getting behind. So the Spider Woman asked them if they would like something to ride on so they wouldn't have to travel on foot, and they said they would.

"Well," she said, "I can make you a tame animal" that would carry your stuff and probably you can have him pack your things and you can walk behind him. If you don't carry any thing on your back you might travel faster."

"Well," the man said, "what could you make it of?"

The Spider Woman said "It has to be a part of you, so you go to that little room with the jar of water and take a bath and whatever rolls off your body—all that dirt—you gather it up and bring it to me."

So this man took a jar of water and went into a little room and started to take a bath. Of course, you know, having travelled many days thinking that he would get to the rising sun, why he never did stop to think about taking a bath and he was awful dirty. All afternoon he spent rubbing himself and all that dirt began to roll off of him. When he got through and gathered it up he almost had a handful. He came out and handed this to the Spider Woman and wondered what sort of an animal it would make and how big it would be, because he thought the dirt that rolled off himself wasn't big enough to make an animal of any kind.

Then the Spider Woman went to work and she brought out a little white robe. She laid this down and put the lump of dirt on it and covered it up with the robe and folded it over. Then she sang the magic songs. Every once in a while she would peek in under this cover and see if it was coming to life, and finally the thing started to move. The Spider Woman finished her songs. She took the little cover off and there was a little gray burro. Well, the Spider Woman told these people that they would have to stay there four days because in four days this little animal would then be strong enough to travel.

Every day the Spider Woman would feed this little animal something and wrap him up. Being a wise old woman, she would feed it some of her medicine—magic stuff—rubbing its legs to give it strength. Finally, in four days, the animal was ready to travel. The people packed up the burro with their stuff and they went on. Well, they found it was much easier to have something packing their stuff than to be packed up themselves.

Having made a burro for these people, this same Spider Woman made a man with knowledge and instructed him to go after these people and help them along, to train animals for them that they might catch up with brother Bahana. But not following the Spider Woman's instructions, this man stole the little burro and went on himself, thinking that he would get ahead of the Bahana and reach the point of the rising sun first. So one day these poor Hopis could not find their animal and they looked for many days. Finally, they found somebody's tracks driving the burro. He had funny shoes and whoever he was, he had slipped up on them and stolen their animal. Now they were made sad because they had to pack their own stuff again. Later, they came upon another Spider Woman who told them that this man was a Castilian who had stolen their burro.

By this time these people had almost forgotten about the rest of the Hopi and they hadn't heard of where they were all this time.

They were traveling away behind and they were rather slow because they would stop to cultivate the land and raise corn to supply them for a few years. They thought that they would build houses and make pottery by which they would mark this land as they went along, because they believed the day would come when their brother would find the rising sun and that they would all come back this way with more power and more knowledge. Of course, they would be true to their brother, but there may be others who would come back with him and they would be the ones who would try to cheat him out of the land, so in order to have some kind of mark in this country they built homes and made pottery.

CHAPTER V
HOW THE HOPI SELECTED SHUNG-OPOVI
FOR THEIR HOME

THE Hopis had forgotten about the other tribes by this time and did not know where they were. They were hoping to see the Eastern Star so that they could settle down and not travel any more. Well, finally the Bear Clan did see the Eastern Star and they were ready to settle down, but they didn't know just where would be a good place for them. They thought that they would do better cultivating by depending on rain, so they went out onto the Painted Desert to Shung-opovi (the place by the spring where the tall weeds grow). Being out here in such a desolate place they thought that they would be safe from other people, who would not think that they had anything worth taking.

By that time the other Hopis were down around the vicinity of Sunset Crater, Canyon Diablo and the Little Colorado River.

After a good many years these other Hopis heard of the Bear Clan being out at Shung-opovi, so the Strap Clan who were settled along Canyon Diablo, thought they would go out and join the Bear Clan. So they started out. When they did start out they stopped along the ridge below Ma-teuvi, which is now called Big Burro Spring. From there they sent off a messenger to Shung-opovi to tell the Chief that his brothers, the Strap Clan, would like to join him.

When the messenger came to the Chief of Shung-opovi and told him what the Strap Clan leader wished to do, he could not very well answer his message just then. So he sent word back that he would like to have the Strap Clan chief come himself. When the Strap Clan leader heard this word he went up to Shung-opovi with his bag of tobacco and his pipe.

Of course, in those days, they had guards that were always on the lookout for someone coming, for fear it might. be an enemy. Well, this man was seen coming and the Chief was notified. He knew who it was, the man being alone, so he went out to meet him and he met him at the place called Teuviovi (point that runs out south of Shung-opovi Day School). When they met there, they greeted one another by smoking their pipes. After they had smoked their pipes, the Strap Clan leader told the chief of the Bear Clan how he had followed his trail and that he had taken his clan name from the same dead bear that he had. So for that reason, he considered himself as his brother and he would like to join his establishment, because he thought being of the same clanship the

Bear Clan was not any greater than the Strap Clan was. So the Bear Clan told him he could go back and bring his people.

Well, the Strap Clan leader went back and told his people this good news and asked the people to get ready, as they would start for Shung-opovi in four days. On the fourth day they started out and when they got to Shung-opovi they were very well received.

When the Strap Clan entered the village they thought they would have the same rights as the Bear Clan but the Bear Clan did not like the way the Strap Clan felt about their rights and the way they were acting, so finally they had to have a council and talk this over. They decided the Bear Clan would give the Strap Clan a chance to become a royal clan and to rule the village. Of course, after this the Strap Clan was always looking forward to this agreement. Now later, the other clans began to drift in. When they came up to the town they would send word up to the chief and the chief would usually send for the leader to come to see him, because it was not his business to go down and meet the people. They had to come up before the chief. He would always ask the leader about his religious rites or ceremonies—of how he had been serving his people in the way of prosperity, if his ceremonies have any effect on the gods and if his ceremonies would bring rain. And of course this chief would have to tell what he did to bring rain or how he did it. Then, if the chief thought he was rather bragging about himself, or exaggerating his ceremonies, he would tell him to stay away, because if he could take care of his people that way, he could get along all right by himself. The chief knew that no human would have such power and that he had to ask the gods or make prayers for rain to make his crops grow.

Many a time some clan leader had to go up to the chief four times before he was permitted to enter with his people. Every time when a band or clan was received, the chief would allot them so much land. The last few clans to arrive were just the common class of people. They didn't have a high priest, or ceremonies of any kind, and they were the ones that had a hard time getting into the village. They were not alloted any land. They wished to have land also, so they asked the chief. The chief asked them what they could do—or what right they had to be given that land. They said that they were willing to have the land on the edges and they would guard his people and keep away the enemies, so since they told him all this, they were given all the outside land which was not alloted to any other clan.

After this was all settled, another clan came along and they were also a common class, and the chief asked them if they had any ceremonies of any kind by which they lived, or by which they prayed to the gods to bring them rain. They said no, they didn't have any and they told him they didn't have any time for ceremonies, they were nothing but warriors and had to fight their way up there, for the country was full of other tribes that were enemies of these people. So the chief said that if they were warriors and had to fight their way up there, they would be his braves. This was the Sun Forehead Clan. Then the chief went to the Parrot Clan (*Gash-wunga*) and asked them if they would give up some of their land to the Sun Forehead Clan, that they too might take their place in guarding the chief's rights and those of his people. The Parrot Clan was very glad to do this, so from then on the Sun Forehead Clan had to be out first if enemies made an attack.

Then, later on, another clan came along, the Sun Clan. They too were without a religion and ceremonies. This Sun Clan was given the same treatment as the clan before them and the Sun Forehead Clan gave up part of their land that the Sun Clan might guard the rights of the people, so to this day, their lands are still on the edge of the Hopi lands.

CHAPTER VI
HOW THE CROW CLAN ARRIVED AND
SETTLED AT MISHONGNOVI

LONG before this time the Crow Clan had made a little settlement at what is called the first Mishongnovi, on the west side of Quang-oufovi Mesa, or Bald Mesa. The leader of this clan was called Mishong, or Black Man, on account of his dark color. They lived there for awhile, but they were much troubled, for there was some sort of a great reptile that lived there, which seemed as if it had no end to it, and sometimes in the morning he would be all over the place, the great coils of him going round and round the little houses on the steep terraced mesa. He had one little pair of wings and Tok-chi-i, he was called. On account of that snake they were having great trouble. It was rather harmless, but they were afraid of it. When this great snake gathered himself together he formed a shape like a plaque and then he would take off into the air and was gone for a long time, and it might be months before he returned again, but when he did return he piled himself up on that little village again. On account of him the people left the place and went to Shung-opovi and settled down about three-fourths of the way to the top of the Mesa. When the Shung-opovi people found out that there were only seven families of them there they called their place the Seventh Point—Chung-ait-tuika.

While living at this place they were constantly asking the Shung-opovi chief if they could join with his people, but he refused them every time, because they were a dark colored people. Of course, they didn't have any land to farm and what little gardening they did was on the bench where there was only a few inches of dirt on top of the rocks. Finally the Mishongnovi leader went to the Shung-opovi chief again.

Now about this time Walpi was established, and when the Shung-opovi people heard about it they decided they would let the Mishongnovi people go to guard the Corn Rock which was a very important shrine.

So the chief of Shung-opovi said, "If you want to become a part of my people, I have a shrine by the Corn Rock and I need someone to take care of it. If you wish to be a part of my people you must settle there."

The chief of Shung-opovi continued, "The eastern star has come up so that we are expecting the Bahana, our savior, a white man. We want to know him when he comes, so I delegate the Crow Clan to look for the Bahana. The Bahana, our savior, will do away with all evil people. But if the Bahana is not the true Bahana it will be your duty to make away with him." So Mishong and his people settled by the Corn Rock, founding Mishongnovi, and the Crow Clan has handed down the idea that they are the ones to look for the Bahana. Other clans joined this pueblo so the Crow Clan became the royal family of Mishongnovi. When Mishong's people were settled there they were given some land to the southeast.

Now the chief of Walpi thought they were taking some of his land, so the Chief of the Shung-opovi went to Walpi and told the Chief that he had the right to give the people that much land as he was the first one to serve them. So then they made a boundary line from one of the points on the North Mesa to the South Mesa. The North Mesa is called Po-noteu-we (shrine that looks like a fat person). The South Mesa is called Aku-haivi (meaning "a little pool or deep rock tank" and here they could easily dip water with a ladle (*aku*) which always hung there.) This seemed to be satisfactory to both sides, so they settled on that question of the boundary line.

About this time all the other villages were just beginning to be established, like Awatovi, and the others on the Jeddito, and it was found that the Awatovi people were speaking the same dialect as the Mishongnovi people. Of course at that time there was nobody at Shipaulovi.

CHAPTER VII
HOW A FAMILY QUARREL LED TO THE FOUNDING OF ORAIBI

LIKE all the other people, the Shung-opovi chief and his brothers were usually having some kind of trouble or argument over something, and about this time he found out that his younger brother was too bold. He was rather taking too much authority upon himself and didn't have much respect for the other people. He never would do much of anything in the way of work, but he would always be down in the fields when the crops were ripe and he helped himself to the things the other people had grown. Since he was one of the royal family no one had a right to say anything to him, and he was always grabbing corn from other people's fields at the time of the harvest and that was where he got his provisions, for he didn't grow anything himself.

Now the people were rather tired of this and they were all turning against him, but no one dared say anything. One day they had baked sweet corn and the men were there husking it, and this man came down and picked out as much as he could carry of the best corn the men had. It happened that his brother, the Chief, was there at the time and his brother, having the same right or being a little above him, called him down. Then all the other men thought that was their chance to say something to him and they all called him down. That hurt him more than anything else and he left all the corn right there and went home.

When night came on he left Shung-opovi. The next morning he was missing and no one knew where he had gone and from then on, they were always looking for him and would send out searching parties but they never could find him. Nobody ever heard anything about him. All the other villages were asked if he had gone to one of them, but he was not in any of them.

One day they went out hunting and at that time Third Mesa was a hunting place where they hunted cottontails among the rock. Now while they were there hunting, they found this man. He was living in one of the little caves. His name was Ma-chito. When they found him they tried to get him to talk but he wouldn't speak to them, so they tried to bring him back home but he would not go with them.

When they got home they told his wife that her husband was over on the mesa and asked her to go and see if she could get him to come home. The next day she went but he told her he would never return to Shung-opovi—that he had left his people for good. He wanted to see how his brother would get along without him, because he considered that he himself had witchcraft power and that it was he that knew all the different songs and all the ceremonies that were being carried on at that time. His wife made four trips over there but she could not get him to come home, so she decided to go over and join him.

So when she got there, they went up on top of the mesa and built up there. From then on, in the other villages, whoever was mistreated or got mad at something went over there to live. When other clans drifted in, Ma-chito didn't have many questions to ask of them, but just brought them in, for he wanted to get ahead of his brother and have more people in a short time.

CHAPTER VIII

HOW THE SPANIARDS CAME TO SHUNG-OPOVI, HOW THEY BUILT A MISSION, AND HOW THE HOPI DESTROYED THE MISSION

IT MAY have taken quite a long time for these villages to be established. Anyway, every place was pretty well settled down when the Spanish came. The Spanish were first heard of at Zuni and then at Awatovi. They came on to Shung-opovi, passing Walpi. At First Mesa, Si-kyatki was the largest village then, and they were called Si-kyatki, not Walpi. The Walpi people were living below the present village on the west side. When the Spaniards came, the Hopi thought that they were the ones they were looking for—their white brother, the Bahana, their savior.

The Spaniards visited Shung-opovi several times before the missions were established. The people of Mishongovi welcomed them so the priest who was with the white men built the first Hopi mission at Mishongovi. The people of Shung-opovi were at first afraid of the priests but later they decided he was really the Bahana, the savior, and let him build a mission at Shung-opovi.

Well, about this time the Strap Clan were ruling at Shung-opovi and they were the ones that gave permission to establish the mission. The Spaniards, whom they called Castilla, told the people that they had much more power than all their chiefs and a whole lot more power than the witches. The people were very much afraid of them, particularly if they had much more power than the witches. They were so scared that they could do nothing but allow themselves to be made slaves. Whatever they wanted done must be done. Any man in power that was in this position the Hopi called *Tota-achi*, which means a grouchy person that will not do anything himself, like a child. They couldn't refuse, or they would be slashed to death or punished in some way. There were two *Tota-achi*.

The missionary did not like the ceremonies. He did not like the Kachinas and he destroyed the altars and the customs. He called it idol worship and burned up all the ceremonial things in the plaza.

When the Priests started to build the mission, the men were sent away over near the San Francisco peaks to get the pine or spruce beams. These beams were cut and put into shape roughly and were then left till the next year when they had dried out. Beams of that size were hard to carry and the first few times they tried to carry these beams on their backs, twenty to thirty men walking side by side under the beam. But this was rather hard in rough places and one end had to swing around. So finally they figured out a way of carrying the beam in between them. They lined up two by two with the beam between the lines. In doing this, some of the Hopis were given authority by the missionary to look after these men and to see if they all did their duty. If any man gave out on the way he was simply left to die. There was great suffering. Some died for lack of food and water, while others developed scabs and sores on their bodies.

It took a good many years for them to get enough beams to Shung-opovi to build the mission. When this mission was finally built, all the people in the village had to come there to worship, and those that did not come were punished severely. In that way their own religion was altogether wiped out, because they were not allowed to worship in their own way. All this trouble was a heavy burden on them and they thought it was on account of this that they were having a heavy drought at this time. They thought their gods had given them up because they weren't worshiping the way they should.

Now during this time the men would go out pretending they were going on a hunting trip and they would go to some hiding place, to make their prayer offerings. So today, a good many of these places are still to be found where they left their little stone bowls in which they ground their copper ore to paint the prayer sticks. These places are called *Puwa-kiki*, cave places. If these men were caught they were severely punished.

Now this man, Tota-achi (the Priest) was going from bad to worse. He was not doing the people any good and he was always figuring what he could do to harm them. So he thought out how the water from different springs or rivers would taste and he was always sending some man to these springs to get water for him to drink, but it was noticed that he always chose the men who had pretty wives. He tried to send them far away so that they would be gone two or three days, so it was not very long until they began to see what he was doing. The men were even sent to the Little Colorado River to get water for him, or to Moencopi. Finally, when a man was sent out he'd go out into the rocks and hide, and when the night came he would come home. Then, the priest, thinking the man was away, would come to visit his wife, but instead the man would be there when he came. Many men were punished for this.

All this time the priest, who had great power, wanted all the young girls to be brought to him when they were about thirteen or fourteen years old. They had to live with the priest. He told the people they would become better women if they lived with him for about three years. Now one of these girls told what the Tota-achi were doing and a brother of the girl heard of this and he asked his sister about it, and he was very angry. This brother went to the mission and wanted to kill the priest that very day, but the priest scared him and he did nothing. So the Shung-opovi people sent this boy, who was a good runner, to Awatovi to see if they were doing the same thing over there, which they were. So that was how they got all the evidence against the priest.

Then the chief at Awatovi sent word by this boy that all the priests would be killed on the fourth day after the full moon. They had no calendar and that was the best way they had of setting the date. In order to make sure that everyone would rise up and do this thing on the fourth day the boy was given a cotton string with knots in it and each day he was to untie one of these knots until they were all out and that would be the day for the attack.

Things were getting worse and worse so the chief of Shung-opovi went over to Mishongnovi and the two chiefs discussed their troubles. "He is not the savior and it is your duty to kill him," said the chief of Shung-opovi. The chief of Mishongnovi replied, "If I end his life, my own life is ended."

Now the priest would not let the people manufacture prayer offerings, so they had to make them among the rocks in the cliffs out of sight, so again one day the chief of Shung-opovi went to Mishongnovi with tobacco and materials to make prayer offerings. He was joined by the chief of Mishongnovi and the two went a mile north to a cave. For four days they lived there heartbroken in the cave, making pahos. Then the chief of Mishongnovi took the prayer offerings and climbed to the top of the Corn Rock and deposited them in the shrine, for according to the ancient agreement with the Mishongnovi people it was their duty to do away with the enemy.

He then, with some of his best men, went to Shung-opovi, but he carried no weapons. He placed his men at every door of the priest's house. Then he knocked on the door and walked in. He asked the priest to come out but the priest was suspicious and would not come out. The chief asked the priest four times and each time the priest refused. Finally, the priest said, "I think you are up to something."

The chief said, "I have come to kill you." "You can't kill me," cried the priest, "you have no power to kill me. If you do, I will come to life and wipe out your whole tribe."

The chief returned, "If you have this power, then blow me out into the air; my gods have more power than you have. My gods have put a heart into me to enter your home. I have no weapons. You have your weapons handy, hanging on the wall. My gods have prevented you from getting your weapons."

The old priest made a rush and grabbed his sword from the wall. The chief of Mishongnovi yelled and the doors were broken open. The priest cut down the chief and fought right and left but was soon overpowered, and his sword taken from him.

They tied his hands behind his back. Out of the big beams outside they made a tripod. They hung him on the beams, kindled a fire and burned him.

CHAPTER IX
RETURN OF THE SPANIARDS TO HOPI COUNTRY. SHIPAULOVI FOUNDED AS A SANCTUARY

AFTER all this had happened the Hopi were sure that the Spaniards were going to come back and make an attack on them and they figured that they would be wiped out. The chief of Shung-opovi thought there should be someone saved who would keep a record of these happenings in the best way they could. Now just about that time the Sun Forehead Clan was admitted into the village. They came from Homolovi. The chief sent one of his relations of the Bear Clan and his family to Shipaulovi and with them he sent half of the Sun Forehead Clan. He told them that this Shipaulovi village would be recognized as an innocent town, and that whenever the Hopi were attacked by any of their enemies whoever wished to live, could go there.

After all this the chief just simply waited for the attack to come from the Spanish, for knowing that he was guilty, he would not hesitate to give himself up to the Spaniards.

He waited quite a long while about 20 years—but nobody knows just how long. Finally the Spanish came. When they did come, instead of going up to the village they camped about three-fourths of a mile below the old Shung-opovi town and the whole village was in terror. The chief went down to the camp to ask them if they had come then to be friends, or to destroy.

The captain of the army told him that they had only come for the guilty. Then the chief said that the whole village was guilty, because everybody that could had put a hand on the priest. Then the captain said that could not be, because there were a good many people in the village and he couldn't understand how everyone could have put a hand on the priest. Then the chief said, if he was guilty all the people were guilty for he was their chief and leader. The captain asked the chief to have all the men of the village descend down there, so the chief called his men to come. When all the men got there, the captain lined them up and then he asked the chief to pick out the men that were really guilty.

Before the chief said a word, the men declared they were all guilty; but the captain would not believe them. During all this excitement there was one Hopi had the heart to come out with the truth. He stepped out and said he didn't like to see all the men get killed, for some of them were too young. They might become good runners or warriors and have long lives to live.

This man turned around to the chief and accused him of simply sacrificing his men because he didn't want to be put to death alone. He said that if he saved some of these men or convinced the Spaniards that these men were not all guilty, he himself would be willing to take the place of the chief and be the leader of the people. He was a man of the Strap Clan, closely related to the Bear Clan to which the chief belonged. This man was angry to think that the chief would sacrifice his men for nothing.

Then after this man had said he would be the leader of the people, he asked the chief to step forward and be honest and point out the ones who were really guilty. But the chief still wasn't man enough to do it, and he was asked four times before he would pick out the guilty men. The men were those who held positions in different kinds of ceremonies. With the Hopi, things like the doing away with the priest are not discussed with the common people—only among the leaders.

When these men were picked out, their hands were tied behind them and they were taken prisoners with the chief. The man of the Strap Clan took his men back to the village and the people coming out to meet them and seeing these men, declared him the chief. The next morning the men that were taken prisoners were shot at sunrise. Then the captain sent word up to the village that if they wished to bury the dead they could come and do it, but the people would not go down for fear they might get killed, so they waited until the Spaniards went away.

The new chief took everything in his hands and went down with some of his men and buried the dead. Each man was buried with his possessions, turquoise and shell beads. In those days the father's relatives would give presents of pottery to be buried with the dead. So they were buried with all those things.

Now the people of Shung-opovi had lived in the same village until the Spanish came back. Then the Strap Clan leader led the people to the top of the mesa and founded the new Shung-opovi, for he was afraid if they stayed down below, there would be more Spanish attacks.

From then on the Strap Clan people were leaders in Shung-opovi. During the next few years things were very prosperous, but it happened that they failed again—another drought came. At this time the people held a council and made an agreement that every clan be given a chance to take their turn at leadership. So from then on, each clan took its turn and it finally came back to the Bear Clan (each clan held leadership for four years) and when their turn was up they refused to give it up for they claimed it was theirs originally. Since they refused to give up their leadership they have remained the royal family ever since.

About this time another company of Spanish soldiers came and old Mishongnovi was still inhabited at that time, for all the people had not yet moved up on top. They stopped on the other side of Mishongnovi and asked the chief if he would make an agreement to let them in. He refused them four times. Then the captain of the Spanish soldiers said he had to destroy their village. Of course the people were very much afraid then, for they had seen what had happened at Shung-opovi and how the Spanish had killed the leaders of the trouble over there. Shung-opovi was then partly in ruins for the people were carrying away the beams to build their new homes on top, but somehow the Spanish didn't make an attack that time but went away again."

After they had gone away the Mishongnovi people wanted to stop up their spring, called *Yo-niai-va* (Antelope Chipmunk), which was a good spring at that time. They closed it up and had a paho-making ceremony. After they made their prayer offerings every man spun some cotton and when this was done they selected four different kinds of pahos and then wrapped cotton yarn over them. It made a round roll, about 10 inches long and about eight inches in diameter. With this they blocked up the water hole. Then in front of it they put a plaque and sealed it up around the edges with sweet cornmeal mush. They did this so that if the Spanish ever came back they would find no water there. This spring was to be opened up when the good white man or his brother came back, but today nobody knows just where the spring really is.

When they had done this they started to move up on top of the mesa, but before they had all moved, the Spanish came back again. Finding no water where they had camped before, they went right into the village and destroyed it. No one was killed and the few people who were left escaped and moved up to the mesa top. Their, the Spanish tried to get to the new village on top, but there was no trail and the people had piled up stones which they rolled down on the Spanish so that they were unable to climb up.

Shipaulovi was pretty well established at this time, but was under a sub-chief of Shung-opovi, as Mishongnovi was too.

After all these happenings the chiefs of the three villages held a council and made an agreement that there should be a limited place where the next white man should stop. This place is where the Sunlight Mission now stands. It was put up to the Mishongnovi chief that it was to be his duty to look out for that. There was also another limited line—between Shipaulovi and Mishongnovi. If any attack should come from the outside on Mishongnovi, whoever wished to save his own life could go over to the Shipaulovi side, where they were not supposed to be touched. Shipaulovi was the place of safety and was not supposed to have any blood stain. No one there could fight and no one was supposed to fight them.

For a long time these two villages were under Shung-opovi, but finally it was too much for them to handle, on account of the great number of ceremonies they were supposed to have. Finally, Mishongnovi was given its freedom. Shipaulovi today is not altogether under Shung-opovi, but the people still go to Shung-opovi for their initiation ceremonies (*Wuwuchime*).

CHAPTER X
THE RETURN OF THE BAHANA, THE WHITE MAN

ALL THIS time the Hopi seemed to know that the real Bahana was coming, but they were warned to be careful and patient, for fear it might not be the true Bahana who would come after the Spaniard or Castilian. So if he ever did come they must be sure to ask him about his books, which they thought would contain his secrets, and it was said that the book of truth would not be on top, but at the very bottom, after all the other books. If he asked the Hopi for the privilege of teaching them his language and taught them how to write, they must be sure to ask that they would like to be taught in the book of truth, because if he was a true Bahana he would quickly consent to teach them of this book. For their belief is, that if he is not the one they are looking for he will refuse to teach them his religion. Now if they learned his religion they would compare it with their religion and ceremonies, and if these were alike they would know that the Bahana had been with them in the beginning.

Most everybody was anxious to see the Bahana come, for they were so afraid that he might not come during their lifetime and they would not be able to enjoy all the benefits that he was to bring back with him-for the Bahana was supposed to bring great knowledge with him. These people were telling their children that the Bahana was wise and with his inventions had reached the rising sun and was coming back to them again, for they had seen the big eastern star and that was a sign and they were waiting for him. Every grandfather and grandmother was telling their children that they were growing so old that they would not see the Bahana. They would tell their grandchildren to go out in the mornings before sunrise with sacred corn-meal to ask the sun to hurry the Bahana along so that he would come soon.

Well, I guess many years had passed, probably a century. You know, some were rather superstitious and they would say that when the Bahana came he would know who was practicing witchcraft and that he would know them by sight. They said that he was to come and make peace and do away with all evil so that there would be no more trouble. And so, for this reason, the people who had so much trouble were the most anxious to see him come.

Well, finally they heard that the Bahana was at Tsehotso (Navajo for Fort Defiance) which means "range of sharp-pointed rocks." He was calling for the Hopi chiefs to come to that place to meet him. Now at that time all the tribes were on hostile terms with one another and it was dangerous. The Hopi wanted to go and see what this Bahana looked like. The chiefs from all the villages went there and they told him if he was the true Bahana they would shake hands and lay down their weapons, for they had a "theory" that when the Bahana came there would be peace forever. Well, at this place they were given cloth of different kinds, flour and sugar and a few tools like axes and knives. That was the first time that they had ever tasted sugar. When they brought these things back home this caused much excitement in all the towns. Of course, they would have to go back and take more men with them but they were always afraid of attacks from the Navajos and the Paiutes. So the Hopis, knowing that the white man was at Fort Defiance and that he had promised to let his soldiers protect the friendly people, knew also that if they were attacked by the Navajos and fighting with them, the soldiers would come. So every time the Navajos made an attack the Hopis would have to fight and if they made a retreat they would follow them up. The Hopis got so that they were good fighters themselves. The Navajos were not much of fighters, for they made up war parties and went places looking for trouble. Well, when they were doing this they thought it was great fun. The Hopi said that if they sighted some hogans they would hide out in the day time and move up at night. These Hopis would have signals like the call of an owl (there are two different kinds of owls—hoot owl and small owl that makes a whistling noise) or a crow. During the night they would circle around the hogans and would signal back and forth imitating the owls or crows to see if the Navajos were all awake. They would surround the place and wait until sunrise before making an attack.

Some old men who used to tell about this said it was great fun and like chasing cottontails on a rocky hill. They (Navajos) would be so scared they couldn't run and all they had to do was to hit them on the head with a club. These old men said that when they had grown old, they knew what a great wrong they had done.

CHAPTER XI
HOW THE HOPI MARKED THE BOUNDARY LINE BETWEEN THEIR COUNTRY AND THAT OF THE NAVAJO

NOW with all this fighting and the Navajo coming in around them, the Hopi were always thinking of their boundary lines and of how they should be marked in some way. But how? What sort of a mark could they put that would be respected by other peoples? It must be something that both the Hopis and the Navajos would remember.

So just at this time there were two men at Walpi who were rivals over a woman named Wupo-wuti. Now both these men were looking for a chance to show this woman how brave and strong they were. Finally they thought of this boundary line and the "theory" of their people that it should be marked in such a way that everyone would always remember. So these two men thought that this was a chance for them to prove themselves and to really do something for their people at the same time. They thought they would plan a fight with the Navajos as near the boundary line as they could get and there they would sacrifice themselves and leave their skulls to mark the line. In this way they thought that they would prove that they were brave and good fighters and they would really be doing something for their people, and so it was agreed upon.

Then Masale (feathers crossed) said they would go to Fort Defiance. So they both made an agreement that they would go early in the fall. Tawupu (rabbit skin blanket) thought they were going alone, but later he found out that there was going to be a party going over. He thought they were sacrificing too many lives, but, of course, he had made the promise to this other man so that he could not tell on him or give him away at that time. The crier made an announcement that whoever wanted to go to Fort Defiance with this party was welcome, and that they must prepare themselves and be ready to go soon. Masale had a son named Hani and he loved him, so he thought that he would take him along. He figured that if he should be killed it might be best for the boy to die also. Of course, this being a time of war, everyone was asked to take his bows and arrows along. Masale asked his boy to come along and to be sure to make some new arrows. The boy, of course, being ignorant of his father's plans, was glad to go with them.

By this time the people had found out that the two rivals were going together to Fort Defiance, and they figured out that there was something going to happen—that they were going out to give themselves away, or sacrifice their lives.

The morning of the day they were starting out, one of the relatives of this boy, Hani, asked him if he was going along with his father and he said he was. This man said to the boy that it would be better for him not to go with them. But Hani said he was all ready and the man, being his father, he was going along with him.

"Well," this relative said, "if you are, I will warn you right now. Wherever you camp you want to be sure where you lay your weapons or your bows and arrows, for your life will be in danger." He told him never to lay his bow and arrows under his head, but that he must lay them at his feet. "Because," this man said, "if you are lying on your back with your bows and arrows at your feet and you are waked up suddenly you will jump up forward. Having your weapons there at your feet you will lay your hands on them every time." He also told him that he must try not to sleep too soundly; that he must remember he was in danger all the time.

Hani, after getting his warning, started out and was the last one to leave. At that time the trail was through Keams Canyon. When he was quite a ways through the canyon, an eagle flew over his head and it was flying low. He thought that if the eagle settled down somewhere on a rock he would kill it and take the feathers along in case he wanted to make some more arrows on the way, so he kind of hid himself in the brush. Finally the eagle landed on top of a rock and Hani crawled toward him and took a shot at him. He did get him and the bird fell from the rock. Hani ran over to the place and found that his eagle was a buzzard. This seemed kind of strange, for he really had seen an eagle. That made him sort of suspicious. He thought it might be a warning or witchcraft, but as he was on his way already, he couldn't very well turn back. Well, finally he came up with the party, in the late afternoon.

That night when they made their first camp he had the warnings in his mind and he couldn't sleep. Anyway, he must have fallen asleep for a while and when he opened his eyes he was wide awake. He heard two men talking but he didn't make any noise and pretended he was sound asleep. He recognized his father's voice and also the voice of the other man, Tawupu. He overheard Tawupu asking his father why he had brought his boy along and his father said he couldn't very well leave him behind because he loved him so dearly. He said that if his boy should refuse to come along with him he would back out too, and he said it would be better for both of them if they got killed. When the boy began to move the two men rushed back and crawled into their beds. Now, after Hani had overheard what the two men had said, he couldn't sleep.

From then on the boy was rather uneasy every night when they made camp. After they lay down to sleep he'd keep awake quite a while because he knew, then, what the two men were up to. All the rest of the party didn't seem to know anything about it. They were ignorant of the plans of the two men.

After several days on the road, they finally reached the place—Fort Defiance. There they were welcomed by the white man and were asked to stay several days with them. There were twelve or fifteen men in the party. Four being the sacred number of the Hopi, they decided to stay four days. On the fourth day, when they were getting ready to go back home, the Bahana gave them flour and sugar and coffee and different kinds of cloth, besides yarns.

So the next morning when they were ready to leave, every burro they had with them was pretty well packed. Before they left they were asked if they would like to have a guard to go along with them. In case they were in any danger, they would have someone to show that they were the friends of the white man and they were not to be harmed, but since they didn't see any signs of danger when they were coming over they refused to take a guard along. Having been granted all their wishes for things that they had wanted for so long, they were very happy when they left there.

They were two days on the road before they reached Ganado, and the night before they reached Ganado this boy, Hani, overheard the two men talking with some other man. This time there were three men sitting around the camp fire quietly smoking. The boy could not really understand just what they were saying because it was all in a whisper. Then , of course, he couldn't help but move and when he did, one man rushed off and the other two men went to bed. One man was an outsider, a Navajo. The next morning the boy was more suspicious than ever, but still he could not ask his father what this night meeting was about.

So that day they traveled all day (on the other side of Ganado). On this day camp was made rather early and they said they wanted to get settled before dark. So they got everything ready before the sun went down, which was northwest of Ganado in the red hills. They said that they would have a good supper that night, so they cooked a great deal of their food that they had gotten at Fort Defiance—with bacon and some beef that they had brought along. Having an early supper, they said they would go to bed soon and would get up early in the morning, for they figured on reaching home the next night.

This man, Masale, the boy's father, seemed very happy that night. Before going to bed they cut a lot of branches off the cedars and brush that was around and put them clear around the camp, as a windbreak, you might say. Against this they put their saddles and all the packs that they had. That night Hani kept awake quite a long time, but he could not stand it very long so he finally fell asleep.

During the night sometime, Hani thought that he was dreaming and that there was a heavy hail storm coming up for he thought that he heard the hail dropping. First he heard it dropping slowly and then faster. When he was wide awake he knew what was going on. They were being attacked and when he did come to, all the men were up. About this time his father spoke at the top of his voice in Apache, then in Navajo and then in Zuni. He was asking who it was that was attacking them. The boy did not forget where to have his bow and arrows every night, so when he did jump up he had his hands right on his bow. By this time arrows were coming from every direction. When Hani was well on his feet all the enemy rushed into the camp, and as this was during the night he did not know who was who. Anyway, he started on a run and they chased after him. It happened that some Navajo had a corn patch near there and in the corn patch he had some squash with very long vines. Hani thought the whole country was full of enemies, so he hid under the vines, breathless and excited. He heard his father make his last groan and he was very angry. Dead or alive, he decided to go back, but found himself with only a few arrows, two or three left. So he ran back to the camp and when he got there he found his father dead, with many arrows sticking in his body. His scalp was gone. He thought that before doing anything else he must find his arrows and he found them rolled up in his blanket. This little blanket was only half the size of a double saddle blanket. Now the enemy thought that he was one of their party so he was not shot at until he had shot at them. As the enemy followed him he ran backward, holding the little blanket in front of him to stop the arrows. The moon was just going down below the horizon and it was getting quite dark.

At first he did not realize that he had been shot, for being a good runner the enemy could not keep up with him, but when he got up to the hills they were rather too steep for him to climb, because he realized then that he was shot, one arrow in his stomach, one in his hip and one between his shoulders. He pulled out two, the one from his hip and the one from his stomach, but he couldn't reach the one in his back. Well, anyway, he thought himself dead when he started to crawl up the hill. When he was halfway up the hill he cried for his dear life and prayed to his gods that if he should die, some day his skull would be found there. He didn't know how many of the party were killed or saved; he didn't know whether they were all dead or not. When he said his prayers, he cried some more, but he couldn't cry very loud, for he'd rather die in peace than have the enemy find him and use a club on him.

As he was going up, it began to show that it was dawn. He could see the daylight over the horizon and he wished that he would not die. If the sun did come up in time, he believed that it would give him strength. Of course, he couldn't help from groaning as he crawled up, and then he heard someone speak to him from the top of the hill, which scared him nearly to death and he thought some enemy had headed him off, so he did not answer. The voice came again and it was in plain Hopi. It said, "Are you hurt badly?" And he said, "Yes." And then the other said, "Will you be able to make it up here?" But he said, "No." So this other man came down and helped him up. When they got up he recognized this man and it was a man by the name of Mai-yaro. Well, this man said to the wounded boy that they would try to travel on together, as he was not wounded. He had been in the party, but had got away safely.

Hani told him to go on and leave him alone for he was done for and was ready to die, but this other man refused to leave him. He said that if the enemy should head them off and follow them, he would be willing to die with him. So they went on walking slowly, and while they were going along, another man named Tochi (Moccasin) joined them. He was hiding too. Hani asked them both again to leave him and run on home but they both ref used. They asked him which of his wounds hurt him most and he said the arrow in his back hurt him the worst. So they thought they would pull this arrow out, but it was stuck fast in the bone. They tried it, but the shaft came off from the point. Then it was even harder to pull out. So they both tried their teeth on it and finally they pulled it out. One of these men was asked to scout ahead and the other to scout behind. So each man was supposed to be about one-fourth mile from the wounded man.

They were going very slowly. Finally they went down into another valley. It was about sunrise. As they were going along Hani saw a rabbit, a little cottontail on the side of the trail, and he wanted to shoot this rabbit because he said he was hungry and needed something to eat. Well, the other man said not to kill the rabbit. He said, "You belong to the Rabbit Clan and you can't kill that rabbit. It might bring you luck if left alive. It might bring us both luck." So he said, "Let the rabbit live."

They thought of a spring around the point, for they were both tired and thirsty. Instead of scouting ahead, the third man, Tochi, had run home. When they got to the spring Mai-yaro would not let the wounded boy have a big drink, thinking that his stomach was injured. When they got kind of cooled off, Mai-yaro thought he would look back over the hill and see if the enemy was following. Before he left, he told the wounded man not to drink any more, for if his stomach was injured badly it would not hold water. But just as soon as he left Hani took a big drink and he felt much better.

Well, Mai-yaro went over the hill and as he looked down on the trail he saw a Navajo walking back and forth over the trail. He watched this Navajo for quite a while and he saw that he was very much discouraged. Well, finally, the Navajo turned back, so Mai-yaro went back to the spring and when he got there Hani told him he had had a big drink and felt better and he asked to have some more.

Then they both started back for the trail. This man, Mai-yaro, said he would go back to the trail and see what the Navajo was doing. When he got where they had seen the rabbit he found that the rabbit was gone. So he investigated there and found that the rabbit had gone over their tracks three times, So the rabbit had disappointed the Navajo who thought the men had passed him in the night long before daylight.

It was about the middle of the day, and it was hot, so they got in among some rocks. Hani was pretty well tired out and he said he would like to lie down for awhile and cool himself off. So he did lie down under one of the rocks and fell right asleep and the other man kept awake. Well, this man on the watch would close his eyes every little while and as he was doing this, he saw the shadow of a little bird on top of a rock. It was a little rock sparrow and it was very much excited about something. The man thought this was a warning to them, so they got right up and started on.

As they were going along it began to show signs that it was going to rain. Clouds were coming up. When it did cloud up they felt very much better, for they were cooled off. Then it started to rain. They thought they would not stop for shelter, but kept right on going while it rained. Finally, it poured down on them and there was a regular cloudburst. It rained so hard on them that it washed all the blood off Hani. He said that he felt very much better, so Mai-yaro asked him to try himself out on a trot.

The man asked him if he felt his wounds hurting him and he said, "No." Then he asked him to go a little faster, and then he asked him again how he felt. Hani said that he felt all right, so Mai-yaro asked him to run as fast as he could. Then he asked him again if the wounds hurt him. Hani said, "No," and thought that he was well, so Mai-yaro said, "Let's go then."

Now when Tochi reached Walpi and told the people what had happened, Hani's mother heard that he had been wounded badly and might die, so she wrapped up some piki and some sweet corn meal and she started out to look for him, all by herself. Now this was a very brave thing for a Hopi woman to do. She thought that she might find him dead somewhere and if she did she would roll his body under a ledge of rock or a bank of earth and cover him up with heavy stones and she would leave the piki and the sweet corn meal there for him.

But near the head of Jeddito Canyon she saw two men coming and then she recognized them for it was her boy Hani and Mai-yaro with him. And when they met they could not help but cry for joy. They hurried on home from there and when they came to the edge of the mesa south of Walpi, they saw clouds of dust in the valley coming toward them. They wondered what it was and thought it was an attack on the mesa. So they said to themselves, if there was an attack they would go on and meet the Navajo. So they went on and were met halfway and they found that this was a war party sent out to help them. When they met the whole party hurried back to the mesa and there at the foot of the mesa the whole village was crying for they found that only six men were saved out of the party that went to Fort Defiance.

Hani chose his godfather at the foot of the mesa, and of course it was Mai-yaro who was the first one to find him wounded, so instead of going to his own house he went with this man to be washed up and cared for the next day. When this was done he fasted four days. On the fourth day he was given his new name, "Hani." From then on he always had in mind to get even with the Navajos in that part of the country, and so he did, for later he led war parties to that country often and brought back a scalp every time. He was considered one of the greatest and bravest men of the Walpi villages.

CHAPTER XII
HOW SOME HOPIS RESISTED SENDING THEIR CHILDREN TO SCHOOL AND THE TROUBLE THAT RESULTED

OUT this time the agency was established at Keams Canyon and of course the Hopis knew that this meant peace. So all the chiefs from every village went there and told the white man that they were his friends and brothers and they told him that they would like to be protected by him from all their other enemies. For this reason they thought the agent ought to settle all their troubles which they had been having right along.

Later, a school was established there and all the Hopis were willing to send their children to school. Everything was going all right until they had an initiation ceremony (*Wuwuchime*) at Shung-opovi and the young men at old Shung-opovi and Shipaulovi were to be initiated. So they were not sent back to school that year and of course, at that time, these ceremonies were not very well understood by the white man, so the agent sent out policemen (two First Mesa men and three Navajos) to fetch the young boys. When they got to Shipaulovi they found the young men in the kiva and they asked the chief to give them up so that they could take them back to school. The chief said he would not let them go until the ceremony was over and he told them that he would be quite willing to let them go then. But the policemen insisted that they must take them at once because they had orders to bring them in. But the chief just flatly refused.

So the policeman said that they would take the chief instead. He said he would be willing to go with them after he had seen his friend, the missionary. So he went off and as he was leaving, he asked the policeman to stay on top of the mesa and wait for him until he came back.

He started off for the Sunlight Mission by way of Mishongnovi. The policemen thought that he was going to fool them, so they followed him and caught up with him as he was going around the village. They took hold of him and dragged him off the mesa, so he did not get to see the chief at Mishongnovi either. He intended that they would both go down to the mission to see what information they could get from the missionary. In both villages there was much excitement and all the people were on the housetops as they were very much troubled to see the chief dragged off the mesa by the policemen.

The three sons of the chief ran out after them and they caught up with them just as they were at the bottom of the mesa, and, of course, they could not help but fight these men to defend their father. But finally they all got to the mission. When they got there, the missionary took the side of the chief and told the policeman to let him go. Then he wrote a letter to the agent asking him to let him know what orders he had given these policemen to come out to do. While he was writing this letter the chief asked him to put in this message to the agent, that he was through with the school and that he would not be his friend any more. And he said that he was a friend of the missionary only and that he would do anything for him. So he said that if the agent were man enough he could come and get his scalp. Then he said, "I am the man, Tawahonganiwa. If you ever want to come out, get no one else but Tawahonganiwa. I am not your friend."

When this was written the missionary enclosed the letter in an envelope and gave it to the policeman to take into the agency. This was how the two factions and all the trouble over sending the children to school was started among the Hopi.

From then on, Chief Tawahonganiwa had many followers in both Mishongnovi and Shipaulovi and every now and then he would hold a council with his fellowmen. Then later, many people of the other villages took up his side, excepting First Mesa.

When they split those that wanted to go to school went right on; but the Chief's relatives had to take his side and held their children back. This was about 1888 or 1889. Every once in a while the agent would send out the policemen. If they were expecting them, the parents would have to go out early with their children to the hiding places under the cliffs. Not finding any children, the policemen would go back.

Finally the policemen thought of the scheme of coming into the villages at night. In that way they got quite a few children and they took them off to Keams Canyon to boarding school. Of course, this was very unpleasant for the Hopis, for they never before had parted with any of their children. So the Chief at Mishongnovi thought that it would be best to let their children be sent to school with their own consent.

About this time, the army (a troop of negro soldiers) was sent out to the Hopi villages to see if they could make the old chief at Shipaulovi change his mind about sending his children to school. They did not stop at Shipaulovi very long, but went on to Oraibi where there were more people. There they were met by the chief, Lololama, and he was very friendly to them and said he was willing to send his children to school. He wanted to take advantage of what the outcome would be of sending the children to school. After he made this agreement Youkioma jumped on him and they quarreled. This was the first time that Lololama had found out that Youkioma was the leader of this other faction. But Lololama, being the chief, said that the children who were old enough to go to the Keams Canyon School could be taken. Now from then on these two men were against each other and each man wanted to see how many followers he could have. These hostile leaders would have meetings at every other village ever so often and they would lecture to the people, telling them that the ones who were sending their children to school would be in worse trouble because the Bahana who established the school was not their true brother who had come up from the underworld with them. If he was, he would have shown the Hopis his written tradition to compare with their tradition. So this faction felt that they would rather wait for their Bahana brother to come with this written story of their ancestors.

This sort of trouble got very bad among the people themselves and the leaders of each faction of course, were working against one another to see who would have the most followers. On account of many good useful things, like tools, such as axes and hoes, clothing and sugar and coffee some of the hostile faction people began falling off, thinking that the idea of being a hostile was just the idea of preventing the people from having these things. Finally it got so there were very few hostiles left at Shipaulovi and Mishongnovi, but there were quite a number at Shung-opovi, so the ones at Shipaulovi moved over to Shung-opovi. This move occurred in 1899.

CHAPTER XIII
HOW HOTEVILLA AND BAKABI WERE FOUNDED

WHILE the Shipaulovi hostiles were living over at Shung-opovi they were very much stronger against the school. The agent would send out policemen every once in awhile to try to get their leader, Tawahonganiwa. Of course those policemen did not have much authority, so they could not take him. He would put up a big fight and his sons were the ones who would do the fighting. These policemen were mostly Navajos.

The move to Shung-opovi occurred after the people had the smallpox and the government was fumigating all the villages. The government people were trying to get these hostiles over to the Toreva school to give them a good cleaning up, so they could give them clean clothes and burn up what they were wearing, but these hostiles did not want to go there, because they did not want to put on what the government would issue to them. So finally the Agent had to send out a regiment, composed of colored soldiers from Fort Wingate. When these soldiers arrived the hostile women made up a lot of piki and took it over to the soldiers to feed them, thinking that the soldiers might recognize them when they came up to the Mesa. The next morning the captain sent over a soldier to warn the people that they must be ready to come right along, otherwise there would be some shooting. But Tawahonganiwa refused to do as he was bid and said he would not go. He said if they wanted to take him they would have to kill him, so he called all his followers, women and all, to one house. Whoever was an officer or priest of some kind in some of the societies would take in an image or emblem to put in the house. One of these families happened to have the image of the war god, Piakonghoya. This little image was put up by the door, for they thought he might have some power to help them. When the soldiers came up on top of the mesa they were lined up about one-fourth mile outside the village and from there the captain sent in policemen to ask these hostiles to surrender. They were asked four times, but they refused every time. So the captain thought it was time to march up. When they got there, they surrounded this house and the captain went to the house himself and asked them if they were ready to surrender and they refused again, so then it was time to take them by force, so he gave orders to the soldiers to take picks and dig around the walls and on the housetops. There must have been about seventy-five or a hundred people in this house. Just as soon as the picks were seen coming through the roofs they all started to run out and as they did this they were taken hold of by the soldiers. The leader was the last one to come out and just as soon as he was outside the door he was grabbed by the soldiers and his five sons piled up on them and the fight began.

They fought there for quite awhile. All the hostile people were fighting with the soldiers, hand to hand. Finally the old chief was knocked out and all the sons had their hands tied up behind their backs. Their father was strapped on to a horse and they were all taken to the Toreva School and there they were given baths and clean clothes and what clothes they had on were taken away and burned.

The smallpox epidemic had not yet spread to Oraibi which was well guarded so that nobody could go there. (The agent's name was Migle and the man in charge of the fumigation, etc., was Sam Shoemaker.) Most of the leading men of the hostiles were put under arrest and taken to Keams Canyon the next day and then on to Fort Defiance. They were kept at Fort Defiance for about 90 days and after that they were sent home, on their agreement that they would behave, themselves. When they got home they turned back and were just as hostile as before they were taken. They said the white man was a fool to let them go, for he was just fooled by them.

They didn't make very much trouble from then on, though their ideas against the schools were just as strong as ever and the two factions would be saying all kinds of things about one another. They were quiet from then on, but, of course, many of their followers began to fall away from the hostiles because they thought that the chief at Shung-opovi had not recognized them, so some of these people went back to Shipaulovi.

The trouble started again in the year 1906, and this was between the same two factions. It started in Shung-opovi and this was during the time of the Bean Dance. The hostiles did not plant their crop of beans with the others and eight days later they came into the kiva to plant their crop. One kiva was divided up—part hostiles and part friendlies. The night of the dance they asked these hostiles to get their plants out of the kiva because some young children who were not initiated into the Kachina ceremony would see the plants. But these men refused to take their plants away because it was against their law to take plants out of the kiva before their time. So in order to have a dance they brought in several wedding robes so as to hide the plants from the children. From then on those people were always fighting one another. So again the hostile leader decided to leave. From there Tawahonganiwa and twenty-five to thirty men and women moved to Oraibi. By this time Lololama was dead and his nephew, Tewaquoptiwa was then chief of Oraibi, but Youkioma was stronger at this time. When they got to the mesa top at Oraibi, Youkioma's men met them. These men sprinkled sacred cornmeal on the path that the Shung-opovi people followed to the village. Of course this was not the proper thing to do, for Youkioma was usurping the chief's function and Chief Tewaquoptiwa did not like it.

The leading men from both sides held council every once in a while trying to see what must be done with these people who were being taken in by Youkioma, and Youkioma always said that he had as much right to do this as the chief. It was his "theory" that he was going to follow out what his great-uncles had taught him of their traditions. This tradition told him that he was to destroy Oraibi or be destroyed himself. He belonged to the Fire or Masauwu Clan. This gave him the idea that his clan ancestor had the power to do almost anything. This clan has the idea that Masauwu can hypnotize people, so he always had said that if any expedition is sent against him all he has to do is to take out a handful of ashes and blow them on the army and they would fall to pieces. Chief Tewaquoptiwa wanted to send these people back to Shung-opovi, but Youkioma, of course, was standing up for them and if Tewaquoptiwa wanted to move them he would have had to move him too. He said that he had already had a site picked out somewhere in the north called Kawishtima (a ruin in a canyon near Navajo Mountain).

As long as he had this site already picked out Tewaquoptiwa wanted to send him there, but Tewaquoptiwa was in doubt that Youkioma would go there. Finally this trouble got so bad that if the two parties should happen to meet out in the street they would start an argument and whoever was passing would stop too and it would get worse and worse.

The people of Oraibi got so that they were very much troubled and impatient and at last they decided to move them out. Right at this time they were having a Snake Dance and Youkioma insisted he would like to be moved away on this day, but Tewaquoptiwa refused to do anything with him on that day because of the ceremony, for he did not want to trouble this religious party. So he set the day for the fourth day after the dance. From the many arguments that all the people had had in the streets both sides had the idea that there would be a fight, so they tried to collect as many weapons as possible-bows and arrows and guns, and to get them ready. Come to find out, Tewaquoptiwa did not have enough men and the hostiles were about three or four times as many as his people. So he called on the Moenkopi people for help and all the other villages of Second Mesa.

The night before the fight both parties stayed up all night for their luck, because this was rather a ceremony. They smoked all night long. When morning came Tewaquoptiwa went to the house where the hostile party was and asked them if they were ready for the day and were willing to put up a fight against his people. He also asked them if any of them would be ready to surrender and follow him. But none would surrender, because of the good sayings of Youkioma and how he was going to take them to a prosperous land.

During these hours of the morning, the men on both sides had rather a creepy feeling about what was going to be the outcome, and the men out in the streets gathered here and there listening to the many arguments. The Oraibi chief made his request four times of the hostile party. Each time he asked them if they would be willing to take the step and leave of their own free will, and that if they would, they would not be bothered or hunted. But each time Youkioma said he would have to be forced to move out. Come to find out, Tewaquoptiwa was a little afraid and he did not have nerve enough to go in and put Youkioma out of the house. So one of the men on the Chief's side was rather tired of all this foolishness that they were going through, so he called the chief, Tewaquoptiwa, a coward and jumped into the house. When he did that the rest of the men followed. When they got in there they got hold of Youkioma and just slung him out of the door. When he landed outside another party picked him up. By this time the men in the street had formed a double line and the men in the house just kept throwing men out and passing them down the line. It seemed as though they were handed out and as if they were unloading sacks of flour or watermelons and passing them on down the line. Every now and then someone would put up a fight but he was pretty well beaten. Now this was kept up until they had emptied the house. When Tewaquoptiwa's men were through they went through the village and got all the hostile women out and drove them to the outside of the village.

On that morning the missionaries had come up and they made the people on both sides give up their weapons and they took them all away. They said it would not be fair for them to have weapons, but they could fight all they wanted, hand to hand.

They passed all the hostiles out of the village and it was something awful on both sides—women and children crying. It might be sisters, it might be brothers, mothers and daughters that were separated. Just about this time one old man, a hostile, came up from his field. The day before he had baked some corn in his ground oven and he had eight burros loaded with sacks of corn, each sack holding about 100 to 150 pounds. When he came to his house no one was at home. Then someone came and drove him out with his burros and when he got out there the hostile people ripped up the sacks and helped themselves. Again Chief Tewaquoptiwa went out and asked them if they were ready to move on. Youkioma said he would not move unless Tewaquoptiwa could push him across the line which he had drawn on the flat rock of the mesa top. So here they had to put up another fight again, to put Youkioma across the line. When the chief was ready to go against them, the hostile men gathered about Youkioma, intending to hold him so that the other side could not move him across the line. Then the fight began, one party pushing toward the village and another pushing away from the village. Tewaquoptiwa had about one hundred men and Youkioma about two hundred. There they pushed back and forth for two hours and a half. When they got out of breath they stopped and then began again. Every once in awhile the pressure would be so great that old Youkioma would rise up in the air. Being quite a bunch of men they were hard to move.

One of the men from Shung-opovi, a friendly who was looking on from a housetop, could not stand it, he was so excited, and seeing one of his relations in the crowd, he dragged him away and threw him up in the air and did it again and again.

Tewaquoptiwa's men found they could pull away their relatives too. They did not like to fight other clans and all this time they had a hard feeling against their relatives who had gone over to the hostiles. By doing this they reduced the hostiles quite a bit, but no one knew why Youkioma was in the midst of the crowd. He must have had some object on either side that he was looking out for. Just as soon as he was pushed over the line, he said, "It is done, I have passed my mark," and all at once they dropped him. When this was done Chief Tewaquoptiwa asked them if they would like to take anything along, food and bedding. He told them they could go back to the village for it, so they did. The men went back and got their bedding and the women got piki and food. All this time the children were crying for something to eat and they were very thirsty. Well, that evening the whole village was like a disturbed anthill. People were everywhere, coming and going and people from other villages were there to see what was going on. You would see a woman with a bundle on her back crying and other people would be making fun of them because they were crying.

Just about sundown they were already to move on-all their burros were loaded and they were pretty well packed themselves. Youkioma took the lead and off they went to the north. They got to Hotevilla just about dark and there they made camp.

CHAPTER XIV
YOUKIOMA

ON THE next day at this place they started to clear out under the trees and cut out the lower limbs so they could have shade. But of course, some of those men who did not really know what this was all about argued here and there and some thought they should go back to Oraibi and make an attack on the Oraibi chief. Somehow the chief of Oraibi heard about this, but by that time the men from Moenkopi had gone back home and he knew he could not very well protect his town if they all came back. So he sent two men out, one to Moenkopi and one to Second Mesa to call for help. But, of course, all the men were out in the field by this time and it was quite late at night when these men heard about it. But anyway they thought they would go there to see if the people had come back to make this attack. When they got there all the men were at the chief's house. There he was, feeding the men on some peaches and melons which were taken from the orchards and fields of the people he had sent away. All night long some of the men were out along the edges of the mesa watching, for they did not know which way the people would come to make the attack. They had guns and what other weapons they could find.

All night long the men took turns going about the edge of the mesa, about six at the north and all at a good running distance from each other, but no enemy had shown up by daybreak so they felt quite sure they were safe.

From then on, all the mesa was pretty well guarded during both day and night and every man coming in from Hotevilla for this things was searched before he was allowed to go into the village.

During all this time the government hadn't interfered until about a month after. Of course, some of the children who had been going to school had gone to Hotevilla and when they tried to get them to go to school, trouble began again. The Hotevilla people would not let their children go back to school, saying they did not have to send the children because they had left the place from which they had been going to school. Every time when the policemen were sent all the people would come out and they could do nothing and had to go back without the children.

About the middle of October of that year, 1906, the army was sent out. They did not go clear to Hotevilla, but made camp at Lower Oraibi. About a couple of days after this they sent word to Hotevilla that they had come to see what the trouble was and if they could help them settle it, they would. Well, Chief Youkioma sent word back to the captain that he did not need his help. The trouble was already settled, but he had moved away from Oraibi. He also said he expected to live in peace, if there was going to be any.

Then the captain sent word back again, asking him if he would mind telling him what had caused him to move. And again Youkioma sent word back to the captain saying he would not tell him unless Chief Tewaquoptiwa would tell him first what this was all about. Then the captain sent for the Oraibi chief. Being friendly to the white man he went right down with his interpreter, and when he got there the captain asked him why he had sent those people away. He said that he had been having so much trouble with them and that they could not get along together in the same village. So the captain asked the chief why it was, and he said it was on account of their not being friendly to the white men and because they did not want to send their children to school. Before the white men had built schools, everything had been going all right. So he said that it was his fault that the trouble had begun some years ago.

The captain said that this chief should not have sent those people away. Since the white men caused the trouble it was for the white man to handle it. The chief thought that he was doing something for his friend, the white man, but he was told that it was wrong to send those people away where there was no shelter, so that he would have to bring them back or serve a term in prison. He said he did not expect to serve a term in prison, for he thought that he was doing something for the government. He told the captain that it was his "theory" that he move the hostile chief out of the village. Youkioma knew that these things were going to happen too and it had happened so. He said that if it had not been for the missionaries who interfered they would have killed each other, Tewaquoptiwa and Youkioma.

The captain said he still had a chance to kill Youkioma, but Tewaquoptiwa said it was all over now. The captain said that that was not the place where the people should settle and he said that Tewaquoptiwa still had a chance to kill Youkioma if he wanted to. He also said that the next morning at sunrise he would give him a chance to do this. He would not let Tewaquoptiwa go home that night and all this time Tewaquoptiwa did not know that he was under arrest.

In the meantime, after nightfall, the captain sent soldiers up in the draw by Bakabi and twenty-five or thirty Navajos on police duty below Hotevilla Spring. In the meantime word was sent to Youkioma that he must be ready to be shot at sunrise the next morning. So about dawn the captain, Tewaquoptiwa, and two Hopi policemen, one Oraibi, and one Second Mesa policeman, and a guard came to Hotevilla and at the sand dune the captain gave automatics to Tewaquoptiwa and to his interpreter.

Youkioma was waiting for them on the top of a sand dune. They slowly moved up on the hostile chief who stood on the top of the sand dune, waiting for his time to come. He was all by himself, but behind the sand dune his men were hidden with all the weapons they could find. They intended to kill Tewaquoptiwa if Tewaquoptiwa killed Youkioma.

When the sun came up the captain told Tewaquoptiwa to walk up to Youkioma, but he refused to move. He was asked four times by the captain, but he was so scared that he could not talk. His jaw was shaking too fast. Since the Oraibi chief could not move the captain asked Youkioma to come over. So he came, not a bit frightened, and the captain asked him if he was ready to be shot. He said he was, for this was the sad day that would be his end. The captain asked Tewaquoptiwa if he was ready to do his duty that he was expected to do, but he would not speak. He was so weak from fright that he could hardly stand up. Then the captain asked Youkioma if he would want to take the gun away from his rival and do away with him, but Youkioma said no, that that was not his "theory". His theory was only that he would get his followers away from the old chief, to a better place. He said the Oraibi chief did not understand his "theory," and that he was all wrong. However, even if he was wrong and had always had in mind about doing away with him, he was willing to let him do it. He was willing to die for his people.

So the captain turned back to Tewaquoptiwa and asked him if he would do it now, since his rival had voluntarily given himself up and was willing to die for his people. The chief said that he would not do it because he said Youkioma must be right and that he himself had made a mistake in thinking of doing away with him. Then Tewaquoptiwa asked the captain what he would do with him if he had killed the old man (Youkioma).

The captain said that Tewaquoptiwa was mistaken in sending the people away like that and he answered that if it was not for this "theory" he would never have done it. Then the captain asked him where he got this "theory" and he said he got it all from his great-uncles. It had been handed down for a good many years and he was chosen to carry this out. The captain said he was sorry to say that his great-uncles must have been pretty mean to have made such a theory and to give it to him to carry it out; that he had been misled and he was not doing anything right for his people or for the government. So the captain told him that this was not only a mistake but a big crime that he had done, to send the people away without anything to eat. Again he asked him if he realized how bad the situation was—that the children were crying for something to eat. Well, the chief said he did realize it then, but it was too late. But the captain said it was not too late; that the houses the people had left were still full of corn and he warned him not to interfere with any men going to Oraibi for food. Tewaquoptiwa agreed to all of this and then he asked the captain if that was all for him but the captain said no. So right there he told him that he was under arrest and that he was going to be taken away some place to serve his term in prison. Tewaquoptiwa asked the captain if he really meant it and he said yes, he had to do it. The chief turned to the captain and asked for mercy and the captain said there was nothing he could do. Then the chief cried like a child and again he asked the captain if he could spend a few days with his people. The captain said that he did not allow his prisoners to spend time with their people but they had to stay around his camp.

The chief said if he was allowed to stay with his people he would show the captain all the different ceremonies that he could perform. He said he would show the captain his most beautiful dance which his people would dance for him. The captain saw he had a chance to see these beautiful dances, so he told the chief not to spend too much time getting the dance up as his time was limited. From then on Tewaquoptiwa got his people to practice a butterfly dance.

During this time the captain returned to Youkioma. He sent for the old man. Youkioma gathered his best men and went to see the captain. When he arrived the captain asked him if he was ready to surrender and send the children to school. The chief said he was not ready for that yet, because he was still expecting to go on to the chosen site for his new village. Again the captain asked him if he would send the children to school so that they would be well taken care of at school and then the others could go on, but Youkioma said no, that he was the father of all and he would leave none behind. The captain said that he must leave them behind if he did not surrender. The chief said that even if he had to serve another term in prison he would go on when he got out again, so the captain said he would send him back home to think it over. The chief agreed to think it over, but said he could not change his mind. When he got home that night and those that went with him broke the news to the people, that was all that they talked of that night. Some had the idea that he would surrender to the captain so as to relieve the trouble of the people.

Now in the next few days there was another division among the people.

After a few days Chief Youkioma was called again and all the men followed him to Kiakochomovi. The captain asked him again if he had changed his mind or decided to surrender. He said, "No." Then the captain asked all the men who came down with Youkioma if they were all with him and would they not surrender. All who were strong with the old chief were asked to step to his side. Before anybody had moved Kiwanimptiwa stepped up and said that he was ready to surrender and that there were some others that would follow him. The captain asked, "Who are they?" Chief Youkioma was put to one side and Chief Kiwanimptiwa on the other side, and the captain said, "Take your choice." Of course there was then a big argument. Some were very undecided because they did not know who was right, but most of them went over to Youkioma's side. After this was done the captain told them that all who went on Youkioma's side were under arrest and would be taken away. All that went on Kiwanimptiwa's side were to be sent back to try to make up with Tewaquoptiwa at Oraibi, so that they could return to their homes.

Youkioma's followers all stayed down at the camp and Kiwanimptiwa's followers went back to Hotevilla. When they came back, they told their families that they had shaken hands with the captain. The next day Kiwanimptiwa went back to Oraibi to see Tewaquoptiwa. When he got there he told the chief what had happened when he had visited the captain and the chief said that he would let them come back but he would like to see all the men who had shaken hands with the captain.

That same night these men went back to Oraibi to have a council with the chief. At this council the chief told them they could come back if they would be willing to send their children to school like the rest of the people and they said they would agree to this.

In a few days they came back to Oraibi with their families and shortly after that the Butterfly Dance took place. On that day all the soldiers were up in the village to see the dance.

The next day after the dance, the police and some soldiers went to Hotevilla to get the children of school age, to send them to Keams Canyon to the school, and on that same afternoon the army broke camp and left Oraibi with their prisoners, Youkioma and his men, and the children. When they arrived at Keams Canyon the captain asked the agent to look the prisoners over and point out the men who had made trouble for him before. On looking them over he picked out Chief Youkioma first. Next was Chief Tewahonganewa of Shipaulovi and all his followers.

So the two chiefs had something like fifteen men picked out with them. Besides these, eleven men were picked out to be sent to Carlysle School (1. Archie Quamala, 2. Glen Chestiwa, 3. Andrew Humiquoptiwa, 4. Joshua Humiyistiwa, 5. Washington Tala-umptiwa, 6. Louis Tiwanima, all from Shung-opovi; 7. William Strong, 8. Albert Tawaventiwa, 9. Quoits-hoeoma, 10. Arthur Ponyaquoptiwa, 11. Tewanimptiwa, from Hotevilla.)

The two chiefs, Youkioma and Tawahonganiwa, with their fifteen followers and the boys were taken on to Fort Wingate. The rest of the men (about one hundred) were left at Keams Canyon.

From Fort Wingate these prisoners were sent to Florence penitentiary. The other eleven men, who were all married, were sent to Carlysle School. Three of the boys, Archie, Andrew, and Louis, had left their wives at Shung-opovi when they went to Oraibi.

When the soldiers went away, Chief Tewaquoptiwa thought that the captain had forgotten him, but when the captain arrived at Fort Wingate he wrote to him and he had to go away, either to Riverside or Phoenix. This was a month after the others had left.

About this time, Tewaquoptiwa had insulted some of the women who came back from Hotevilla and of course Kiwanimptiwa could not stand for this, so he called together all his followers, men, women, and all, about fifteen or so families and when he got them together, he asked them how long this had been going on, and they said, ever since they had come back. They said that the chief had always said to them that if they wanted to stay in that village they had to do as the Oraibi people asked them to, whether they wanted to or not. After hearing all this from the women folk Kiwanimptiwa went and called Chief Tewaquoptiwa in and when he did bring him in he said that the women had told him what he had been doing. Tewaquoptiwa said it was not so, but the women stood right up and told him it was so and there was no use f or him to try to hide it. Then, of course, after that there was an argument. Finally, the chief told them that they did not have to stay there, but could go any place they wanted to—to Hotevilla or any place else.

They knew that after having left Hotevilla they could not go back there, so the next day, Kiwanimptiwa went out to look for a site. First he went to a spring, Meumeushva, below Hukovi. Then he came back upon the mesa and went to Bakabi. Finding that place with plenty of water and wood he decided to take his people there, so when he came back he told his people they were to move the next day.

The next morning all their burros were packed up with their stuff. (This was almost the middle of October.) When they got there, the Hotevilla people hearing of it, did not like it because after splitting away from them they were coming back to a place so near them.

Of course, this being the fall, the weather was getting cold and the best they could do was to find a little shelter along the edge of the cliff and a few of them were under the ledge. Of course in both places, Bakabi and Hotevilla, the people were busy trying to put up houses of some kind. In Hotevilla the women had to do all the work, for there were just a few old grandfathers left to help them.

Mr. Lemon, the agent, after hearing about this trouble again at Oraibi, came right out and sent Tewaquoptiwa to Riverside. They just keep him there and he did a little work. After sending him to Riverside School the agent went back to Hotevilla and picked out all the Shung-opovi families and sent them back to their homes.

Kiwanimptiwa thought he should have help from the government, since he had shaken hands with the captain and made friends with the white man, so he went to the agency to ask for help. When he got there he told the agent he would like him to see if he could help him out and the agent asked him in what way. The chief said he would like some lumber for doors and windows. Well, the agent thought it was rather wise of him to call on him for help, so he ordered some ready-made doors and windows. But these windows and doors did not come until the spring, about April. Of course, at both places, the people had a hard time during the cold weather. They had built little shelter places of stone with what cedar beams they could get, and they got through the winter pretty well and not many people died. The Hotevilla people had taken some of their beans from Oraibi and with burros they had dragged them over. The women went back and forth every day and carried their doors and their metates. The Oraibi people had taken all their string-beans and jerky.

The men at Keams Canyon were set free about April. They were let out in time to plant their crops. The men sent to Florence were kept there about a year and a half. Along with these men was one man they thought was a witch, Quoitsventiwa, and he would slip out of his cell (mysteriously) once in a while. Once he got out and ran away from the prison, but they caught him again, up in the mountains. While they were there, of course, their leaders—Youkioma and Tawahonganiwa,—always would refuse to answer whenever the warden or superintendent would ask them if they were ready to surrender and be sent back home. The others were quite young, and having left their families behind they wanted to go home, and so of course they were always having trouble among themselves.

Finally, the two chiefs surrendered and were sent home, but after they came home they had a feeling that they were not respected—especially those that came from Shung-opovi.

Everything went well for about a year at Hotevilla and Shung-opovi. Then the children came home from school in the summer. At Hotevilla houses had been built by this time. When the school opened in the fall, the people, would not let the children return. The policemen went out but returned without the children. Again the army was called in. One company arrived and went to Hotevilla, caught the children, and then went on to Shung-opovi. At Shung-opovi the hostile group ref used to send their children and hid them. After that the children of the hostile group were not allowed to go home in the summer.

From then on, everything went well. The old chief at Shipaulovi, Tawahonganiwa died at Shung-opovi about 1920, and his followers all mixed with the other people. When Tawahonganiwa became hostile Sikia-litstiwa became chief of Shipaulovi.

Later Youkioma was again arrested and taken to California because he refused to have the sheep dipped—he thought it was bad for the sheep and he thought the dipping caused the scab. He was arrested and sent to Keams Canyon. There were about fifteen men from Hotevilla, mostly sheep owners.

When his time came to be released, Mr. Daniels, the agent, called him into the office at Keams Canyon and asked him if he was ready to go back home.

The old chief said, "Yes, but I will never change my heart and the idea of making a friend of the white man. I am old now and I am not able to serve any more terms in prison. As far as my "theory" is concerned, I think that I have carried it out well for my great-uncles who gave me this theory to carry out. When I go back to my people I will ask them or my relatives if they will carry this on, but I think that they will not do as well as I have done, because they will be afraid. They will not be men enough to do it, but whoever does step in and take my place in prison I think will be Chief Tewaquoptiwa, because he will carry on and make trouble for you as he did for me, and if he ever does serve a prison term, I wish to see if he is as brave as I am and will stand as much as I have stood to this day. So I am through. From now on I hope to live in peace and die in peace." He did.

HOW THE CROW CLAN BECAME ALSO THE KACHINA CLAN

ORIGINALLY, the home of the Crow Clan was somewhere in the forest at the foot of the San Francisco Peaks. There were seven families and they were a dark people. Now, often in the night they would hear something moving about far away in the woods, making a strange noise and they wondered who it was. The leader of the village wanted to find out about this strange sound, for he knew that no animal made that kind of a sound, like a deep growling (for in those days this person wore a bell made out of mountain sheep horn, which rattled and could be heard a long distance).

So finally the Chief said he would send out a few boys who were good runners, to spy around and see who this person could be. And so one night he did send out seven of them into the forest. They wandered around and finally, away in the distance, they heard the strange noise, far up at the top of the peaks, coming down from point to point and they were frightened. The noise came on, passed them and came down on the flat and traveled on toward the village. The boys saw that it was someone, but they feared that it might be a man of great power who would kill them and they did not try to catch him.

So this man, or whoever it was, came close to the village again and finally went away up the mountain. Now someone said to the Chief that this person, whoever he was, that came from the peaks must surely live up there, so that it would be well for him to hold the ceremony of the "Paho making." So he called the High Priest and had him make prayer offerings.

After thinking it over the Chief decided to send one of his nephews with the offerings so that. if he found anyone on the peaks and harm should come to the youth, as he was a relative, there would be no trouble.

So he called his nephew and gave him the pahos and told him to go up the mountain and give the pahos to anyone that he might find there. Now they got the youth ready next morning and painted him in reddish clay and tied a prayer plume on his head. Every man who had made a prayer offering went and placed it on a white buckskin and after they were all delivered there, they wrapped them up nicely and gave them to the youth together with a sack of sacred corn meal. Before the boy started, the Chief told him that if there were supernatural beings up there, to tell them that the Chief had sent them a message. He would like to ask if they were gods or other spirits and if they were, he would like to communicate with them. If they were spirits, then the people would worship them and accept their advice, because he knows himself, who must have control of the weather.

So the youth started out, but before he commenced to ascend he came upon the old Spider Woman. The Spider Woman spoke to the youth, but he could not see her anywhere, so she peeped a little more out of her hole and she said to him, "Come in."

But the youth looked down and said sadly, "How can I, the hole is too small." So she said, "Stick in your foot and wriggle it around a little." He did as she told him and the hole grew larger and he went down into her pithouse.

The wise old Spider Woman said to the youth, "My poor boy, I am sorry for you. You have been sent up there on a difficult journey and I am afraid you are going to have a very hard time. You will have to do the best you can. There are four dangerous places that you must pass, guarded by 'terrible beings.' I will give you a charm which will make these creatures harmless and you can pass in safety." She handed him the root of a plant and told him how to use it. Whenever he came up one of these guards (it might be a mountain lion, a bear, or a terrible snake) the Spider Woman charged him to chew the magic root and spray it out upon the creature and he would immediately become mild and gentle. Then the old woman gave him a little fluffy feather and directed him how to use it, and told him which way to go.

So the youth started out and traveled upward about three quarters of the way when he discerned a very faint trail and it was difficult to follow. All at once he thought of the little feather that the old Spider Woman had given him and how she had told him that it would go before him and show the way. So the youth took out his feather and let it go and it rose in the air and flew along before him, very slowly, so that he could easily follow it.

No sooner had he started than he came to the first guard. A great mountain lion lay across his way and when he saw the boy he growled in his throat and crouched ready to spring upon him. The youth was frightened but he remembered the old Spider Woman's words and he quickly chewed the magic root and sprayed it out upon the angry lion and at once the beast lay down and it seemed as if he had never noticed the boy.

Now all this time, the little feather danced along ahead of the youth and presently they came to the second guard, a giant grizzly bear. Of course you know, this animal is very fierce and the boy was even more afraid than he had been of the mountain lion, but he quickly chewed more of the magic medicine and sprayed it out over the bear and at once he became quiet and the youth passed on.

Finally, with the feather going before he reached the top of the mountains and there he found a kiva. This kiva was guarded by two snakes, a great rattler, and a small rattler more deadly than the first. When they saw him approaching they coiled ready to strike and the boy stopped a long way off and felt very much discouraged and he forgot about his magic medicine. But the little feather had gone on ahead and stopped over the two snakes on top of the kiva. Now the snakes looked at the little feather and then at the youth and they thought that the feather was the boy's spirit. Then the youth remembered his charm and sprayed the snakes and they quieted down, uncoiled and crawled away from the entrance to the kiva.

The feather entered the kiva and the youth followed. One lone man was sitting by the fire-place and he did not notice the youth. So the boy stood by the ladder and waited and presently the man saw him and asked him to be seated. The youth had a pipe which he filled with tobacco, lit it at the fire and passed it to the old man, who took four puffs and all the tobacco was used up; but the odor of the tobacco filled the room. Now he asked the youth where he had come from and who had sent him and the youth said that his uncle, the Chief, had sent him to find out who it was that visited the village and returned to the peaks each night.

The old man said, "I know who you mean, he is my scout. He is away today, but he will soon come home. At any rate, I am the head man here."

So the boy said, "If you are the head man here, I have brought you the prayer offerings the Chief and High Priest and the other head men have made for you."

Well, the old man said that he was very glad that the offerings were made for him, because his people prized them very highly and he took the bundle and opened it and spread the plaques with the pahos on them out in front of him in the middle of the kiva. Then he said to the youth, "Watch me closely and see what I do. Do you see this paho? It was made by a man with a bad heart—I will cast it behind the ladder. But the maker of this paho has a good heart—I will place this in front of the ladder. Now I will call my people and pass these offerings around to them."

So he opened the north, west, south, and east doors of the kiva and as he did this, many people came in and the youth saw that this was a large under-ground dwelling with only one opening through the kiva to the upper world. The youth was surprised to find that, as the head man handed around the pahos, there were certain ones for certain people and that there were just enough for every one.

Finally, the head man asked the youth why his people down there had sent the offerings and what it was they wanted. Well, the boy said that his people wanted to find out who it was that lived up there and if they might be supernatural beings. And they answered him and said that they were the Kachinas, and being Kachinas they had control of the weather, like the rain and the storms.

Now the Kachinas said that they would teach the youth the Kachina dances so that he could show his people down below how to hold Kachina dances and make them a part of their religion.

So the youth was asked to stay for four days and during those four days and four nights he was shown the different dances and he was asked to study them so that he could paint the faces on the ceremonial masks when he returned. So the old man dressed the youth in full costume and they danced to the north, west, south, and east.

Then the youth, who had heard about the Germ God (Muiaingwa) now recognized the old man as the Germ God himself. Then the Germ God told the youth that if he would stay with them for awhile he would teach him how to make masks out of a white material and he told him that he must also learn how to make the costumes and belts and how to prepare the paint. The Germ God said that the youth must also learn their songs and then he said, "This ceremony will surely bring rain if you do as we do up here."

Now after he had learned these dances and memorized the painting and the songs and all that was necessary, he was sent back to his home. Before he left the kiva, he was told that he and his relatives would now be a Kachina Clan. Well, the youth said that they were already the Crow Clan, but the head man said that they had a Crow Kachina and told the boy to tell his uncle, the

Chief, that they must make pahos to the Kachinas whenever they held a dance.

When they had told him all this he was sent back. While he was gone his people had been uneasy for four days, for they knew the forest was full of wild animals. When he returned, they were glad.

The youth went to the kiva and the Chief was waiting for him there. The Crier was sent out to call the people to come to the kiva and when the men gathered in the kiva the youth told them how he had been taught the songs and the painting of the masks and how the Kachinas had control of the rain and wished the people to make prayer offerings for them whenever they prayed for rain and held a Kachina dance.

And so the Crow and Kachina Clans brought these dances to the Hopi.

THE LEGEND OF PALOTQUOPI

MANY years ago when the Hopis were living down at Palotquopi they were very progressive and prosperous, on account of having water, and having an irrigating system from the river which flows through that country. There they had taxation by means of doing some donation work on the canals and ditches at certain times of the year. They did not have so many ceremonies then and their most sacred one was Laconti (Basket Dance). In this dance baskets were used, like the ones of Second Mesa today. This ceremony always took place late in the fall and it had always brought them rain and heavy snow up in the mountains. And also their Jejellti (social dances) were not many, the most joyous one was the Butterfly Dance. Being prosperous in their way of living everything was plenty, and why shouldn't they be happy and amuse themselves in some way? So, from one of the kivas, they held a Butterfly Dance with which the spectators were very much pleased. Everybody was talking about it, so the dancers again put it on for two more days, then they thought they would pass it on to the next kiva. So they asked the men of the other kiva to carry on the same dance, and when they had danced, these men passed it on to the next kiva, and so it went around like that until it came back to the kiva from where it was started. In this kind of a dance only the young maidens are supposed to dance, but by this time some of the young married women were taking part and instead of putting it on during the day time in the plaza, they were dancing in the kiva at nights, so they were having a great time of their lives, and it went on from bad to worse. Nobody cared who was whose wife or husband, and finally they got the wife of their chief. In those days the chief or any high priest was not supposed to take part in social dances or was not to be seen in the kiva with the rest of the people. As it was their general rule that they must have patience, and above all must bear in mind peace, and think and pray for prosperity in the years to come, for they knew that the people of any race must have good supplies of food and water to keep their bodies in strong physical condition to defend themselves against an enemy attack. They were good fathers and watched over their people carefully. They were patient and neither heard nor spoke evil. No matter what the people would do or how bad they might be, they were always comforted. But as this dancing went on, it was carried too far and all the rest of the priests had gone crazy except Chief Tawayistiwa, himself. This chief they had, was quite a young man; he had only two small children, and these babies being neglected they would cry at night when they woke up, so the father would take them to the kiva to get the mother to nurse the younger one. When they were quieted down the father would take them back to bed again. On these trips to the kiva at night his wife would sometimes ask him to come down into the kiva and look on while they danced, and of course knowing the law and his duty he always had refused. All these things got so heavy on him that he could bear it no longer, so one evening he went and called on his nephew, Siwiyistiwa, who had grown up to be a good strong young man. While this madness was with the people, men and women of mature age had pleaded with their sons and daughters, telling them of the wrong and crime that they were doing against their father, the chief, and themselves. But it was of no use, it only caused the younger people to lose respect for them, and then the old people were ill-treated, spit upon and fed on the leftovers, which were not very much, for the house duties were neglected by the young women. All this was unbearable for the aged people and for the Chief. So he called at the house of his nephew. He was welcome and seated himself by the fireplace. Siwiyistiwa got up from his seat and handed his uncle a bag of tobacco which hung on the wall near by, and this the uncle smoked. After finishing his smoking, the youth asked him what he had come for.

"Yes," said Tawayistiwa, "after long wanderings in my mind about our children (people) it seems like I am forced to come and have to depend on you to 'sacrifice' yourself, not for the good of any one, but for all—everybody here in my town."

"Yes, you certainly have a lot of patience," said the youth, "to hold out this way, what with all I have seen and know of your wife. I did not want to tell you because I did not wish to be the cause of the weight of your wrath. Because of the sympathy that I have for you I am willing to do what you have come to ask of me."

"I thank you, my nephew," said the Chief. "Thank you. First of all I would like to know if you are strong on your running."

"Yes," said Siwiyistiwa, "I am quite strong."

"All right," said the Chief. "Of course you may be, but I still want you to gain some more strength and speed. So from tomorrow on, you will start to do your running to the foot of the mountain ridge and back. That is quite a distance away, so the best way to time yourself would be by the rising of the sun. For a few mornings the sun will rise before you get back here, but if you are gaining by and by you will get back here away before sunrise, so be sure to get up at the same time in the mornings and be off. I will call again in a few days and will tell you what we will do next."

After the Chief had gone Siwiyistiwa was rather a little worried, but of course, with the Hopi in those days the uncle was over the nephews and nieces. Whenever he asked anything of them it had to be done. While the boy was preparing himself, he didn't know for what, his uncle too was getting things ready for him. The youth was gaining strength and speed and was very light on his feet and he was getting back to the village away before the sun would come up over the horizon. Then Tawayistiwa again went to see his nephew and when he got there he found the youth was waiting for him.

"Come right in and have a seat," said his nephew, getting up and handing him a bag of tobacco as usual. After smoking a pipe he said to the boy, "Again I am here, hoping to find you with more strength and speed."

"Yes," said his nephew, "I have gained some."

"Very well," said his uncle, "I have everything ready for you, so tonight you can come over to my house and there I will tell what to do. But be sure to come after everybody goes to the kiva."

Late that night Siwiyistiwa went to his uncle's house. Upon entering, the Chief took him away into the back room. There they sat down and there his uncle smoked his pipe solemnly over the pahos which he had prepared. Then he said, "Here I have these things ready for you and tomorrow morning early you will take these pahos out with you toward the same direction you have been going and up over the mountain ridge. On the other side is an open range. There you will come upon a herd of deer. Look them over carefully, then make your selection of a young buck with a pair of good weapons (horns), but wait for the sun to appear. Now watch very closely and just as it peeps over the horizon run into the herd. It is those weapons that you are going to get for me, so be sure to keep after your selected buck until you run him down, then after cutting off his two front horns you will deliver to him these pahos that I have here made ready for him, and also my message."

The next morning Siwiyistiwa went out to where he was directed and when he got there he went over the mountains and there in the open he saw a herd of deer. He looked them over very carefully while he was waiting for the sun to rise and just as the sun peeped over the horizon he ran into them and how they made the dust fly! But he kept after them along the side of the mountain range so as to keep them away from the rocky hills. The deer kept falling away one by one, until at last his selected buck was left alone. Now finally this deer gave out and lay down. The boy jumped on him quickly and took hold of his horns and turned his head over. But alas, the deer cried, "Mercy me, have a heart," in plain Hopi, which was of course a very astonishing thing to the youth and he held his breath for a moment. Then he said to the deer, "I am not going to hurt you, I am not going to kill you, I only want your horns, your weapons. My uncle, Tawayistiwa, would like to have them, so he has sent me out here to get them but I don't know why."

"Mercy be upon us!" said the deer. "Has he lost his mind and forgot his 'theory' and law, and is he angry with us all, and will he use my weapons to destroy his town?" Then he sank down in sorrow and in sympathy for all that were ignorant of the coming calamity. Shedding quite a few drops of tears, he then looked up and said, "Take my weapons, but please do not use your knife, because you will hurt me. Just give them a little twist and they will slip off and another pair will grow out again soon."

"Thank you," said the youth as he took off the horns. Then he brought forth his bundle and said to the deer, "Here, I have some pahos which my uncle, Chief Tawayistiwa, has made and sent them to you, hoping to make you all happy. He also said that all you people (game) living down here in the lower country must get to moving and drift over to the higher mountains to the northeast, that you may be saved, so take these pahos to your people and tell them what the Chief has said about moving."

The deer got up and went away with the bundle of pahos which he distributed among his people and told them about the Chief's message, which of course, was a great grief to them all.

The youth went on home taking the two horns which he had taken from the young buck. When he got home Tawayistiwa was waiting for him and as he entered the doorway, "Thanks," said the Chief. "Thanks that you have come already. I did not quite expect you so soon, but you have proved yourself strong and swift. All right, have a seat." As the youth seated himself the Chief got out his bag of tobacco and pipe and then he said to his nephew, "If you have anything that you have brought me you may lay it here before me that I may give it a welcome smoke." So the boy laid the two horns down on a plaque on the floor before the Chief. He was very much gratified with the little horns as though they were for some benefaction of his people. After smoking his pipe, the Chief asked Siwiyistiwa about his trip and the boy told him all about it.

After hearing his nephew's story of his trip, Tawayistiwa said, "You have done well, but there is some more to be done and I have everything ready, so tonight when you come again I will tell you what you will do next."

Late that evening the boy went back to his uncle, and when he got there his uncle was waiting for him. As he entered the house he was welcomed. The Chief was already smoking and the boy seated himself by his uncle. "The weight of all this worry is getting heavier every day as I am preparing these things and I am sad to think that here I am working only for the punishment of my children (people) but this will be the only way out of the trouble and it is necessary to sacrifice you." As he said this he could not help but cry. Tawayistiwa had made masks for him, each one different—Kachina, Yaponcha, Masauwu, and one portion was of fat meat. "Tonight you will wear these masks, one upon another, and carry these weapons of the deer, and you will go the same direction where you have been going for your running, up the mountain range where there is some wood. Build your fire there and when you get enough live coals, take one and put it in the mouth of the top mask and blow on it and this will give the look of having eyes of fire and your fire will be seen from the pueblo. Then come running and when you get here, come through the small south alley and run up the ladder to the top floor of this house. Up there you will find corn in metates. Start grinding for a few moments and then go down again and out the same way. If the men in the kiva be brave and big-hearted they will come out and try to catch you.

With these instructions Siwiyistiwa was dressed up in a dreadful and fearful costume and he went out to where he was directed. He built a fire and the people seeing it from the village wondered who or what it was having a big bonfire, and by the reflected firelight the people could see, even at that distance, something standing in the glow.

The fire went down lower and lower and finally it died out. Then they saw a light coming toward the town, coming closer and closer. When it came up they saw that this terrible being had eyes of fire and those who saw him fell with fright in their doorways or wherever they happened to be. He entered through the alley into the plaza and went to the Chief's house, where he ascended to the top floor and could be heard grinding corn. Then down he came and went out again toward the direction he had come from. Now it happened that there was a little boy who was just thought to be an outcast and he was with some other boys who were looking down at the dance from the kiva top. This boy was not at all frightened and saw everything. He called down into the kiva to the dancers and told them that some dreadful ghost had come, but everybody called him a liar and would not believe him.

This boy, whose name was Kochoilaftiyo (Poker Boy) was just a poor boy and was living with his old grandmother. Regardless of what Kochoilaftiyo had told the people in the kiva about the ghost, the dancing went on with full force until morning. But that day, everybody was telling about this terrible ghost and so the young men declared that they could catch the ghost that night.

After dark the young men placed themselves in many hiding places from where they might leap out at the ghost. But when he came, they all fell down with fright and after coming to they ran for their lives. Kochoilaftiyo was watching the dance from the kiva top, wrapped up in his little mouse skin robe and he was not a bit scared. The young men tried for two nights, but alas, the creature was so frightful that he could not be caught.

The next day the little boy told his grandmother about the ghost. "Grandma," Kochoilaftiyo said, "for three nights some frightful ghost has been coming to the village and the young men have tried to catch him but all have failed."

"It is time," said the old lady, "that we get our warning because of what has been going on. This is a warning of punishment or some calamity which will fall upon us all and it will be something that no one can escape."

"Tonight," said the boy, "they will lay for him again and I would like to be with them. If he is caught I would like to see what he is. It must be something more than man who can handle this thing with magic or witchcraft power."

"So go," said the grandmother, "and get me a sumac branch." Kochoilaftiyo obeyed his grandma and went out after a little branch. When he came back with it the old woman brought out from the back room her materials of feathers and cotton yarns of which she made two prayer plumes and put them on this sumac twig and with her little pipe she smoked her earnest prayer over her offering to the gods. "Take this, my son," she said to the boy, "to the Masauwu shrine and set it therein and pray for the best, but before you leave look around carefully and if you find there Masauwu's digging stick, pick it up and replace it with this one. This is the exact duplicate of it." As she said this she handed him an old digging stick pretty well weathered. Kochoilaftiyo took the stick and the prayer offering to the shrine. There he placed the pahos, looked around carefully, and seeing the stick he picked it up and replaced it with his grandmother's. Then he came back. The grandmother was very thankful for the stick. "This stick of Masauwu's is a wand of power and with it you might be able to knock down that ghost. So, my dear child," said the old woman, "it may be best that you station yourself in the narrow alley through which he comes and goes."

That evening after dark Kochoilaftiyo, instead of going to the kiva top to look on the dance, went into the alley to wait for the ghost. As he was sitting there in the dark someone came and the boy looked and alas, there was Masauwu himself, standing before him and Kochoilaftiyo was stunned with fright for a moment and could not speak. "You certainly did a wise thing," said Masauwu to the boy, "by taking my stick, but here is something that will hide you and keep you from being seen," and he handed him four grass brush bristles and advised him what to do. Kochoilaftiyo was very thankful and he sat down with the bristles in one hand, the stick in the other, and waited for his chance on the ghost. Now; some of the strong young men had also stationed themselves outside the village to await the coming of the ghost. At the same time, the dancing was still going on in the kiva. Toward midnight the ghost was seen coming and all the supposed brave-hearted fell down with fright, but Kochoilaftiyo was still himself. When the ghost passed him he got up and waited for his return and got ready for the attack. The ghost jumped off the house, ran into the alley, and with all his might Kochoilaftiyo struck him with Masauwu's stick and knocked him down. As he fell, the boy was on top of him and he held his breath for he was half scared then. Finally he asked, "Who are you?"

"It is I," said the ghost, "but don't ask me more, but take me into the kiva. In there you will see who I am."

As they walked over to the kiva the dancing was on with full force, and when they got on top Kochoilaftiyo called in and he was not heard on account of the beating of the drum and again he called at the very top of his voice. This time he was heard, so he said, "Be courteous to this guest who is my companion for I am not alone." Hearing Kochoilaftiyo's voice, the whole kiva became silent and all held their breath. Finally a voice called out, "Come in. Come right in."

The ghost started down the ladder first with Kochoilaftiyo following him, and the people in the kiva were all looking up to see what was coming in. When the ghost exposed himself to the firelight the people were stricken with fright and fell to the floor. One by one, when they came to, they crawled out of the kiva. Only a few old men were left and the ghost and Kochoilaftiyo seated themselves in front of the firelight. Seeing this frightful creature the old men hung their heads and were silent.

Finally, one of them spoke and said, "For all our conduct of crime it is already too late and we must suffer and who knows what will become of us. Perhaps we may learn from this man, whoever he is, but we can do nothing. Call our father, the Chief," and at this request Kochoilaftiyo went out and called the Chief. He pretended to be very much surprised at being called away in the night, but he took his bag of tobacco and his pipe and went to the kiva with the boy. Coming, he seated himself on the left side of Kochoilaftiyo and before anyone else, he lit his pipe of tobacco and started smoking. Having taken four puffs of smoke out of his pipe he passed it on to the rest of the old men. The pipe went around and was finished up, and then the chief spoke and said, "My dear fellowmen, I wondered why I was called at this time of the night, but I see that you have someone with you."

"Yes," said one of the old men, "this ghost has been coming for the last three nights and this being his fourth night he is caught. He has been going up to your house to the top floor. Therefore, perhaps you might explain to us the meaning of all this. Though we know that we have done wrong against you, we are wondering now if this might not mean more than just to stop this dancing, and worry is upon us now."

"Of all this I do not know," said the chief, "and also the meaning of it I cannot explain. So without any further questions take the masks off the man that we may see who he is." Kochoilaftiyo was asked to take the masks off and as he came to the piece of fat meat the Chief said to put it aside as it is food that the men in the kiva may cook and eat. As the last mask was taken off they saw that he was the Chief's nephew, Siwiyistiwa, his only nephew, and alas he hung his head and wept.

"Being your own nephew," said the kiva chief (Kiva mongwi), "take him and do what you want with him."

"No," said the Chief, "him I deliver unto you."

Said the kiva chief, "You being our chief, we cannot do otherwise from your wishes, so we demand your advice."

"If you do," said the Chief, "I advise you to bury him alive in the plaza in front of the shrine, with all his masks, before the day comes. But be sure and make a good job of it that he may not escape."

At this command Kochoilaftiyo went out and dug a hole deep enough that Siwiyistiwa's head would be covered under ground when he was sitting down. When he had done this he went back to the kiva and brought Siwiyistiwa out to the plaza and buried him, but before he had him all covered up Siwiyistiwa asked him to come there for four mornings and to take a look for signs of the approaching disaster.

That night the whole town was weary and the old men and women of good mind were stricken with fear. The next morning Kochoilaftiyo went to look at the grave, and behold, there was Siwiyistiwa's hand sticking up out of the grave with four fingers open, which meant that something would happen in four days. The second morning he went again and saw that there were three fingers up and one finger down or closed. Now every morning one more finger would be closed down, until on the fourth morning all the fingers had been closed and his whole hand had disappeared under the ground. The day was gloomy. Clouds were gathering in the skies overhead and around the grave the earth was all wet and boggy. Toward noon it began to rain, coming down heavier and heavier, and then out of the grave a great water serpent of enormous size appeared and stood swaying back and forth and also, at every corner of the plaza others appeared but they were not quite of the size of the one at the shrine, who had come up out of the grave. Now water came shooting up out of the corners of the plaza where these serpents stood swaying, and soon there was water everywhere. The rain kept up and the waters were raising higher and higher. Now the people began to move to the higher ground, taking what they could in the way of food and bedding, and there was much suffering and fear, and all this continued for four days. The only thing they could do was to look at their village standing in the midst of the water, where the great serpent was still swaying back and forth. Of course, the people were in great trouble and hated to leave their homes but still this serpent was so fearful and they wondered if it ever would go away. With weary thoughts of sadness the men set to work making their prayer offerings of many pahos, and when this was done the Chief asked of the people who would be willing to sacrifice their children, because they must make all this offering to the Great Serpent and ask him to make peace. Now who would part with beloved children? There was a great hesitation among the people, but being the request of the Chief a boy and a girl of six years of age were chosen who were, of course, of clean hearts and innocent. These two were given a tray of pahos and told to walk out into the water toward the great serpent while the people watched with sadness and tears in their eyes. When they had reached this monster he sprang up and coiled himself around the two children and sank with them into the water, which was of course a very terrible sight to the people watching from the hills.

Now everybody was very much discouraged, and though they hated to leave their homes and property they finally gave up all hope and decided to leave the country, but before starting they called a council to select their new chief or leader, because at this time the Chief considered himself guilty of the disaster and no longer worthy to lead his people and the people too felt the same way, but because of the wrong they had done no one dared to say anything. So finally the Chief himself asked the boy, Kochoilaftiyo, to be the chief and as he had been just an outcast, but had done a brave act, he was now looked upon as more than just a human being, on account of his wise Spider grandmother.

"I pray you," said Kochoilaftiyo, "I am not worthy to lead you. I am only a Kocholabi (fire poker) and do not consider myself good enough to take your authority, to be your chief and leader."

"It is not who you are, or what you are that I am considering. It is because of your innocence and the simplicity of your heart that I wish you to be our chief from now on."

"Well," said Kochoilaftiyo, "will you and the people ever forsake me?"

"No," said the Chief, "your wishes and footsteps will be our path and here with my tiponi you shall lead our people."

"I shall not take yours," said Kochoilaftiyo, "I and my grandmother have our own in which we believe and trust and it is without stains of evil. Therefore, we shall take no other in its place. So you shall keep yours. Your kind request and offer of your highness and royalty unto us, we shall not accept, because we will always be looked upon as who we are and what we are and always will be considered as such and no other but that. Why not ask your brother, Tawahongva? I think it is best that your clan should keep this royalty and continue as our chiefs and leaders. As it is today, on this very day we all feel guilty and not worthy to be your children (people) so it is for you and your clan to consider whether you will have mercy and forgive us. We are willing to follow you again. Therefore, I, Kochoilaftiyo, demand for the people that this man, Tawahongva, your brother, be our chief and leader from this day on, as we feel that it is not right for any other clan to take the royalty away from your clan."

"Very well," said Tawayistiwa, "I think you for your great and earnest consideration for my clan, and so your demand for Tawahongva, my brother, to be our chief, is fulfilled." After these last words, Tawayistiwa picked up his tiponi and handing it to his brother, Tawahongva, declared him chief and leader of the people.

When this was done, the people were somewhat relieved of their weariness. Tawahongva set to work and made his pahos or prayer plumes. With these and his sacred corn meal he drew his line or path over which the people were to journey toward the northeastward.

Now, with all this worry and grief two parents had forgotten their children, a brother and sister. These two little children had been sleeping and wakened up while the water was still high. They cried for their mother and father and not only that they were hungry too. So they got up and searched about for something to eat, and finally they found some piki which they ate. By this time the water had gone down a good deal so the two children came down off their house and went around into the plaza and alas! there they saw the great serpent swaying back and forth and they were very much frightened. They stood still for awhile, looking at the monster in great fear, and then suddenly the serpent spoke to them, saying, "Come, be not afraid, I am not going to hurt you. It is sad to see that you two children have been left behind, so be not afraid and come." The serpent was being very sympathetic in asking the children to come, so finally they came up to him. "Please, don't be afraid of me. I am Siwiyistiwa and I am not going to hurt you. I called you here to me to tell you where your parents and the rest of the people have gone. They left here many, many days ago, going toward the northeast, heading for a place called

Situqui (Flower Butte) and it is best for you to follow them. You cannot live here because very soon there will not be anything more to eat. If you ever catch up with your people it is likely that you will not recognize your father and mother, so I will tell you their names. Your father's name is Koyoungnu, and your mother's is Sackmunima, and they too will not recognize you and they will ask you your names, so young man, you are Tiwahongva and you, his sister, you are Tawiayisnima, so above all remember your parents' names and your own. Now, you go up over there to the northeast corner house of this plaza and climb the ladders to the very top floor. Up in there you will find some big birds sitting upon the shelves. You must bring them out and let them fly toward the same direction that your people have gone. The feathers of those birds will be used for making pahos of all kinds by your people."

The two children went up to the house as they were directed, and to their surprise they found some odd looking birds with no feathers on their heads, and the ends of their tail feathers were still covered with the foam from the water which had turned them white, and away over in one corner there sat still another bird looking somewhat the same as the others, but the ends of his tail feathers were not white. After letting these birds down from their roosts they spoke to the children, saying, "We all thank you, Tiwahongva and Tawiayisnima, for we are the innocent elderly people. We could not swim and so here we had turned into birds and we are now the turkeys, and from now on our feathers will be helpful to your people for making prayer offerings to the gods."

"And I am the buzzard," said the other strange bird, and with my feathers, after all the sacred ceremonies the members will be 'discharmed' and they will also be used for 'discharming' the sick and evil among all the people. And again we all thank you for letting us down and out, so here we go, and good-bye." As they flew away the buzzard went up and circled around overhead four times to "discharm" the ruined town, then he followed the rest of the birds away toward the northeast. After the birds were gone Tiwahongva and his sister went back to Siwiyistiwa, the serpent, for some more instructions.

"Now," he said to them, "you go up to the west corner and up at the very top floor you will find some sweet corn meal and some piki and also a small robe and gourd to carry your water in. Bundle all that up in the little robe and come back here to me." So they went up there and got what was there.

When they came back again, the serpent said to them, "Now you are ready to go and if you catch up with your people tell them that I, Siwiyistiwa, am now a supernatural being and have power and will do anything for the people in the way of prosperity—I can send them rain and in fact, anything like that will be yours for the asking, so tell them to make pahos for me and set them out anywhere toward this direction, but remember, they must call me by name at the very top of their voices that I may hear and know. Now, like this, 'Siwiyistiwa, here I have made pahos for you. We know and remember your message of promise which was sent to us by Tiwahongva and Tawiayisnima, so please fulfill now your promise of sending us rain for the benefit of our crops and the people, and so forth.' Then the pahos and the message will always be received. Now, I warn you not to look back till you get away over on the other side of the hill. If you do, something might happen to you, so be sure to remember not to look back. Farewell. Take good care of your sister." Tiwahongva and his sister than started out on their long journey and they didn't know where they were going but they were traveling on their way. Being so young, it was hard for them to travel, especially for the little sister, so Tiwahongva would carry her on his back awhile and then let her down again and they would go on like that all day. It was still daylight in the evening when they decided to make camp and were just about opening their bundle of lunch when they heard a loud roaring noise overhead and they were very much frightened and wondered what it could be. Tiwahongva held his sister tightly to his breast, and behold, someone had descended from the heavens all clothed in a glittering costume of ice that sparkled like silver and his head and face shone like a star. He spoke to them and said, "Do not fear, I am So-tukeu-nangwi, the heavenly God and because of the sympathy I have for you I have come to help you, so come get on this shield (Yo-vota) of mine and let us be on the way." When they had climbed onto the shield, up they went into the heavens. The two children had their eyes closed all the way up, until they got there and when they opened their eyes they could see for many miles and everything was grand.

"Now," said So-tukeu-nangwi, "I know you are tired and hungry, so you may now eat," and he cut up a nice ripe muskmelon and set it before them and they ate very delightedly.

When the darkness had covered the earth again this God said to them, "Look to the far north and you will see firelight. There is where your people are now. It does not look so very far away, but that is many, many days journey and you are too young and do not know that this is a big undertaking for you. For this reason, I went to get you and brought you up here, because I know you are too young, but you must understand me and I know you will. I am the wisdom and knowledge and above all else you must have faith in me—faith and trust, honesty and truth. Without faith you shall know nothing. If you have faith your prayers for your people will always be answered, and from now on my teachings will come to you in dreams and there will be more and more as you grow older."

The next morning So-tukeu-nangwi had made everything ready for them to take along upon their journey—seeds of all kinds for the coming season. Said he, "When the spring comes, the warm weather, these seeds you will broadcast outside around the village and they will grow and bear fruit that everybody may eat and they may save the seeds for their own use. Be like the others, play like the other children, but always together. When you catch up and get to your people they will not know you. They have already given you up and have forgotten all about you. Look carefully among them. Your father has a mole under his eye on the right side of his face and your mother has a bunch of gray hair in front on the left side of her head. By these marks you will recognize your own father and mother and you will run to them. These seeds and other things which I have placed in this bundle of your robe must never be handled by anyone, especially this little 'tiponi' (emblem) which needs your particular care. It is this 'tiponi' that you will always set up when you perform my ceremony for the benefit of your people. Now let us be on the way. I will take you close up to your people, that you may camp just for one night, then in the morning after all the meal is over you will be there. They have got their town built now, so you will go straight into the plaza."

The two children had a grand ride on Yovota (shield) and were landed just about a quarter of a day's trip from the town. So-tukeu-nangwi then said, "Farewell" to them and went back up into the heavens.

The next day Tiwahongva and his sister walked into the plaza of the new town. There they stopped and the people stared at them and wondered who they were and where they had come from, so they notified the crier to call out and let the people know, so that they would come to the plaza to see that somebody had come. When the people came, they surrounded them.

Then Chief Tawahongva came forward with a heavy heart of sympathy, "Now, you my people," he said, "is there anyone here that remembers or could recognize these children and tell us who they are and whom they belong to? Is there any parent here that had forgotten or had given them up as dead at the time of the flood, back down at Palotquopi. They must belong to somebody. Who shall claim them? If nobody will, I will now leave it up to them and see if they, themselves, remember and can recognize their own father and mother. Now look carefully among us and see if you know anyone or remember anybody." So the brother and sister looked for the mole on the faces of the men and for the gray hair on the women, by which they were to detect their parents, and all at once they recognized them and with tears in their eyes they ran up to their parents, saying, "You are my father and you are my mother. We are your son and daughter. My name is Tiwahongva and mine is Tawiayisnima."

"My dear children!" cried their parents with tears and they caught hold of them and held them close to their breasts, which of course struck the hearts of all the people and the whole town cried for joy. They were taken to the home of their parents with their little bundle of sacred things and of this they warned them that they must never touch it or open it. To be sure of safe keeping they took it away into the back room and hung it up in the corner.

Thereafter they lived very happily with their parents and the rest of the people. Day after day the wisdom and knowledge was coming to them clearer and clearer so that when the spring came and the days got warmer they did everything that So-tukeu-nangwi had told them to do. They broadcast the seeds and on them it rained and rained. Then the sun came out and shown brightly on them and heated them and caused them to germinate, and in a few days the little plants sprang up. While these Nasiwum (brother and sister) would play around with the rest of the children they were always telling them not to pull up the plants for they would bear fruit for the people. And every few days it would rain, which kept the plants growing quite fast and all about the town it was all green. Soon the people were noticing the blossoms beginning to bloom on these plants of many kinds and having all these fruitful plants around them they were very happy and when these were ripe and mature everything was plentiful and the people gathered them all in. They lived there happily for a number of years but as they were really heading for Situqui they decided to move on, and so again they were on the long journey and ahead of them they would always send their scouts—men who were good runners and whose duty it was to look for new sites. On their travels they were protected because So-tukeu-nangwi was with them. This time their new location was at Nuvaquayotaka (Chavez Pass—a butte with snow belt on). Here again they lived very prosperously. But knowing that this was not to be their destination they moved on up to Homolovi (east bank of the Little Colorado river, near Winslow). There they were divided into many groups and established their villages here and there.

Their life here was miserable on account of many mosquitos. These insects caused deaths, especially to the young children, so they moved on still looking for Situqui, going through the country that is called the Moqui Buttes, on to Paquaichomo (Water Dust Hill) which is within a few miles of the present Hopi towns, around the First and Second Mesa district. Southeast of them was Awatovi, which was a good sized town but was now in ruins. From this place, Paquaichomo, they sent the scouts back to find the rest of the people who also had left the Homolovi district. It was thought that they might have gone in other directions and sure enough they were found in many different places in small groups. These scouts were sent back to tell them that the Chief and his group were now in sight of Situqui (Walpi), so Chief Tawahongva was calling all his people together. Finally, most of them came on but some of them had already gone to Sioki (Zuni). Tawahongva then sent his messengers to the chiefs of all the different towns asking for permission to be admitted into their villages and to become a part of their people. So to each town a message went, to Walpi, Mishongnovi, Shung-opovi and Awatovi. When the messengers came back with. the news none of the replies were satisfactory and they all felt sad and realized that they were in a very difficult position, being as they were in somebody else's territory. The only thing to do now was to divide themselves equally into groups and go to these towns and try to enter, so then each group had to select their leader or spokesman. In each group was an equal number of each clan, as the Corn, Cloud, Tobacco, Eagle, Sun-forehead, Sand and Bamboo clans. With the group which went to Shung-opovi, Nasiwum (brother and sister Tiwahongva and Tawiayisnima) and also Kochoilaftiyo and his grandmother went. Each group was now hoping for the best, so they camped within a short distance of these towns and then asked for mercy and to be permitted to enter in and become their people, but the answers from the chiefs were of no satisfaction. Four being the limit of time to do anything or to ask for anything, these people were very much troubled and discouraged on the third day of their request at all these places. The chief at Shung-opovi did not know that he was discarding the best of these groups who were coming to his people, the two Nasiwum who had the wisdom and knowledge of So-tukeu-nangwi and also Ko-choi-laftiyo and his wise old grandmother. Here at Shung-opovi each clan was admitted in, one after another, the Sun-forehead clan was the last to enter. On this last day Nasiwum were more than discouraged—they had given up all hope, and said that they would stay just where they were and they refused to enter into the town. But Kochoilaftiyo and his grandmother went in with the rest. In a few days Nasiwum had disappeared and no one knew where they had gone. At Mishongnovi and over at Awatovi these people had less trouble of being permitted to enter. But at Walpi they had received the same kind of treatment, or even worse than at Shung-opovi, so it was hopeless to try again and they decided to move on to Siotuka (Onion Point).

By this time, old man Masauwu got anxious and excited, so he rushed up to the town to see the people who had taken his name for their clan. He told them that these people whom the chief of Walpi had refused were religious and were honest in their ceremony and that it would bring rain. Said he, "You must not forget and must remember that I am the one that owns this whole territory. The chief here has no more right than just of his town. I am the man that has all the right to say what I think, so hereafter, whoever comes shall enter and stay. With compassionate feelings in my heart I ask for two of your good runners to rush down there and head them off. They are leaving right now."

When these two runners reached them at Tawapa (Sun Spring) their scouts had already gone ahead. Tawahongva and his people had destroy all the crops of the Walpi's because their people had received such disagreeable treatment from the chief. While all this was going on, it was clouding up very heavily overhead and the people had divided themselves—all the women folk on one side and the men on the other. The women had formed in a circle and were singing and dancing the Basket Dance and while this was going on the storm clouds had gathered so heavily that the day was growing very dark and cold and then it started snowing and it kept coming on heavier and heavier. All through the storm and the dancing the two Masauwu clansmen had pleaded earnestly with Tawahongva and his people, telling them that this chief who had refused them was only a sub-chief under Masauwu.

"To make you understand," said the two men, "we are telling you all, Masauwu has all the right here and it is his earnest message of sympathy that we have brought to ask you to come and live with us. We trust and worship him. What the chief has done unto you by this he has only hurt himself and lost his self respect. So trust that we, with all our hearts, are telling you the truth and asking you all earnestly to come with us."

"Well," said Tawahongva, "will it be that you will consider and respect us as you do yourselves as a people? Otherwise we will not turn back to go with you. My scouts have already gone."

"We honestly and truly say that you will have the same right as we have, so over what land your scouts have trotted, this is given unto you. It is yours forever."

During all these pleadings the dancing by the women was kept up and the snow by this time had fallen over a foot deep. At last Tawahongva consented for all his people to return to Walpi or Situqui and all at once the snowstorm turned into rain—a real cloudburst which washed away the snow in a very short while and now the waters were rushing down off the hillsides from the Walpi Mesa. All this water had drained down into the flats and that made nice fertile farming land for the people. Now from that day on to this day, the descendants, generation after generation, of these people from Palotquopi have been living here at these different Hopi villages. But Situqui is no more. This Situqui was where the present Walpi is now situated. There used to be a big sand dune covering this whole mesa and the butte that you see there today was covered, heaped up with sand, and every summer it would be covered with flowers of many different varieties. Later all this sand was drifted away off this mesa, by strong winds, and these sand dunes are now away over above Wepo Spring and are still slowly drifting on.

YAPONCHA, THE WIND GOD

ANY years ago the Hopi were very much troubled by the wind. It blew and blew all the time. The sand drifted away from their fields, and they tried to plant their crops but the wind would sweep the soil away before the seeds would even start to germinate. Sadness and worry were upon everybody and they made prayer offerings of many pahos but there were no results.

Many councils were held by the old men in the kivas, where they smoked their pipes earnestly and asked one another why it was that their gods should turn such strong wind upon them. And after awhile, they decided that they would ask the "little fellows" (the two little War Gods Po-okonghoya and Palongahoya, his younger brother) to help them. Now these "little fellows" were called in. When they came in they wanted to know why they were called. The Hopis said that they needed their help, something must be done to the wind. The "little fellows" said yes, they would see what they could do to help the people.

They told the men to stay in the kiva and make many pahos. Then the "little fellows" went to their wise old grandmother, the Spider Woman, and they asked her to make some sweet corn meal mush for them to take along on a journey. Of course they knew who Yaponcha (the Wind God) was and where he lived—over near the Sunset Mountain in the big cracks in the black rock.

When the corn meal mush was made they came back to the kiva and found the pahos were ready and also the ball which they always liked to take along to play with wherever they went, and the bows and arrows had been made for them, because it was much like going on the warpath for them. So the arrows were of bluebird feathers which were considered most powerful in those days.

The two "little fellows" set out toward the San Francisco Peaks. The old men went with them as far as the Little Colorado River and there they sat down and smoked their pipes.

The little warriors went on and on, playing with their ball. They reached the home of the Wind God, Yaponcha, on the fourth day. The Wind God lived at the foot of Sunset Crater in a great crack in the black rock, through which he is ever breathing and does so to this day. They threw the pahos into the crack and hurriedly took out their old grandmother's sticky cornmeal mush, and they sealed up Yaponcha's door with it. Now he was awfully angry, and he blew and blew, but he could not get out. The "little fellows" laughed and they went home, very pleased with themselves, indeed.

But bye and bye, the people in the villages began to feel that it was very hot. It was getting warmer and warmer every day. Down in the kivas it was so awfully hot that the men came out and the people came from their houses and they stood upon the housetops and looked and looked toward the San Francisco Peaks, to see if there were any clouds coming. But there wasn't even the tiniest bit of a cloud to give a pleasant shadow, and not a breath of air, and the people thought that they would smother.

They thought they must do something right away, so the men made some more pahos and called the "little fellows" again and they begged them to go back to Yaponchaki (House of Yaponcha) right away and tell him that there must be peace, and then give him the pahos and let him out, because this heat was much worse even, than the wind. So the "little fellows" said that they would go and see what could be done to make things better.

On the fourth day they arrived at the house of Yaponcha and they talked together and decided that the best thing to do would be to let Yaponcha have just a little hole open, just enough to let him breathe through, but not large enough for him to come out through, altogether. So they took out some of the cornmeal mush and right away a nice cool wind came out, and a little white cloud appeared and went over across the desert toward the Hopi towns.

When the "little fellows" got home again to the villages, everybody was pleased and they have been very grateful ever since. Ever since that time the winds have been just right, and just enough to keep the people cool without blowing everything away.

Ever since then prayer offerings of pahos, to this day, are made to the Wind God, Yaponcha, in the windy month of March by the chiefs and high priests of the three villages of the Second Mesa.

THE KANA-A KACHINAS OF SUNSET CRATER

AT old Mishongnovi the people lived and at the San Francisco Peaks the Kachinas were living. Over in the old town of Mishongnovi there was a young maiden who would not give up to any young man. Her parents were getting old and the father was not able to do as much work as he used to, so he wished that his daughter would get married. But she had refused all proposals from the young men in her town and also from all the towns around. The old man, her father, was very much discouraged to think of all these young men who had tried their chances with the maiden and had met with failure.

Sometime after this, at the San Francisco Peaks, a young Kachina man heard about this. So he thought he would go over to Mishongnovi and propose to the maiden. When evening came he started out across the desert over to the Hopi towns, but being unknown in the town, he was very much in doubt of what the outcome of his undertaking would be. When he did get there some time early in the night, he found the maiden grinding corn up in the second floor of her house. He went in and stood around for awhile and finally sat down. Then he asked her to stop for a moment and listen, because he would like to speak to her. But she would not stop and just kept on grinding. But finally, after awhile, she did stop grinding.

"Why did you stop?" asked the youth.

"You asked me to stop," said the maiden. "Where are you from?"

"I am from the west," he said, and at this, she thought that he was from Shung-opovi. She saw that he was a very handsome looking young man.

Now the parents, in the room below, had noticed that their daughter had stopped her grinding and they wondered, for they thought that something unusual must be happening up there, but they dared not go up to see what or who it was who had come to see the maiden. Now the girl thought that it was getting late, so she asked the young man to go on to bed and as the boy was going out through the door, she asked him to come back and see her again. She herself now came downstairs to bed and the parents asked her who the young man was. She said she did not know him, though she had asked him to come back again to see her.

Now the very next night the youth went back to see the maiden again and found her grinding corn the same as usual. The parents heard someone go up the ladder and walk over the roof to where their daughter was grinding. She stopped her work and then they thought that it must be the same young man who was there the night before. They hoped that the maiden might be interested in this handsome youth and indeed he did interest the maiden. So she asked him again, "Where is your home?" And he said as before, "Over in the west," and again she thought that he meant that he lived in Shung-opovi.

Now the maiden liked this handsome youth very much indeed. She said, "In four days I will go back with you. I will be prepared by that time So come back upon that day and take me to your home."

When the fourth day came, she prepared herself and had her hair done up in butterfly wings (poli-ia-na) and got ready some corn meal and some piki, which she must take with her on her journey. When the boy came everything was ready and he took the tray of corn meal while she carried her piki. They started out and when they got outside of the village the youth said, "Wait awhile, I will see if we can travel easier and faster than we could walk, for we have some distance to go."

He then reached into a little pouch which he was carrying and pulled forth something and threw it from him, westward, across the country, and the maiden saw it was a rainbow like a path before them and she was very afraid. But she had already started out with him and she could not turn back.

"Now let us get on," said the youth, and when they stepped upon it, the rainbow drew itself up to the other end and when they landed they found that they were close to the Little Colorado River. From there again the youth threw his magic in the same direction. The rainbow appeared and they mounted it again and this time they landed on the south side of Palotsmo, Sunset Crater, or the home of the Kana-a Kachina. Here there was a little cloud hiding itself among the pine trees and he was a Kana-a Kachina and he spied the Kachina youth from the San Francisco Peaks taking a Hopi girl with him. The maiden was weary and begged to take a rest and asked the youth to wait a little where he was, for her.

She walked away some distance and presently she heard a voice which seemed to come from under her feet. The voice said, "Be careful, so you may not step on me." And the maiden stopped and looked about her but could not see anyone. It was the Spider Woman who spoke to her, and as the maiden moved to one side, she saw the light down in a little kiva where the good Spider Grandmother lived. She asked the maiden to come in and when she entered the Grandmother said to her in deep sympathy, "My dear child, I have to tell you because you do not know, being only a child. Down in my heart I sympathize with you very deeply. You are out on your first trip and it may be your last trip, and you may not ever see your father and mother again. We cannot hesitate very long. Now I am going with you and I am prepared to go. If we win or lose I am willing to die with you. The youth is a Kachina from San Francisco Peaks and when you reach his home the Kachina people will give you some very difficult tasks to perform, and without my help you would surely fail. Quickly, put me in your ear and let us be on our way." The little Spider Woman was so invisible inside of the Hopi maiden's ear that she could not be detected by anyone, even a Kachina youth.

When the maiden joined the boy again, he threw the rainbow up towards the Peaks and they mounted upon it to take another leap. Now all this time the Little Cloud who was hiding in the pines, knew what was going on, for this little cloud was one of the Kana-a Kachinas who lived in the Sunset Crater. This time the youth and the maiden landed right close to a great kiva far up in the Peaks and they descended from the rainbow and walked up to it.

The youth approached the opening and calling in, he said, "Be courteous to this guest who is my companion, for I am come and am not alone."

And a voice called out from the kiva, "Come in, come right in."

They went in and there they found one old lone man sitting by the fire in the fire-place. The old man begged the young maiden to sit down, and getting up he spread out his own wildcat skin robe for her to sit down upon. Now the whole kiva was very quiet and after she had seated herself she noticed that the youth had disappeared and she did not know where he had gone.

The old man was slowly poking into the fire trying to get more light and he called out saying, "Mother of the House and you, young maiden, come forth. Some stranger has come and she has entered into our kiva."

All this time the Spider Grandmother was whispering her advice into the ear of the Hopi maiden and telling her what she should do.

Now from the north side of the kiva a handsome woman came forth. She seemed suspicious, although she acted with great politeness. The grandmother of the Hopi maiden had already told her of the character of this woman called Hahai-i Wu-uti.

Now the maidens of the house came forth also, and they served her with food and when she was through they cleared it away.

By this time it was quite late in the night, so the old man said, "It is time to go bed," and the handsome Kachina woman, Hahai-i, then opened the door on the north side of the kiva and she asked the maiden to enter and she told her that this was the room where she was to sleep. Now this was the place where the North Wind lived, and as Hahai-i was leaving the room, she said to the maiden, "It is quite cold in here but you will have to do the best you can to get through the night."

Just as soon as the door was closed the Grandmother hastily pulled out some turkey feathers from the bosom of her dress and putting one down on the ground, she asked the girl to lie down on top of it. Then she put one over her, one at her feet, then at her head, and one on either side. And the maiden soon fell asleep, for she was very tired, and the good little Grandmother's turkey feathers kept her warm. Now the wind was blowing very hard all night and it hailed and it snowed and when she woke in the morning she was under a pile of snow. Just as she became awake, Hahai-i opened the door and peeked in, thinking that the maiden had frozen to death. But finding her still alive, she was surprised and asked, "How did you rest ?"

"Very comfortably," said the maiden, and she got up and went out into the kiva room. No sooner had she done this than she was shown to the *mata* (the place for grinding corn) and instead of corn Hahai-i came out with a basketful of icicles and put them into the *mata* for the maiden to grind. The poor maiden felt very cold and unhappy to think she had to grind these icicles and then she thought of her turkey feathers and she took one in each hand with which she would hold *mata-ki* (the mano) so that her hands would not get cold. The icicles were very cold and hard to grind, but she had to go on; she had to grind and grind. The icicles were cold and slick and she could not hold them between the two rocks. Every once in a while Hahai-i would come and take a look to see if she was getting the icicles melted, which she had intended the maiden to do.

Now the Spider Grandmother took a bit of her magic root of an herb and put it in the girl's mouth and asked her to chew it well and then spray it over the icicles. She did this, and no sooner had it touched the icicles than they melted and turned into water in the mata. Now this was the maiden's first test, and when Hahai-i came again and saw what the bride-to-be had done, she was glad. The maiden continued to do this for four days and she spent four nights in the cold room with the North Wind. At the end of four days she finished her test and it was found that she had won over the Kachinas, so she was married to the youth who had brought her there from Mishongnovi. The Grandmother was glad to have been able to serve the Hopi maiden and bring her successfully through her trials. She had put up many jars of water for the Kachinas by grinding the icicles and snow.

Now the maiden's wedding robes and many other presents were brought to her and she was ready to be sent home. Many Kachinas were to go along with her to carry the presents to Mishongnovi, and the bride and bridegroom were dressed in their wedding robes.

This day was rather a joyful day for the bride for she thought of how wonderful the Spider Grandmother had been and how she had helped her to win. And now she was going back home and taking her husband along. And she was very thankful indeed to the little old woman.

On the way back to Mishongnovi at Sunset Crater, the girl stopped just as she had done on the way over and walked away a little to take a rest. But this time, she took her little Grandmother back to her home, and when they got there they both cried for joy. For the last time the girl thanked her again. The Little Cloud who detected the couple on their way up to the San Francisco Peaks was again hiding in the pines and he saw everything that took place.

Now during these four days the parents of the maiden had been very much worried because they did not know where she had gone. So in Mishongnovi this was rather an exciting afternoon for the people to see this girl who had been missing so long coming home with the Kachinas and bringing all kinds of presents. The Kachinas gave all their presents to the villagers and then returned to their home.

From this time on the Hopi were very prosperous for a number of years until finally the men of one kiva, and these were the troublemakers of the village, plotted to see how they could break up the happiness of the Kachina youth and the Hopi maiden and win her love away from her husband. These wicked men made a costume exactly like that which the Kachina man wore and so one day, one of these young men dressed up like him and went to see the Kachina's wife while he was away. On his return he found that his wife cared for someone else, but she herself did not know that it was another man because of the costume and everything being exactly like her husband. So the Kachina man, without making any further trouble, told his wife that he had to go away to his home in the San Francisco Peaks and back to his own people, and so he did. But as he was leaving, he took one of the longest ears of corn from the stack in the house and carried it back with him to the San Francisco Peaks.

Two years later a famine came upon the Hopi people. They prayed and prayed for rain and held ceremonies of many kinds, all of which were of no use. No result came from any of them.

Finally Kana-a Kachinas at Sunset Crater, felt compassion for the people and took mercy upon them. Now they knew that the Mishongnovi maiden had not been treated fairly and they knew of all the hard tests that she had had to go through in the kiva of the San Francisco Mountain Kachinas, and they did not think it right for these Kachina people to bring this terrible calamity upon the whole people. The Kana-a Kachinas then took much sweet corn and strung it up with yucca and many other good foodstuffs. They came across the desert to the Hopi villages to make the people happy and to relieve their hunger. Now when they got there they went dancing through the streets and distributed their sweetcorn and food to the people. But they asked the people not to eat everything up that day which they had received and told them that each family must leave an ear of corn in the corner of their empty storage room.

All the people were made happy and glad so they asked these Kachinas not to go back to their Sunset Crater home, but to live with them always there. But they, being supernatural beings, could not do this, so of their own choice, they went to a little butte which stands by Mishongnovi today, and they opened it up and went in. So that to his day the little butte is called Kana-a Katchin-ki.

Waking up the next morning, to their wonder, the people found that their empty rooms were full of corn and from then on joy was with the people again. After this the Kana-a Kachina dance was celebrated every year until 1902.

THE LADDER DANCE AT OLD SHUNG-OPOVI

The present Hopi pueblo of Shung-opovi has occupied its present site since about 1700. Previous to that time, the pueblo straggled over the foothills at the mesa base. About a hundred yards west of this pueblo, over a sharp ridge, lay the old walled-in spring called Shungopa, the spring that gave the name to the pueblo, and which went dry in the 1870's at the time of a landslide which caused a local earthquake.

About a hundred yards south of this spring stands a large boulder. On the top of this boulder can be observed three holes in a row, each hole being about a foot in diameter and between a foot and two feet deep. Hopi tradition associates these holes with a Hopi ceremony now extinct call the Ladder Dance.

THERE WAS one kiva at old Shung-opovi known as the Ash Pile Kiva. They knew but one dance and that was called the Coal Kachina dance. This kiva was composed of not well-to-do people. Not having many costumes, all they had to wear for kilts were old dresses discarded by the women. The men in the kiva gave the Coal Kachina dance so often that it grew monotonous to see those Coal Kachinas. So one day they made an announcement that they would give another kind of dance in four days. The men in the other kivas said that only some more Coal Kachinas would come into the kiva. About a day after the announcement was made, the boys went out hunting. While they were out, one of the boys got away from the party, and, as he was going around, he jumped a rabbit out of a bush and he chased after it. The rabbit just kept going westward and the boy just kept following it. Well, the rabbit finally got into one of the shrines above Burro Springs, and the rabbit went around back of the shrine and the boy thought the rabbit was all in and tired and ready to lay down. When he got around the shrine he saw a kiva. When he looked in he asked if the rabbit had gone in there. The men who were there said "Yes," and they asked the boy to come in.

When he got in there, they sat him down beside the fireplace and gave him a welcome smoke. When he finished that they told him they had sent the rabbit out to get him and bring him there because they were rather sorry that the men in the other kivas made fun of the Ash Pile Kiva. Then they told him they would like to have two or three of the boys go over to the San Francisco Peaks. There they would show them different kinds of Kachina dances from which they could choose which of the dances they would have in their kiva. So they asked the boy to go right back home and tell the rest of the men of his kiva.

When he came home he went right into the kiva. Well, he told these men what he had seen at the shrine and what news he had been told. He asked the old men to make some prayer offerings which they would take over to the San Francisco Peaks to the main Kachina Kiva and said this must be kept secret from the other people who would be expecting to see the Coal Kachina dance again. They stayed up late to make their prayer offerings so that the boys could start out early for the San Francisco Peaks before the rest of the village woke up. So they came to the foot of the main peaks that day. The next morning about dawn they started to climb and at sunrise reached the kiva. When they got there they were asked to come in, and there they found the same men that the boy saw at the shrine at Burro Springs. So, as usual, they were given their welcome smoke. The men said that they would show them different kinds of dances without losing much time for there was now little time before the dance at Shung-opovi.

So they danced many dances for them and the boys liked the ladder dance very much. Well, the men at the kiva said the dance was difficult because the dancers had to climb a limber young Douglas fir tree. Finally the boys decided to ask these people if they could not do it for them. The people agreed to do the ladder dance themselves because it would be so difficult for the people at Shung-opovi. So when they did agree to do this they sent the boys back, but they asked them to take back home with them two young Douglas firs each about a foot high. They told them that when they got home, they were to find a rock on which to plant these two trees. When they got home with the two firs they brought them into the kiva and the men in the kiva performed a ceremony of welcoming the firs and the boys by smoking.

The next morning the boys took the two trees and went up to the rock which they thought would be best to plant the trees on. That morning the whole village noticed the two trees on top of the rock and wondered what was going to happen. One by one they went to look. There was an old man up there on watch so that no one could hurt the trees. Everyone who went asked him what they were for but he told them not to be too anxious until night came.

That day towards evening the Kachinas began to come out of the kivas. They kind of paraded around the village. At that time the men from the Ash Pile Kiva came out all wrapped up in their blankets. These men went out to meet the real Kachinas who came from the San Francisco Mountains. By that time it was clouding up. These men met the Kachinas at the place called Lonatchi, a spring which lies about a mile west of Old Shung-opovi. When they met them, the Kachinas told the men they must hide out that night so that he people would believe that they were putting on the dance. So they decided they would stay there and the Kachinas would go to the village and the men could follow after dark.

This old man at the rock under the two fir trees would sprinkle cornmeal on the trees and they would grow about an inch or two, and by that time the Kachinas got there they were quite tall trees. In this ceremony each Kachina was in a different costume, except that the two who were to climb the trees were dressed alike. When the people saw the Kachinas on the hill around the rock, they all ran up there. They carefully observed the performance. They were trying to figure out who the Kachinas were. They resembled men in the different kivas. The two Kachinas climbed the trees. The trees were so slender that the Kachinas swayed back and forth. They climbed while the rest sung around. It seemed as if the two trees had a spirit as the two Kachinas swung back and forth. The song that the Kachinas sung, the people of Shung-opovi still sing.

Well, after this performance they went to the village. They paraded around and entered the kiva. Then rain came down. The rest of the kivas felt jealous. Every once in awhile they would send up a man to peep in to see if it were true that the men in this kiva were putting on the dance. About midnight the dance started. All the Kachinas from the other kivas were out. But the men from the other kivas did not dance. They just put away their costumes and followed the new Kachinas around. And then by that time the men who were supposed to put on the dance came in. They watched the dance too and were not recognized.

After the dance was over the Kachinas went back into the kiva. They were supposed to go down the Sipapu and go home that way. So the next day after the dance this kiva was given praise because they had put on a great dance, different from anything that had ever been seen. From that day this kiva was recognized because of this dance, whereas, before they had never been recognized by the people of the village. From then on the people at Shung-opovi held this kind of a dance every four years until the town was abandoned (between 1680 and 1700).

THE LADDER DANCE AT PIVAHONKIAPI

Northwest of Oraibi, seven or eight miles, on that broad terrace which so conspicuously encircles many of the Hopi mesas, about 200 feet below the rim, lie the ruins of two pueblos. The nearest to Oraibi occupies a point which projects from the mesa and is called Hukovi, "The Place of the Winds," or "Windy Point." Two miles farther along the ledge, at the base of a large rock, the pueblo of Pivahonkiapi covers the shelf.

Potsherds tell us that Hukovi and Pivahonkiapi were occupied in the twelve hundreds. We, therefore, assume that the two pueblos were abandoned, like so many others in northern Arizona, because of the great drought of 1275 to 1299 which shows so well in Dr. A. E. Douglass' studies of the tree rings.

About these pueblo ruins, Hopi traditions cluster. At Hukovi the girls were beautiful but bad. At Pivahonkiapi among the gamblers lived a handsome youth. At Achamoli, halfway between Hukovi and Oraibi, lived the two little war gods, sons of the Sun, Po-okonghoya and his brother, Palo-onghoya, with their grandmother, the Spider Woman. What more can you ask as the basis for a story!

About 100 yards east of Pivahonkiapi can be observed eight circular holes, about eight inches in diameter, cut in the rock at the cliff edge. About one of these holes the rock has cracked. The Hopi believe that these holes belong to the "ladder dance."—Ed.

A Pivahonkiapi there dwelt a handsome young man. Two miles away on Windy Point lived two girls in the pueblo of Hukovi. These girls wanted to marry this handsome youth, but he would not look at either of them. This made them mad.

They knew that he was to take the part of a Kachina in a "ladder dance" to be held at Pivahonkiapi in March. The girls thought that this would be a chance to destroy him.

The dance was announced and the dancers practiced the songs in the kiva for eight days. Four days before the ceremony, two youths were selected to go to the San Francisco Peaks which the Hopis call Nuvatekiaovi (The Place of Snow on the Very Top) to get two fir trees, and one of the youths was the handsome young man.

On the way to the peaks they followed a trail and because they were tired they stopped to rest. The handsome youth stepped aside off the trail. Here he met the Spider Woman. She said, "I am in sympathy with you because I know what is going to happen to you. Change your pahos (prayer offerings) as the ones you are carrying are bad. Cast them somewhere and take mine and put them in the shrine. If you don't do that, the witches will surely get you. On your way home, stop and see me."

Returning to the trail he joined his companion and went on to the peaks and placed the pahos in the shrine. There they selected two small fir trees about two feet high.

On his way back the handsome youth remembered to stop and call on the Spider Woman. He left his companion by the trail and hunted up the old woman. The old woman said, "Take the pipe of your father and make smoke so the clouds will hide our path from the witches." So he lit his pipe and she brought him to her kiva. He set down his trees and sat on a skin. "My dear grandchild," said the old woman, "do as I say or your last day will be the day of the ceremony."

She handed him some medicine and said, "The wise men will sing and the tree will grow too fast. Chew this medicine and spit it out on the tree, so the tree may be limber but it will not break." Then she gave him a little light white feather of an eagle and placed it under his heart so that it would make him lighter.

By this time the sky was covered with clouds and he rejoined his companion. He did not say much because he was worried. That night they got home and entered the kiva with their two fir trees. All the men smoked and when they stopped, asked them what they saw in the way of prosperity. They said that they saw good flowing water, so the old men knew that the summer would be good.

While this was going on the old Spider Woman, (she was a great old woman), sent word to the other Spider Women that lived near Pivahonkiapi (she sent the message by way of dreams) to send out her two little war gods, Po-okonghoya and his brother, Palo-onghoya-her grandsons-to look over the place where the tree was to be planted.

As they were small boys no one would notice them as they played with the other children of the village. The boys investigated and discovered that the girls of Hukovi had cracked the rock about the hole in which the tree was to be planted. They hurried back to their grandmother and reported.

"If that is the case," said the old Spider Woman, "I will have to go there and see. I have not got a thing to mend that rock with. One of you boys run and get an ear of baked sweet corn." When the boy had found it, she ground it up as fine as she could. Then she mixed the meal into dough—like the finest clay. When this was ready the day of the ceremony had arrived.

The Kachinas put on their costumes at the mesa foot as they were supposed to come from the San Francisco Peaks. Everyone gathered on the house-tops watching them climb up the mesa. While everyone's attention was so occupied, the old Spider Woman and the boys tried to mend the crack in the rock with the dough. When it was mended, she gave some medicine to the two boys who chewed it up and spat it out on the crack and blew on the crack.

As soon as they had finished, the Kachinas entered the village and marched about the two kivas four times.

In this ceremony, you must know, the leading Kachina, though a man, takes the part of a Kachin-mana (Maiden). In this dance the leader was a notorious wizard who was being paid by the girls of Hukovi to do crooked work.

After making the rounds of the kiva, the Kachinas marched to the place on the edge of the cliff where the trees were to be planted. The Kachin-mana carried the two little trees. When the Mana gave the handsome boy the wrong tree, and the other boy the right tree, he knew the wizard was trying to get him. Both boys laid the trees down on the rock. Someone said something and the leader and everyone looked the other way and the boys exchanged the trees, He knew his tree for it had a feather fastened to one of the leaves.

The trees were now planted in the holes that had been prepared. The Kachinas, standing in a row, started to dance and sing. Slowly the trees began to grow. They grew and grew until they reached 25 to 30 feet high. The two Kachinas that were to climb, one of them being the handsome boy, stood by the trees. Finally the Kachin-mana, the wizard, told them to climb. The young man trusted the old Spider Woman. He chewed the medicine and spat on the tree and climbed slowly. When he reached the top the tree swayed back and forth. All the people on the house-tops thought that the tree would break and he would go over the cliff. He came down and danced and then went up again. When he came down and danced he climbed the tree the third time, swinging back and forth. The girls from Hukovi were on the house-tops with the inhabitants of the village. They wondered why the rock did not give way. When he climbed the fourth time the leader told the youth to climb faster and swing back and forth harder, and swing good and hard with all his might. But still the tree did not break nor the rock crack. When he had climbed down the leader told him to go up a fifth time, but someone had counted so the chief said that was enough as they had gone up the four ceremonial times.

Later the two young men who had climbed the trees took the prayer offerings and started back to the San Francisco Mountains to place them in the shrine. The rest of the Kachinas entered the kiva with the men of the pueblo and all smoked.

Before the men had entered the kiva, the girls from Hukovi hired a wizard to cut the beams in the back part of the kiva. They were mad at the leader of the Kachinas, the Kachin-mana, and the boy. They did not know that he was already on his way to the peaks.

While the smoking ceremony was on, the kiva roof caved in. Everyone was killed but one poor old man far back in one corner who was not a man of high standing but was a common person who never rushed up in front. This old man dug his way out.

The village was in trouble. All the men were killed except the two youths and the old man. Well, of course you know, everyone was sad for many days. The old man knew that everyone was sad so he thought he would do something. So the old man went off by himself and practiced a dance under the cliff. While he was practicing, a girl found him, and he asked her to join him in the dance. She accepted so the old man went to work and made a mask so no one would know her. He took some corn, boiled it well, late one afternoon. He fixed up the girl as well as himself in a Kachina costume. The old man told her to hold out all the nerve she could. When they went to the plaza, the people saw them come. All the people started to cry, but soon got all right. Then the old man and the girl danced and gave out presents of corn.

That night the handsome youth was outside the pueblo where he went every night. He heard something and lay still. He listened. He heard a sound coming closer and closer. It finally came and passed by. It was a ghost dressed in white. He was scared and fainted. After laying insensible for a while, he came to himself. He followed the ghost to the village. When he got to the plaza, the ghost was sitting on the shrine. It was a woman ghost. He went up and asked her why she was there and where she had come from.

She said, "I come from the Colorado River. I come because I sympathize with the people of Pivahonkiapi. I have nothing for you but if you wish to get even with the girls of Hukovi, I would like to help you. I would like to have a prayer plume from everyone in the pueblo and I ask you to have them made this very night. You must keep it a secret why they are to be made."

So the youth went from house to house and every woman made a prayer plume (paho). The boy collected them and gave them to the ghost and said, "We have done what you asked us to do." The ghost took the prayer offerings and thanked him. She said, "I will do everything that you ask me to do. Now what do you want me to do? I can drive them eastward or I can drive them westward. I can even drive them over the cliff." The boy said, "Drive them westward."

Then the ghost went over to Hukovi and she made a noise as if she were dying. She rolled on the ground and moaned. This scared the people. Some boys said they were not scared and offered to kill the old ghost.

The next night the boys lay in wait for her and when she started to moan they got scared and ran away. Everyone got scared. The ghost came back six or seven nights. The people could not sleep for her moaning, so they decided to leave the pueblo.

They packed up their belongings and left the village. The ghost drove them westward. They camped for the night by the Dinnebito, Wash at Bang-wu-wi (Mountain Sheep Cliff). The old ghost came again and kept them awake. But they could not move that night on account of the children.

The next day they moved to near where the Dinnebito Store is and camped. The ghost came early and kept them awake till daylight. Again they started on, and on the third night camped by the Little Colorado River. The ghost came just after sundown because she was near her home and kept them awake till dawn.

At daylight they started on again and camped in the Cinder Hills. Still the ghost came after them. The fifth night they camped by Mormon Mountain. The ghost followed them. On and on they went, crossing the Big Colorado into California. They say that their descendants are now the Mission Indians of California.

DR. FEWKES AND MASAUWU
THE BIRTH OF A LEGEND

*In the autumn of 1898, the late Dr. Fewkes, archaeologist of the
Smithsonian Institution, was staying at Walpi, one of the Hopi
Indian Pueblos. In the annual report of the director of the Bureau
of Ethnology his visit is noted as follows:*

*"In November, Dr. J. Walter Fewkes repaired to Arizona for the
purpose of continuing his researches concerning the winter
ceremonies of the Hopi Indians, but soon after his arrival an
epidemic of smallpox manifested itself in such severity as to
completely demoralize the Indians and to prevent them from
carrying out their ceremonial plans, and at the same time placed
Dr. Fewkes in grave personal danger. It accordingly became
necessary to abandon the work for the season."*

*The Hopis at Walpi have another story of the cause of Dr.
Fewkes' departure.—Ed.*

ONE OF the most important of the Hopi winter ceremonies is
the Wuwuchim which comes in November. At a certain time
during the ceremony the One Horned and the Two Horned
Societies hold a secret rite in a certain part of the pueblo, and all
the people who live on that plaza go away and close their houses.
No one may witness this ceremony, for Masauwu, the Earth God,
is there with the One Horned Priests who do his bidding in the
Underworld and the Spirits of the dead are there and it is said
that anyone who sees them will be frozen with fright or paralyzed
or become like the dead.

Masauwu owns all the Hopi world, the surface of the earth and
the Underworld beneath the earth. He is a mighty and terrible
being for he wears upon his head a bald and bloody mask. He is
like death and he clothes himself in the raw hides of animals and
men cannot bear to look upon his face. The Hopi say he is really a
very handsome great man of a dark color with fine long black hair
and that he is indeed a great giant. When the Hopi came up from
the Underworld and looked about them in fear, the first sign which
they saw of any being of human form, was the great footprints of
Masauwu. Now Masauwu only walks at night and he carries a
flaming torch. Fire is his and he owns the fiery pits. Every night
Masauwu takes his torch and he starts out on his rounds, for he
walks clear around the edge of the world every night.

Dr. Fewkes had been in the kiva all day taking notes on what
he saw going on there. Finally the men told him that he must go

away and stay in his house for Masauwu was coming, and that part of the ceremony was very sacred and no outside person was ever allowed to see what was going on. They told him to go into his house and lock the door, and not to try to see anything no matter what happened, or he would be dragged out and he would "freeze" to death. So he went away into his house and he locked the door just as he had been told to do and he sat down and began to write up his notes.

Now suddenly he had a queer feeling, for he felt that there was someone in the room, and he looked up and saw a tall man standing before him, but he could not see his face for the light was not good. He felt very much surprised for he knew that he had locked the door.

He said, "What do you want and how did you get in here?" The man replied, "I have come to entertain you."

Dr. Fewkes said, "Go away, I am busy and I do not wish to be entertained."

And now as he was looking at the man, he suddenly was not there any more. Then a voice said, "Turn your head a moment," and when the Doctor looked again the figure stood before him once more, but this time its head was strange and dreadful to see.

And the Doctor said, "How did you get in?", and the man answered and said, "I go where I please, locked doors cannot keep me out! See, I will show you how I entered," and, as Dr. Fewkes watched, he shrank away and became like a single straw in a Hopi hair whisk and he vanished through the key hole.

Now Dr. Fewkes was very much frightened and as he was thinking what to do, there was the man back again. So he said once more to him, "What do you want?", and the figure answered as before and said, "I have come to entertain you." So the Doctor offered him a cigarette and then a match, but the man laughed and said, "Keep your match, I do not need it," and he held the cigarette before his horrible face and blew a stream of fire from his mouth upon it and lit his cigarette. Then Dr. Fewkes was very much afraid indeed, for now he knew who it was.

Then the being talked and talked to him, and finally the Doctor "gave up to him" and said he would become a Hopi and be like them and believe in Masauwu, and Masauwu cast his spell on him and they both became like little children and all night long they played around together and Masauwu gave the Doctor no rest.

And it was not long after that Dr. Fewkes went away but it was not on account of the smallpox as you now know.

Although Dr. Fewkes never reported this story to the outside world, the Hopis now tell that he related it to the priests in the kiva the next day after the strange occurrence. We can see how in less than forty years a legend had its birth.—Ed.

Navaho Myths, Prayers, and Songs
By Washington Matthews

Table of Contents

ALPHABET.

The characters used in this work, in spelling Navaho words, are given below, with the value assigned to each character.

VOWELS.

a has the sound of English a in father.

ä has the sound of English a in hat. has the sound of English a in what.

a̱ has the sound of English e in they. In some connections it varies to the sound of English e in their.

ë has the sound of English e in then.

i has the sound of English i in marine.

ï has the sound of English i in tin.

o has the sound of English o in bone.

u has the sound of English u in rude.

ai unmarked, or accented on the i (aí), is a diphthong having the sound of English i in bind. When it is accented on the a (ái), or has a diaeresis (aï), it is pronounced as two vowels.

ow has the sound of English ow in how. It is heard mostly in meaningless syllables.

A vowel followed by an inverted comma (ʻ) is aspirated, or pronounced with a peculiar force which cannot be well represented by adding the letter h.

CONSONANTS.

b has the sound of English b in bat.

d has the sound of English d in day.

d represents a strongly aspirated dental sonant. It is often interchanged with d.

g has the sound of English g in go, or, in some connections, the sound of English g in gay.

g has a sound unknown in English. It is the velar g, like the Arabic ghain, or the Dakota g.

h has the sound of English h in hat.

h has the sound of German ch in machen. It is sometimes interchanged with h.

k has usually the sound of English k in koran; but sometimes the sound of English k in king.

l has the sound of English l in lay.

l has a sound unknown in English. It is an aspirated surd l, made with the side rather than with the tip of the tongue. It is often interchanged with l.

m has the sound. of English m in man.

n has the sound of English n in name.

n has the effect of French n in bon. It has no equivalent in English.

s has the sound of English s in sand.

s has the sound of English sh in shad. It is often interchanged with s.

t has the sound of English t in tan.

t represents a strongly aspirated dental surd. It is often interchanged with t.

w has the sound of English w in war.

y has the sound of English y in yarn.

z has the sound of English z in zone.

z has the sound of English z in azure. It is often interchanged with z.

c, f, j, p, q, v, and x are not used. The sound of English ch in chance is represented by t*s*; that of English j in jug by d*z*.

EDITOR'S NOTE.

In the latter part of the year 1902 the late Dr. Washington Matthews entered into an arrangement with the Department of Anthropology of the University of California, through its head, Professor F. W. Putnam, in accordance with which he was to devote the remainder of his life to the preparation of a large amount of unpublished material which he had accumulated during the many years of active life among the North American Indians. In accordance with the agreement, this material was received by the Department of Anthropology shortly after the lamented close of Dr. Matthews' life.

It was the good fortune of the editor to spend some days in Dr. Matthews' company during the autumn of 1903, when plans were formed for the completion and publication of certain material. The texts of a number of prayers and songs, for the most part connected with the ceremony of the Night Chant, had been recorded hastily, and required the aid of a Navaho to bring them into proper condition for publication. Since Dr. Matthews' health would not permit of a trip to the Navaho country and his increasing deafness rendered the acquisition of information from native sources difficult, the editor undertook the work of revision. The first trip made in 1904 to the Navaho country was unsuccessful because of the serious illness of Hatali Natloi, the priest from whom the texts had been originally obtained. A second trip during January of the present year resulted in the accomplishment of the task, but alas! too late for the completed work to pass under the critical hand of its author. The editor must the therefore assume the responsibility for the addition of certain lines to the texts, for the substitution of certain words made at the dictation of Hatali Natloi, for the alteration of the orthography of a few Navaho words, and for the choice, here and there, of one of the two possible renderings suggested by the author. It is needless to say that the free translations are the unimprovable work of the author.

Berkeley, Cal., April 14, 1906.

A TALE OF KININAÉKAI:

ACCOUNTING FOR THE ORIGIN OF CERTAIN PRAYERS AND SONGS OF THE NIGHT CHANT.

INTRODUCTION.

In my work entitled "The Night Chant, A Navaho Ceremony," I give translations of four myths (or, more properly, of three myths and a variant) that belong to the ceremony described. These may be called the great or fundamental myths of the ceremony; but, in addition, there is a great number of minor myths, accounting for the origin of certain minor rites, and of different groups of songs of sequence and other matters. We may never reasonably hope for the collection and translation of all these myths.

The following tale accounts for the origin of one of these groups of songs, namely the Tsénit*si*hogan Bigï'n or songs of the Red Rock House, and perhaps for the origin of some of the ritual observances.

In "The Night Chant" I say, when describing the rites of the second day: "When the party returns to the medicine lodge, the patient sits in the west, for he has still further treatment to undergo. The chanter applies pollen to the essential parts of the patient, puts some in his or her mouth, takes a pinch of it on his own tongue, and applies a little of it to the top of his own head. These applications of pollen are all timed to coincide with certain words of the accompanying song." Song F that follows is what may be called a pollen song, for it is sung when pollen is applied. I explain, in notes, where and when different applications of pollen are made as the singing progresses. I cannot say if there are other pollen songs; but probably there are.

THE LEGEND.

In the ancient days, there were four songs which you had to sing if you would enter the White House. The first was sung when you were ascending the cliff; the second, when you entered the first doorway; the third, when you walked around inside the house; and the fourth, when you were prepared to leave. You climbed up from the ground to the house on a rainbow. All this was in the old days. You cannot climb that way now. In those days, *Hayolkál* Askí, Dawn Boy, went there on a rainbow.

In the ancient days, there lived in this house a chief of the house. There were four rooms and four doors, and there were sentinels at each door. At the first door there were two big lightnings, one on each side; at the second door there were two bears; at the third door there were two red-headed snakes, which could charm you from afar, before you got near them; and at the fourth door there were two rattlesnakes.

Of course few people ever visited the place, for if the visitor were not a holy one some of these sentinels would surely kill him. They were vigilant. The chief of the house and his subordinates had these songs, by the power of which they could enter and quiet the sentinels, who always showed signs of anger when any one approached them.

Dawn Boy got leave from *Hastséyalti* to go to White House. *Hastséyalti* instructed him how to get there, taught him the prayers and songs he must know, and told him what sacrifices he must make. These must include fragments of turquoise, white shell, haliotis, and cannel-coal, besides *destsí* corn-pollen and larkspur pollen, and were to be tied up in different bags before he started. "When you get into the plain, as far off as the people of White House can see you, begin to sing one of these songs and a rainbow will form on which you may walk," said *Hastséyalti*.

Dawn Boy then set forth on his journey. When he got to Dzi*l*danístíni, or Reclining Mountain, he got his first view of the White House, and there he began to sing. Reclining Mountain is, today, far from White House; you cannot see one place from the other; but in the ancient days the world was smaller than it is now, and the people of whom I speak were holy ones. When he had finished the song a rainbow appeared, as *Hastséyalti* had promised, spanning the land from Reclining Mountain to White House. As he walked on the rainbow, a great wind began to blow, raising a dust that blinded the sentinels at White House and prevented them from seeing Dawn Boy when he entered.

There was a black kethawn at each side of the door and a curtain hung in the doorway. When he entered the house, he walked on a trail of daylight and he sprinkled pollen on the trail. The people within became aware of the presence of a stranger and looked up. *Hastséyalti* and *Hastséhogan*, the Talking God and the House God, who were the chief gods there, looked angrily at him, and one said: "Who is this stranger that enters our house unbidden? Is he one of the People on the Earth? Such have never dared to enter this place before." Dawn Boy replied: "It is not for nothing that I come here. See! I have brought gifts for you. I hope to find friends here." Then he showed the precious things he had brought and sang this song:

SONG A. (Free translation.)
1. Where my kindred dwell, there I wander.
2. Child of the White Corn am I, there I wander.
3. The Red Rock House, there I wander.
4. Where dark kethawns are at the doorway, there I wander.
5. With the pollen of dawn upon my trail. There I wander.
6. At the yuni, the striped cotton hangs with pollen. There I wander.
7. Going around with it. There I wander.
8. Taking another, I depart with it. With it I wander.
9. In the house of long life, there I wander.
10. In the house of happiness, there I wander.
11. Beauty before me, with it I wander.
12. Beauty behind me, with it I wander.
13. Beauty below me, with it I wander.
14. Beauty above me, with it I wander.
15. Beauty all around me, with it I wander.
16. In old age traveling, with it I wander.
17. On the beautiful trail I am, with it I wander.

Then he gave them the sacred things he had brought with him, and *Hastséyalti* said it was well, that he was welcome to remain, and they asked him what he wanted. "I want many things," he replied. "I have brought you pieces of precious stones and shells; these I wish wrought into beads and strung into ornaments, like those I see hanging abundantly on your walls. I wish domestic animals of all kinds, corn of all kinds, and plants of all kinds. I wish good and beautiful black clouds, good and beautiful thunder storms, good and beautiful gentle showers, and good and beautiful black fogs."

The chiefs thanked him for his gifts, and asked him whose song it was that enabled him to come to White House,—who it was that taught it to him. But he had been warned by his informant not to reveal this, so he answered: "No one told me; I composed my songs myself. They are my own songs." "What is your name?" they asked. "I am *Hayolkál. A*ski, Dawn Boy," he replied. "It is well," said the holy ones. "Since you know our songs you are welcome to come here; but rarely does any one visit us, for there are but two outside of our dwelling who know our songs. One is *Hastséyalti* of Tsé`intyel, in this cañon, and the other is *Hastséyalti* of Tse`ya*hó*dïl*y*ïl in Tse`gíhe.

Then *Hastséhogan* sent for a sacred buckskin, and one son and one daughter of each of the two gods, *Hastséyalti* and *Hastséhogan* spread the skin for Dawn Boy to stand on. Thus do we now, as the gods did then. As he stood, *Hastséhogan* taught Dawn Boy the White House prayer, as follows:

PRAYER No. 1. (Free translation.)

I.

1. In Kininaékai.
2. In the house made of dawn.
3. In the story made of dawn.
4. On the trail of dawn.
5. O, Talking God!
6. His feet, my feet, restore (or heal).
7. His limbs, my limbs, restore.
S. His body, my body, restore.
9. His mind, my mind, restore.
10. His voice, my voice, restore.
11. His plumes, my plumes, restore.
12. With beauty before him, with beauty before me.
13. With beauty behind him, with beauty behind me.
14. With beauty above him, with beauty above me.
15. With beauty below him, with beauty below me.
16. With beauty around him, with beauty around me.
17. With pollen beautiful in his voice, with pollen beautiful in my voice.
18. It is finished in beauty.
19. It is finished in beauty.

II.

2. In the house of evening light.
3. From the story made of evening light.
4. On the trail of evening light.
5. O, House God!
(The rest as in I, except that lines 12 and 13 are transposed.)

III.

5. O, White Corn Boy!
(The rest as in I.)

IV.

5. O, Yellow Corn Girl!
(The rest as in II.)

V.

5. O, Pollen Boy!
(The rest as in I.)

VI.

5. O, Grasshopper Girl!
(The rest as in II, with "It is finished in beauty" four times.)

When they had done, Hastséhogan said: "You have learned the prayer well; you have said it properly and you have done right in all things. Now you shall have what you want." They gave him good and beautiful soft goods of all kinds, all kinds of good and beautiful domestic animals, wild animals, corn of all colors, black clouds, black mists, male rains, female rains, lightning, plants, and pollen.

After he had said the six prayers (or six parts of a prayer) as he bad been taught, he prayed in his mind that on his homeward journey he might have good pollen above him, below him, before him, behind him, and all around him; that he might have good pollen in his voice. The holy ones said: "We promise you all this. Now you may go."

As he started he began to sing this song:

SONG B. (Free translation.)
1. To the house of my kindred, there I return.
2. Child of the yellow corn am I.
3. To the Red Rock House, there I return.
4. Where the blue kethawns are by the doorway, there I return.
5. The pollen of evening light on my trail, there I return.

6. At the yuni the haliotis shell hangs with the pollen, there I return.

7. Going around, with it I return.

8. Taking another, I walk out with it. With it I return.

9. To the house of old age, up there I return.

10. To the house of happiness, up there I return.

11. Beauty behind me, with it I return.

12. Beauty before me, with it I return.

13. Beauty above me, with it I return.

14. Beauty below me, with it I return.

15. Beauty all around me, with it I return.

16. Now in old age wandering, I return.

17. Now on the trail of beauty, I am. There I return.

He continued to sing this until he got about 400 paces from White House, when he crossed a hill and began to sing the following song:

SONG C. (Free translation.)
Held in my hand. (Four times. Prelude.)

1. Now with it Dawn Boy am I. Held in my hand.

2. Of Red Rock House. Held in my hand.

3. From the doorway with dark kethawns. Held in my hand.

4. With pollen of dawn for a trail thence. Held in my hand.

5. At the yuni, the striped cotton hangs with the pollen. Held in my hand.

S. Going around with it. Held in my hand.

9. Taking another, I walk out with it. Held in my hand.

10. I walk home with it. Held in my hand.

11. I arrive home with it. Held in my hand.

12. I sit down with it. Held in my hand.

13. With beauty before me. Held in my hand.

14. With beauty behind me. Held in my hand.

15. With beauty above me. Held in my hand.

16. With beauty below me. Held in my hand.

17. With beauty all around me. Held in my hand.

18. Now in old age wandering. Held in my hand.

19. Now on the trail of beauty. Held in my hand.

II.

3. From the doorway with the blue kethawns. Held in my hand.

4. With pollen of evening for a trail thence. Held in my hand.

5. At the yuni, the haliotis shell hangs with pollen. Held in my hand.

(The rest as in I, except that 14 and 15 and also 16 and 17 change places.)

By the time he had finished this song he was back at Dzi*l*danístíni, whence be started on his quest and from which he could see Depéntsa and the hills around Tse`gíhi. Then he began to think about his home, and he sang another song.

SONG D (Free translation.)

There it looms up, it looms up, it looms up, it looms up. (Prelude.)

1. The mountain of emergence looms up.
2. The mountain of dawn looms up.
3. The mountain of white corn looms up.
4. The mountain of all soft goods looms up.
5. The mountain of rain looms up.
6. The mountain of pollen looms up.
7. The mountain of grasshoppers looms up.
8. The field of my kindred looms up.

He thought it was yet a long way to his home, so he sat down to eat some food he had brought with him. Then he sang another song, one of the Be*z*ín*y*asin or Food Songs, as follows:

SONG E. (Free translation.)

Ína hwié! my child, I am about to eat. (Three times. Prelude.)

1. Now *H*astséyal*t*i. His food I am about to eat.
2. The pollen of dawn. His food I am about to eat.
3. Much soft goods. His food I am about to eat.
4. Abundant hard goods. His food I am about to eat.
5. Beauty lying before him. His food I am about to eat.
6. Beauty lying behind him. His food I am about to eat.
7. Beauty lying above him. His food I am about to eat.
8. Beauty lying below him. His food I am about to eat.
9. Beauty all around him. His food I am about to eat.
10. In old age wandering. I am about to eat.
11. On the trail of beauty. I am about to eat.
Ína hwié! my child. I am about to eat. Kolagane. (Finale.)

When he had finished his meal, he sang another of the Bezínyasin, a song sung in these days when pollen was administered in the rites.

SONG F. (Free translation.)

Ína hwié! my grandchild, I have eaten. (Three times. Prelude.)
1. *Hastséhogan*. His food I have eaten.
2. The pollen of evening. His food I have eaten.
3. Much soft goods. His food I have eaten.
4. Abundant hard goods. His food I have eaten.
5. Beauty lying behind him. His food I have eaten.
6. Beauty lying before him. His food I have eaten.
7. Beauty lying above him. His food I have eaten.
8. Beauty lying below him. His food I have eaten.
9. Beauty lying all around him. His food I have eaten.
10. In old age wandering. I have eaten.
11. On the trail of beauty. I have eaten.
Ína hwié! my grandchild. I have eaten. Kolagane. (Finale.)

Dawn Boy how crossed a valley to Tse`gíhi, and as he crossed it he sang another song the burden of which was "Hozógo nasá, in a beautiful manner I walk."

When he got to the edge of the cañon he looked across it, and there he saw his mother, his father, his sisters, his brothers, and all his relations. They espied him from afar at the same time, and they said: "Hither comes our elder brother. Hither comes our younger brother," etc., and *Hastséyalti*, who first taught him the songs and sent him forth on his journey, said: "Sitsówe nada`, my grandson has returned home." Then his father, who had gone inside to spread a sacred buckskin for him, came out again.

Dawn Boy sang a song when he was at the door of the house, the burden of which was, "Sagán si níya, I approach my home," and after he entered he sang "Sagán si nidá, in my house I sit down."

Hastséyalti entered the house after him, and then all the neighbors crowded in and sat down. The old man and the old woman said: "My son, tell us your story;" and *Hastséyalti* said: "Tell us the story of the holy place you visited, where no stranger ever dared to venture before." Dawn Boy bade them sing a song and promised when they were done singing he would tell his story. The father then sang a song the burden of which was "Diiá *ti silnaholne* se, this person will tell me a story."

When the song was finished, Dawn Boy said: "My grandfather, my mother, my father (etc.), what you said was true. It was in truth a holy place that I visited. I did not at first believe that it was such; but now I know that it is.", Then he related all his adventures as they have been already told.

After he had related his story, they made preparations to have a ceremony for him. They made him stand on a sacred buckskin, even as the people of White House had done. As he stood on the footprints, drawn in pollen, he said this prayer:

PRAYER No. 2. (Free translation.)

1. Dawn Boy am I, I say.
2. Soft goods of all kinds, my moccasins, I say.
3. Soft goods of all kinds, my leggins, I say.
4. Soft goods of all kinds, my shirt, I say.
5. Soft goods of all kinds, my mind, I say.
6. Soft goods of all kinds, my voice, I say.
7. Soft goods of all kinds, my plumes, I say.
8. Soft goods of all kinds, hanging above me, I say.
9. Hard goods of all kinds, hanging above me, I say.
10. Horses of all kinds, hanging above me, I say.
11. Sheep of all kinds, hanging above me, I say.
12. White corn, hanging above me, I say.
13. Yellow corn, hanging above me, I say.
14. Corn of all kinds, hanging above me, I say.
15. Plants of all kinds, hanging above me, I say.
16. Dark clouds, good and beautiful, hanging above me, I say.
17. Male rain, good and beautiful, hanging above me, I say.
18. Dark mist, good and beautiful, hanging above me, I say.
19. Female rain, good and beautiful, hanging above me, I say.
20. Lightning, good and beautiful, hanging above me, I say.
21. Rainbows, good and beautiful, hanging above me, I say.
22. Pollen, good and beautiful, hanging above me, I say.
23. Grasshoppers, good and beautiful, hanging above me, I say.
24. Before me beautiful, I go home, I say.
25. Behind me beautiful, I go home, I say.
26. Above me beautiful, I go home, I say.
27. Below me beautiful, I go home, I say.
28. All around me beautiful, I go home, I say.
29. In old age wandering, I am, I go home, I say.
30. On the trail of beauty, I am.

31. In a beautiful manner, I am.
32. It is finished in beauty.
33. It is finished in beauty.
34. It is finished in beauty.
35. It is finished in beauty.

The ceremonies performed were some of those which now occur in the rites of the Night Chant, on the last morning when the great nocturnal dance is finished.

1. Sïké holó ládïn nasá ga
My kindred | where are | there | I wander. |
2. Sïké holó ládïn nasá woya
My kindred | where are | there | I wander. |
3. Sïké holó ládïn nasá ga
My kindred | where are | there | I wander |
4. Sïké holó ládïn nasá woya
My kindred | where are | there | I wander. |
5. Nadánlkai biyáze si nïsli'n yégo nasá woyen
White corn | its son | I am. | | I wander. |
6. Tsénitsehogan ládïn nasá
Red Rock House | there | I wander.
7. Ketáni dïlyï'l danadïnla' ládïn nasá woyen
Kethwan | dark | hangs down | there | I wander. |
8. Hayolkál íye tadïtdi'n íye bïl bikeétin ládïn nasá woyen
Dawn | | pollen | | with | its trail | there | I wander. |
9. Yúnigo nídeká bikénadeskaiye taditdi'nye bïl dasilá ládin
nasá woyen
Behind the fire | cotton fabric | with strips on a white ground | pollen | with | hanging | there | I wander. |
10. Baaíya yégo nasá woyen.
I have | them | I wander. |
11. Tanalágola nayuné` bïl tsenánëstsa yégo
A second thing | from within | with it | I went out |
12. Sáan hogán ládïn nasá woyen
Old age | house | there | I wander. |
13. Hozó hogán ládïn nasá woyen.
Happiness | house | there | I wander |
14. Sïtsï'dze hozó yégo nasá woyen
Before me | happily | | I wander |
15. Sïkéde hozó yégo nasá woyen

Behind me | happily | | I wander. |

16. S'iya'gi *hozó* yégo nasá woyen

Beneath me | happily | | I wander |

17. S'ïkï"ge *hozó* yégo nasá woyen

Above me | happily | | I wander |

18 S'ïnáde dáa*l*tso *hozó*ne yégo nasá woyen

Around me | all | happily | | I wander. |

19. Ka̱t sáa*n* nagaí bïke ka̱t bïké *hozó* si nïs*l*ínne yégo nasá woyen

Now | old age | travelling | now | its trail | happily | I become | | I wander |

Prayer No. 1.
I.

1. Kininaekaígi

House of horizontal white in.

2. *H*ayo*l*ká*l* be*h*ogángi

Dawn | house made of, in.

3. *H*ayo*l*ká*l* beda*h*onikági

Dawn | having its foundation of, in.

4. *H*ayo*l*ká*l* bekeétin

Dawn | its trail marked with.

5. *H*astséyalti!

O, Talking God!

6. Bïké s'ïké nas*l*ín

His feet, | my feet | have become.

7. Bïts*á*t s'ïtsát nas*l*ín

His limbs, | my limbs | have become.

8. Bïtsï"s s'ïtsï"s nas*l*ín

His body, | my body | has become.

9. Bï"ni s'ï"ni nas*l*ín

His mind, | my mind | has become.

10. Bïné s'ïné nas*l*ín

His voice, | my voice | has become.

11. Béitsos séitsos naslín

His plumes, | my plumes | have become.

12. Bebïtsï"d*z*e *hozó*ni besïtsï"d*z*e *hozó*

With before him | beautiful, | with before me | beautiful.

13. Bebïkéde hozóni besïyakéde *hozó*

With behind him | beautiful, | with behind me | beautiful.

14. Bebiyá *hozó*ni besiyá *hozó*

With below him | beautiful, | with below me | beautiful.

15. Bebïkígi *hoz*óni besïkígi *hoz*ó

With above him | beautiful. | with above me | beautiful.

16. Bebïná *hoz*óni besïná *hoz*ó

With around him | beautiful, | with me around | beautiful.

17. *T*adïtdín bebïzáhago *hoz*ódi ai besïzáhago hozó nasï's*l*in

Pollen | with in his voice | beautiful, | that | with in my voice beautiful | I become.

18. *Hoz*ó na*h*ast*l*ín

In beauty | again it is finished.

19. *Hoz*ó na*h*ast*l*ín

In beauty | again it is finished.

II.

1. Kininaekaígi

House of horizontal white in.

2. Na*h*otsói be*h*ogángi

Horizontal yellow | house made of in.

3. Na*h*otsói beda*h*onikági

Horizontal yellow | having its foundation of in.

4. Na*h*otsói bekeétin

Horizontal yellow | its trail marked with

5. *H*astséhogan

O, House God!

(The rest as in part I, except that lines 12 and 13 are transposed.)

III.

1. Kininaekaígi

House of horizontal white in.

2. *H*ayo*l*kál be*h*ogángi

Dawn | house made of in.

3. *H*ayo*l*kál beda*h*onikági

Dawn | having its foundation of in.

4. *H*ayo*l*kál bekeétin

Dawn | its trail marked with.

5. Nadán*l*kai Askí

O, White Corn | Boy!

(The rest as in part I.)

IV.

1. Kininaekaígi
House of horizontal white in.
2. Na*h*otsói be*h*ogángi
Horizontal yellow | house made of in.
3. Na*h*otsói beda*h*onikági
Horizontal yellow | having its foundation of in
4. Na*h*otsói bekeétin
Horizontal yellow | its trail marked with.
5. Nadán*l*tsoi Atét
O, Yellow Corn | Girl!
(The rest as in part II.)

V.

1. Kininaekaígi
House of horizontal white in.
2. *H*ayo*l*kál be*h*ogángi
Dawn | house made of, in.
3. *H*ayo*l*kál beda*h*onikági
Dawn | having its foundation of, in
4. *H*ayo*l*kál bekeétin
Dawn | its trail marked with.
5. *T*adïtdín Askí
O, Pollen | Boy!
(The rest as in part I.)

VI.

1. Kininaekaígi
House of horizontal white, in.
2. Na*h*otsói be*h*ogángi
Horizontal yellow | house made of, in.
3. Na*h*otsói beda*h*onikági
Horizontal yellow | having its foundation of, in.
4. Na*h*otsói bekeétin
Horizontal yellow | its trail marked with.
5. Anï*lt*ani Atét
O, Grasshopper | Girl!
(The rest as in part II, with "Ho*z*o na*h*ast*l*ín" repeated four times.)

SONG B.

1. S̈iké bogán ládïn nasdás
My kindred | their house | there | I return.

2. S̈iké bogán ládïn nasdá gose
My kindred | their house | there | I return. |

3. S̈iké bogán ládïn nasdás
My kindred | their house | there | I return.

4. S̈iké bogán ládïn nasdá gose
My kindred | their house | there | I return. |

5. Nadánltsoi biyáze si nïslín yégo nasdás
Yellow corn | his child | I | am | I return.

6. Tsénitsehogan ládïn nasdá gose
Red Rock House | there | I return.

7. Ketáni dolï'zi danadïnlá ládïn nasdá gose
Kethawn | blue | hangs down | there | I return. |

8. Nahotsói tadïdín bïl bekeétin ládïn nasdóse
Evening light | pollen | with | its trail marked | there | I return.

9. Yúnigo hadáte tadïtdín bïl dasilá` ládïn nasdóse
Behind the fire. | haliotis | pollen | with | hanging | there | I return.

10. Baaíya yégo nasdóse
Having them | | I return.

11. Tanalágole nayoné` bïl tsënánëstsa yégo nasdóse
A second thing | from within | with it | I went out | | I return.

12. Sáan hogán ládïn nasdóse
Old age | house | there | I return.

13. Hozó hogán ládïn nasdóse
Happiness | house | there | I return.

14. S̈ikéde hozóni yégo nasdóse
Behind me | happily | | I return.

15. S̈itsï'dze hozóni yégo nasdóse
Before me | happily | | I return.

16. S̈ikéde hozóni yégo nasdóse
Beneath me | happily | | I return.

17. S̈ikígi hozóni yégo nasdóse
Above me | happily | | I return.

18. S̈ináde daáltso hozóni ládïn nasdóse
Around me | all | happily | | I return.

19. Ka̱t sáan nagaí ka̱t bïké hozóni si nïslín ládïn nasdóse

Now | old age | traveling | now | its trail | happily | I | become | there | I return.

(Followed by a refrain of meaningless words.)

SONG C.
PRELUDE.

Sïlá sïlá këlyá ananan. (Repeated four times.)

My hand | my hand | it lies | in.

1. Kat bïl Hayolkáli Askí si nïslín sïlá kë'lya

Now, | with it | Dawn | boy | I | have become | my hand | they lie in.

2. Tsénitsehogan ládïn sïlá kë'lya

Red Rock House | there | my hand | they lie in.

3. Ketáni dïlyï'l danadïnla' ládïn sïlá kë'lya

Kethawn | dark | hangs down | there | my hand | they lie in.

4. Hayolkáli tadïtdín bïl bekeétin ládïn sïlá kë'lya

Dawn | pollen | with | its trail marked | there | my hands | they lie in.

5. Yúnigo ndéka, bïkénadëskaiye tadïtdín bïl dasilá` ládïn sïlá kë'lya

Behind the fire | cotton fabric | with stripes on a white ground | pollen | with | hanging | there | my hands | they lie in.

6. Si baaíya yégo sïlá kë'lya

I | having them | | my hands | they lie in.

7. Tanalágola nayúne` bïl tsënánëstsa sïlá kë'lya

A second thing | from within | with | I went out | my hands | they lie in.

8. Sáan hogán ládïn sïlá kë'lya

Old age | house | there | my hands | they lie in.

9. Hozó hogán ládïn sïlá kë'lya

Happiness | house | there | my hands | they lie in.

10. Si bïl nadïstsá` yégo sïlá kë'lya

I | with | set forth for home | my hands | they lie in.

11. Si bïl nayëstá yégo sïlá kë'lya

I | with | go homeward | | my hands | they lie in.

12. Si bïl nanëstsá` yégo sïlá kë'lya

I | with | reach home | | my hands | they lie in.

13. Si bïl nanësdá yégo sïlá kë'lya

I | with | I sit down | | my hands | they lie in.

14. Sïtsï'dze hozógo yégo sïlá kë'lya

Before me | happily | | my hands | they lie in.

15. S̈ïkéde *hoz*ógo yégo s̈ïlá kë'lya

Behind me | happily | | my hands | they lie in.

16. S̈ïyági *hoz*ógo yégo s̈ïlá kë'lya

Beneath me | happily | | my hands | they lie in.

17. S̈ïkíge hozógo yégo s̈ïlá kë'lya

Above me | happily | | my hands | they lie in.

18. S̈ïnáde daáltso *hoz*ógo yégo s̈ïlá kë'lya

Around me | all | happily | | my hands | they lie in.

19. K̲at sáa*n* nagaí k̲at biké *hoz*óni s̈ï n̈ïsli'*n* yégo s̈ïlá kë'lya

Now | old age | traveling | now | its trail | happily | I | become | | my hands | they lie in.

REFRAIN.

Ananaiye s̈ïlá s̈ïlá kë'lya s̈ïlá s̈ïlá kë'lya ananan

| my hands | my hands | they lie in | my hands | my hands | they lie in. |

II.

3. Ketáni do*l*ï'*z*i danadïnlá` lád*ï*n s̈ïlá kë'lya

Kethawns | blue | hang down | there | my hands | they lie in.

4. Nahotsói *t*adïtdí*n* bï*l* bekeéti*n* lád*ï*n s̈ïlá kë'lya

Evening light | pollen | with | its trail marked | there | my hands | they lie in.

5. Yúnigo *h*adáte *t*adïtdí*n* bï*l* dasilá` lád*ï*n s̈ïlá kë'lya

Behind the | haliotis | pollen | with | hangs | there | my hands | they lie in.

The remainder as in stanza I, except that lines 14 and 15 change places.

SONG D.
PRELUDE.

*H*aineya nagaí naa` naaí oyéye naaí oyéye

| | Stands up, | stands up, | | stands up. |

Naaí oyé naaí oyéyea`.

Stands up. | | stands up. |

1. *H*ad*j*inaí dzïl nayiáyi`

They came up | mountains | loom up.

2. Hayo*l*kál dzïl nayiáyi`

Dawn | mountain | looms up.

3. Nadán*l*kai dzïl nayiáyi`
White corn | mountain | looms up.
4. Yúdi dzïl nayiáyi`
Soft goods | mountain | looms up.
5. Nï'*l*tsa dzïl nayiáyi`
Rain | mountain | looms up.
6. *T*adïtdí*n* dzïl nayiáyi`
Pollen | mountain | looms up.
(Anï*l*tani dzïl nayiáyi`)
Grasshopper | mountain | looms up.
7. Aíye diné *s*ikéyo bikéya niaíye nizóni yaaíye
That | people | my country | their country | looms up |
beautifully | it stands.
8. Aíye diné *s*ikéyo *h*okéya a*l*tsó hozóni nayiáyi
That | people | my country, | their country | all |
beautifully | looms up.

REFRAIN.

*H*aineya oooo naaia, etc.

SONG E.
PRELUDE.

I'na hwié *s*iyá*z*e eena saadïlní*l*
| | my child, | | cook for yourself.
1. *H*asd*z*é*l*ti bisté sadïlní*l*
*H*astséyalti, | his lunch | cook for yourself.
2. *H*ayo*l*ká*l* bïtadïtdí*n* bisté sadïlní*l*
Dawn | his pollen, | his lunch | cook for yourself.
3. Yúdi bidolyágo bisté sadïlní*l*
Soft goods | abundant, | his lunch | cook for yourself.
4, Nt*l*í*z* bidolyágo bisté sadïlní*l*
Hard goods | abundant, | his lunch | cook for yourself.
5. Bitsí*n* na*h*ozógo bisté sadïlní*l*
Before him | happily, | his lunch | cook for yourself.
6. Biké na*h*ozógo bisté sadïlní*l*
Behind him | happily, | his lunch | cook for yourself.
7. Biyáge na*h*ozógo bisté sadïlní*l*
Above him | below happily, | his lunch | cook for yourself.
8. Bikíge na*h*ozógo bisté sadïlní*l*
Above him | happily, | his lunch | cook for yourself.
9. Biná na*h*ozógo bisté sadïlní*l*

Around him | happily, | his lunch | cook for yourself.
10. Sáa*n* nagaí bisté sadïlní*l*
Old age | traveling | his lunch | cook for yourself.
11. Biké *hoz*ó bisté sadïlní*l*
His trail | happily, | his lunch | cook for yourself.

REFRAIN.
I'na hwié *s*iyázi sadïlní*l* olagáne
| | My child | cook for yourself.

SONG F. POLLEN SONG.
PRELUDE.
I'na hwié *s*itsówe eena saanë*l*yá`
| | | My grandchild | | | I have eaten.
1. *H*ast*s*é*h*ogan bisté saanë*l*yá`
*H*ast*s*é*h*ogan | his lunch, | I have eaten.
2. Nahotsói bi*t*aditdí*n* bisté saanë*l*yá`
Evening light | its pollen, | his lunch | I have eaten.
3. Yúdi bidolyágo bisté saanë*l*yá`
Soft goods | abundant, | his lunch | I have eaten.
4. Nt*l*íz bidolyágo bisté saanë*l*yá`
Hard goods | abundant, | his lunch | I have eaten.
5. Biké na*h*oz*ó*go bisté saanë*l*yá`
Behind him, | happily, | his lunch | I have eaten.
6. Bits*í*n na*h*oz*ó*go bisté saanë*l*yá`
Before him | happily, | his lunch | I have eaten.
7. Biyáge na*h*oz*ó*go bisté saanë*l*yá``
Below him | happily, | his lunch | I have eaten.
8. Bikíge na*h*oz*ó*go bisté saanë*l*yá`
Above him | happily, | his lunch | I have eaten.
9. Biná na*h*oz*ó*go bisté saanë*l*yá`
Around him | happily, | his lunch | I have eaten.
10. Sáa*n* nagaí bisté saanë*l*yá`
Old age | traveling, | his lunch | I have eaten.
11. Biké hozó bisté saanë*l*yá`
His trail | happily, | his lunch | I have eaten.

REFRAIN.
I'na hwié *s*itsówe saanë*l*yá` kolagáne
| | My grandchild, | I have eaten. |

PRAYER No. 2.

1. *Hayolkál Aski'* nïsli'ngo adïsní`
Dawn | boy | I am, | I say.

2. Yúdi *al*tasaí *s*ïkégo adïsní`
Soft goods | of all kinds, | my moccasins, | I say.

3. Yúdi *al*tasaí *s*ïst*l*ego adïsní`
Soft goods | of all kinds, | my leggins | I say.

4. Yúdi *al*tasaí *s*iégo adïsní`
Soft goods | of all kinds, | my shirt | I say.

5. Yúdi *al*tasaí *s*ínígo adïsní``
Soft goods | of all kinds, | my mind, | I say.

6. Yúdi *al*tasaí sïnégo adïsní`
Soft goods | of all kinds, | my voice, | I say.

7. Yúdi *al*tasaí seetsósgo adïsní`
Soft goods | of all kinds, | my plumes, | I say.

8. Yúdi *al*tasaí *s*i da*h*azlágo adïsní`
Soft goods | of all kinds, | me, | they will come to, | I say.

9. Nt*l*íz altasaí *s*i da*h*azlágo adïsní`
Hard goods | of all kinds | me, | they will come to, | I say.

10. Lin altasaí *s*i da*h*azlágo adïsní`
Horses | of all kinds | me | they will come to, | I say.

11. Debé altasaí *s*i da*h*azlágo adïsní`
Sheep | of all kinds | me | they will come to, | I say.

12. Nadán*l*kai *s*i da*h*azlágo adïsní`
White corn | me | it will come to, | I say.

13. Nadán*l*tsoi *s*i da*h*azlágo adïsní`
Yellow corn | me | it will come to, | I say.

14. Nadá*n* altasaí *s*i da*h*azlágo adïsní`
Corn | of all kinds, | me | it will come to, | I say.

15. Nanisé altasaí *s*i da*h*azlágo adïsní`
Growing things | of all kinds, | me | they will come to, | I say.

16. Kos dï*l*yï'*l* yasóni *s*i da*h*azlágo adïsní`
Clouds | dark | beautiful, | me | they will come to, | I say.

17. Nï*l*tsabaká yasóni *s*i da*h*azlágo adïsní`
Male rain | beautiful, | me | it will come to, | I say.

18. A` dï*l*yï'*l* yasóni *s*i da*h*azlágo adïsní`
Cloud | dark | beautiful, | me | it will come to, | I say.

19. Nï*l*tsabaád yasóni *s*i da*h*azlágo adïsní`
Female rain | beautiful, | me | it will come to, | I say.

20. Atsïnïlt*lï's* yasóni *s*i da*h*azlágo adïsní`
Lightning | beautiful, | me | it will come to, | I say.
21. Natsílït yasóni *s*i da*h*azlágo adïsní`
Rainbow | beautiful, | me | it win come to, | I say.
22. *T*adïtdí*n* yasóni *s*i da*h*azlágo adïsní`
Pollen | beautiful, | me | it will come to, | I say.
23. Anïl*ta*'ni yasóni *s*i da*h*azlágo adïsní`
Grasshoppers | beautiful, | me | it will come to, | I say.
24. S̈ïtsï'dze *h*ozógo naságo adïsní`
Before me | happily, | I travel, | I say.
25. S̈ïkéde *h*ozógo naságo adïsní`
Behind me | happily, | I travel, | I say.
26. S̈iyági *h*ozógo naságo adïsní`
Below me | happily, | I travel, | I say.
27. S̈ïkígi *h*ozógo naságo adïsní`
Above me | happily, | I travel, | I say.
28. S̈ïnáde daá*l*tso *h*ozógo naságo adïsní`
Around me | all | happily, | I travel, | I say.
29. Sáa*n* nagaí nïslíngo naságo adïsní`
In old age | wandering | am I, | I travel, | I say.
30. Biké *h*ozógo nïslíngo naságo adïsní`
Its trail | happily | am I, | I travel, | I say.
31. *H*ozógo naságo adïsní`
Happily | I travel, | I say.
32. Ho*z*ó na*h*ast*l*ín
Happily | it is finished.
33. Ho*z*ó na*h*ast*l*ín
Happily | it is finished.
34. Ho*z*ó na*h*ast*l*ín
Happily | it is finished.
35. Ho*z*ó na*h*ast*l*ín
Happily | it is finished.

A PRAYER OF THE SECOND DAY OF THE NIGHT CHANT.

I.

1. From the base of the east.
2. From the base of the Pelado Peak.
3. From the house made of mirage,
4. From the story made of mirage,
5. From the doorway of rainbow,
6. The path out of which is the rainbow,
7. The rainbow passed out with me.
S. The rainbow raised up with me.
9. Through the middle of broad fields,
10. The rainbow returned with me.
11. To where my house is visible,
12. The rainbow returned with me.
13. To the roof of my house,
14. The rainbow returned with me.
15. To the entrance of my house,
16. The rainbow returned with me.
17. To just within my house,
18. The rainbow returned with me.
19. To my fireside,
20. The rainbow returned with me.
21. To the center of my house,
22. The rainbow returned with me.
23. At the fore part of my house with the dawn,
24. The Talking God sits with me.
25. The House God sits with me.
26. Pollen Boy sits with me.
27. Grasshopper Girl sits with me.
28. In beauty Estsánatlehi, my mother, for her I return.
29. Beautifully my fire to me is restored.
30. Beautifully my possessions are to me restored.
31. Beautifully my soft goods to me are restored.
32. Beautifully my hard goods to me are restored.
34. Beautifully my horses to me are restored.
34. Beautifully my sheep to me are restored.
35. Beautifully my old men to me are restored.
36. Beautifully my old women to me are restored.
37. Beautifully my young men to me are restored.
38. Beautifully my women to me are restored.
39. Beautifully my children to me are restored.

40. Beautifully my wife to me is restored.
41. Beautifully my chiefs to me are restored.
42. Beautifully my country to me is restored.
43. Beautifully my fields to me are restored.
44. Beautifully my house to me is restored.
45. Talking God sits with me.
46. House God sits with me.
47. Pollen Boy sits with me.
48. Grasshopper Girl sits with me.
49. Beautifully white corn to me is restored.
50. Beautifully yellow corn to me is restored.
51. Beautifully blue corn to me is restored.
52. Beautifully corn of all kinds to me is restored.
53. In beauty may I walk.
54. All day long may I walk.
55. Through the returning seasons may I walk.
56. (Translation uncertain.)
57. Beautifully will I possess again.
58. (Translation uncertain.)
59. Beautifully birds . . .
60. Beautifully joyful birds
61. On the trail marked with pollen may I walk.
62. With grasshoppers about my feet may I walk.
63. With dew about my feet may I walk.
64. With beauty may I walk.
65. With beauty before me, may I walk.
66. With beauty behind me, may I walk.
67. With beauty above me, may I walk.
68. With beauty below me, may, I walk.
69. With beauty all around me, may I walk.
70. In old age wandering on a trail of beauty, lively, may I walk.
71. In old age wandering on a trail of beauty, living again, may I walk.
72. It is finished in beauty.
73. It is finished in beauty.

II.

1. From the base of the south.
2. From the base of the San Mateo mountain.

(The rest as in Part I, except that 65 and 66 and also 67 and 68 are transposed.)

III.

1. From the base of the west.
2. From the base of the San Francisco mountain.

(The rest as in Part 1.)

IV.

1. From the base of the north.
2. From the base of the San Juan mountains.

(The rest as in Part II; but "It is finished in beauty" is repeated four times.)

TEXT AND INTERLINEAR TRANSLATION.

1. *Haá` biyáden*
The East | from its base.
2. Dzïlnadzï'ni biyáden
Pelado Peak | from its base.
3. *Hadáhonige behogánden*
Mirage | house made of from.
4. *Hadáhonige bedahonikáden*
Mirage | having its foundation of from.
5. Natsílït dadïnláden
Rainbow | the doorway from.
6. Natsílït biké dzétïn
Rainbow | its trail | the passage out.
7. Natsílït sïltséïndel
Rainbow | with me it went out.
8. Natsílït sïldáindidel
Rainbow | with me it went higher.
9. Daiké hot`él elnígi
Field | broad | in the middle
10. Natsílït sïlnáhindel
Rainbow | with me it returned.
11. *Sóhogan bitsíhastigi*
My house | from where it could be seen
12. Natsílït sïlnáhindel
Rainbow | with we it returned.
13. *Sóhogan sitkíge*
My house | its roof

14. Natsílït sïlnáhindel
Rainbow | with me it returned.
15. Sóhogan dzeetín
My house | the entrance
16. Natsílït sïlnáhindel
Rainbow | with me it returned.
17. Sóhogan bahastláde
My house | just inside
18. Natsílït sïlnáhindel
Rainbow | with me it returned
19. Sóhogan honïshá`de
My house | the hearth
20. Natsílït sïlnáhindel
Rainbow | with me it returned.
21. Sóhogan yahalnígë
My house | the center
22. Natsílït sïlnáhindel
Rainbow | with me it returned.
23. Hayolkál bësóhogan ntsitlági
The dawn | with my house | fore part
24. Hastséyalti sïlnaneské`
Talking God | with me he sits.
25. Hastséhogan sïlnaneské`
House God | with me he sits.
26. Tadïtdín Aski sïlnaneské`
Pollen Boy | with me he sits.
27. Anilta'ni Atét sïlnaneské`
Grasshopper | Girl | with me she sits.
28. Hozógo Estsánatlehi samá bananestsá
Happily | Woman Who Rejuvenates | my mother | for her I
return.
29. Hozógo sókon sïnastlín
Happily | my fire | is restored to me.
30. Hozógo sinalyée sïnastlín
Happily | my possessions | are restored to me.
31. Hozógo soyúde sïnastlín
Happily | my soft goods | are restored to me.
32. Hozógo sintlíz sïnastlín
Happily | my hard goods | are restored to me.
33. Hozógo sïlín sïnastlín
Happily | my horses | are restored to me.

34. *Hozógo* sidebé sïnast*lín*
Happily | my sheep | are restored to me.
35. *Hozógo* sa*h*astúe sïnastlín
Happily | my old men | are restored to me.
36. *Hozógo* sizáni sïnastlín
Happily | my old women | are restored to me.
37. *Hozógo* sitsilké sïnastlín
Happily | my young men | are restored to me.
38 *Hozógo* sídzíke sïnastlín
Happily | my young women | are restored to me.
39. *Hozógo* saltsíni sïnastlín
Happily | my children | are restored to me.
40. *Hozógo* bï*l*hinisnáni sïnastlín
Happily | my wife (or husband) | are restored to me
41. *Hozógo* sinantaí sïnastlín
Happily | my chiefs | are restored to me.
42. *Hozógo* sikéya sïnastlín
Happily | my country | is restored to me.
43. *Hozógo* sidaiké sïnastlín
Happily | my fields | are restored to me.
44. *Hozógo* sagán sïnastlín
Happily | my house | is restored to me.
45. *H*astséyalti sï*l*naneské'
Talking God | with me he sits.
46. *H*astséhogan sïlnaneské'
House God | with me he sits.
47. *T*adïtdín Askí sïlnaneské'
Pollen | Boy | with me he sits.
48. Ani*lta*'ni Atét sïlnaneské'
Grasshopper | Girl | with me she sits.
49. *Hozógo* nadán*l*kai sïnastlín
Happily | white corn | is restored to me.
50. *Hozógo* nadán*l*tsoi sïnastlín
Happily | yellow corn | is restored to me.
51. *Hozógo* nadándotl̈izi sïnastlín
Happily | blue corn | is restored to me.
52. *Hozógo* nadán a*l*tasaí sïnastlín
Happily | corn | of all kinds | is restored to me.
53. *Hozógo* nasádo
Happily | may I walk.

54. Da*l*ádji*n* (?) nahatígo nasádo
All day long | | may I walk.

55. *T*así akena*h*otlédo nasádo
Thus | becoming again | may I walk.

56. *H*ozógo da*l*ási nahádo
Happily | |

57. *H*ozógo ase na*h*otlédo
Happily | | I will get again.

58. *H*ozógo dasé ïndïntëso
Happily | (?) | (?)

59. *H*ozógo ay*á*s indantáhi danditségo nasádo
Happily | birds | (?) | (?) | may I walk.

60. *H*ozógo ay*á*s ba*h*oz*ó*ni danditségo nasádo
Happily | birds | joyful | may I walk.

61. *T*adïtd*í*n bekeétin nasádo
Pollen | its trail marked with | may I walk.

62. Ani*lt*a'ni bide*s*ísgo nasádo
Grasshoppers | about my feet | may I walk.

63. Da*t*ó bide*s*ísgo nasádo
Dew | about my feet | may I walk.

64. *H*ozógo nasádo
Happily | may I walk.

65. *S*itsídze *h*ozógo nasádo
Me before toward | happily | may I walk.

66. *S*ïkédze *h*ozógo nasádo
Me toward behind | happily | may I walk.

67. *S*iyádze *h*ozógo nasádo
Me toward below | happily | may I walk.

68. *S*ikï'dze *h*ozógo nasádo
Me toward above | happily | may I walk.

69. *S*ïná taá*l*tso *h*ozógo nasádo
Me around | all | happily | may I walk.

70. Sáa*n* nagaí biké *h*ozógo neslíndo nasádo
Old age | wandering | its trail | happily | I will be | may I
walk.

71. Sáa*n* nagaí biké *h*ozógo nasïst*l*íngo nasádo
Old age | wandering | its trail | happily | again living |
may I walk.

72. *H*ozó na*h*ast*l*ín
Happily | it is restored.

73. *H*ozó na*h*ast*l*ín

Happily | it is restored.

II.
1. Sadaá` biyáde
The south | from its base,
2. Tsódzïl biyáde
Mt. San Mateo | from its base.

(The rest as in part I except that lines 65 and 66, and 67 and 68 are transposed.)

III.

1. Iná` biyáde
The west | from its base,
2. Dokooslít biyáde
San Francisco Mt. | from its base.
(The rest as in part I.)

IV.

1. Náhokos biyáde
The north | from its base
2. Debéntsa biyáde
San Juan Mts. | from its base

(The rest as in part II except that "Hozó nahastlín" is repeated four times.)

A PRAYER OF THE FOURTH DAY OF THE NIGHT CHANT.

I.

1. Tse`gíhi.
2. House made of the dawn.
3. House made of evening light.
4. House made of the dark cloud.
5. House made of male rain.
6. House made of dark mist.
7. House made of female rain.
8. House made of pollen.
9. House made of grasshoppers.
10. Dark cloud is at the door.
11. The trail out of it is dark cloud.
12. The zigzag lightning stands high up on it.
13. Male deity!
14. Your offering I make.
15. I have prepared a smoke for you.
16. Restore my feet for me.
17. Restore my legs for me.
18. Restore my body for me.
19. Restore my mind for me.
20. Restore my voice for me.
21. This very day take out your spell for me.
22. Your spell remove for me.
23. You have taken it away for me.
24. Far off it has gone.
25. Happily I recover.
26. Happily my interior becomes cool.
27. Happily I go forth.
28. My interior feeling cold, may I walk.
29. No longer sore, may I walk.
30. Impervious to pain, may I walk.
31. With lively feelings may I walk.
32. As it used to be long ago, may I walk.
33. Happily may I walk.
34. Happily with abundant dark clouds, may I walk.
35. Happily with abundant showers, may I walk.

36. Happily with abundant plants, may I walk.
37. Happily on a trail of pollen, may I walk.
38. Happily may I walk.
39. Being as it used to be long ago, may I walk.
40. May it be happy (or beautiful) before me.
41. May it be beautiful behind me.
42, May it be beautiful below me.
43. May it be beautiful above me.
44. May it be beautiful all around me.
45. In beauty it is finished.
46. In beauty it is finished.

II.

10. Dark mist is at the door.
11. The trail out of it is dark mist.
12. The male rain stands high upon it.

(With the exception of these lines and lines 40 and 41, which change places, the second part of the prayer is identical with the first. At the end it has "In beauty it is finished," repeated four times.)

TEXT AND INTERLINEAR TRANSLATION.

1. Tse`gíhi
Tse'gihi
2. *Hayolkál* be*h*ogán
Dawn | house made of.
3. Na*h*otsoí be*h*ogán
Evening light | house made of.
4. Kósdïlyïl be*h*ogán
Dark cloud | house made of.
5. Ni*l*tsabaká be*h*ogán
Male rain | house made of.
6. A"dïlyïl be*h*ogán
Dark fog | house made of.
7. Nï*l*tsabaád be*h*ogán
Female rain | house made of.
8. *T*adïtdín be*h*ogán
Pollen | house made of.
9. Anï*lt*ani be*h*ogán
Grasshoppers | house made of.
10. Kósdïlyïl dadïnlá'

Dark cloud | doorposts.

11. Kósdïly*ïl* bïké dzeétin
Dark cloud | his road | the exit.

12. Atsïnit*lís* yíke dasizíni
Lightening | on top | standing up.

13. *H*astsébaka
O, Male Divinity!

14. Nigél is*lá*`,
Your offering | I make.

15. Nadíhila`
For you I have prepared.

16. *S*ïké saádï*lil*
My feet | for me restore.

17. *S*ïtsát saádï*lil*
My legs | for me restore.

18. *S*ïtsís saádï*lil*
My body | for me restore.

19. *S*ï'ni saádï*lil*
My mind | for me restore.

20. *S*ïné saádï*lil*
My voice | for me restore.

21. *T*ádïsd*zin* naalíl saádï*lil*
This very day | your spell for me | you will take out.

22. Naalíl sa*h*anéïnla`
Your spell | for me is removed.

23. *S*ïtsád*ze* tahï'ndïnla`
Away from me | you have taken it.

24. Nïzágo nast*lín*
Far off | it has gone.

25. *H*o*z*ógo nadedisdá*l*
Happily | I will recover.

26. *H*o*z*ógo sïtáha dïnoké*l*
Happily | my interior | will be cool.

27. *H*o*z*ógo tsïdïsá*l*
Happily | I shall go forth.

28. Sïtáha *h*onezkázigo nasádo
My interior | being cool | may I walk.

29. Dosa*t*éhigo nasádo
No longer sore | may I walk.

30. Dosohodi*l*nígo nasádo
Impervious to pain | may I walk.

31. Saná` nislíngo nasádo
My feelings | being lively | may I walk.
32. Daalkída kitégo nasádo
Long ago | as it was | may I walk.
33. *Hozógo* kósdïlyïl *s*enahotlédo nasádo
Happily | clouds dark | receiving again | may I walk.
34. *Hozógo* nasádo
Happily | may I walk.
35. *Hozógo s*edahwiltíndo nasádo
Happily | having abundant showers | may I walk.
36. *Hozógo* nánise *s*enahotlédo nasádo
Happily | growing plants | receiving again | may I walk.
37. *Hozógo t*adïtdín keheetíngo nasádo
Happily | pollen | its trail | may I walk.
38. *Hozógo* nasádo
Happily | may I walk.
39. *T*asé *a*lkídzi *a*honílgo nasádo
Thus | as it used to be | it having happened | may I walk.
40. S̈itsídze *hoz*ódo
Before me | may it be happy.
41. S̈ikéde *hoz*ódo
Behind me | may it be happy.
42. S̈iyáde *hoz*ódo
Below me | may it be happy.
43. S̈ikide *hoz*ódo
Above me | may it be happy.
44. S̈iná taáltso *hoz*ódo
Around me | all | may it be happy.
45. *Hoz*ó na*h*astlín
Happily | it is restored.
46. *Hoz*ó na*h*astlín
Happily | it is restored.

II.

10. A`dilyil dadïnlá`.
dark fog | door posts.
11. A`dilyil biké dzeétin
Dark fog | its trail | the exit.
12. Niltsabaká yíke dasizíni.
Male rain | on top | standing up.

(The second part of the prayer is identical with the first part except that lines 40 and 41 change places and the lines given above take the places of the corresponding lines in part I. The concluding lines are said four times instead of twice.)

THE STORY OF BEKOTSIDI.

Békotsïdi and Sun Bearer (Tsínihanoai) made all the animals while they were sitting together in the same room,— Békotsïdi in the north, Tsínihanoai in the south. While the former was making a horse, the latter was making an antelope, and this is why the antelope is so much like a horse. It has a mane and no small back toes as the deer has.

Both of the gods sang while they were at work, and this was the song that Békotsïdi sang to bless all that he was making. It was the first song which he sang at this work.

1. Now Békotsïdi, that am I. For them I make.
2. Now child of Day Bearer am I. For them I make.
3. Now Day Bearer's beam of blue. For them I make.
4. Shines on my feet and your feet too. For them I make.
5. Horses of all kinds now increase. For them I make.
6. At my finger's tips and yours. For them I make.
7. Beasts of all kinds now increase. For them I make.
8. The bluebirds now increase. For them I make.
9. Soft goods of all kinds now increase. For them I make.
10. Now with the pollen they increase. For them I make.
11. Increasing now, they will last forever. For them I make.
12. In old age wandering on the trail of beauty. For them I make.
13. To form them fair, for them I labor. For them I make.

After he had made the animals, he sang another song the refrain of which is "Kat hadzídila`, now they are made." As the animals began to breed, he sang another song appropriate to this, and when they were multiplying abundantly, he sang a fourth song, the burden of which was Keanádildzïsi, which means, they are multiplying.

While Day Bearer was making the horse and domestic sheep, Békotsïdi was making antelope and bighorn. While Day Bearer was making a goat, Békotsïdi was making a cow. While the former was making a deer, the latter was making an elk. Then Day Bearer began to make a mule and Bekotsidi began to make a donkey, and the former said: "I shall stop with this; I shall make no more." But Békotsïdi said, "I shall continue my work." Then he made the jack-rabbit, the small rabbit, the prairie-dog, the wood-rat, and many more animals.

No pictures were drawn of Bekotsidi and no one masquerades in his form. His appearance is not known.

Four songs and no more belong to this tale. If you want a fine horse, sing the second and third songs, say a prayer, and you will get the horse. In your prayer specify the color and kind of a horse you desire., It will come to you from the house of Day Bearer.

The name Békotsïdi signifies "He tries to catch it." He got his name while he was out hunting. An indecent story is told to account for this.

The first iron-gray horse was made of turquoise, the first red (sorrel) horse of red stone (carnelian ?), the first black horse of cannel coal, the first white horse of white shell, and the first piebald horse of haliotis shell. So horses are now, according to their color, called after the different substances of which the first horses were made, Thus the Navahoes speak of doli̇'zi lin. (turquoise or gray horse), bástsïli lin (red stone or sorrel hors e), bászïni lin (cannel coal or black horse), yo*l*kaí lin (haliotis or spotted horse).

The hoofs of the first horse were made of tse`hadáhonige, or mirage stone, a stone on which paints are ground. Such stones are added to earth from six sacred mountains to form their most potent medicine. A shaman will not treat a diseased horse without this. It is used, too, when they pray for increase of stock and increase of wealth.

TEXT AND INTERLINEAR TRANSLATION.
SONG A.
PRELUDE.

E'ya aíya éya aíya ai eena
E'ya aíya éya aíya ai Ba*h*atsidïlés
| | | | | For them I make.
1. Ka*t* Békotsïdi ka*t* si nïs*lín* Ba*h*atsidïlés
Now | Békotsïdi | now | I | am. | For them I make.
2. Ka*t* Tsí*ni*hanoai bigé ka*t* si nïs*lin*'go Ba*h*atsidïlés
Now | Day Bearer | his son | now | I | am. | For them I make.
3. Ka*t* Tsí*ni*hanoai bit*lól*(el) do*li̇*'zigo Ba*h*atsidïlés
Now | Day Bearer | his beams | blue. | For them I make.
4. S̈ïké la*t*á ka*t* niké níti Ba*h*atsidïlés

My feet | ends of | now | | your feet run into. | For them I make.

5. *Lin* a*l*tasaí k<u>a</u>t la nadïldẕï's̓i Ba*h*atsidïlés

Horses | of all kinds | now | | are increasing. | For them I make.

6. S̓ïla la*t*á k<u>a</u>t nïlá níti Ba*h*atsidïlés

My hands | ends of | now | your hands | run into. | For them I make.

7. Díni a*l*tasaí k<u>a</u>t *l*a nadïldẕï's̓i Ba*h*atsidïlés

Animals | of all kinds | now | | are increasing. | For them I make.

8. K<u>a</u>t ayás do*l̓*i'zi k<u>a</u>t *l*a nadïldẕï's̓i Ba*h*atsidïlés

Now | birds | blue | now | | are increasing. | For them I make.

9. Yúdi a*l*tasaí k<u>a</u>t *l*a nadïldẕï's̓i Ba*h*atsidïlés

Soft goods | of all kinds | now | | are increasing. | For them I make.

10. K<u>a</u>t bïtadïtdín bï*l* *l*a nadïldẕï's̓i Ba*h*atsidïlés

Now | its pollen | with | | are increasing. | For them I make.

11. Kéa` nadïldẕï's̓i k<u>a</u>t dóni`dïnës Ba*h*atsidïlés

More and more | are increasing | now | they will last forever. | For them I make.

12. K<u>a</u>t sáa*n* nagaí k<u>a</u>t bike hozóni. Ba*h*atsidïlés

Now | in old age | wandering | now | its trail | beautiful. | For them I make.

13. Tentíngo *l*a` baanïslé Ba*h*atsidïlés

To make them well | | for them I do it. | For them I make.

REFRAIN.

Baanaslési e*n* a*n* etc.
For them I make. | |

PROTECTION SONG.

(To be sung on going into battle.)

I.

Now, Slayer of the Alien Gods, among men am I.
Now among the alien gods with weapons of magic am I.
Rubbed with the summits of the mountains,
Now among the alien gods with weapons of magic am I.
Now upon the beautiful trail of old age,
Now among the alien gods with weapons of magic am I.

II.

Now, Offspring of the Water, among men am I.
Now among the alien gods with weapons of magic am I.
Rubbed with the water of the summits,
Now among the alien gods with weapons of magic am I.
Now upon the beautiful trail of old age,
Now among the alien gods with weapons of magic am I.

III.

Now, Lightning of the Thunder, among men am I.
Now among the alien gods with weapons of magic am I.
Rubbed with the summit of the sky,
Now among the alien gods with weapons of magic am I.
Now upon the beautiful trail of old age,
Now among the alien gods with weapons of magic am I.

IV.

Now, Altsodoniglehi, among men am I.
Now among the alien gods with weapons of magic am I.
Rubbed with the summits of the earth,
Now among the alien gods with weapons of magic am I.
Now upon the beautiful trail of old age,
Now among the alien gods with weapons of magic am I.

TEXT AND INTERLINEAR TRANSLATION.
I.
PRELUDE.

Sinaháse nagée nagée alíli ka̱t bïtása
My thoughts run. | Alien gods, | alien gods | weapons | now
| I walk among them.

A'yeyeyeyahai`
(Meaningless).

1. K_at Nayénëzgani si nïs*lín* nitá`
Now | Nayénezgani | I | am | people among.
nagée nagée alíli k_at bïtása
alien gods, | alien gods, | weapons | now | among them I
walk.

2. Dzï*l* *h*otsï's tsï'da hwe*z*taníta`
Mountains | tops of | truly | I am rubbed with,
nagée nagée alíli k_at bïtása
alien gods, | alien gods, | weapons | now | among them I
walk.

3. K_at sáa*n* nagée k_at biké hozóni si nïs*lín*
Now | in old age | wandering | now | its trail | beautiful | I
| am.
nagée nagée alíli k_at bïtása
alien gods | alien gods | weapons | now | among them I
walk.

II.

1. K_at *T*óbad*z*ists*í*ni si nïs*lín* nitá`
Now | *T*óbad*z*ists*í*ni | I | am, | among them
nagée nagée alíli k_at bïtása
alien gods, | alien gods | weapons | now | among them I
walk.

2. Tó` *h*otsï's tsï'da hwe*z*taníta`
Water | tops of | truly | I am rubbed with.
nagée nagée alíli k_at bïtása
alien gods, | alien gods | weapons | now | among them I
walk.

3. K_at sáa*n* nagée k_at biké hozóni si nïs*lín*
Now | in old age | wandering | now | its trail | beautiful | I
| am
nagée nagée alíli k_at bïtása
alien gods, | alien gods | weapons | now | among them I
walk.

III.

1. K_at Bëlïndzïnot*l*is si nïs*lín* nitá`
Now | Bëlïndzïnot*l*is | I | am | among them.

nagée nagée alíli ka̱t bïtása
alien gods, | alien gods | weapons | now | among them I
walk.
2. Ya *h*otsï's tsï'da hwe*z*taníta`
Sky | top of | truly | I am rubbed with,
nagée nagée alíli ka̱t bïtása
alien gods, | alien gods | weapons | now | among them I
walk.
3. Ka̱t sáa*n* nagée ka̱t biké hozóni *s*i nïs*lí*n
Now | in old age | wandering | now | its trail | beautiful | I
| am,
nagée nagée alíli ka̱t bïtása
alien gods, | alien gods | weapons | now | among them I
walk.

IV.

1. Ka̱t A'ltsodoniglehi *s*i nïs*lí*n nitá`
Now | A'ltsodoniglehi | I | am, | among them,
nagée nagée alíli ka̱t bïtása
alien gods, | alien gods | weapons | now | among them I
walk.
2. Ni` *h*otsï's tsï'da hwe*z*taníta`
Earth | top of | truly | I am rubbed with,
nagée nagée alíli ka̱t bïtása
alien gods, | alien gods | weapons | now | among them I
walk.
3. Ka̱t sáa*n* nagée ka̱t biké hozóni *s*i nïs*lí*n
Now | in old age | wandering, | now | its trail | beautiful |
I | am,
nagée nagée alíli ka̱t bïtása
alien gods, | alien gods | weapons | now | among them I
walk.